Ink under the Fingernails

The publisher and the University of California Press Foundation gratefully acknowledge the generous support of the Peter Booth Wiley Endowment Fund in History.

Ink under the Fingernails

PRINTING POLITICS IN
NINETEENTH-CENTURY MEXICO

Corinna Zeltsman

UNIVERSITY OF CALIFORNIA PRESS

University of California Press
Oakland, California

Library of Congress Cataloging-in-Publication Data

Names: Zeltsman, Corinna, 1983– author.
Title: Ink under the fingernails : printing politics in nineteenth-century
    Mexico / Corinna Zeltsman.
Description: Oakland, California : University of California Press, [2021] |
    Includes bibliographical references and index.
Identifiers: LCCN 2020051226 (print) | LCCN 2020051227 (ebook) |
    ISBN 9780520344334 (cloth) | ISBN 9780520344341 (paperback) |
    ISBN 9780520975477 (epub)
Subjects: LCSH: Printing industry—Political aspects—Mexico—Mexico
    City—19th century.
Classification: LCC Z244.6.M6 Z45 2021 (print) | LCC Z244.6.M6 (ebook) |
    DDC 338.4/7686209725309034—dc23
LC record available at https://lccn.loc.gov/2020051226
LC ebook record available at https://lccn.loc.gov/2020051227

Manufactured in the United States of America

30 29 28 27 26 25 24 23 22 21
10 9 8 7 6 5 4 3 2 1

CONTENTS

ILLUSTRATIONS

FIGURES

TABLE

Introduction

IN THE FIRST DAYS OF 1865, a police officer ripped an anonymous broadside from a Mexico City wall and sent it to his superiors. The short text plunged readers into the middle of a complex political debate. Its author, expressing dismay, advised the national government not to scuttle diplomatic talks with the Vatican (see figure 1).[1] Government sources had recently hinted that negotiations to restore good relations between Mexico and Rome might be breaking down, generating a flurry of concern about the actions of Mexico's new ruler, the Hapsburg prince-turned-emperor Maximilian.[2] Just months after being placed on a Mexican throne by the troops of Napoleon III of France, Maximilian's headstrong dealings with the Vatican and plan to create a national church had begun to erode the confidence of the conservatives and clergy who had helped bring him to power.[3] President Benito Juárez, who led the republican resistance from his base in Northern Mexico, had rejected the emperor's authority, and large swaths of Mexican territory remained unsubdued. Now this anonymous broadside added pressure from yet another angle, a position captured in its author's choice of pseudonym, "A Christian Liberal." Claiming to represent "general opinion," the author argued that ordinary Mexicans favored good relations with Rome and wanted to resolve, rather than exacerbate, the conflicts that had wracked the nation in recent years over the power and status of the Catholic Church.

Recognizing the text as a public rebuke of the emperor, city officials moved quickly to investigate the broadside's source and contain its spread. Similar copies had already been identified on street corners around the capital, yet the single sheet of paper did not provide much information to help the authorities. The author's decision to use a nom de plume established the broadside's political commitments but also masked the author's identity.

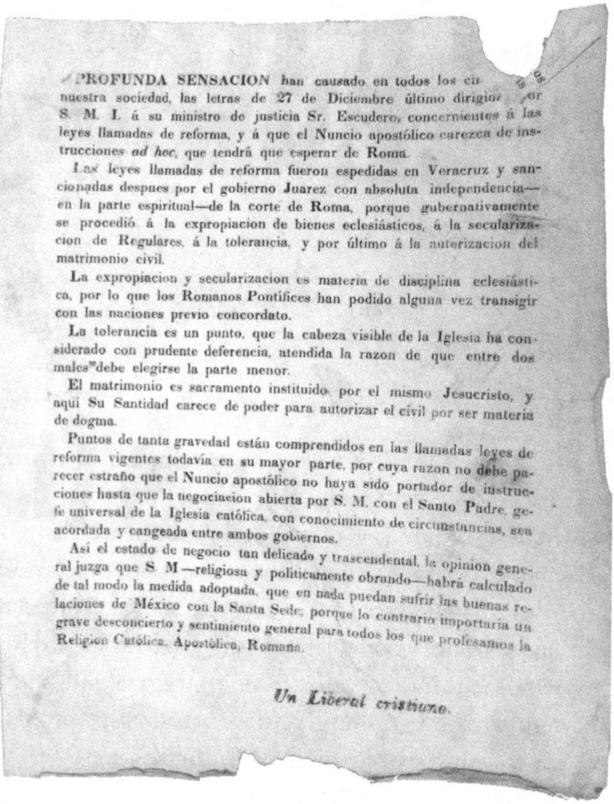

PROFUNDA SENSACION han causado en todos los ci?
nuestra sociedad, las letras de 27 de Diciembre último dirigi?? ?or
S. M. I. á su ministro de justicia Sr. Escudero, concernientes á las
leyes llamadas de reforma, y á que el Nuncio apostólico carezca de ins-
trucciones ad hoc, que tendrá que esperar de Roma.

Las leyes llamadas de reforma fueron espedidas en Veracruz y san-
cionadas despues por el gobierno Juarez con absoluta independencia—
en la parte espiritual—de la corte de Roma, porque gubernativamente
se procedió á la expropiacion de bienes eclesiásticos, á la secularizacion de Regulares, á la tolerancia, y por último á la autorizacion del
matrimonio civil.

La expropiacion y secularizacion es materia de disciplina eclesiástica, por lo que los Romanos Pontífices han podido alguna vez transigir
con las naciones previo concordato.

La tolerancia es un punto, que la cabeza visible de la Iglesia ha con-
siderado con prudente deferencia, atendida la razon de que entre dos
males debe elegirse la parte menor.

El matrimonio es sacramento instituido por el mismo Jesucristo, y
aqui Su Santidad carece de poder para autorizar el civil por ser materia
de dogma.

Puntos de tanta gravedad están comprendidos en las llamadas leyes de
reforma vigentes todavia en su mayor parte, por cuya razon no debe pa-
recer estraño que el Nuncio apostólico no haya sido portador de instruc-
ciones hasta que la negociacion abierta por S. M. con el Santo Padre, gefe universal de la Iglesia católica, con conocimiento de circunstancias, sea
acordada y cangeada entre ambos gobiernos.

Asi el estado de negocio tan delicado y trascendental, la opinion general juzga que S. M —religiosa y politicamente obrando—habrá calculado
de tal modo la medida adoptada, que en nada puedan sufrir las buenas relaciones de México con la Santa Sede; porque lo contrario importaria un
grave desconcierto y sentimiento general para todos los que profesamos la
Religion Católica, Apostólica, Romana.

Un Liberal cristiano.

FIGURE I. Recto of broadside *Profunda sensación* (Mexico City, 1865).
Archivo General de la Nación, Mexico City.

The broadside's printer should have included a name and address on the
document, as required by law. This mechanism provided officials with an
important tool of accountability. Here, however, the broadside's creators had
purposefully omitted any publication information, making verification
impossible. These strategies ensured that the investigation would come up
short, but official anxieties about public criticism in print allowed the ephemeral document to endure in the archive. Within a day, the broadside had
traveled from a Mexico City street corner through the chain of command
and onto the desk of one of the nation's top officials, the minister of the
interior. Filed away after the case went cold, it joined a vast corpus of controversial ephemera preserved among the papers of official power.

FIGURE 2. Verso of broadside *Profunda sensación*, with layers of previously posted broadsides attached. Archivo General de la Nación, Mexico City.

On the verso of the broadside, another story emerges. There, the physical traces of at least three other broadsides can be seen embedded in fragmented layers of ink, paper, and paste (see figure 2). Bold letters and novelty typefaces selected to draw the eye hint at an urban landscape where printed texts acted as routine provocateurs that worked through the city's built environment.[4] As a Mexico City governor once complained, broadsides posted on street corners and church doors provoked "disorders from the disputes of those that read them, some defending the pros, and others the cons of their content."[5] The governor had observed how printed documents could galvanize political discussions, blurring the boundaries between oral and literate modes of communication in a society with low literacy levels. These discussions could become heated and cacophonous, too, a feature embodied in the layered verso of the broadside. The slather of starch, paper, and fragmentary words offers a visual and material complement to the oral cacophony described by the governor. It captures something of the spirit with which print's nineteenth-century creators and users ignored the ideals of rational, measured debate that Mexico's lawmakers invoked when they described how freedom of the press was supposed to function. Instead, the actors who engaged print aimed to utterly obliterate their opponents. With a tug and peel, local officials entered the political game as well, ordering subordinates across the city to "rip off the pasquinades and apprehend whoever posted them."[6] Zealous enforcers occasionally added chunks of wall plaster to the archival record.

As anxious officials attempted to track down the culprits behind broadsides like this, they illuminated a contentious field of political exchange that flourished around texts printed in the urban core of Mexico City: the field of printing politics. After Mexico's independence in 1821, individuals and factions of all stripes embraced the printing press as a weapon in their broader struggles over power. In spite of the fact that most Mexicans could not read, political actors poured energy and resources into printing in order to advance proposals for the new nation, challenge rivals, and immortalize themselves in the public record. Printing was by no means a new technology, especially in Mexico City, which hosted the oldest Western printing tradition in the Americas. Since the founding of the first press there around 1539, the city's printers had collaborated with the powerful royal and religious officials who clustered in the urban core, contributing to the expansion and consolidation of colonial rule, Catholicism, and a local creole intellectual community.[7] Mexico City remained the preeminent national center of publishing after independence. The collapse of the Spanish regime, however, transformed the relationship among printers, authors, the state, and the church, ushering in an era characterized by uncertainty and heated debate. As printing intertwined with emerging networks of urban politics that crisscrossed the nation's capital, a familiar media form, rooted in Hispanic political culture, gained new urgency and possibility.[8]

In the eyes of its elite nineteenth-century users, print had a powerful role to play in shaping the present and future of the nation. After independence, Mexican intellectuals and statesmen, in step with peers across the Americas, identified printing as an essential tool to educate a population largely deprived of formal schooling. Projecting enlightened attitudes that predated independence, reformist commentators hopefully described print's ability to represent and shape public opinion, forming a check against government tyranny or abuses of power. Creating viable domestic publishing industries, nation builders agreed, could help new polities develop collective identities and secure intellectual and cultural autonomy from Europe.[9] Not all observers shared the same optimistic sensibilities toward print as a didactic aid or check on state power. While some extolled the press's transcendent ability "to spread the seed of virtue to all corners, establish the principles of justice and make nations happy with the immense benefits of civilization," others emphasized its potential to incite violence, undermine Catholic piety, or erode the established order when used incorrectly.[10] The appearance of competing attitudes toward the medium reflected the competing political and ideological projects that emerged in the ferment of the early national era. Yet the fact that virtually all political actors embraced printing in spite of their concerns reveals a shared construction of the technology as both a symbol and an engine of social and civilizational achievement that could be used to effect calculated change.[11] Print's modernizing potential seemed matched only by its power to conserve ideas for future generations, forming the raw materials from which histories would be written. One Latin American statesman conveyed this sense of gravity when he described the press's lofty power to make words "pass triumphantly across the ocean and the centuries."[12]

The realities of printing brought such high-minded discursive formulations down to earth. After all, those who hoped to harness print's power needed access to an actual printing press and the embodied knowledge of skilled artisans in order to publish. And this meant confronting the gritty pragmatics associated with running a printing business in nineteenth-century Mexico: the politics of printing itself. The artisans and workers who kept the presses running had to be paid, yet the owners of Mexico City's printing shops faced numerous challenges. In the neighboring United States, economic growth, urbanization, and rising literacy rates propelled the expansion and industrialization of the printing trades and the emergence of publishing, type founding, and press manufacturing industries with national and international reach throughout the nineteenth century.[13] In independent Mexico, however, the collapse of the colonial economy, compounded by debt, foreign invasions, and political instability, meant that local printers worked in more constrained circumstances and could not count on a steadily growing consumer market for print. By the end of the nineteenth century, imperfect government statistics pegged national literacy rates at just 17 percent.[14] While literacy was more widespread in Mexico City, the nation's center of power and wealth, readers were not necessarily paying customers. Adding to these challenges, printers had to assume considerable risk to import expensive machinery and supplies like metal type and paper from abroad.

As they confronted economic realities, printers embraced politics as central to their heterogeneous business strategies. Doubling as publishers, they developed and managed partisan newspapers and cultivated connections to politicians and religious patrons that might yield lucrative contracts. Printers forged individual and collective personae as they tangled with rivals in the public arena, framing and shaping the contours of political debates in the process. Close observers, like noted historian and bibliographer Joaquín García Icazbalceta (1824–1894), lamented that the politicization of Mexico's printing trades detracted from nobler publishing endeavors.[15] Yet printing politics offered printers income, visibility, and a degree of power. It also brought them under the scrutiny of wary or openly hostile officials, whose unpredictable behavior could spell ruin for the entire printing shop community.

State and religious authorities based in the capital looked upon printing shops as suspicious places, at once familiar and frustratingly beyond official control. Even as they approached printing as an essential political tool, they struggled to channel and neutralize the challenges that materialized on the shop floor. Uruguayan literary scholar Ángel Rama famously argued that urban elites used technologies like writing and printing to rule over majority illiterate societies in colonial Latin America, wielding literate power from within the "lettered city."[16] This configuration, he and others contend, morphed but endured throughout the nineteenth century as nation builders worked to construct a political system ruled by respectable, propertied, literate men, or *hombres de bien*.[17] The printing shops that operated at the heart of the lettered city, however, fostered a more democratic worldview at the intersection of intellectual and manual labor. On the shop floor, a cross section of urban society collaborated to transform written texts into printed ones. There, formally educated editors and upwardly mobile journalists rubbed elbows with self-educated type compositors, skilled press operators, and illiterate shop servants. Successful printing shop owners, many of whom began as apprentices, leveraged their skills and connections to become well-known public figures. Some even gained seats in local and national government, acquiring clients of their own as they rose in stature.[18] Over the course of the nineteenth century, printing shop communities embraced a liberal discourse that celebrated these exceptional printers as "men of talent," home-grown examples of merit-based social mobility that challenged the stigma associated with manual labor and reflected positively on urban working communities.

As they gained influence and visibility, printers faced criticism and outright scorn from social superiors, especially when they tangled over politics. When Mexico's most powerful conservative statesman, Lucas Alamán, brought charges against radical printer Vicente García Torres (1811–1894) for defamation in 1849, for example, he denounced the printer's "failure to act as a gentleman and lack of education" to the judge overseeing the case.[19] Confronted later with the printer's defense, Alamán pulled rank, accusing his adversary of making arguments that "while tolerable in the exercises of beginner schoolboys, are in very bad taste and unworthy of the consideration of the Courts." Such comments reveal the thinly veiled class prejudices harbored by political elites, who sought to put upstart printers in their place. These prejudices endured in spite of the intellectual project, with roots in the eighteenth-century Enlightenment, to reconfigure work in a positive light.[20] Like artisans across Latin America who deployed the egalitarian language of liberalism and republicanism to challenge the stigma against manual labor in the nineteenth century, printers emphasized their honor, respectability, and patriotism to defend their presence in the public sphere.[21] However, they often found themselves caught between dueling negative depictions unique to their craft and its relationship to words, being viewed either as partisan lackeys or unprincipled mercenaries willing to print anything for a profit.

Negative characterizations of printers also reflected the frustrations of officials who struggled to regulate the complex world of print production and confront its social implications, which they found especially troubling given Mexico's climate of political instability. The politics of the early republican era involved spirited contests over the form and direction of the new national government, in which urban popular sectors played a visible role. In the first decades after independence, presidential administrations frequently collapsed midterm, and lawmakers rewrote the constitution multiple times as conflicts between federalists and centralists, exacerbated by foreign interventions and government penury, provoked regional revolts and military intervention. By the 1850s these fluid struggles would mutate and expand to full-scale civil war, with Mexicans divided over the role of the Catholic Church in national affairs. In the midst of this instability, postindependence governments across the political spectrum—from radical to conservative, republican to monarchist—all proclaimed their support for "freedom of the press," professing a shared commitment to liberal principles. Yet their language, actions, and related laws established clear limitations and boundaries around printed expression. National officials, hoping to channel print at its source, enacted a dizzying succession of press laws, executive decrees, and juridical interpretations bearing on printing. The Catholic Church, a major actor in the political struggles surrounding nineteenth-century nation building, also attempted to shape publishing in the public arena and behind the scenes.

The laws, cases, and policies that affected printing, accumulating steadily throughout the nineteenth century, reflected officials' enduring concern about the power of print. Famed pamphleteer José Joaquín Fernández de Lizardi (1776–1827) captured the resulting climate of uncertainty felt among print communities when he sardonically recast freedom of the press as "danger of the press" in one of his fictional dialogues.[22] While Lizardi wrote this analysis in 1820, when press freedom was still relatively new in Mexico, its basic premise continued to resonate throughout the nineteenth century, as a revolving cast of officials struggled to develop a stable regulatory regime. By the late nineteenth century the administration of Porfirio Díaz had consolidated a more powerful state over thirty years in power, strengthening the ability of government to oversee and tame printing politics. Yet the legal framework that regulated printed speech remained in flux until 1917, when the Mexican Revolution forced a reevaluation of the nation's press laws.

Mexican authorities' inability to stabilize the laws governing printed speech over nearly a century reveals printing as a key yet underexplored node of conflict in Mexico's process of state formation. For those in power, print posed a dilemma. Even as they hoped to channel printed expression in order to contain political challenges, officials also depended on the printing press to wage their own political struggles against rivals, run the government, and create an archive of state achievements. After attempts to create a printing office inside the National Palace failed in 1828, the national government turned to Mexico City printers to produce the official materials of statecraft, from letterhead to the state's mouthpiece, the government gazette. The Ministry of the Interior, which monitored Mexico City's world of printing and pursued press infractions, also oversaw the government's own printing operations, negotiating the minutiae of its many contracts with local printers and fretting over its inability to fully control the state's own printed image. Officials thus acted as both regulators of print and participants in the contentious politics associated with printing. This juggling generated a central, enduring tension that helps to explain government actions toward printing and the press. Joining political rivals, church officials, upwardly mobile journalists, printing shop owners, and a diverse cast of artisans and workers, officials in the emerging national state competed over the ability to access and command print production.

RETHINKING PRESS FREEDOM AND POLITICAL CULTURE THROUGH PRINTING

By examining struggles over printing, *Ink under the Fingernails* explores Mexico's nineteenth-century history through a new lens. It reconstructs the practical negotiations, legal debates, and discursive maneuvers that unfolded in the back rooms, printing shops, government offices, courts, and streets of the capital around print production and regulation, from the late colonial era to the Mexican Revolution of 1910. The book's attention to practices not only reveals the wide range of actors, from powerful presidents to humble type compositors, whose lives were bound up in these struggles; it also sheds new light on the political, ideological, and social conflicts that accompanied postindependence state formation. As students of the nineteenth century know well, the advance of liberalism and the ways it was embraced in theory and negotiated in practice have constituted a central focus of recent histories about Mexico and Latin America.[23] Revising older narratives about liberalism's supposed incompatibility with Mexican realities, regional studies have emphasized how urban sectors and rural peasant and indigenous communities built local liberal (and, in some contexts, conservative) political cultures as they confronted a variety of state-building projects.[24] The printing shop is a particularly dynamic site from which to reexamine these contingent processes in Mexico's urban core. It is a space where familiar categories often used to explain Mexico's political trajectory break down. Printing shops were microcosms of urban society, complicating distinctions between elite and popular sectors. Members of every faction and institution commissioned the medium, revealing printing as a "political arena" and a shared "instrument of practical politics."[25] Yet even as this broad engagement reflected the emergence of a public sphere facilitated by press freedom, the terms of debate were far from settled. Indeed, printing became a practice around which the outlines of broader ideological, institutional, and sociocultural conflicts took shape, not just as a clash of textual positions but in contests over the material reproduction of texts.

Indeed, we cannot understand struggles over a "free press" in nineteenth-century Mexico without taking seriously their material and laboring dimensions. Current scholarship on Mexico has begun to move beyond the contents of press laws toward examining broader legal institutions like the press jury in order to analyze interactions between state and civil society.[26] Yet by focusing on journalists and the abstract category of the press, these studies have not only overlooked the full range of printed forms that engaged politics, such as ephemeral *papeles públicos*, serialized fiction, government decrees, printers' specimens, and bureaucratic documents; they have also underestimated the degree to which nineteenth-century officials cared about regulating the practical processes of printing as a means to regulate printed speech. Lawmakers repeatedly discussed how best to channel print at its source, and officials used legal and extralegal action to target printing shop communities. In public, actions against printing shop communities became a central theme—rather than simply a footnote—in political debates about press freedom and power.

Broader questions about the nature of labor, intellect, and agency in relation to texts shadowed politicized debates about print and its regulation. Printing shops presented lawmakers with a complex challenge. Many minds and hands participated in the production and distribution process from start to finish. Press laws defined specific categories like authors, publishers, printers, and *responsables* (responsible parties) in order to ensure that some individual could be held responsible for any infractions at the end of the day. Arguments in congress, the courts, and the press, however, reveal a lack of consensus not only about the rules of who should be held responsible for printed texts, but also about the very categories used to describe the field of textual production in the first place. On the one hand, the question of whether an author or a printer bore responsibility for a controversial text— whether "moral" or "mechanical" creation mattered more and what counted as each—loomed, unresolved, over printing politics. On the other hand, printers proved notoriously slippery under questioning, defying categorization. A single individual might recast himself in multiple ways or describe printing shop practices differently to fit the circumstances, reflecting the strategic and situational deployment of legal and professional categories.

By bringing printers into the picture, this book offers new insight into historical struggles over the meanings of freedom. Efforts to regulate printed speech did not flow in one direction, after all. Printers attempted to shape legal interpretation and the letter of the law through their political activities and in the argumentative strategies they used to contest official actions. They also had the means to construct multifaceted identities in moments of crisis, having recourse to their own presses and, often, the sympathies of other members of the trade. Despite their partisan entanglements, printers' search for autonomy from state and religious officials emerged as a constant theme in the postindependence era, overlapping with and departing from broader efforts to set rules around public debate. Throughout the nineteenth century, they emerged as theorists in their own right, competing with officials and writers to redefine "press freedom" as the freedom to operate and work in a printing business without persecution or government interference.

Centering issues of production also yields new information about the networks of patronage that crisscrossed the divide between state and civil society in Mexico, complicating the Habermasian ideal of an independent public sphere produced by market forces.[27] Printing shops were businesses, to be sure, yet their full range of economic strategies similarly fits poorly with the vision of print capitalism sketched out in Benedict Anderson's famous argument linking the market-driven proliferation of newspapers with the rise of horizontally organized national imaginaries in the Age of Revolution.[28] A more sustained look at the political economy and culture of printing in Mexico shows a broader constellation of factors at work, and thus contributes to recent efforts to understand print's multiple trajectories and meanings in specific historical contexts.[29] In a world where only a narrow sector of the population could afford newspaper subscriptions, printers juggled job printing—contract work and commissions—with capital investments and support from political patrons.[30] Not everyone commissioned print in order to turn a profit. (Indeed, profits were rare enough to delay the emergence of a robust, domestic book publishing industry, like the one that developed in nineteenth-century France.[31]) Some freely distributed their pamphlets and ephemera to friends, members of congress, or popular audiences in order to advance specific goals. Officials sometimes subsidized authors by paying their printing costs. The state buoyed newspapers by ordering subscriptions and paid out hefty sums to those with the right connections for all sorts of ephemera. And the sizable church business some printers captured should also be considered a dimension of printing politics, since broader political objectives often animated religious printing.[32]

In short, political networks and objectives played a major role in driving the business of printing in nineteenth-century Mexico. Unlike the North Atlantic narrative that assumes printing expanded steadily throughout the nineteenth century as markets expanded, Mexico exhibited a multifaceted "print clientelism," wherein urban patronage connections helped power production and shaped consumption. For the first half of the nineteenth century, the growth of printing remained modest at best, punctuated by great spikes of activity corresponding to momentous political and legal changes or gathering conflicts: the advent of press freedom in 1820, for example, or the political crisis following Mexico's defeat by the United States in 1848. Only as economic stability and expanded state patronage combined with new technologies in the late nineteenth century did the printing trades expand at a more measurable clip.[33]

These observations have implications for how we conceptualize the role of print within Mexico's nineteenth-century political culture and society. Situating the medium within its contexts of creation and exchange reveals new information about the social reach of certain genres and documents, showing how the contents of printed material moved beyond the exclusive purview of elites through secondhand circulation, recitation, and rumor.[34] Yet access to specialized technologies like writing and printing also allowed a narrower set of actors to distinguish themselves as full participants within these networks, reinscribing power hierarchies in the process.[35] Beyond the framework of literacy/orality, print's symbolic associations with the rituals of power and performance of status—rituals developed through colonial rule and reworked after independence—also left it open to appropriation from below.[36] The medium refracted the hopes and fears of a cross section of urban society.

Take José Agustín Arrieta's 1851 painting, *Tertulia de Pulquería*, which illustrates elite anxieties around print through a scene of tavern reading. The painting, an example of *costumbrismo*, the literary and artistic genre depicting popular customs and local color, shows members of the popular class arranged around a table set with *pulque* and snacks, where they drunkenly discuss and brandish political ephemera (see figure 3). The subject in the top hat—a marker, along with literacy, of his higher social standing—decodes a cartoon for two companions. The two men on the right, bearded and cloaked, engage in a furtive side conversation. The central figures cackle as they consume political satire in mixed company; the woman, a *china poblana*, a stock figure of the village girl of questionable moral character, clutches her breast and rolls her head back in ecstatic laughter. The painting's subjects, who consume satirical newspapers that actually circulated in mid-nineteenth-century Puebla, read and react emotionally to the materials they encounter.[37] The newspapers signal their growing political awareness, yet the individuals gathered at the table appear ill-equipped to assume the role of sober, informed citizens. Paintings such as this would have hung in the houses of elite patrons,

FIGURE 3. José Agustín Arrieta, *Tertulia de Pulquería*, oil on canvas, 1851. Courtesy of the Colección Andrés Blaisten, México.

who could observe the lively, popular scene from a safe distance, drawing moral lessons about the dangers posed by incendiary print-out-of-place.[38] The image seems aimed at justifying elite interventions in society to safeguard political order, whether through educational efforts to create model citizens, restrictions on voting and vagrancy laws, or the policing of print. Yet it also yields a counter-reading, proposing everyday life as a democratizing arena in which printed materials meet unanticipated audiences, generating animated conversation and political ferment through intimate networks of exchange.

PRINTING SHOP INTELLECTUALS

Social ferment and contestation also churned behind the scenes of literate production. With mules powering large presses by midcentury and ink, grease, and solvents potentially everywhere, printing was a gritty and pungent business. Amid the noisy racket and intense smells of Mexico City's printing shops, a unique workplace culture took shape, breaking down easy distinctions between manual and intellectual labor and muddying class hierarchies. Viewed holistically, these spaces encompassed such a wide array of jobs and social horizons that they resist easy categorization. Shop owners and managers with business savvy and craft expertise, formally or marginally educated editors and journalists, literate-worker compositors and proofreaders, skilled press operators and mechanics, poor apprentices, and low-paid workers who folded newspapers, ran errands, and salvaged type that had been *empastelado* (pied, or scattered on the floor)—all contributed to making printed materials. These different roles, each requiring its own specialized knowledge, claimed unequal compensation and prestige, generating internal tensions. And printing shops possessed their own exclusionary logics. In Mexico, women managed and owned printing shops as the daughters, wives, or widows of printers, continuing colonial-era practices.[39] They played an active role behind the scenes in numerous ways, from petitioning government officials for restitution of canceled contracts or release of imprisoned family members, to laboring as servants, bookbinders, and street vendors. Yet few appear in accounts of shop life or received public recognition. Printers in Mexico, furthermore, informally barred women from activities like type composition. The only feminine actor in printing shop lore, indeed, was the press itself, which printers allegorized in poems and newspaper articles as the obedient daughter, nurturing spouse, wise grandmother, or patron saint of the corporate community. The marginalization of women on the shop floor, combined with the gendered construction of the press, solidified the printing shop's identity as a male space of sociability. The collaborative work rhythms of printing, meanwhile, generated homosocial camaraderie and friendships that crossed socioracial lines, encouraging exchanges of ideas and practices. Among the shop's diverse ranks, after all, many shared an ambition for advancement through association with the printed word.

Printing shops nurtured the careers of upwardly mobile journalists, many of whom leveraged writing and political ties to become state functionaries or influential statesmen. Journalists, lacking the wealth of *hombres de bien*, embraced romantic notions of authorship as a form of cultural capital, crafting public reputations around the values of creative autonomy and individual valor.[40] This celebration of creative freedom, however, sat in uneasy tension with the economic and political compromises required in the printing business, a tension embodied (and parodied) in the literary image of the young, idealistic journalist forced to clip out articles from old newspapers to fill the next day's columns. "We worked like scribes, not like writers," the protagonist in Emilio Rabasa's 1888 novel *El cuarto poder* complains, finding himself in this ego-crushing situation. "We were not artists, but rather workers."[41] The protagonist's disavowal of manual labor, construed here as mindless drudgery, reveals the subtle lines of distinction journalists drew as they built cultural capital.

Printers, however, disputed the assumption that the ink under their fingernails disqualified them as thinkers or full participants in the lettered city. Compared to other working groups, they produced a wealth of textual commentary that reflected their engagement with literate culture, enlightened ideas, and liberal narratives. The owners of printing businesses not only shaped legal debates about press freedom, they also intervened in politicized conversations about taste and national identity as publishers. Groundbreaking studies have highlighted their role as cosmopolitan intermediaries who framed international literature, news, and popular entertainment for local audiences.[42] While publishing controversies fueled accusations about the destabilizing effects of printers' economic interests, printers countered by cultivating the public image of impartiality through new strategies—like sending letters to the editor to their own newspapers or cooking up anonymous third-party reviews—that construed the press as a supposedly neutral marketplace of ideas. Type compositors, too, embraced elements of liberal discourse over the nineteenth century, celebrating education and hard work as avenues to self-improvement.[43] Though these literate workers rarely had the chance to assume a public voice in print, they seized special opportunities to display their knowledge and ideas, like the celebration of an employer's birthday, the anniversary of a mutual aid society's founding, or the creation of a type specimen catalog. Through a variety of texts, compositors rejected the characterization of their work as an uncreative pursuit. In the 1870s, they emerged as leading voices in the new urban worker press, where they described themselves as "the interpreters of thought" who "perfected" authors' muddled and unintelligible ideas.[44]

Printers' textual interventions and self-representations open a window onto the cultural imaginary and intellectual world of a unique sector of Mexico's artisanal and working communities. They cohered, on the one hand, into a shared craft mythology about how printers carried the noble legacy of Gutenberg forth into the new nation.[45] Ignacio Cumplido (1811–1887), Mexico's most illustrious printer, for example, narrated a visit to Gutenberg's birthplace as a spiritual pilgrimage, describing an emotional encounter with a statue of "that [immortal] man who redeemed the human race from igno-rance" in his travel memoir.[46] Arguments about printers' social importance emerged not only through the self-aggrandizing cult of Gutenberg but also via a deeper analysis of their working relationship to words. Beyond leverag-ing liberal discourse that recognized manual labor's productive input to the economy, printers elaborated creative, craft-inflected formulations that demanded recognition and respect for their intellectual activities. By claim-ing textual production for themselves, they expressed what Jacques Rancière describes as the worker's "dream of moving to the other side of the canvas": to depict the world as one wishes and thus "[retain] sovereignty for himself."[47] The resulting portrait reimagined intellectual production not through the paradigm of romantic individualism, a common theme among journalists and authors, but as a composite, collaborative activity.

This book continues printers' exploration of the links between creativity and craft by asking how they shaped meaning not just through but also beyond literacy.[48] Typographers determined format, page layout, and design, adapting international styles they encountered through transnational professional networks. These decisions coalesced into conventions that linked material forms with literary and political genres, shaping readers' expectations by framing texts in recognizable ways.[49] As Roger Chartier notes, the meaning of texts "depends upon the forms through which they are received and appropriated by their readers (or listeners.)"[50] Paper sizes, printing technolo-gies, and the constraints of time and money placed parameters around printers' creative endeavors, yet a broader pursuit of novelty—visible in the proliferation of type designs that clamored for viewers' attention throughout the nineteenth century—opened space for creative appropriations in typogra-phy and title page design.[51] Furthermore, Mexico City's location on the edge of the Atlantic circuits through which printing technology moved demanded resourcefulness to overcome the challenges associated with delayed and dam-aged shipments or shortages of type. Finally, the printing shop opened path-ways for learning through reading and listening associated with composing and proofreading texts, yet its activities also cultivated haptic sensitivity, visual acuity, and problem-solving skills. Few chroniclers of Mexico City's print world recognized the value of printers' knowledge, nor did practitioners con-sider it fully in manuals or treatises. Approaching print with attention to the practitioner's perspective, however, opens avenues for understanding the social, formal, and even embodied dimensions of nineteenth-century printing politics.[52]

Printing politics emerged during the upheaval of Mexico's independence era as the medium became newly charged with possibility and the long-negotiated rules surrounding its production and use broke down. In tracing the shifting relationships and negotiations among printers, authors, and officials, the following chapters examine a long process of state unraveling and reconstruction, which unfolded throughout the nineteenth century. Mexico City is an ideal place to study these transformations, since it remained the preeminent site of publishing even after printing technologies became more widespread around the national territory. The process of state building challenged printers yet opened unprecedented opportunities to participate in the nation's emerging political culture, where, as semiautonomous actors, they influenced legal interpretations and frameworks, intellectual and working-class cultures, and the look and materiality of political debate.

To construct this narrative, I have drawn from a range of sources, many of which have never been analyzed. Government and church communications attest to ongoing efforts to channel and harness the power of printing, betraying officials' aspirations and anxieties alongside their collaborations with Mexico City's printers. Press laws and judicial opinions show how debates over legal concepts like responsibility and authorship shifted over time, while court testimony preserves printers' own strategic positioning in relation to law. State contracts and records from the government printing shop, combined with notarial documents and surviving records from the papers of the Abadiano bookselling family, open a window onto printers' business and labor practices. All of these unpublished sources provide the context for a series of case studies which, by examining publishing controversies and important events or moments, reconstruct the politics of printing as they unfolded on the ground. These episodes underscore key features of nineteenth-century printing politics, such as calculated provocation, reprinting, and the evasion or strategic claiming of responsibility for texts. Collectively, they call attention to multifaceted contexts of textual reproduction and consumption and how the material, visual, and performative dimensions of print combined with textual content to suggest meaning. The cases also make visible the historical construction of the figure and myth of the printer, which emerged in tension with simultaneous efforts to marginalize printers in the public sphere.

At the beginning of the nineteenth century, Mexico's colonial printers cultivated close ties with royal and religious officials, who served as both regulators and important patrons of print. Chapter 1 introduces the politics of loyalty that shaped printing in Bourbon Mexico City during a period of court-sponsored, enlightened reform. Manuel Antonio Valdés (1742–1814), the publisher of the semiofficial *Gazeta de México*, exemplified this politics, elaborating discourses about enlightened print in the service of viceregal glory and imperial stability. Valdés's loyalties endured even after Napoleon's 1808 invasion of the Iberian Peninsula unleashed forces that threatened his exclusive monopoly over the news. As chapter 2 argues, printers' loyalties also weathered the decade of insurgent warfare that broke out in 1810. After all, it was royalists who flooded their presses with new business, while insurgents struggled to even acquire printing presses in order to create alternative symbols of political legitimacy in the rural hinterlands. When the Spanish Empire's liberal revolution brought press freedom laws to Mexico, however, certainties about both printers' commitments and imperial legitimacy wavered. One of the first printing scandals, over an 1820 anti-viceregal broadside written by the son of a high-ranking colonial official and reprinted in Mexico City by Alejandro Valdés (1776-1833), reveals an emerging climate of distrust that framed early negotiations over press freedom.

Chapters 3, 4, and 5 delve into the contentious printing politics that exploded in the early republican era, a period that remains one of the least examined in Mexican historiography. Collectively, these chapters trace the birth of the printer as a modern public figure and explore the cat-and-mouse struggles that characterized state and church attempts to channel public debate at the printing shop. Chapter 3 examines the strategies authors and printers developed to circumvent regulation, which officials policed through the legal category of "responsibility" for printed texts. Focusing on the fallout over a pamphlet that called for replacing Mexico's republican system with a foreign-led monarchy, the chapter shows how Cumplido used his legal case to argue that press freedom depended on printers' freedom from state persecution. Chapter 4 examines the politics of printing in relation to the Catholic Church, which retained censorship powers over religious texts yet struggled to enforce them in the face of state inaction. García Torres's reprinting of the scandalous French anti-Catholic novel and global best seller *Mysteries of the Inquisition* shows how printers courted controversy in order to remake the legal and cultural landscape, while leveraging liberal ideas about private property as a wedge against church power. Chapter 5 examines the emerging state's efforts to establish its own tools of self-representation through a national printing office in Mexico City. While the government printing shop failed soon after independence, the invading French regime headed by Maximilian reopened its doors, and successive liberal governments co-opted it as a tool of state formation. The trajectory of state publishing efforts reveals the challenges that vexed officials' efforts to harness the power of printing.

The government printing shop also opens a window onto the elusive working world of the shop floor, explored in chapter 6. As a triumphant liberal party consolidated its hegemony after 1867, workers engaged and pushed to expand the definitions of citizenship and belonging both on the job and in their free time. As contributors to the worker press that flourished during the "Restored Republic" and first presidential term of Díaz, type compositors grappled with their working relationship to words and ideas while demanding greater respect and remuneration. A unique 1877 type specimen, created as a tool of bureaucratic accountability in the government printing shop, shows how printers narrated Mexico's history through the lens of liberal victory, positioning themselves as its privileged interpreters.

Restrictions on printing increased as Díaz consolidated power and began to construct a more powerful, centralized state during his lengthy second tenure (1884–1911). The Porfirian regime's emphasis on technology in the service of progress inflected new strategies for corralling debate through the criminalization of press infractions and seizures of printing presses. Chapter 7 explores late nineteenth-century changes in the politics of printing and considers how printer-publishers like Daniel Cabrera (1858–1914) and Filomeno Mata (1845–1911) contested press seizures, paving the ground for the reworking of press laws during the Mexican Revolution. The revolution that swept Díaz from power in 1911 restored an older, liberal set of press laws, rejecting late nineteenth-century modifications. These new-old laws revived fundamental tensions that had plagued nineteenth-century governments, yet their innovations also reflected printers' long-term efforts to redefine press freedom as printers' freedom.

ONE

The Politics of Loyalty

THE PRINTER MANUEL ANTONIO VALDÉS spent the last days of 1803 preparing a public address to the new viceroy of New Spain. He distributed his remarks in the form of a preface to subscribers of the *Gazeta de México*, the semiofficial newspaper he had overseen for nearly twenty years thanks to an exclusive royal privilege. Valdés had seen a series of colonial administrators come and go, and his text followed the formula he had perfected over time. Emblazoned with an engraving of the new viceroy's coat of arms, the preface appealed to his patron for support, describing the *Gazeta* abjectly as "a shapeless and almost lifeless body."[1] If his newspaper was an ailing patient, Valdés suggested that the viceroy held the cure. The *Gazeta*, though infirm, could "reanimate itself and appear with the most pleasing aspect if Your Excellency pledges the influence of your power to protect it." The preface linked the revival of the newspaper to the success of New Spain itself. Not only did Valdés construe the *Gazeta* as a metonym for the body politic; he also described his editorial efforts as "enriching posterity with news, which perhaps will be lost eternally to memory" otherwise. Although he positioned himself humbly as a mere *"curio* or copyist" who organized news that he received from officials, thus strengthening their authority, Valdés also mused, more grandly, that "perhaps the day will come in which [these] volumes will have a special place on the shelves of *literatos."* Aligning his activities with a forward-looking project to arrange, preserve, and eventually glorify the present, the printer nudged the viceroy toward generosity.

The printer's preface captures the rhetorical strategies that framed publishing in colonial Mexico during an era of enlightened reformism. It is no coincidence that Valdés appealed to his sponsor using medical and aesthetic metaphors. These references gestured toward broad scientific, intellectual, and artistic transformations that by 1803 were already well underway across the Spanish Empire, linked to a series of sweeping reforms implemented by the Bourbon monarchs. In the second half of the eighteenth century, the Bourbons pursued a multifaceted plan to increase revenues, shore up military defenses, and centralize and modernize imperial governance, all with the goal of improving Spain's flagging position vis-à-vis its imperial rivals. The Bourbon reforms had a practical and utilitarian cast aimed at strengthening and generating positive returns for the crown. They found expression in the crown's embrace of broad objectives like "public happiness," a concept developed in intellectual circles that held the interests of ruler, state, and subjects to be synonymous and viewed imperial improvement as a mutually reinforcing process.[2] These ideas underpinned official support for scientific inquiry and sanction of economic societies, literary groups, and periodicals developed by residents of the Americas. The *Gazeta de México*, created at the impetus of a Mexican-born printer, reveals links between newspapers and the broader process of imperial reform. By connecting his publishing activities to the success of viceregal officials and the empire, Valdés translated enlightened theory into practice.

The preface also shows how the concept of loyalty simultaneously greased the wheels of publishing and served as a "meaningful political relationship" that shaped interactions between printers and the state.[3] Printers like Valdés embraced a politics structured around loyalty in part because they depended on good relationships with royal officials as a precondition of doing business. In Mexico and across the Spanish Empire, publishing generally required prior permission from religious and royal officials.[4] Furthermore, a system of licensing and privileges regulated access to the colonial market, shaping the economics of publishing and generating fierce competition among the owners of printing shops, an intimate community that, in Mexico City, numbered between two and five during the late eighteenth century. Classic accounts of the public sphere tend to connect the emergence of newspapers with political movements that challenged the ancien régime. Thanks to their economic independence from authorities, newspapers could become vehicles for anti-absolutist or anti-colonial critique. In late colonial North America, for example, printers' business interests aligned with protest movements against the British Crown.[5] In Bourbon Mexico City, however, most printed speech—as opposed to other forms of communication—was authorized from above. Valdés reinforced this system from below when he linked his newspaper with public happiness, underscoring the importance of consensus, patronage, and political capital as preconditions for entrance into the realm of public discourse.[6]

Enlightened ideas also appealed to printers because they offered opportunities for social repositioning. New theories about the manual arts allowed printers to envision themselves as complementary contributors to intellectual life, rather than its servants. Influential Spanish reformer Pedro Rodríguez de Campomanes (1723–1802), for example, described printing as an "auxiliary art" in an effort to elevate its status.[7] New policies promoted useful arts like printing as contributing to Spain's economic and intellectual development. New aesthetic sensibilities—especially the neoclassical typography and design promoted by the Royal Academy of San Carlos, founded in Mexico City in 1781—allowed printers to show themselves as promoters of good taste. More broadly, eighteenth-century reformers challenged the rigidity of social hierarchies based on birth and caste, arguing that individuals' merits and services to the crown justified changes to their status.[8] Valdés's self-characterization as a useful copyist and archivist whose *Gazetas* would serve as source material for the unwritten histories of the future speaks to how these intellectual and policy reorientations captured printers' imaginations, reflecting a certain discursive democratization elaborated within the framework of empire.[9]

Yet deeper hierarchies endured in spite of crown-sponsored reforms that identified printing as a strategic imperial priority, and meritocratic discourses had their limits, revealing the unevenness of reform. An episode from 1809 shows new lines of exclusion taking shape against a backdrop of political upheaval. The Napoleonic invasion of 1808 rocked Spain, already weakened by disastrous wars with its imperial rivals. King Fernando VII abdicated the Spanish throne that year, triggering a crisis that rippled across the empire as subjects wondered where political authority and legitimacy lay. In Mexico City, as in the Iberian Peninsula and in other parts of the Americas, the king's abdication provoked political conflicts and competing plans for resolution. Discord grew as some Mexican-born creoles advocated for greater autonomy in the absence of a monarch. Amid the unrest, news and opinions from Europe became both a potentially valuable commodity and a matter of pressing imperial security, since officials viewed the *Gazeta de México* as a key tool for shaping public opinion and maintaining elite loyalty. Valdés, a creole, found his long-held privilege to print the news under attack. The Bourbon reforms had opened space for printers to develop new public personae in eighteenth-century Mexico. The crisis of 1808, however, tested printers' ability to capitalize on enlightened arguments about authorship, service, and merit as the political ground shifted beneath their feet.

THE FOUNDATIONS OF PRINTERS' LOYALTY

The legal framework around publishing played an important role in shaping printers' relationships to authorities in New Spain. The law detailed royal and religious oversight of print production through a dual- or triple-pronged structure of censorship and licensing. All manuscripts were supposed to be reviewed by the readers of Mexico's Inquisition before printing could begin.[10] They also required a license from the viceroy, who in Mexico City acted on recommendations from the Metropolitan Cathedral. Members of religious orders needed additional approval from their superiors. These requirements generated continuous contact and collaboration among printers, authors, and officials, ensuring that locally made print emerged as the product of negotiation and consensus. Political conflicts and debates over orthodoxy—72 percent of authors who published in Mexico City during the seventeenth and eighteenth centuries were clergy members—often unfolded before a work was released or rejected.[11] Inquisition officials, however, relied on printers to police orthodoxy in several ways. They trusted printers to prepare inventories of their stock, allowed them to expurgate problematic passages from works that had been censored after printing, and expected them to comply with the bureaucratic formalities of obtaining licenses from the viceroy on behalf of authors.[12] Authors and printers, in turn, emphasized consensus by publishing censors' reports, licenses, and privileges as preliminary materials preceding a text or in a work's imprint information. Censors' reports, after all, were book reviews that attested to the merits of a text, often in glowing terms. By presenting the judgments of prominent religious scholars alongside the approval of civil authorities for public view, authors and printers formed a web of authority around a printed text.

The political economy of printing, too, linked printers' fortunes to royal officials and commercial networks on both sides of the Atlantic. Printers needed royal permission to establish their businesses in Mexico and had to import from Spain presses and supplies that could not be fabricated locally. The crown taxed imported paper and banned its local production to generate trade revenue.[13] Beginning in the eighteenth century, furthermore, the crown enacted protectionist tariffs to encourage book production on the Iberian

Peninsula, allowing books printed in Spain to be imported tax free to the Americas and undercutting local book publishing. Mercantilist policies presented printers based in New Spain with certain challenges. Importing paper, for example, produced periodic shortages and raised the costs of printing, generating complaints from authors.[14] Yet by shaping the parameters of printers' local activities, these policies also opened opportunities for profiting through imperial networks. Through relationships with counterparts in Spain, printers became important intermediaries in the transatlantic book trade, often doubling as booksellers.[15] Instead of competing with European publishers, they served local institutional needs and markets, which expanded in the eighteenth century.[16] The mechanism of the privilege, furthermore, linked printers' economic fortunes to the viceroy and monarch, establishing them as royal clients. Privileges served numerous functions. From the perspective of recipients, securing a privilege gave an individual or corporate body monopoly rights to publish a particular work for a span of time, including across generations, which bolstered the chances of making a profit by cordoning the market. In addition to regulating access to markets, privileges also generated revenue for the state, cut expenses for the crown through outsourcing of official printing, and knit together communities through patronage.[17]

A brief census of Mexico City's eighteenth-century presses clearly shows the links to official patronage. The Calderón printing dynasty had dominated Mexican printing throughout the seventeenth century through its monopoly on producing *cartillas* (texts used for religious and literacy education), yet the family's fortunes eroded as new arrivals from Spain contested its market dominance in the eighteenth century.[18] José Bernando de Hogal, a Spaniard who established a press in the 1720s in Mexico City, attained the exclusive title of printer for the Holy Crusade and aggressively challenged the Calderón heir, María Candelaria de Ribera's, privileges.[19] In the middle of the eighteenth century, two new presses briefly expanded the colonial printing community. However, the experimental press of Juan José Eguiara y Eguren, founded as a humanistic project to support local intellectual endeavors, folded with its owner's death and was absorbed by the heirs of the Calderón dynasty. A press started at the Jesuit Colegio de San Ildefonso earned revenue through commissioned work yet closed after the order's expulsion from Spanish territories in 1767.[20] On the other hand, Mexican-born Felipe Zúñiga y Ontiveros, who founded a press in 1761 with his bookseller brother Cristobal, achieved robust success by gaining a privilege for a new *Guía de Forasteros* (Traveler's guide) and a popular almanac, which he published each fall in quantities exceeding twelve thousand copies, muscling out competitors with his royal monopoly.[21] In his private journal, Zúñiga y Ontiveros gloated when his rival, José Antonio de Hogal, failed to win a petition for expanded privileges.[22] Privileges could, of course, be revoked. When officials caught Hogal participating in a fraudulent scheme with royal lottery officials in 1780, he lost his privilege to print the lottery tickets.[23] Such misfortunes could seriously harm the viability of a printing business, since lucrative state contracts were essential sources of income.

The vertical links that structured printers' relationships with royal and religious officials paralleled social organization inside the printing shop itself. Printing shop owners, who may or may not have possessed trade expertise, and skilled overseers exercised authority over *oficiales* (roughly, journeymen), apprentices, and servants in the workshop.[24] Some amassed considerable fortunes through their multifaceted business dealings. At least two Mexico City printers in the seventeenth and eighteenth centuries were slave owners.[25] Prominent printing families had members in the clergy, and descriptions in colonial registers usually listed printers as *españoles*, a marker of whiteness and status that encompassed individuals born in Spain or their creole descendants born in the Americas of Spanish parentage.[26] For those associated with the laboring side of the business, whose racial status remains obscure, social mobility was possible but rare. Unlike in North America, where journeymen printers like Benjamin Franklin expanded their opportunities by traveling within the colonies, Mexican presses operated in just two cities before the final decades of the eighteenth century: Mexico City and Puebla.[27] While Mexico's colonial printing offices were large and well-equipped, the high capital requirements, bureaucratic hurdles, and limited markets prevented most *oficiales*—like the two pressmen depicted in a rare portrait from eighteenth-century Lima—from starting workshops of their own (see figure 4).

The language of loyalty permeated the cultural expressions of Mexico City printing shops, framing the creative imaginations that flourished there. Coexisting with workplace hierarchies based on skill and position, a shared expressive repertoire emerged in the city's printing shops that celebrated printers' literary talents and explored the intersection of texts and their visual or typographic forms—always deployed in the service of temporal or spiritual patrons. This repertoire took shape in ephemera printed to commemorate birthdays, marriages, and special events. Although too few to warrant a guild

FIGURE 4. Rare representation of a colonial Spanish American printing shop, 1701. The engraving, with a bit of creative license, shows two printers using a common press to print a heart-shaped remembrance of the recently deceased monarch Carlos II. José de Buendía, *Parentación real al soberano nombre e inmortal memoria del Católico Rey de la Españas y Emperador de las Indias . . .* (Lima: Por Ioseph de Contreras, impressor real, del Santo Oficio, y de la Santa Cruzada, año de 1701). Courtesy of the John Carter Brown Library.

or religious confraternity of their own, printers nevertheless used their access to the press to craft professional identity while emphasizing vertical bonds.[28]

Printers' exercises, which mobilize both textual and visual elements, open a window onto strategies of communication and aesthetic values that circulated both within and beyond the craft community. In 1782, for example, the printing shop of the Jáuregui family produced a complex specimen to debut its newly imported typefaces, featuring a poem in the voice of a would-be author seeking the patronage and protection of the Virgin (see figure 5).[29] The poem describes Mary, who is depicted in an engraving as the Mater Dolorosa pierced by suffering, as an ideal benefactress, since she serves as both a book and a printer (*impresora*) of sacred history. Indeed, Mary's grief is so strong that she displaces the very "iron of the press" itself, printing with the red ink of blood. The poem ultimately claims not just the Virgin's protection but also the approval of God himself:

Heavenly Father above,
APPROVED it with his Science,
And released it to the public,
With his ROYAL PRIVILEGE:
In accordance with the ORIGINAL,
Made worthy with her sorrows;
Thus it is advised
To the pious Reader:
That it is written with skill,
And has no *errata*.

Allá el Padre Celestial,
Con su Ciencia lo APROBÓ,
Y al público lo sacó
Con su PRIVILEGIO REAL:
Conforme a su ORIGINAL,
Con sus Dolores conviene;
Por eso se le previene
A su piadoso Lector:
Que está escrito con primor,
Y *fé de erratas* no tiene.

Throughout the poem, the legal framework, political economy, and quotidian practices of printing gain spiritual meaning through their association with the Virgin and Christ. The poem implies that its text rises above the earthly realm of censorship; the poem is perfect (printed without errors) because of its divine approval. Yet it also elevates censorship and privileges as acts of divine patronage.

The poem's extended metaphor about the Virgin-as-printer/press takes shape through an ornate typographical composition that offers a parallel argument. While type composition in straight lines and right angles is a straightforward task, creating rounded forms like circles and hearts with rectangular pieces of type requires time and ingenuity. Here, rounded shapes composed with typographical ornaments cover the page, evoking the baroque's use of organic forms or the elaborate facade of Mexico City's cathedral (1749–1768), designed to inspire religious devotion by stimulating the senses with opulence.[30] Individual shapes frame the poem into stanzas organized by number, each presenting a different typeface. The numeric system directs the reader to follow a pattern that jumps from side to side across and down the central axis, evoking, perhaps, the form of a cross and the motions of crossing oneself as one reads. The type composition therefore not only

FIGURE 5. *Demostración de los tamaños de letra y adornos de una nueva imprenta madrileña* (Mexico City: En la imprenta de la Calle de San Bernardo, 1782). Image property of the Biblioteca Nacional de España.

performs artisanal mastery but also encourages the reader to engage with the text as an embodied spiritual exercise. The Jáureguis' type specimen represented one item in a wide-ranging genre of printing shop literature that referenced and riffed on trade practices as a platform for public expression. As Marina Garone has argued, such productions may have been the outgrowth of competition among workshops, yet they also represented public performances of printers' broader loyalties.

Print workers, too, engaged related forms of discursive positioning, preserved remarkably in rare late colonial ephemera. In one sonnet printed on a loose sheet of paper, printing shop workers honored the birthday of "their beloved Patron," whom they depicted as a benevolent father figure who gives lessons to a printing press.[31] While the sonnet's typography and structure demonstrated the workers' knowledge of poetry's formal conventions, its content showcased their creativity. In the sonnet, the press, feminized and anthropomorphized as the printer's daughter, promises to listen in "reverent silence" as she absorbs her father's teachings. The press, in turn, represents the printing shop's workers, who reveal themselves in the poem's final stanzas as their patron's real-world "Clients" and pledge their silence as a marker of respect for their employer. The poem's parallel between the silent, feminized press and the printing shop workers mobilizes gender norms to establish the workers as subordinate to and dependent upon Valdés, like an obedient daughter. In exchange for his paternalistic protection, the workers grant their love and compliance, conceptualizing the workshop as a hierarchically organized family or "moral community," despite the absence of formal corporate structures.[32]

These and similar surviving ephemera emphasized the culture of consensus that shaped publishing in New Spain, yet residents had other opportunities to cultivate their critical sensibilities toward royal and religious authorities. The book trade brought works published abroad to fill the libraries of local elites and literate artisans. While the Mexican Inquisition monitored ships' cargoes for works deemed unorthodox or heretical, enforcement of the Index of Prohibited Books remained uneven and generally unpopular.[33] Thus, controversial texts printed abroad circulated in spite of periodic decrees published by the Inquisition. Oral and written communications, too, undermined official attempts to police the sphere of debate that flourished alongside formal censorship. Handwritten satirical pasquinades and libels appeared posted on walls or circulated from hand to hand, especially at moments of political tension, like during the 1767 expulsion of the Jesuits, which garnered criticism from Mexico's elite.[34] Personal correspondence shared news and information

across oceans and within the Americas. Letters became increasingly important when, after the outbreak of the French Revolution, the viceroy increased
scrutiny of printed materials and tried for a time to create a blackout on political commentary about France, enacting what Gabriel Torres Puga calls a
"politics of silence." Censorship, indeed, relaxed and intensified in relation to
imperial events and anxieties. Mexico's Inquisition, anxious about revolution
and the expansion of French publishing, issued a barrage of decrees prohibiting over three hundred titles published in France, Spain, and the Netherlands
between 1790 and 1809.[35]

Despite the Inquisition's considerable efforts to shape reading habits in an
era of revolutionary upheaval, efforts to establish orthodoxy in all aspects of
colonial life were always partial, sometimes contradictory, and subject to
changing official priorities and conflicts.[36] Inquisitors, too, tempered their
prohibitions with a degree of flexibility, to be deployed through the familiar
concession of the license to read prohibited works.[37] Even the popular printed
materials of everyday religious devotion could be harnessed to challenge or
circumvent authority in micropolitical contexts. Religious prints—like small
images of the Virgin, Christ, or saints sold as loose sheets or as part of *novena*
booklets—were not carefully supervised by officials, in spite of their ubiquity
in colonial society.[38] These familiar objects formed a key component of the
devotional practices of ordinary Mexicans, representing another important
source of printers' income. Their mystique turned them into tools of spiritual
intercession but could also inspire unorthodox uses at the hands of poor
devotees, who slipped them under the altar cloth, placed them on the body
to cure ailments, or used them to fend off abusive local officials.[39] This
broader field of critical exchange and appropriation throws printers' official
loyalties into relief.

REFORMING PRINT, REFORMING EMPIRE

Transformations in the second half of the eighteenth century generated new
interest in the relationship between printing and empire. In his influential
1775 educational treatise *Discurso sobre la educación popular de los artesanos y
su fomento*, enlightened reformer and royal adviser Campomanes argued that
Spain's future rested on its ability to remake itself as a nation of producers.[40]
In order to transform Spanish consumers into productive, efficient subjects,
he argued, Spain needed a broad program of rational, state-supported

technical education. State education, Campomanes believed, would wrest the trades from the traditional, stifling authority of guilds, spurring progress that would revitalize Spain's economic fortunes. Among the areas ripe for reform, he identified the "auxiliary arts, such as writing, the printing press, engraving, the art of making dies and punches, the casting of letters, the manufacture of paper, [and] the materials of book binding." "These arts," he explained, "prosper or fail according to the progress of national education that occupies them."[41] Spain's success, in turn, depended on reconfiguring cultural attitudes about the skilled trades, historically viewed as inferior or degraded by virtue of their association with labor. "How harmful is the distinction between liberal and manual arts," Campomanes argued, "as if it were possible to write or print a book without the mechanism of writing or the press."[42]

Campomanes's program to uplift and reform the manual arts through education and state investment represented an important current in the broader intellectual milieu of the Spanish Enlightenment, one that shaped reformist policies enacted by the Bourbon monarchs. The Bourbons, who had come to power earlier in the eighteenth century, intended these reforms to centralize governance, modernize economic infrastructure, and reshape the empire's corporatist society.[43] Reforms affected administration in the colonies in countless areas, generating both opportunities and local resentments as they restructured the colonial bureaucracy, tax policies, trade rules, military organization, social opportunities, and the relationship between church and state. Rulers also funded new intellectual pursuits in the Americas, like scientific expeditions and the founding of court-sponsored educational institutions devoted to utilitarian and artistic pursuits in Mexico City, including the Royal Mining College and the Royal Academy of San Carlos.[44]

Even before the publication of Campomanes's treatise, the Bourbons had already begun a concerted effort to modernize peninsular printing, which they viewed as essential for facilitating and stimulating intellectual production. Spanish printing, type founding, and papermaking industries had long been overshadowed by other centers in Europe, but this became a problem only after Spain lost the Spanish Netherlands—including the publishing center of Antwerp—in the succession wars of the early eighteenth century. By the middle of the eighteenth century, Fernando VI started to encourage book production in Spain, enacting protectionist tariffs on imported Spanish-language books to help local trades.[45] Carlos III, encouraged by his advisers and observing France's official printworks, sponsored a series of typographical projects focused on turning Madrid into an up-to-date publishing center. The crown acquired matrices—the molds used to cast individual letters of type—from France and subsidized local craftsmen to develop their own. To make a matrix, engravers first carved a positive letterform onto the end of a steel rod, or punch, which would then be hammered into a softer metal to create the negative matrix, into which hot lead would be poured to cast type.[46] This required specialized training, and noted punch cutters received royal stipends to develop matrices, which were then used to produce type for a new royal printworks, the Imprenta Real, established at the Royal Library in 1761. The crown further centralized production by recouping the various privileges that had been distributed over the years to printers who produced royal materials.[47] As the state approached printing through the lens of enlightened reform, it also consolidated its presence as the trade's primary sponsor.

The reforms of the eighteenth century aimed to strengthen peninsular printing, but Mexico City printers engaged the process, too, as consumers and improvisers. In the late eighteenth century, local printers imported and used types and matrices produced by the Imprenta Real, updating their designs.[48] Some experiments in type founding occurred in Mexico City, but most printers entrusted agents with considerable sums to furnish and update their stock with supplies from Spain. At the same time, one of the chief participants in the peninsular printing reforms, Jerónimo Antonio Gil, arrived in Mexico City on a royal commission. Gil, trained as an engraver, had produced thousands of punches while working at the Royal Library in Madrid; his type designs were among those imported to Mexico. After being named head engraver of the Mexico City Mint, Gil traveled there in 1778 and soon founded a school of engraving that became the colony's first fine arts academy, the Academy of San Carlos.[49] Gil, though a contentious figure, exercised considerable influence over the artistic milieu that formed around the academy, spurring the expansion of neoclassical taste in Mexico.[50] In 1784 he petitioned the viceroy to establish a printing shop modeled after Spain's Imprenta Real, hoping to extend his influence. Yet the viceroy denied Gil's request, perhaps because the privileges of local printers would conflict with the activities of a new state-sponsored institution.[51]

Mexico City printers' engagement with Gil's notions of neoclassical taste varied, adapted or reimagined in some circumstances but gradually embraced over time. The type specimen explored in figure 5, for example, deployed type designed by Gil with neoclassical principles in mind. The specimen informed audiences that this type had been acquired along with a "new Madrid press," highlighting its cosmopolitan connections. Yet the document configured

ESTATUTOS
DE LA
REAL ACADEMIA
DE
SAN CARLOS
DE NUEVA ESPAÑA.

EN LA IMPRENTA NUEVA MEXICANA
DE DON FELIPE DE ZUÑIGA Y ONTIVEROS,
AÑO DE CI‫כ‬. I‫כ‬CC. LXXXV.

FIGURE 6. *Estatutos de la Real Academia de San Carlos de Nueva España* (Mexico City: En la Imprenta Nueva Mexicana de Don Felipe de Zúñiga y Ontiveros, 1785). Courtesy of HathiTrust.

these typefaces in a dizzying baroque display, filled with exuberance and ornament, which classicizing reformers like Gil shunned. In contrast, the title page of the statutes of the Academy of San Carlos, printed just three years later at a different press, used blank space to dramatic effect, cutting out content typical of Mexican title pages, like dense ornamental borders and detailed textual information (see figure 6). This new style favored a spare composition that highlighted the qualities of the individual letterforms and their composition on the page, often with a single illustration like a bow or a floral bouquet. Variation in typography likely reflected printers' strategizing in relation to consumer preferences and expectations, and announcements about the arrival of new types from Madrid alerted potential patrons to printers' participation in the court-sanctioned project of aesthetic reform.[52] By the end of the eighteenth century, the sparer neoclassical style, focusing on letterforms while shunning dense ornamentation, frequently framed scientific and religious scholarly works, directing viewers' attentions to the text itself. This typography reflected the broader enlightened project to curtail ostentatious display and baroque sensuality in favor of the more austere aesthetics promoted by royal academic institutions.[53]

New kinds of printed matter, too, reflected royal support for enlightened reform in Mexico City. The semiofficial *Gazeta de México,* published twice monthly at the impetus of the printer Valdés beginning in 1784, exemplified the rise of a periodical culture that intertwined with official objectives. This was not the first attempt to formalize a vehicle for news in Mexico. Information and newsworthy accounts had long circulated sporadically in various printed forms throughout the colonial era: as broadsides, *relaciones de sucesos,* and other genres. Several periodical projects emerged in the 1720s to 1740s, and again in the 1760s when scholar José Antonio Alzate y Ramírez (1737–1799) published the *Diario literario de México,* dedicated to scientific themes and funded by his inheritance.[54] Viceregal authorities temporarily shut Alzate down in the wake of the Jesuit expulsion, leaving Mexico City without a serial of its own for two decades. When Valdés unveiled his recently approved plans for a new periodical, he emphasized the *Gazeta*'s usefulness above all.

The *Gazeta de México* refracted the outlooks and objectives of its principal architects, revealing overlapping understandings of empire and its relationship to news. The viceroy, Matías de Gálvez (1783–1784), conceptualized an empire of information in which the newspaper's "various news: arrivals, departures, ships' cargoes and natural productions; elections of prelates, mayors; cannon appointments and other notable distinctions that occur in this extensive country" could facilitate commerce and strengthen local governance.[55] The *Gazeta,* he implied, also brought Mexico into a cosmopolitan sphere of enlightened exchange, "in imitation of the Court of Madrid and others in Europe."[56] Carlos III, who approved the project in 1785, hoped the *Gazeta* would deepen his knowledge of empire, suggesting that it could be augmented with "some articles that treat with exactitude geographic points in the country and curiosities of its natural history."[57] By expanding the king's scientific knowledge, the newspaper would improve his ability to govern overseas possessions.[58] The *Gazeta*'s creator, Valdés, conceptualized the newspaper as a vehicle that served two interlinked constituencies: his official patrons and local readers. He dedicated the first issue to the viceroy, describing the newspaper as a testament to the improvement projects the viceroy had already spearheaded in New Spain. By recording their success, the *Gazeta* would "archive these useful documents for posterity."[59] At the same time, the newspaper could serve local readers by improving communications and information-sharing practices. Thanks to orders from the viceroy, the quality of the *Gazeta*'s information was sure to be more reliable since it emanated from official sources, Valdés argued. The newspaper, Valdés hoped, could "save friends the labor of mutually writing news, or the curious the [task] of archiving it by some method."[60] Valdés's addendum to the prologue left no doubt about the well-heeled audiences he imagined addressing: he invited individuals to submit notices advertising the sale of houses, haciendas, and slaves and for lost and found jewels. The newspaper's materiality, too, underscored Valdés's arguments about its function. He imagined his paginated *Gazetas* carefully compiled and bound at year's end into a leather volume, adorned with a title page, index, and sometimes a preface, that would endure for future generations as testaments to New Spain's vibrancy in an enlightened empire.

The *Gazeta* offered Valdés an opportunity to craft a new identity. Even as he published the newspaper, Valdés also managed the Zúñiga y Ontiveros press. Yet through this new venture, Valdés gained the title of "author" of the *Gazeta*. What, for Valdés, did authorship entail? In his first prologue, Valdés described how he facilitated the exchange of information, downplaying his personal credentials in an elaborate display of modesty. "I don't sell myself as an erudite Historian," explained Valdés, "but rather as a general amanuensis for those who take my printed matter."[61] Defending himself with caveats, he promised to "display my docility and deference" when faced with justified criticism. Valdés defined authorship around the selection and organization of information. His show of humility acknowledged his position on the fringe of Mexico's intellectual communities. Yet his prologues established a new public figure that, emerging from the laboring milieu of the printing shop, spoke with the backing of royal authority.

The semiofficial nature of the *Gazeta*'s news apparatus nevertheless challenged Valdés from the outset. Early on, he complained that individuals writing anonymously or with cryptic names had been sending in news items directly to the printing shop for publication. Concerned that he could be seen as responsible for misleading the public with unverified news, Valdés instructed readers to submit writings to their local officials for vetting.[62] Yet relying on local officials for the news presented its own problems. Valdés occasionally skipped issues, blaming the scarcity of news. Indeed, this became a persistent complaint in the semiregular dedications issued at year's end in honor of a succession of viceroys. In his dedication to the 1788 series, for example, Valdés praised the new viceroy for reminding local officials to remit their news and permitting the inclusion of additional content to fill space.[63] Such repeated exhortations underscored the links between the periodical and the largesse of its official patrons. So too did the economics of publishing. In exchange for an annual fee for the privilege, Valdés apparently received a subsidy of paper—always the largest share of printing costs—from the viceroy.[64] Subscriptions, paid announcements, and publicity for other publishing ventures also sustained the *Gazeta*.[65] It remained the sole local printed vehicle for news, over which successive viceroys maintained a degree of control, for two decades.[66]

Having a semiofficial publication aided viceregal authorities amid the climate of uncertainty that accompanied the French and Haitian Revolutions. The French Revolution, in particular, raised Spanish authorities' anxieties about publications perceived to threaten imperial stability. Concern that works by French philosophes would lead readers in the Spanish Americas to question political and religious authority showed that officials perceived imported texts as potential agents of unrest. Yet printers in Mexico City betrayed little of the daring shown by New Granadan Antonio Nariño, who translated and oversaw the printing of one hundred copies of *The Declaration of the Rights of Man* in 1794, before thinking better of his actions and destroying the edition.[67] Instead, the *Gazeta de México* observed the viceroy's news blackout during the Revolution, before filling in with anti-French coverage after Spain entered war with France.[68] At the height of the war in 1794, the *Gazeta* doubled its output by reprinting news excerpted directly from the *Gazeta de Madrid*, likely handpicked by the viceroy. The choice to reprint news from Madrid meant that it reached colonial audiences with up to five months' delay, perhaps long after reports conveyed through letters and merchant networks. Yet reprinting was not only aimed at informing local audiences; the viceroy encouraged the practice in order to shape local interpretations of events, strengthen transatlantic ties, and urge residents of New Spain to act patriotically by donating to the war effort. Indeed, the issues of the *Gazeta* ballooned in 1794 and 1795 not only with official battlefield reports from Europe, but also with long reports of contributions made by locals to the royal treasury. In these lists, humble artisans who donated less than a peso earned recognition alongside the wealthiest luminaries. Subscribers of the *Gazeta*, however, eventually grew tired of bankrolling royal donor lists, which quickly consumed the paper allotment for the twenty-four issues that filled a year's subscription. Reader complaints led Valdés to change the subscription system to make donor lists optional. The end of the war brought an end to the reprinting of European news and a return to familiar rhythms and content, refocused on local events.

THE MONARCHICAL CRISIS OF 1808

The *Gazeta de México*'s status as a semiofficial newspaper made it a site of conflict and contestation after political crisis generated imperial uncertainties in 1808. Napoleon's occupation of the Iberian Peninsula that year sent shockwaves across the Spanish Empire. The event destabilized the foundations on which Valdés's exclusive news privileges rested. For one, the invasion generated speculation in Mexico City that even official news might be a lucrative business, since residents craved information about events unfolding across the Atlantic. At the same time, the crisis provoked shifts in authority behind the scenes, which threatened the public image and patronage ties Valdés had cultivated over his long career.

In the decades preceding the 1808 crisis, the *Gazeta*'s publisher had become a wealthy man. Besides operating Mexico City's first coach-for-hire service and sending his son to Guadalajara to found that city's first press, Valdés owned haciendas in the Valley of Mexico.[69] As the nineteenth century dawned, however, his privileges faced competition, as new actors sought to expand the scope of printed news and test its local markets. In 1805, journalistic entrepreneurs received permission to start a daily newspaper, the *Diario de México*. Often described as Mexico's first modern newspaper, the *Diario*— the brain child of creole lawyers Jacobo Villaurrutia and Carlos María de Bustamante—used a playful, sarcastic tone that created a feeling of intimacy lacking in the staid formality of the *Gazeta*.[70] While Valdés constantly emphasized his loyalty to royal officials, the *Diario* poked fun at his deferential prologues and at the broader realities of colonial censorship. "Prologues only serve to make offerings and promises, and to give excuses in advance," wrote the editors in their own antiprologue, which obliquely mocked the *Gazeta*. "What is the point of promising, if one can't comply? And if one has to comply, what is the point of promising?"[71] The new daily, printed at a rival press, attracted nearly seven hundred subscribers in its first year of production, revealing readers' interest in nonofficial content.[72] This popularity clearly preoccupied Valdés, and he partnered with Juan López Cancelada, a peninsular-born Spaniard, to update the *Gazeta*.

Three years after Valdés first partnered with Cancelada, Napoleon's occupation of the Iberian Peninsula spurred an unprecedented crisis. When Spanish prime minister Manuel Godoy allowed Napoleon to march across Spanish territory in 1808, Napoleon seized the Spanish throne, forcing the abdication of Fernando VII in March and placing his own brother in power. Local governments in both Spain and the Americas, refusing to recognize Napoleonic rule, rushed to fill the power vacuum by forming governing juntas. In Mexico City, the crisis put new pressure on Viceroy José de Iturrigaray (1803–1808), himself a protégé of the disgraced Godoy and widely rumored to be corrupt. Local elites were already disgruntled that Spain had been siphoning New Spain's church wealth to finance ongoing wars with England and France. Now, suspicions about Iturrigaray's skimming of these funds took on darker significance.[73] Competing plans soon emerged for how to solve the crisis of legitimacy, provoking tensions among elites and revealing schisms between creoles and Spanish-born *peninsulares* over the question of local autonomy. In September, Spanish merchant elites allied with Mexico's peninsular-dominated Audiencia (high court) staged a coup against the viceroy, whom they accused of sympathizing with the autonomist agenda of the creole-controlled Ayuntamiento (city council). The new viceroy, Pedro de Garibay (1808–1809), curtailed creole movements for autonomy.

The upheavals of 1808 also played out in the pages of the press. The first reports of Fernando's abdication, received from Spain that summer, were newspaper accounts that provoked uncertainty over their authority and reliability.[74] Iturrigaray's hesitations and retractions further fueled rumors and speculation over his own loyalties and motivations. As news of Spanish resistance to Napoleon followed, the *Gazeta* and the *Diario* published declarations of loyalty and exhortations to patriotism from around the viceroyalty. The viceroy soon announced that the *Gazeta* would publish special supplements that would recognize financial benefactors without crowding out the information that readers craved.[75] By resurrecting official wartime policies designed to inspire patriotic sentiments and further largesse, the viceroy also proclaimed his own loyalties as he navigated a complex political situation.[76] News reports in the *Gazeta* and the *Diario* bolstered the portrait of a unified society with descriptions of residents' spontaneous displays of patriotism, noting how they wore cockades and brooches in support of the king. Advertisements hawked lockets, portraits, and medals bearing the king's face, to be worn on the body or hung from city balconies.[77]

The politics of loyalty generated new business opportunities for members of Mexico City's printing trades in the second half of 1808. While the *Gazeta* reproduced authorized briefings, all the city's printers took advantage of the patriotic flurry to reissue pamphlets from Spain and Havana that criticized Napoleon and expanded the field of political commentary. Mexico City residents, for example, could purchase satirical cartoons that mocked Napoleon, just like their counterparts in Spain. In one scatological engraving, a peasant representing Spain crouched with dropped trousers on the "summit of generosity," from which he defecated onto Napoleon's desk as England looked on, an expectant voyeur (see figure 7). While the general railed against "Ungrateful Spain!," the peasant slyly apologized for the meagerness of his offering, which rained down upon a draft of the constitution Napoleon had prepared on Spain's behalf. Mocking Napoleon's pretensions as a giver of laws, the print's descriptive text explained that while Napoleon had triumphed elsewhere with "lies and tall tales, in Spain his plan fell to shit (*se cagó*)." Though satire had long troubled colonial officials, who feared its subversive power, its use in support of Spain was hardly problematic. Indeed, its commissioner, Cancelada—Valdés's editorial collaborator—proudly informed viewers that the print resulted from his investment, having asked the engraver to include an inscription along the print's right edge that it had been produced "at the expense of D. J. L. Cancelada."

Cancelada, the editor of the *Gazeta de México* during the 1808 crisis, had perhaps commissioned the anti-Napoleonic cartoon as part of his own strategic display of loyalty, for recent events had landed him in serious trouble. Since 1805, he had helped Valdés manage and modernize the *Gazeta*. He had started off as an occasional contributor, advising Mexicans on household methods for waterproofing shoes and curing snakebites.[78] After he became a regular collaborator, however, he acted as Valdés's heavyweight, defending the latter's monopoly over the news. He had briefly managed to shut down the *Diario* by complaining to the viceroy that the daily had infringed on the *Gazeta*'s news privilege.[79] Before long he had garnered a controversial reputation, and in 1807 he faced the Inquisition on charges of blasphemy for one of

FIGURE 7. Larrea, *Napoleon trabajando para la regeneración de España, la cual represen-tada en un patriota le paga agradecida el beneficio*, engraving, 1809. Ministerio de Cultura y Deporte. Archivo General de Indias. MP-Estampas, 51.

his publications.[80] The Inquisition dismissed the charges, but the censor described Cancelada as "publicly and notoriously reputed as scatterbrained and a gossip."[81] In November 1808, following the coup against Viceroy Iturrigaray, Cancelada tried to get the *Diario de México* shut down for a sec-ond time, accusing its cofounder not only of privilege infringement but also of seditiously plotting to use the newspaper as part of a creole scheme "to publish independence."[82] The strategy backfired. Viceregal authorities launched an investigation and, after an initially sympathetic reception, deter-mined that Cancelada had cynically framed his rival as a radical separatist in a byzantine attempt to eliminate the *Diario* and boost the *Gazeta's* fortunes. Cancelada, a partisan of the Spanish contingent that had orchestrated the coup, had misjudged the new viceroy, Garibay. Officials censured him with a fine or two-month jail sentence.

As Cancelada stared down a possible prison sentence, his collaborator, Valdés, faced accusations by the archbishop of Mexico that he had failed to perform his duties as the official government printer.[83] The accusations revolved around donor lists, which, by order of the previous viceroy, Valdés was supposed to print as supplements to the *Gazeta* to recognize the financial donations made by locals to the Spanish cause. Valdés had, indeed, been publishing regular lists of donors, along with their contribution sums, as *Gazetas Extraordinarias*, special editions published once or twice per month in addition to the regular *Gazeta*. Yet according to the archbishop, people had been complaining that their names had not been published, meaning their acts of patriotism and generosity went unrecognized by fellow readers. The archbishop argued that without these regular recognitions in the *Gazeta* proper, patriotic sympathy might falter. The printer, he directed, must publish at least two pages of donor lists in each edition of the *Gazeta* from now on.

The printer responded to the archbishop's complaint in a letter to the new viceroy, drafted with Cancelada, which suggested that it was not the *Gazeta* but rather government policy that needed reform. The men accused the state of having abandoned its side of the patronage pact. While viceroys in decades past had underwritten the costs of producing the *Gazeta* by paying for the paper, the men explained, this support had since lapsed, and now sales alone supported the newspaper. "One cannot pay nothing and make demands against another's work and income," they claimed, explaining that only a contract with public subscribers dictated the contents of the *Gazeta*.[84] As experience had taught them, subscribers preferred to "learn about political news" and had no interest in paying for donor lists. Arguing that financial independence conferred them autonomy over news content, Cancelada and Valdés simultaneously reaffirmed the importance of patronage by pressing to reform and expand their privilege to publish the news. Asking the viceroy for a monopoly to reprint all political content from Spain, they complained that other presses had "gained a fortune" in recent months by reprinting Spanish broadsides and pamphlets about the Napoleonic invasion while they remained saddled with a five-hundred-peso annual fee for the *Gazeta*. Wagering that their considerable services to the crown would strengthen their case, the men pushed the viceroy to either subsidize the official news apparatus or clear the way for greater earnings in the private sector by extending their monopoly over all political content from Spain. Otherwise, they boldly refused to follow the archbishop's order to print donor lists without payment in advance. The specter of a *Gazeta* governed only by the publishers' economic contract with readers became a tactic for renegotiating the status quo.

Unfortunately for Valdés and Cancelada, Spanish officials soon removed and replaced the viceroy to whom they had complained with none other than Mexico's archbishop, Francisco Javier Lizana y Beaumont (1809–1810), the very individual who had taken umbrage at their work in the first place. The viceroy-archbishop, consulting with legal experts in the Audiencia, reviewed their outstanding petition. Promisingly, one *fiscal* (crown attorney) argued that the government indeed depended on the *Gazeta*, as the paper with the widest domestic circulation, to publicize its donor lists, which made contributors happy and encouraged others to "show their zeal and liberality for the cause of the sovereign and the state."[85] Nobody, the official admitted, would pay to purchase a list of donors if such a list were to circulate separately; hence, the fate of the donor lists was bound to the *Gazeta* for logistical reasons, and he recommended approving a subvention. Yet the official also proposed a new idea for saving costs, suggesting that the government could authorize the creation of a second government newspaper, peeling off the privilege to print political news from Europe to start a *Gazeta del Gobierno* at the treasury's expense that could also print the donor lists. Thus, the editors of the *Gazeta de México* would be relieved of their burden, and the government would be freed from paying them back. By the fall of 1809, officials had received three proposals from printers and would-be publishers, and they looked favorably upon the bid launched by Francisco José de Noriega, a deacon and lawyer of the Audiencia. Noriega criticized the *Gazeta de México*, suggesting that its creators had taken advantage of a recent climate of tolerance "to speak arbitrarily about whatever the editor wants."[86] Instead, he could better oversee the delicate task of "forming public opinion and . . . instructing inhabitants of the realm." He also promised to cover all of the costs of the newspaper while publishing any official news the government saw fit to include, free of charge. By October, Noriega had received a new privilege.

A PRINTER DEFENDS HIS PRIVILEGES

Valdés's contestation of his lost privilege reveals how the disruptions of 1808 destabilized the networks he had cultivated since the creation of the *Gazeta de México* in 1784. After explaining the history of the privilege, which had been customarily reinforced by successive viceroys, he appealed to the viceroy-archbishop in the language of loyalty.[87] The printer detailed his lengthy services to the crown, which included cost savings on official printing commissions, sending his son to Guadalajara to establish its first printing shop when it would have been more profitable in Mexico City, and lowering the price of corn on his haciendas to prevent unrest during recent periods of famine. The printer's petition argued that his substantial investments had directly served the crown's economic and strategic political interests.

Describing himself as old and infirm yet always working at his printing shop, and responsible for many dependents, Valdés begged the viceroy not to give his privilege to Noriega. Otherwise, he warned, costs of official decrees and the *Gazeta* would both rise, to the detriment of consumers. Mentioning a lawsuit, Valdés hoped to sway the viceroy through a combination of appeal to his status as a model industrious subject, his history of service, and a threat that played to official concerns about local resentment. Rising costs for the news and other official imprints would surely be unwise policy in a time of political crisis, he implied.

The redistribution of Valdés's privilege was almost certainly linked to politics, since the printer offered to match Noriega's terms. It took several weeks, however—as the printer, his rival, and viceregal authorities negotiated over the decision—for officials to develop an argument to justify Valdés's dispossession. Emerging conceptions of intellectual property provided the key. After numerous exchanges, an *oidor* (judge) for the Audiencia questioned whether Valdés even held an exclusive privilege to the *Gazeta de México* at all. In his opinion, Valdés only held a license, which granted him permission to publish content from the *Gazeta de Madrid*.[88] And Valdés had simply reprinted much of this content, so that the *Gazeta de México* had almost come to resemble its Madrid counterpart. Where was the evidence of the printer's own contributions? The *oidor* pointed to recent policies advocated by Carlos III, which had favored the exclusive privileges of authors and their heirs over those enjoyed by institutions or corporations. "Since Valdés is not the Author in the true sense of this word," he reasoned, he could hardly claim a privilege. "Valdés himself said in a dedication to his *Gazetas* that he was a curious copyist who sought to put the events presented to him in order." Furthermore, Valdés seemed unable to keep up even with the basics of the news. In 1805 he had justified his appointment of Cancelada as the *Gazeta*'s editor under the logic that he was too busy to carry out the organization of the newspaper. If this were so, the official reasoned, then the government was justified in finding someone else to publish its *Gazeta*. In the *oidor*'s eyes, Valdés was being greedy, attempting to monopolize printing to the detriment of the crown's interests. "This is purely a question of governance," he argued, that could be fixed, in the reformist spirit of Carlos III, by eliminating "those monopolies and literary cartels (*estancos*) to give stimulus to the application of the area of printing."

This exchange challenged all of the arguments upon which Valdés had built his career as a gazetteer. His own writings, published to craft a public persona that juggled his status as printer and creator of the *Gazeta*, had been used against him. While Valdés had described the activities of collecting, organizing, and publishing as proper to authorship, the official reframed these activities as simply copying, leveraging ideas about intellectual property rooted in original, individual textual creation. Antitrust language justified cutting ties with a long-term contractor, and Valdés saw himself painted not as an industrious subject of empire but as a backwards impediment to productivity. The viceroy-archbishop, who had displayed his annoyance with Valdés months before, approved the dismantling of his claims over the official news and granted Noriega permission to publish the new *Gazeta del Gobierno*.

In response, Valdés wrote to officials in Spain, appealing to law, custom, and loyalty.[89] He described himself as the holder of a privilege established long ago by decree and strengthened over time by custom. The new viceroy-archbishop, however, had trampled this privilege in an action that smacked of cronyism, since, according to Valdés, the new *Gazeta*'s publisher was actually the viceroy's personal servant. Nepotistic practices, he argued, harmed Spain's image as an empire of law. The printer asked Spanish officials to reverse the viceroy's action, to extend his privilege to his heirs, and to grant him the exclusive privilege for European news as well. In the meantime, however, Valdés ceased publishing the *Gazeta*, which passed into new hands as the *Gazeta del Gobierno*. In a veiled farewell to longtime audiences printed on the last page of the final issue, Valdés promised to send subscribers their biannual indices, "as proof of thanks from the Author ... for the steadfastness with which they have favored him over the twenty-five years that he has enjoyed the honor of overseeing this newspaper."[90] While Valdés contested his lost privilege, his collaborator, Cancelada, faced prison and expulsion from the colony. The outspoken editor had fallen afoul of the viceroy-archbishop thanks to public criticisms that he had launched, perhaps imprudently, as his business dealings were under scrutiny.[91]

Before Cancelada's forced repatriation, the viceroy-archbishop himself wrote to Spanish officials to explain the situation and defend his dismissal of Valdés, whom he argued lacked the necessary cultural capital to publish the *Gazeta*.[92] In his telling, the newspaper had fallen into "decadence" by 1805. This, combined with the conflict over printing donor lists, had led viceregal officials to seek a new solution, and Noriega—the new editor—had proved well suited to the "grave task" of publishing official news. As the viceroy-archbishop argued, "the author of the old *Gazeta* is an elderly printer who has exercised this trade alone his whole life, and thus lacks the necessary knowledge to carry out such a delicate commission." Further proof of Valdés's unsuitability for the royal commission lay in his having associated with all sorts of questionable people, including Cancelada, a "man of a restless disposition, and without learning [*sin literatura*]," as editorial collaborators. Cutting through the political charges that swirled around the privilege for printing, the viceroy spoke to Spanish officials in the language of status, undermining the printer Valdés's activities by emphasizing formal education as the cultural capital required of the office of gazetteer. On the other hand Noriega, an educated man, was well suited to the task. It seems that the reformist discourses about the complementarity between the manual and liberal arts, which Valdés had negotiated as the *Gazeta*'s printer and author, held little purchase amid the priorities of the powerful.

It took nearly half a year for officials in Spain to receive and rule on Valdés's case. In the intervening period, Spanish officials relieved the viceroy-archbishop of his duties. Lizana y Beaumont had alienated New Spain's peninsular merchant elite and pro-Spanish factions, who complained to their contacts across the Atlantic and secured the archbishop's dismissal.[93] While the viceroy-archbishop had attempted to realign royal patronage, punishing Valdés for his association with Cancelada, the council of the Spanish Regency favored reliable familiarity over promises of a new and improved news apparatus for its colonial subjects. Perhaps the council believed one of Cancelada's supporters, who warned darkly that the new editor of the *Gazeta del Gobierno* harbored autonomist leanings and would use the newspaper to promote "the disunion of the Metropolis."[94] On July 1 the council, now based in Cádiz, issued its ruling on the *Gazeta de México*, reversing the former viceroy's policy, affirming printer Valdés's privilege over the news, and ordering the suppression of Noriega's license. Mexico's Audiencia, governing in the interim, acknowledged the decision in early September, just days after a new viceroy, Francisco Javier Venegas, had landed at Veracruz to assume his post. For Valdés, however, the confirmation of his privilege offered cold comfort; he never produced the *Gazeta* again.

CONCLUSION: THE PRINTER'S PLACE IN THE
SHIFTING POLITICS OF EMPIRE

The Valdés case revealed the enduring power of privileges in the late colonial political economy of printing. Though a material struggle, the conflict was inseparable from broader concerns about political loyalty and imperial security, which loomed in the minds of officials and subjects alike amid the uncertainties of the 1808 crisis. While historians agree that the crisis of 1808 generated an outpouring of support for the Spanish monarch across the empire, the immediate aftermath of the Napoleonic invasion revealed divergent perspectives and expectations in New Spain. The conflict surrounding the privilege to print the news adds to our understanding of this process. According to the editor Cancelada, Mexican creoles who threatened his privileges—from the editor of the *Diario de México* to the viceroy-archbishop himself—also threatened the stability of the Spanish Empire. His communiqués to Spain expressed a righteous superiority that he thought would play well with his compatriots. Viceregal officials viewed the news as an important element of imperial stability they hoped to control, but they wanted to distribute the costs (and potential rewards) of information to their clients. As the political crisis changed the economic stakes of publishing, officials looked for new ways to regulate the news and control flows of information. The printer Valdés found himself caught in the middle, hamstrung by his association with a provocative *peninsular* whom he had hired to modernize his newspaper.

The conflict also shows some of the heterogeneous currents of the Spanish American Enlightenment in action. Participants deployed liberal discourse in the same breath as they requested new monopolies, scrutinized the definitions of usefulness and individual merit, and wielded or questioned certainties about law and custom. Even as these discourses circulated in often mercenary ways, the rules and practices surrounding news, information, and print in Mexico were on the brink of change. Ten days after local officials received the Regency's order to restore Valdés's privileges in 1810, a violent peasant revolt led by the parish priest Miguel Hidalgo in the name of the king broke out in the inland province of Guanajuato, raising the stakes of official calculations. In Spain, the Regency convoked the Cortes, a medieval representative body, at Cádiz to rule in the king's absence. By the end of the year, the Cortes had, among other proclamations that embraced liberalism for Spain, declared freedom of the press and heralded a new legal regime that promised to sweep printing privileges into oblivion. Yet across the ocean in New Spain, press freedom would follow a somewhat different path, shaped by the violent insurgency that would transform into wide-scale civil conflict.

Cancelada, meanwhile, lobbied to return to New Spain to establish a press and requested the restitution of his position as the editor of the *Gazeta de México*, making false claims in an attempt to recover his fortunes. In 1811 he published a short history that blamed the 1810 Hidalgo uprising on Viceroy

Iturrigaray and the Mexico City Ayuntamiento, reviving his accusations that pro-autonomist creoles had sowed the seeds of discontent.[95] The Ayuntamiento complained to Spain about Cancelada's treatise, and official reports commented unfavorably on his suitability for any royal commission, noting his "indiscretion."[96] Cancelada's former targets sued him in revenge, but officials stopped the suit for its politically sensitive nature, since it centered on peninsular-creole animosities at a deeply inconvenient moment.[97] José Servando Teresa de Mier, a Mexican-born priest and liberal thinker exiled for his unorthodox ideas, cited Cancelada's lies as the impetus for writing his own *History of the Revolution in New Spain*, published pseudonymously in London, a city that, along with Philadelphia, became a printing hub for exiled critics from around Spanish America.[98] Cancelada lived out his days in Spain, publishing a lengthy history of Mexico's independence wars based on his witnessing of the events surrounding the coup against the viceroy.[99]

Valdés, on the other hand, did not live to see the outcome of the conflict, though his son Alejandro would inherit the challenges of navigating the uncertainties accompanying the declaration of freedom of the press. Alejandro commemorated his father's death in 1814 with a portrait that, commissioned at the height of Mexico's war for independence, underscored the deceased printer's royal credentials (see figure 8). The portrait depicts its subject in the act of composing or editing a bit of verse. Dressed elegantly, he stands in a spare working space, supplied with a high table, inkwell, and bookshelf full of bound volumes at his back. Perhaps Valdés is correcting a proof for publication, comparing a manuscript copy to a printed example held in his left hand. Typical of late colonial portraiture, Valdés is depicted in full figure, a composition that showed the subject as a representative of a recognizable social group rather than an individual whose unique character is emphasized through careful attention to the face.[100] Yet unlike previous portraits of *letrados*, Valdés appears with his quill suspended in midair, a move that Tomás Pérez Vejo argues heralded the reimagining of the modern intellectual as an active creator of texts rather than a scholar associated with academic institutions.[101] Only the portrait's text reveals the connection between the subject and his broader professional life, describing him as the "Royal Printer to his Majesty, May God Protect Him" and "Author of the Gazeta de México."

The portrait offers an argument that is not only about the shifting basis of intellectual identity but also about the printer's role within this world. Depicted here is an idealized portrait of the printer, who, embodying the spirit of industriousness and intellectual improvement that underpinned the

Manuel Antonio Valdés Murguía y Saldaña. Impresor de Cámara de su M.[?] que D. G. Autor de la Gazeta de Mexico In
... Cortes de Providencia nació en esta Capital en el día 17 de Julio del año de 1742. fueron sus Padres D. Miguel Benito Valb...
... Villa de Piña en el Concejo de Langrebó Obispado de Obiedo, y su Madre D. María Murguía y Tabera ... para presente...
... D. Alexandro Valdéz el año de 1814. que fue en el que murió día 8 de Abril.

FIGURE 8. Ignacio Ayala, *Manuel Antonio Valdés Murguía y Saldaña*, oil on
canvas, 1814. Secretaría de Cultura, INAH, Mexico. Reproduction authorized
by the Instituto Nacional de Antropología e Historia.

court-sponsored Enlightenment in the Spanish Americas, devotes his endeavors to royal service and the improvement of knowledge in the empire *as a letrado*. Kelly Donohue-Wallace shows how the commissioned professional portraits of Mexico's most renowned enlightened artistic practitioners, like engraver Gil and sculptor Manuel Tolsá, featured tools of their crafts in the composition.[102] Valdés's portrait emphasizes instead the literary side and the finished product, the effort of textual composition and writing, but reveals nothing of how these elements would be converted into useful form through the manual labor, materials, and machinery of the printing shop. Thus, the portrait reveals a deep ambivalence about the printer's social status, suggesting that Spanish intellectuals' efforts to reconfigure the manual arts had not completely succeeded. Its representative strategy, which seems a direct response to the viceroy-archbishop's dismissal of Valdés as an old printer who "lacks the necessary knowledge" and formal education to carry out his work, provides early evidence of printers' public positioning in relation to intellectual production. The role of the printer would come under intense scrutiny during the conflicts of the following decade, which brought a greater degree of autonomy to the world of publishing and serious challenges to the colonial regime in Mexico.

TWO

Negotiating Freedom

IN 1813, A LETTER CAME into the possession of José María Morelos, a priest and the main leader of a rural insurgency fighting to establish an independent government in Mexico. The letter, written by the archbishop-elect of Mexico, Antonio Bergosa y Jordán, had been printed in Mexico City before traveling south to the town of Chilpancingo, arriving two months later at Morelos's headquarters. The archbishop's text exhorted Mexico's priests to assist with counterinsurgency efforts by instructing Mexicans in religious and royal obedience and combatting the insurgency's "impious maxims of rebellion and anarchy."[1] Brought to Morelos's attention, the archbishop's text elicited a clear response. The insurgent leader replied by adding a series of annotations to the printed page followed by his signature and rubric (see figure 9). "Return this," Morelos ordered, "since this Archbishop is not elected by the legitimate American government because the Regency of Spain only commands in its own house." Morelos's directive, preserved along with several sarcastic jabs as marginalia, defiantly rejected the archbishop's moral authority and claimed political legitimacy for an American government that did not even exist on paper. It would be several months more before insurgents would convene the Congress of Anáhuac in Chilpancingo, where they formally declared independence from Spain and drafted a constitution.

Morelos's emphatic annotations were probably never seen by the archbishop. Indeed, the material traces of the exchange between Morelos and Bergosa y Jordán underscore the communication difficulties facing the insurgent cause, in stark contrast with the archbishop's situation. Out in the rural hinterlands, insurgents struggled to acquire and maintain a poorly equipped press without expertise or essential supplies like parts and paper. As

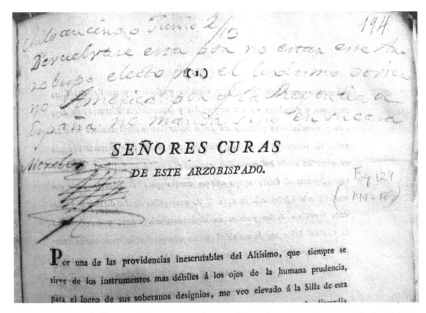

FIGURE 9. Detail of printed letter returned to sender, with marginalia written by José María Morelos, 1813. Archivo General de la Nación, Mexico City.

revolutionary movements across the Atlantic world deployed printed texts like newspapers, pamphlets, and clandestine literature to question the legitimacy of absolutist and colonial regimes in the late eighteenth and early nineteenth centuries, Mexico's top insurgent leader resorted to marginal commentary to advance his critique.[2] Bergosa y Jordán, on the other hand, had the resources of the largest printing hub in the Spanish Americas at his disposal. Having fled from Oaxaca after insurgents captured the city, the archbishop made use of Mexico City's presses to publish and republish numerous pastoral letters, sermons, and appeals against the insurgency. This disparity stared insurgent leaders in the face as they set about the task of constructing their own political authority in the form of a constitution, printed on a press smuggled out of Mexico City with type founded helter-skelter in Oaxaca.[3] The insurgent constitution would never hold sway, and Morelos was soon captured and executed by a firing squad. Morelos's paper adversary, Bergosa y Jordán, presided over his Inquisition trial and condemnation.

As the story of rival yet unequal communication strategies suggests, printing technology played a central role in the violent political struggles that unfolded in Mexico and across the Spanish Empire as autonomist and independence movements challenged absolutist and colonial rule from within. In

Mexico, royalists and insurgents alike viewed print as a medium essential for constructing and maintaining loyalty. Inside the urban core, printed fora like the *Gazeta de México* had formed one component of the public sphere that had taken shape under the auspices of viceregal patronage during the late eighteenth century. Censorship and privileges, however, kept criticism of government largely off the printed page. As violent challenges to established authorities broke out, the medium gained new importance. Historians have focused on how print, by circulating revolutionary ideas within the Atlantic world, sparked revolutionary change in the Spanish Americas, transforming readers and proximate audiences, even in contexts without presses.[4] Yet the case of Mexico shows that printing mattered because it served as a technology of power and source for constituting and negotiating legitimacy that came up for grabs amid the messy context of war, Spain's liberal political revolution, and imperial disintegration.[5]

Print as a medium rooted in social realities—rather than just as a vehicle for ideas and political discourses—was fully entangled in broader struggles over the foundations of authority and the definitions of freedom and rights in the Age of Revolution.[6] While the aftermath of the 1808 monarchical crisis had strengthened the position of hard-line Spanish loyalists in Mexico, the convocation of the Cortes in Cádiz in 1810 opened space for liberals to reimagine the foundations of imperial sovereignty, producing experiments in constitutionalism and renewed enthusiasm for local autonomy in government affairs, especially among Latin America's creole elites.[7] The crisis also precipitated violent anti-colonial movements across the empire that quickly sought outright independence from Spain. In Mexico, the evolving radical character of the rural anti-colonial insurgency initiated by the 1810 Hidalgo Revolt—its empowerment of Mexico's multiracial majorities, defiance of traditional authorities, embrace of abolitionism, and support of universal male suffrage—led urban creoles to recoil in spite of their autonomist leanings.[8] Thus, as they embraced a set of liberal guarantees associated with their new, privileged status as imperial citizens, most urban elites showed little inclination to convert the emerging watchwords of liberty and equality into solidarity with insurgents like the mestizo Morelos.

Although Mexico's rural insurgencies and Spain's empire-wide liberal revolution are often explored separately, their influence on how residents of Mexico used and understood print intertwined. Insurgents' attempts to wrest the printed symbols of political authority from royalists generated an outpouring of counterpropaganda in Mexico City, unleashing optimism among urban intellectuals about printing's potential as a technology of popular and individualized persuasion rather than the stuff of elite networking or information aids deployed within familiar webs of authority. At the same time, the 1812 Cádiz Constitution (revoked in 1814 but restored in 1820) introduced new press freedom laws around the empire that fundamentally shifted well-heeled, urban residents' own relationship to printing, generating new rights-based demands. After the initial euphoria surrounding the reenactment of the constitution in 1820, pressing questions remained unresolved. Urban residents repudiated the insurgency, yet wondered how much a citizen in good standing could conceivably say in print. Writers like José Joaquín Fernández de Lizardi, who envisioned new opportunities to expand their influence and the scope of political debate, asked how printers' close connections to royal officials and market power shaped the parameters of freedom. Printers like Alejandro Valdés, who depended on viceregal business yet benefited from the growing interest in publishing, worried about public perceptions and official responses to potentially sensitive texts. And officials struggled to find strategies that could contain criticism in print with the newly available tools of press laws. The 1820 publication of a simple broadside, *El liberal a los bajos escritores*, put all of these questions into motion. Released anonymously by what turned out to be the son of a high-ranking colonial official and reprinted in Mexico City at the impetus of a sympathetic reader, the broadside boldly condemned the viceroy. The resulting episode reveals how struggles over printing and its symbolic dimensions lay at the core of broader struggles over power, authority, and rights on the eve of independence.

PRINT AT WAR

The outbreak of a rural insurgency against the viceregal regime challenged the culture of consensus surrounding printing and spurred reflection about the relationship between print and authority. Long before the rise of periodical culture in the Bourbon era, Spanish rulers and officials had used printing to construct and enforce their power. Royal and inquisitorial decrees, printed (or reprinted after a Spanish original) in Mexico City, circulated along the routes of viceregal administration as tools of governance, promulgating laws and edicts and communicating official directives. These routes connected the capital with urban centers around the viceroyalty, extending as far afield as the Philippines. *Cordilleras*, written documents passed through the bureaucratic chains of command and signed by each official recipient before being returned to the original sender, recorded the itineraries of printed orders as they traveled from Mexico City out into removed rural territories—where no printing presses existed—and back.[9] Local officials would read and display these orders from the pulpit during church services and post them in customary places in urban centers with large populations. In towns too small to receive their own copies, decrees might be written out by hand using a style that mimicked the typographical conventions of print.[10] These documents conveyed legal directives that might be flagrantly ignored, yet they also played an important, visible role in the rituals of authority. Besides conveying directives within official hierarchies, they also mediated power relations between officials and ordinary residents.[11]

The Hidalgo Revolt, which broke out in Mexico's Bajío region in September 1810, disrupted these circuits of governance. Coming on the heels of the monarchical crisis, the revolt exploded onto the political scene, the largest in a series of plots staged against the viceregal regime since 1808. Initiated by the disaffected and reputedly libertine parish priest Miguel Hidalgo after a conspiracy he participated in was betrayed by one of its members, the revolt called for the defense of Fernando VII against Napoleon and an end to bad viceregal government. Appealing to market-goers in the town of Dolores, Hidalgo rallied a multiethnic group of followers to his cause, attracting indigenous peasants, rural laborers, and social sectors disillusioned by economic hardship and resentful of the Spanish minority who wielded power in everyday affairs. After ransacking the city of Guanajuato, a force of up to sixty thousand— painted by elite witnesses as a mob of murderous *indios* put up to their actions by rebel leaders—marched on Mexico City, before turning back and being repelled and scattered by Spanish troops.[12] The initial revolt would transform into a decade-long civil conflict, led by a mostly creole directorate but drawing forces from rural groups who joined the struggle either for ideological reasons or because it resonated with deep-seated grievances and efforts to defend local land and community against colonial elites.[13] While a brutal counterinsurgency campaign gained the upper hand after 1814, royalists never successfully stamped out the rebellion.

In the early stages of the conflict, insurgents broke the royal monopoly on print production, transforming the medium into a part of wartime strategy and unsettling colonial officials. Their proclamations and news bulletins, which contradicted royal communications, presented a platform to appeal to potential followers—advocating the abolition of slavery and *papel sellado* (stamped paper required for legal writings and an unpopular source of royal tax revenue).[14] Initially, insurgents commissioned or commandeered printing shops when they captured major cities—first in Guadalajara and later in Oaxaca—and used the presses to issue thousands of copies of manifestoes, proclamations, passes, various iterations of a government gazette, and all manner of bureaucratic documents.[15] They then distributed these materials through insurgent networks, occasionally sending them into the urban center of viceregal control, reversing the flow of printed materials that characterized typical circuits of governance. In 1811, for example, officials arrested an indigenous man reported for smuggling insurgent propaganda into Mexico City hidden in a false-bottomed box filled with lard.[16]

Insurgent efforts to harness print, especially after a counterinsurgency campaign pushed them out of major cities, underscores the importance they placed on the medium as a symbol of political legitimacy. As royalist troops drove them from Guadalajara and Oaxaca, insurgent leaders had to rely on two *imprentillas*, small, portable printing presses that they spirited out of urban areas and into rural headquarters.[17] On the move and in danger of capture, the leader in charge of printing operations described the press as "sluggish" and lamented the difficulties of keeping it up and running.[18] Printing far away from major centers where equipment and expertise might be acquired presented the insurgents with enormous challenges, especially when royal troops seized parts from one of the two *imprentillas*.[19] Nevertheless, insurgents continued working in the rural hinterlands to construct material symbols of political power, including minting currency, engraving official seals, and printing a constitution that never went into effect. Lack of paper sometimes threatened to make the insurgent press irrelevant. After 1814, when insurgent activity had been brutally curtailed by royalist troops, holdout commanders tried to get their hands on this critical imported material, even attempting to learn how to make it themselves.[20] There is evidence that by 1816 the insurgent directorate distributed printed materials to local groups, who sold them as a fundraising activity.[21]

As their efforts reveal, insurgent leaders viewed printed materials through a lens similar to that of their royalist counterparts, appropriating familiar genres and forms—like the official decree—to advance their goals in increasingly adverse circumstances. A comparison of viceregal and insurgent decrees reveals key conventional similarities (see figures 10 and 11).[22] Like the viceregal example, the insurgent decree capitalized the first line of text, leading with the name of the issuing official. Its creators also ended the communiqué

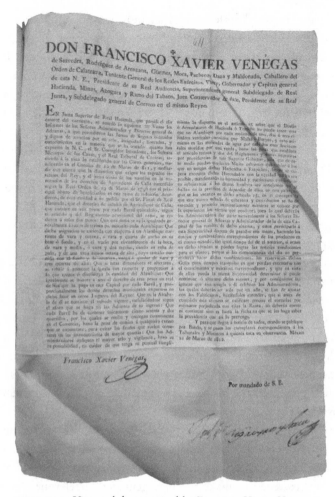

FIGURE 10. Viceregal decree issued by Francisco Xavier Venegas in
Mexico City, 1812. Archivo General de la Nación, Mexico City.

with the date of issue and included the hand-drawn rubrics of officials,
authenticating the printed document. The insurgents also innovated, however, illustrating their decree with an engraving of the coat of arms of
the Supreme National American Junta, which featured the neo-Aztec symbol of an eagle perched on a cactus. Crowned and surrounded by instruments
of war, the eagle is positioned atop a bridge bearing the initials N.F.T.O.N.
(Non fecit taliter omni nationi), a phrase associated with the Virgin
of Guadalupe.[23] With this coat of arms, insurgents sought to mobilize
Catholic and pre-Columbian symbolism to inspire loyalty to a new, American

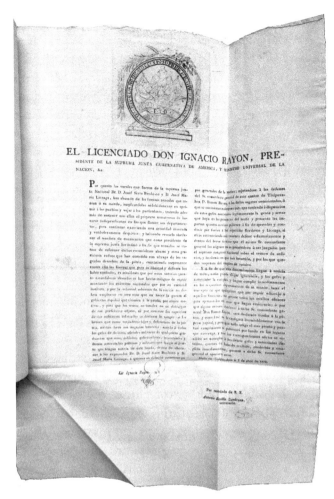

FIGURE 11. Insurgent decree issued by Ignacio Rayón in Tlalpuxahua, 1813. Archivo General de la Nación, Mexico City.

political community. Yet the details of the image are difficult to discern due to the poor quality of the printing, and the artist's draftsmanship of the eagle is clumsy at best. While the insurgents embraced printing to spread their political platform and encourage loyalty, their experiences in rural Mexico revealed the desperate position of their cause.

Viceregal officials responded to the insurgency not only with military power, but also by underwriting an outpouring of counterinsurgent messages that, issued in the months after the Hidalgo Revolt, emphasized the royalist command of printing.[24] Royalists used a number of tactics as they engaged print as a form of propaganda. News in the government gazette downplayed rebel success to boost morale among military commanders and their troops.[25] Mexico City–based writers directed missives to a wider swath of urban residents in an attempt to prevent solidarity from forming between middling social sectors and their rural counterparts, appealing discursively to familiar notions of authority and directing condescending mockery at insurgents.[26] Some financed their anti-insurgent publications by soliciting subscriptions from individuals, whose names would be printed in the finished work as a public demonstration of their loyalist credentials.

Beyond Mexico City, royalist propaganda circulated through official channels, as the viceroy distributed printed materials to religious authorities around Mexico for use in their sermons or for dissemination in their diocese. In 1812, for example, one of the crown's most zealous propagandists, Agustín Pomposo Fernández de San Salvador (1756–1842), distributed two thousand copies of his *Disillusionments Directed to the Insurgents of New Spain* to bishops from Sonora to Guatemala with approval and financing from the viceroy, who also received one hundred personal copies to share.[27] Propagandists hoped religious officials would incorporate their ideas at the pulpit, and religious officials developed their own anti-insurgent sermons, which they reprinted as pamphlets, redirecting a common practice toward more immediate political ends. Printed texts thus complemented, enhanced, and reproduced oral forms of persuasion emanating from official sources.

Among the ranks of royal propagandists, the insurgency also prompted reflections about audience, authorship, and print's potential to speak directly to individuals, rather than through the mediating influence of priests. Writers like Fernández de San Salvador revealed their enlightened intellectual formations and royalist perspectives as they imagined printed materials restoring reason—and along with it, social order—to Mexico's rebellious rural hinterlands. In an 1812 prospectus printed to raise funds for a forthcoming volume, the propagandist explained that he "writes not for the wise, but rather for poor ignorants deceived by astute seducers."[28] He emphasized that his latest production—a volume printed small "so that it can be carried in the pocket or even hidden if necessary"—could be used not only by traditional authorities like priests, fathers, schoolteachers and employers, but more importantly by those who skipped or did not have access to church services. Fernández de San Salvador even imagined his pocket edition reaching insurgents and prompting them to abandon their fight.[29] Here, the propagandist created new scenarios for authors, readers, and printed texts.

Rather than mediating and strengthening preexisting authority structures, texts would now rebuild them on the individual level, even in the absence of traditional social relationships. In this scenario, the author acquired new power as a secular authority, able to persuade through texts alone.

Enlightened royalists like Fernández de San Salvador encountered an increasingly skeptical supporter in Viceroy Félix Calleja (1813–1816), especially as royal forces gained the upper hand against the insurgency and enthusiasm for financing propaganda campaigns waned. When the propagandist requested support from Calleja in 1814, he submitted an anonymous letter directed mysteriously to his doorstop by a rural resident desperate for more anti-insurgent propaganda. The letter argued that sending an outpouring of printed materials to the countryside would generate a "prodigious consumption" that "will snuff out this terrifying revolution sooner than with bayonets and bullets."[30] The viceroy, however, expressed doubts. Calleja explained that the government could not afford to distribute official printed materials for free, and surely no one would pay for Fernández de San Salvador's pamphlets. "The unfortunate thing," he argued, "is that there is no disposition for buying rational works. If they sold, *hombres instruidos* would not need further encouragement; and you know this truth all too well."[31] Alluding to the propagandist's own publishing failures, the viceroy rejected the possibility that print could shape public opinion in Mexico without financial underwriting. While Fernández de San Salvador imagined that his work would generate new demand, the viceroy argued that markets had to exist already in order for propaganda to work. In spite of his skepticism, however, Calleja did help the propagandist distribute his pamphlet to various officials around the viceroyalty. Acknowledging receipt of a stack of copies, one Puebla official thanked the viceroy but echoed his doubts, warning that "it is impossible to promise any great results."[32]

New attitudes toward print's potential emerged during Mexico's independence wars. While insurgents appropriated the symbols of royal power by establishing their own parallel (if markedly inferior) printing apparatus, royalist propagandists showed their enlightened influences when they imagined reaching out to rural audiences in unmediated ways to change people's minds with printed pamphlets and broadsides. Viceregal officials increasingly showed ambivalence, especially when faced with footing the bill for printing costs. During the conflict, printed materials moved through new geographic circuits of distribution and became objects of heightened scrutiny and potential. Yet the material realities of production and consumption meant that vast media campaigns would never take off as propagandists imagined. Instead, the establishment of press freedom laws, first for a brief moment in 1812 and again in 1820, would refocus official attention on the role of print as a medium for conducting politics in the urban centers where production and reading publics already clustered.

INAUGURATING PRESS FREEDOM IN
THEORY AND PRACTICE

Against the backdrop of civil war, new laws bearing on printed expression arrived in Mexico, further destabilizing certainties about print's uses and raising questions about the power and influence of printers. Initially decreed in Cádiz as part of the liberal revolution unfolding at the Cortes, the law permitted the discussion of political themes in print and abolished censorship mechanisms like royal licenses and Inquisition review. The new law generated much public debate about what press freedom was, both as an abstract element of an emerging political system and as a set of practices. Intellectual historians situate the embrace of greater press freedoms within a broader process of imperial transformation starting at Cádiz and spreading throughout the Spanish Americas, during which writers working after 1808 came to see themselves as representatives of public opinion, developing new discursive practices in their publications that challenged absolutism.[33] Yet Mexico's specific political and publishing contexts shaped the unfolding of new laws, discourses, and practices on the ground, influencing residents' calculations about how they could use print in relation to imagined publics and colonial authorities.

The fitful trajectory of press laws in Mexico did not align neatly with the course of Spain's liberal revolution, a fact that generated uncertainty and complaints in Mexico.[34] The Cortes passed press freedom legislation in 1810, proclaiming that "all bodies and particular persons, of whatever condition and state they may be, have the freedom to write, print, and publish their political ideas without need of license, revision, or any approval prior to publication" within certain limits.[35] In Mexico, however, Viceroy Francisco Javier Venegas (1810–1813) refused to enact the law in the colony, pointing to the Hidalgo Revolt and its threat to Spanish rule. He resisted pressure for two years, finally relenting in September 1812, when he promulgated a constitution that had been ratified earlier that year by the Cortes.[36] A small group of individuals tested the waters after September. Creoles Carlos María de Bustamante and Lizardi both debuted new periodicals, *El Juguete Rabioso* and *El Pensador Mexicano*, respectively, that embraced open political commentary and critique, referencing Enlightenment thinkers who had been expressly prohibited by the Inquisition. Within two months, the viceroy suspended press freedom, as well as elections that had swept a slate of pro-autonomist creoles to power on the Mexico City Ayuntamiento.[37] Bustamante fled Mexico City to join the insurgency, and Lizardi served many months in jail after he criticized the viceroy. Lizardi continued to publish, this time under the watch of censors, praising the viceroy in an attempt to reduce his prison sentence and eventually shifting to fiction in order to avoid conflicts with authorities.[38] Texts published in other parts of the empire, where press laws remained in effect, continued to circulate in Mexico, but in 1814 Fernando VII regained the Spanish throne and suspended the constitution altogether.

The brief 1812 opening did not radically transform Mexico City publishing practices, yet its closing lingered in the minds of political observers, who responded to the loosening of controls on printing for the second time in 1820 with a mixture of elation and concern. That year, a military revolt in Spain successfully challenged the king's power and forced him to reinstate the constitution, inaugurating a new period of experimentation with expanded press freedom. In the second half of 1820, a barrage of loose printed material—a collection of short pamphlets and broadsides that contemporaries described generally as *papeles públicos*—fluttered through Mexico City's streets, heralding the legal change with exuberance. In contrast to the extensive foot-dragging in 1812, officials rapidly repromulgated the law in 1820, prompting a rush to work out the broader implications and practical uncertainties of the new legal regime.[39]

In the flood of pamphlets published in subsequent weeks and months, writers expressed enthusiasm about the new rules—part of the constitutional mania that swept across Mexico—along with concern over the potential moral consequences. One anonymous author betrayed his anxieties in a pamphlet that described freedom of the press as "a breath of reason, not a release of passions: it is a ventilation shaft to the light of understanding, not a drain to the malice of the will: a channel to noble ideas and thoughts, not a sewer of delinquent and crude feelings."[40] This passage, while echoing royalist propagandist Fernández de San Salvador's arguments about print as a tool of reason, raised concerns that unrestrained printing could unleash dangerous passions. In the right hands, press freedom could edify and uplift; if abused, it could degrade or debase. Yet the pamphleteer ultimately deflected concerns about the potentially dangerous effects of press abuses on Mexico's society by turning rhetorically to the law as a safeguard. He obliquely referenced insurgent propaganda when he admitted that print could spread falsehoods and misinformation, since "not all the individuals of a population are capable of discerning, nor have sufficient instruction to judge what they read."[41] Yet the law, he argued, would channel writers' behavior in salutary directions.

The public writers who first made use of expanded press freedom in 1820 countered the specter of violence and upheaval that stalked their discussions by positioning themselves as an "intelligentsia" that would initiate ignorant Mexican publics into the age of reason.[42] Many of the early pamphleteers, like Lizardi, emerged from middling urban sectors and defended the right to publish opinions developed outside the traditional centers of intellectual authority.[43] Wielding the equalizing rhetoric of rights and freedoms, writers nevertheless drew discursive distance from their audiences as they defined a new role for themselves as educational reformers. "It is now time (wise writers of Mexico)," inveighed one pamphleteer, addressing his peers, "that you use your intelligence for the enlightenment of the low and ignorant *pueblo*."[44] The folksy dialogue—used to present competing perspectives and featuring ordinary Mexicans, often speaking in mock dialect—soon emerged as a favored teaching tool by writers who imagined themselves speaking to broad publics.[45] Through the dialogue, writers tried to set the parameters of political debate and acceptable behavior, claiming moral authority for themselves. Thus, characters like the fictional Don Ruperto, who raised the specter that limitless press freedom would produce social dissolution, found their counterparts in the upstanding Printer, who reassured readers that cooler heads would prevail under the guiding spirit of the law.[46]

As writers publicly defended the law's ability to channel public expression toward rational debate, local officials laid the actual apparatus for legal enforcement. When press freedom went into effect in New Spain in June 1820, the viceroy urged "moderation, decorum, and circumspection."[47] In July, the government gazette republished the original 1810 decree and 1813 rules delineating press freedom and its limits.[48] These rules had established the rights of individuals to publish, as long as they did not commit libel or calumny, subvert the law, or violate public decency or morality. Mexican delegates to the Cortes had pushed in 1812 for greater specificity to clarify these broadly subjective categories and guard against official retribution, yet the laws had been passed without clarification.[49] The specific criteria for any violations of press law, therefore, would be determined by a regional *junta de censura*, a censorship board comprised of five individuals. In June 1820, officials reinstated Mexico City's provisional *junta de censura*, which would gradually be fully appointed.[50] They also named a new *fiscal de imprenta*, a press prosecutor, to monitor print materials and report any violations to a local judge, who would forward appropriate cases to the junta for review.[51] Mexico City's three major printers, Juan Bautista de Arizpe, Valdés, and Mariano Zúñiga y Ontiveros, received instructions to send copies of all materials produced in their printing shops to the press prosecutor's attention.[52] In October, the Cortes issued a new set of rules that clarified procedures associated with press freedom in greater depth, but many of the basic principles endured from 1813.[53] The Inquisition was abolished in 1820, for instance, but publishing on religious matters would continue to require the permission of church censors, although the law laid out an appeal process that vested ultimate authority in the Cortes.[54] The 1820 law also described limits to printed speech in five areas, counting conspiracy against state religion or the monarchy, threats to public peace or incitement to rebellion, incitement against the law or legitimate authority, obscenities or indecency, and libel or injury against private persons as abuses of press freedom.[55]

A period of accommodation extended throughout the summer and into the fall of 1820 as officials implemented the regulatory framework for press freedom. The first press prosecutor resigned his post after three months, and his replacement complained that nobody had sent him any printed material to review.[56] New notices delivered to Mexico City's printing shops—which had doubled from three to six since July, one stocked with a captured insurgent press auctioned off by royal authorities—met with apologetic excuses.[57] Their administrators informed officials that they had misunderstood the rules and expected the author of a printed work to send copies to the press prosecutor for review.[58] For writers, too, events from 1812 offered few lessons to carry forward into 1820, beyond the fact that press freedom had been quickly revoked and its principal experimenters jailed. Against this backdrop of uncertainty, Mexican writers began to publish.

THE EMERGING POWER OF PRINTERS

As a growing community of writers began to share their political opinions in 1820, they confronted the costs and unexpected logistics of publishing, which generated debate about the rights associated with press freedom. Someone had to pay for printing in order to enter the field of debate, but just who that someone might be remained an open question. Cultural entrepreneurs like Lizardi, who emerged as one of the principal commentators of 1820 and embodied the reformist spirit, hoped that readers would end writers' dependence on patronage or personal wealth as a precondition for publishing. In the prologue to his 1816 satirical novel, *El periquillo sarniento*, he slyly dedicated the book not to "His Excellency, His Lordship, or at least Mr. Somebody," but rather to his readers, "offering it as a fitting tribute to your noble (money's) worth."[59] Lizardi imagined that public sales could liberate writers from the constraints of patronage, and writers, in turn, would elevate the public. In practice, however, writers faced a more complex reality. The Bourbons had made significant investments in public primary education by the end of the eighteenth century.[60] Yet for all of writers' talk about enlightening the Mexican *pueblo*, expanding freedoms did not generate a spate of new readers overnight, eager to spend on tutelage via the printed word. Furthermore, while three new second-rate printing businesses now offered services in Mexico City, three familiar printers remained dominant figures in the trade. To their chagrin, writers discovered that printers had quite suddenly gained new importance as gatekeepers to the world of public opinion.

A public dispute between two writers and Alejandro Valdés, Manuel Antonio Valdés's heir and one of Mexico City's most prominent printers, sowed suspicion that printers' loyalties might pose a threat to writers' new freedoms. Soon after press laws lifted censorship rules in 1820, the journal *El Conductor Eléctrico* published an angry letter to the editor complaining about the printer Valdés's business practices. *El Conductor* was the brainchild of Lizardi, who in the years since his 1812 imprisonment had built a reputation in Mexico City as a public writer and literary entrepreneur. Lizardi had collaborated frequently with Valdés, who had published *El periquillo* to commercial success in 1816, before the viceroy censored its final volume. Yet by 1820 their relationship had become strained. Sales of Lizardi's second novel had failed to cover production costs, and Valdés had sued Lizardi's financial backer to recoup his losses.[61] Lizardi seemed to be thinking of his fraught relationship with Valdés when he published the angry letter, which he framed for journal readers with a careful disclaimer. "Public editors," explained Lizardi, "are not responsible for the outside opinions they print in their newspapers and that they should print with impartiality, as long as they are not contrary to Religion and they are assured with the signatures of their authors."[62]

The angry letter, written by a reformer who signed only J. G. T. P., took aim at printers like Valdés for "putting unjust obstacles in front of authors" when they should be "the most liberal and contribute to the enlightenment of the public."[63] The letter writer's experiences at Valdés's printing shop led him to conclude that Mexico's printers should actually be counted among the ranks of the *serviles*: toadies of the recently extinguished absolutist regime. When the letter writer had brought a manuscript to be published, he received an exorbitant price quote demanding half the profits on top of the costs of production. Alas, the other printing shops in the capital were all full with business, and the writer encountered hard terms, which, Valdés's administrator told him, were due to the fact that "we earn more printing *cartillas,* for which there is a license, than for those papers that only give us a miserable profit."[64] With his reference to *cartillas*, instructional texts historically printed under royal privilege, the angry writer painted Valdés as an avaricious creature of the ancien régime. He underscored the point by describing how he left the shop in a rage, "not only because [the printer] demanded that I pay what is neither just nor customary, but due to the despotic fashion in which I was treated." J. G. T. P.'s brief communiqué raised the critical point that being allowed by law to publish did not guarantee that one would be able to afford to do so, especially in a transforming literary market where printers had gained leverage amid a flood of would-be public writers. Indeed, the author claimed that printers' prices were worse than "the censorship we used to suffer." Arguing that an author's right to publish at a reasonable rate represented a core value of the new press law, the letter writer accused printers of dampening its spirit.

The printer Valdés responded to this criticism by issuing a pamphlet, *La prensa libre*, that refuted the charges and reframed the terms of debate. Redirecting the conversation from the accusations of price gouging launched by J. G. T. P., he focused instead on the printer's contractual obligation. Valdés explained that he had actually inflated his price quote not because he feared the manuscript in question would sell poorly, but because no other printer in town had wanted to publish it. The hard terms were only a pretext for diplomatically denying service, which Valdés had no qualms admitting publicly. The angry letter writer, Valdés explained, had misunderstood the meanings of the "free press" referenced in his pamphlet's title. Rather than infringing on authors' press freedom, which he dismissed as "a very different thing," Valdés instead described the printer's freedom to serve the customers he liked.[65] Just as an author might choose the printing shop in which to have a work produced, so too might a printer choose what patrons to serve, regardless of the new constitution. "The owner [of a printing shop]," he argued, "will be obligated to print in general, and not precisely the works of a determined person, since doing this depends on his will."[66] Pointing to Europe to enumerate various publishing scenarios—like purchasing rights from authors or sharing profits in exchange for financing—Valdés schooled Mexico City's would-be public writers on participating in this new world. Those who didn't like his policies could take their business elsewhere. For good measure, he mocked his critic for being a nobody whose works failed to "make the presses sweat," and distributed his pamphlet with a "free of charge" notice, displaying his power in a context where access to the press had gained a premium as demand ballooned overnight.[67]

Valdés's pamphlet reconfigured the issues raised by the angry letter writer, proclaiming the start of a new era of publishing shaped by printers' influence. While J. G. T. P. described the monopolistic power of printers as impeding the free flow of authors' ideas, Valdés recast printers' discrimination as beneficial to society, since it kept bad writings out of the public sphere. The letter writer claimed that Valdés had violated "just" and "customary" norms surrounding printing by charging exorbitant fees, yet Valdés brushed these categories aside as relics of a bygone era. Rather than linking himself to the censorship practices of the old regime, Valdés founded his actions in the language of political economy, mobilizing ideas about free will and contractual obligation to justify his conduct. Throughout this debate, the contents of J. G. T. P.'s rejected manuscript remained undiscussed, a fact that generated considerable ambiguity. Had the printer scorned his text because it was written in poor taste and would surely flop on the market, or because it contained potentially controversial propositions? By defining the issue in purely economic terms, Valdés skirted the question of printers' political loyalties.

Having facilitated the exchange between the printer and his critic as the editor of *El Conductor Eléctrico*, Lizardi took it upon himself to establish a set of ground rules for publishing in his next issue. These new norms, he suggested, would diminish future conflicts of interest between writers and printers, rationalizing Mexico's world of printed debate. Lizardi dismissed Valdés's arguments categorically, explaining that printers should serve the entire public without discrimination, since printers "are not censors nor judges of works."[68] Writers, on the other hand, should stay out of printing shops. Lizardi complained that Mexico City's writers had gravitated toward publishing anonymously, concerned about the risks of taking responsibility for their texts yet at the same time desperate for public recognition. "I have noticed," he grumbled, "that many [writers] frequently go to the printing shops, talk about their paper, they see it, they re-read it, they correct it, they might even be at the time of its sale in the same bookstore, where they take account of the profits it made them, publicly and without the least hesitation."[69] All of this posturing annoyed Lizardi, who had personally suffered the consequences of publishing controversial ideas when he was imprisoned in 1812.

Besides reflecting his own resentments, Lizardi's comments open a window onto a lively world of intellectual production, located in Mexico City's printing shops and bookstores, which the writer wanted to reform. Here, authors and shop workers rubbed elbows, and a spirit of titillating anticipation swirled around print at a time when authors still hesitated to openly claim credit for their texts amid uncertainties around press freedom. This was a world not just of printed debate, but also of urban performance—of seeing and being seen at the printing shop or bookstore—that Lizardi worried would undermine the smooth operation of laws governing press freedom.[70] Around the same time that he made this observation, Lizardi developed his own plan to rationalize the messy world of intellectual exchange with the Public Reading Society, which he founded in 1820.[71] For one *real*, individuals could enter the reading room, centrally located near the *zócalo*, and peruse all the latest printed works over the course of the day. Lizardi's business model, a self-financing subscription system, targeted two potential audiences: those who came to the reading room, and those who subscribed to a daily service that delivered current reading material to their homes for private consultation. Thus, Lizardi envisioned a two-tiered world of urban reading, in which wealthy, discriminating patrons could opt out from associating with social inferiors while simultaneously underwriting the broader public project. Those who came to the reading room, for their part, would be required to follow a series of rules, including reading silently and not marking any of the papers on display. Lizardi's reading room would be a quiet space of study, disturbed only by the rustling of papers or scratching of quills used to take notes (on separate sheets of paper supplied by the house)—a far cry from the printing shops and bookstores, where gossip and literary reputations were discussed alongside machinery and merchandise.

Lizardi's vision of a rationalized world of print production and public reading sought to bring order and respectability to a boisterous world of urban social exchange, yet the project, for all its vision of social uplift and discipline, remained a pipe dream. His reading room failed, and by September he publicly admitted that printers showed no interest in consigning themselves to the roles he had prescribed for them.[72] In a new issue of *El Conductor Eléctrico*, Lizardi explained that he had run into the same dilemma faced by the angry letter writer J. G. T. P. at the hands of a different Mexico City printer. Indeed, he suspected that the city's printers were colluding to shut him out of the publishing market altogether. "Printers are by definition public persons," he complained, "destined to serve the public that fattens them, especially in Mexico, where by virtue of being three, they are all rich."[73] Lizardi's argument that printers should serve customers "without deference or preference," just as bakers sell bread, fell on deaf ears.[74] By October he was publishing in the neighboring city of Puebla, fuming in his footnotes that he had indeed been locked out of Mexico City's print economy.[75] In the meantime, at least Puebla printers—"more generous than my compatriots"—welcomed would-be authors with open arms.[76]

As Lizardi and his colleagues grumbled over their inability to rationalize publishing and reading in Mexico City, they shed light on a context wherein the power of printers could overrun authors' access to publishing, even, it seems, when they had the financial resources to pay for the printing. Their conflict with Alejandro Valdés, who served as an alderman in the new constitutionally elected municipal government while doing significant business with the viceregal regime, not only showed that authors and printers conceptualized their rights in competing terms; it also raised the question of where printers' loyalties lay in a world without prior censorship. The fallout over an explosive political critique—reprinted by Valdés's own printing shop—would force the issue of printers' relationship to the viceregal government out into the open in September 1820.

INSUBORDINATE REPRINTS AND THE PERILS OF PRESS FREEDOM

A broadside printed in the fall of 1820 became one of the first texts to test the limits of official tolerance toward printed criticism. *El liberal a los bajos escritores* (The liberal to low scribblers) emerged on September 27 from the very same Puebla printing shop where Lizardi had published his angry critique of Mexico City printers. The single-sided document accused Mexico's "slavish writers" of "prostituting your pens in clumsy adulation" to Viceroy Juan Ruíz de Apodaca (see figure 12).[77] Its author, a soldier who signed the initials F. M., went on to criticize his commanding officer and the viceroy himself for failing to fully implement the provisions of the constitution, arguing that the establishment of local city councils and elections represented mere tokens of

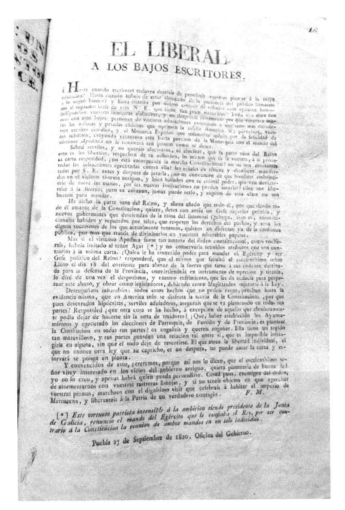

FIGURE 12. First printing of F.M., *El liberal a los bajos escritores* (Puebla: Oficina del Gobierno, 1820). Archivo General de la Nación, Mexico City.

genuine constitutional spirit. The critical broadside articulated a new style of political discourse, conducted publicly and assertively through the printed word. It claimed to reject sycophantic appeals to the viceroy by "men fascinated by the old vice-ridden system" in favor of direct critique and straight talk. The broadside's design, stripped of any adornment, underscored this message. Its production also reflected emerging tensions in the relationship between printers and royal officials, brought on by the loosening of restrictions on printing. As its imprint information revealed, the broadside had been issued by the shop of Pedro de la Rosa, a prominent Puebla printer who advertised his royal privileges by describing his press as the "Printing Office of the Government." That the government's own authorized printer should release such a critical text spoke to a potential realignment in publishing practices put in motion by press freedom laws, a development that authorities in Mexico City confronted once the broadside reached the capital.

The trajectory of the Puebla broadside opens a window onto the practical dilemmas that challenged royal officials even as it illuminates broader struggles over political authority made acute by expanded press freedom. The broadside arrived in Mexico City within the week, where it came to the attention of the press prosecutor, who quickly sent it to a judge for review.[78] In his accompanying letter, the prosecutor explained that he strongly suspected that the broadside represented a "slanderous libel" of the type described in the new press laws.[79] Using the legislation as a guide, he exhorted the judge to investigate the broadside's production, confiscate any copies he could find, and determine who was responsible for the text.[80] Turning to the more immediate matter of how to stop the text from circulating further, the prosecutor urged the judge to send notice to Mexico City's printing shops, warning them not to reprint the controversial item. Aware that such a move seemed to violate the laws of freedom of the press—especially because the item had not yet been judged by the *junta de censura*—the prosecutor couched his logic in another legal statute. "It would be enough to warn [printers]," he reasoned, "that said writing is a property that no one can take advantage of without the license of the author as disposed by the Cortes and published here by edict."[81] The prosecutor thus invoked intellectual property statutes—described in 1813 legislation—that protected authors' rights as a mechanism to control printed speech.

The prosecutor's letter, written during a moment of legal transition, revealed anxiety over the as yet untested political consequences of press freedom. His attempt to develop a legal justification for enacting a roundabout form of censorship shows how officials tried to wield the new liberal laws to control information. The growing phenomenon of reprinting—a practice that first proliferated in 1808 during the Napoleonic invasion and flourished again in 1812 and 1820 as Mexico City printing shops reissued texts received from Spain—clearly preoccupied the prosecutor, who worried that *El liberal a los bajos escritores* would soon find a larger audience in Mexico City. Yet reprinting received no special mention as a phenomenon with political implications in the Spanish legislation. This helps explain the prosecutor's creative invocation of intellectual property laws, deployed not by an author protecting individual rights, but as an official strategy to contain the multiplication of printed criticism.

Indeed, reprinting challenged officials' capacity to contain the developing controversy with the tools afforded by law. By the time the *junta de censura* had convened to respond to the judge's notification, the controversial Puebla broadside had already been reissued as a pamphlet by the Mexico City printing shop of Valdés. Forwarding a copy of the local reprint to the junta, the judge exhorted members to rule on the text within the next two days.[82] Just one day later, the junta condemned the broadside as a "slanderous and calumnious libel" against the viceroy.[83] Taking action, the judge ordered the confiscation of any printed copies of the text and sent his court scribe to investigate the reprint's production at Valdés's printing shop within the next twenty-four hours.[84] He also called for a full inquiry into the object's dissemination, instructing his scribe not only to ascertain the print run and names of any buyers or subscribers, but also to track down the pamphlet in the city's "stands or stores where it is known papers are sold."[85] In addition, he ordered the prohibition printed up in the newspaper and placed on notice boards, warning any possessors to hand in their copies within three days.

When the court scribe arrived at Valdés's home later that day, the printer shooed him away. Valdés had been elected to the city council after the restoration of the constitution in 1820.[86] Due to official business with the city council, he claimed, he was "ignorant of the governance of his establishment," having turned over daily management of his shop to an administrator.[87] The administrator, whom the scribe found in Valdés's printing shop just off the central *zócalo*, presented the three remaining copies of the pamphlet on hand. The individual who had ordered the reprinting, he explained, had done so multiple times, and the printing shop had produced two thousand copies in total. These copies had then been distributed to vendors throughout the city. Referencing his printer's log, the administrator revealed the signature of Don Manuel Galán, a lieutenant from Tres Villas who lodged on nearby Donceles Street. After checking the bookselling stalls in the Portal de Mercaderes, the arcade lining the *zócalo* where public papers were normally sold, the scribe turned up only one large cache of pamphlets and a few copies in Lizardi's public reading room.

Because the individual behind the broadside's reprinting, Galán, held a military affiliation, officials rescinded his case to an *auditor de guerra* (military judge advocate), who wrote to the viceroy with a plan of action for Galán's imprisonment and the continued confiscation of printed materials in the capital. While the viceroy approved the judge advocate's plans, he informed him that Galán had already been remanded to the citadel by his own order. The viceroy, it seems, had moved preemptively to assert his authority in the developing case. Meanwhile, nearly two thousand pamphlets circulated throughout the city and its environs, out of official reach and on the move.

The controversial text generated an immediate response in Mexico City, and a number of writers began to issue a flurry of pamphlets that countered the accusations advanced in *El liberal a los bajos escritores*, which quickly became required reading for the capital's literate elite. One of the first refutations appeared on October 6, just one day after the pamphlet had been declared libelous, in a text titled *Muzzle on the So-Called Liberal* and printed in the shop of Valdés, the same printer who had reissued the original tract. Valdés used his privileged access to dispel the rumors about his involvement in the affair, attaching a rhyming epigram to the end of this pamphlet, which he addressed as "The printer to the respectable public":

He who attacks virtue
With such crazed daring
Understands neither virtue
nor APODACA.

Quien á la virtud ataca
con tan loco atrevimiento,
no tiene conocimiento
ni de ella, ni de APODACA.

"The insolent paper printed in Puebla and reprinted in my house," explained Valdés, "is worthy of the fire."[88] Valdés excused himself for allowing the controversial text to pass through his presses, justifying his own lack of oversight and defending his administrator who, overwhelmed with work, had simply followed legal protocol.

Valdés's apologetic addendum spoke to the challenges of navigating the printer's position when the outcomes of press law violations were as yet unknown. On the one hand, his poetic flourish in support of the viceroy performed public loyalty. As a printer with patronage ties to the viceregal administration, he had no interest in inciting the viceroy's ire, which the controversial broadside had clearly done. As a member of the newly elected city council, he publicly upheld the constitution and press freedom. Yet the text also navigated the uncertain position of the printer in relation to a broader public that already knew about his willingness to stop manuscripts from being published in his printing shop, an unpopular behavior under the new legal regime. Valdés had already refused to print certain texts because of their contents; why had he not exercised such judgment in this particular case? Was he a viceregal critic? Had he finally embraced the spirit of production advocated by Lizardi, serving customers like a baker, or had he simply made a mistake by failing in his unofficial censorship duties? Implying the latter, Valdés rushed to smooth over his actions by disavowing the publication. His embarrassment surely grew the following day, when officials released a supplement to the government gazette that reproduced the judge's orders to confiscate the pamphlets and investigate their printing in Valdés's shop.[89]

Meanwhile Galán, who was responsible for reprinting the pamphlet, wrote his own self-defense from behind bars, which he sent to be printed in the newly established office of J. M. de Benavente y Socios.[90] Like Valdés, Galán took steps to explain himself and justify his decision to publish what he knew would be a controversial broadside. Galán claimed that far from this being a political decision, poverty had forced his hand. Imprisoned on charges of collaborating with insurgent leaders in Guanajuato (which he denied), Galán had taken a salary cut and turned to publishing as a way to make some cash. "It is true that it contains scandalous propositions against our worthy Viceroy," he admitted, "but I decided to profit by this means, so that they should arrive to his notice, so that being summoned, I might make him see up close the state of my misery, and the delay in the dispatch of my suit, which causes it."[91]

Like Valdés, Galán pulled back the curtain on his publishing activities in order to shape the reception of the controversial *El liberal*. By confessing and explaining his economic woes, Galán endeavored to generate sympathy, lessen punishment, and downplay any potential affinity with *El liberal*. At the same time, his discursive strategies reveal how printed items with broad political resonance could become entangled, through the act of reprinting, in micropolitical dramas. Galán used his pamphlet to speak to the viceroy directly, shifting from a general exposition to the language of petition as he threw himself at the viceroy's feet and begged for mercy in the public eye. His own small story—itself related to disgruntlement over the outcomes of the internal conflict—amplified and interwove with the larger story of a brazen critique of viceregal power. Thus, metacommentary about publishing, including discussions and justifications of the motivations behind a text's production, became part of the grammar through which reputations and political relationships were negotiated in public, as printed items provoked legal action and concrete political response.

Valdés's and Galán's apologetic disavowals joined a growing discussion that unfolded over the following weeks as Mexico City writers commissioned a spate of pamphlets that commented on *El liberal*'s text, with titles like *Sobre el papel de Puebla El Liberal a los bajos escritores*; *El americano sincero en defensa del Exmo. Virey, Conde de Venadito ofendido en el papel titulado, El liberal a los bajos escritores*; *Otro liberal a los bajos escritores*; and *El tercer liberal a los bajos escritores*. These pamphlets' titles performed their authors' political loyalties in relation to the original pamphlet, generating a dense web of intertextual commentary that extended from serious political tracts to teasing, moralizing poetry.[92] One pamphlet, composed in rhyming verse, obliquely chastised *El liberal* for disrespecting an authority figure. "Whether you write with a *liberal* pen or a *servile* pen, you shouldn't write badly about anyone."[93] These texts addressed broader questions of authority and the implementation of the constitution through analysis of F.M.'s words and actions: *El liberal* had become the central node of debate.

As speculation swirled in the capital, Puebla officials received instruction to commence their own parallel investigation into the broadside and turned up Lieutenant Félix Merino as the F.M. responsible for the broadside. Like Galán, Merino was a member of the military and, significantly, the son of the intendant of Valladolid, a highly ranked, loyal colonial official.[94] His case passed to a judge advocate, who requested a copy of the new press freedom laws, having never seen them since they had been promulgated. This case would be charting new ground. Merino, it turned out, was already imprisoned on charges of insubordination in the fort of Loreto, located in the hills north of Puebla.

As the investigation developed, Puebla officials moved to confiscate any broadsides they could find. After visiting the printing shop of Pedro de la Rosa, however, they learned from the administrator that all of the original six hundred copies had already been sold.[95] Within the week, Puebla officials announced that they had posted nineteen printed notices advising local residents of the ban and ordering owners to turn over their copies.[96] While several residents complied with the order, the news seemed only to fan the flames. Puebla residents showed their support for Merino's position in writing and other direct actions. A copy of the broadside confiscated by officials, for instance, bore a marginal annotation with its writer's mocking address to the viceroy: "Poor you, *tata* (old man); resign, because they'll take it from you soon enough."[97] The intendant of Puebla expressed consternation over a steady stream of visitors to the fort. "The gathering of people of all classes that went with frequency to visit Lieutenant Don Félix Merino in his arrest at the fortification of Loreto," he worried, "could compromise public tranquility, because both those that visited him and the masses (*vulgo*) could, through an erroneous belief, persuade themselves that his imprisonment springs from persecution for being a defender of the constitution."[98] Merino's developing case revealed how his act of printing intertwined with other insubordinate actions to disrupt military discipline and, in the eyes of officials, threaten the very fabric of the social and political order.

Merino, for his part, was unapologetic and seemed to revel in further opportunities to speak his mind. Surely being the son of a prominent royal official emboldened the young officer. In mid-November he published a second broadside that took aim at the *junta de censura*, accusing it of violating press laws, which he argued should serve as a check on the tyranny of government.[99] Merino ended his pamphlet by calling for "Constitution or death," rejecting charges that he was a revolutionary and defending himself as a "good Spaniard" who only wanted the laws to be respected.[100] Explaining that everyone already knew who he was anyway, Merino revealed his identity in a final flourish.

Merino refused to back down from his criticisms of the viceroy, even when he faced closed-door questioning for his actions in late November, where he vehemently challenged the charge of libel that had been added to his ongoing case. He claimed that his paper was indeed "founded in public opinion" and used the opportunity to directly challenge the viceroy, offering a laundry list of examples—including the case of Rafael Dávila, another viceregal critic recently imprisoned for his own pamphlet, *La verdad amarga, pero es preciso decirla* (The truth embitters, yet it must be told)—as evidence that the viceroy had indeed disrespected the constitution. Denying the charges that he had committed defamation by calling the viceroy a "despot" and using italic type to describe him sarcastically as *Virtuous Apodaca*, Merino pointedly argued that the viceroy indeed lacked public virtue.[101]

In December a military court in Mexico City convened to decide Merino's fate, its members consulting various reports prepared by government officials that discredited Merino's arguments. One official had advised that Merino's act of printing while imprisoned meant that the broadside was necessarily part of his broader crimes of insubordination. Not only had he committed a crime by insulting his commanding officer in print; he had dared to publish at all while already behind bars. The proof of insubordination was self-evident, and the dangers were significant. "If a subaltern," the prosecutor assigned to the case reasoned, "dares so brazenly not only to disobey the Supreme Authority, the Captain General, the Viceroy, but also to insult them openly in public papers, what can other authorities and Military Chiefs expect from their subordinates?"[102] Military officials fixated less on the question of libel and more on how the act of publishing a critique itself constituted a violation of authority and the chain of command. The following day the military court's members unanimously found him guilty. One of the voting judges described Merino as lacking "the respect and subordination the Laws establish for good order, without which society would be endangered by anarchy."[103] The court sentenced Merino to be shipped back to Spain, where he would be held under arrest for four months until he moderated his stance.

Merino's case revealed that top-ranking officials had reason to worry about freedom of the press. When viceregal authorities hoped to use aspects of liberal law—like libel prohibitions and intellectual property rules—to channel and contain opinions expressed in print, printers like Valdés publicly avowed themselves to be potential partners in the task. Yet an examination of how Merino's text actually gained circulation reveals that even the most trustworthy printer could not be counted on to contain critical texts, and the speed of print's dissemination outpaced officials' first attempts to reckon with the emerging world of political discourse made possible through press freedom. Such incidents cast doubt—from the perspective of officials—on the nature of their long-standing relationship to Mexico's printers and suggested this relationship would need to be renegotiated under the new legal regime.

Looking back in his influential 1851 *Historia de Méjico*, conservative statesman and scholar Lucas Alamán assigned a fair amount of power to the pamphlets that circulated in the fall of 1820, a period that preluded the collapse of the viceregal regime. "The pamphlets that each day were published in use of freedom of the press," he argued, "contributed much to augment this agitation of spirits, with the strangest titles and in which, in the style best suited to make an impression on the masses, incited them to revolution."[104] Alamán blamed Mexico's *junta de censura*, whose members he accused of excessive liberality, for allowing controversial statements carte blanche. Alamán's assessment, reflecting his conservative distrust of politics linked to popular mobilization, misread the junta's more measured activities while overstating the ability of printed texts to reach mass audiences. Merino's case does seem to have elicited a response not only from readers with pesos to spare and writers with the means to publish rebuttals, but also from a broader swath of Puebla society that expressed its support through actions that troubled military officials. The archival record surrounding Merino's case, however, shows that twenty-six hundred copies of his text were printed in total. Far from targeted at "the masses," this quantity represented the upper range of typical print runs and provided enough copies to reach well-heeled readers in Puebla and Mexico City, where they generated significant conversation and official action at the highest level. Instead, the pamphlet—like the flurry of printed documents that crisscrossed in and out of the printing shops and booksellers' stands clustered in Mexico City's core—contributed to the breakdown of the viceregal regime by voicing public criticism that, in provoking a response, revealed the limits of the regime's tolerance amid fears of a broader disintegration of its legitimacy, especially among urban elites and within the ranks of its own military hierarchy. The regime's unwillingness to perform liberality toward *El liberal*'s printed critique widened this growing rift.

CONCLUSION: FREEDOM OF
THE PRESS BE DAMNED

The case of Félix Merino intertwines the two threads of Mexico's independence era. As the first major controversy to test press laws enacted in 1820 as part of the Spanish Empire's liberal revolution in Mexico, it showed urban elites the official limits of published speech in a colonial public sphere stalked by the specter of independence. A pamphlet published later that year, critical of the actions of the *junta de censura*, reflected on the limits of tolerance when it appended a mock advertisement for a guide to help neophytes learn how to judge printed works for themselves. This handy reference volume, available at the fictional Have-a-Care Bookshop and titled *Instruction to Quickly Understand Whether a Work Is Good or Bad; Revealing the Key Words That Allow One to Determine, with Certitude, the Fate of Any Text*, could serve residents of Mexico as they navigated the potentially hazardous waters of press freedom.[105] The events surrounding the publication of Merino's pamphlet, written in the midst of a stubbornly persistent (if weakened) insurgency, also suggest that the climate of protracted warfare, along with Merino's military affiliation, shaped official responses to his proposition. Although Merino felt vested with the right to express his critique in print, after a decade of conflict in which the medium had been mobilized as a weapon of war, officials regarded the boundaries of public speech with greater caution. Merino's pamphlet, after all, targeted not the rural insurgency, which had been largely contained, but rather his social peers: members of an educated group of authority figures whom he hoped to reconfigure into a new community of readers outraged by viceregal abuse.

Concerns over the potentially destabilizing force of print among the local elite led royal officials to take action against select writers, provoking criticism about their willingness to uphold the constitutional principles of the new legal order. Further cases beyond the initial Merino incident confirmed this appraisal in the eyes of the Mexico City publics that read and wrote in 1820. Dávila, another critical pamphleteer, was imprisoned in November on charges of libel and sedition.[106] His pamphlet, *La verdad amarga*, bolder in argumentation than Merino's though less polemical in its style, criticized the colonial regime's failure to back constitutional guarantees in Mexico and repeatedly raised the specter of independence for the Americas behind professions of love for Fernando VII.[107] As in the Merino case, Dávila's pamphlet generated intertextual commentary, including printed petitions addressed to the viceroy requesting his release from prison.[108] These cases led one pseudonymous pamphleteer to question the integrity of Mexico's *junta de censura* and criticize its emerging practice of stopping reprints from circulating before following proper legal protocol. It advised writers to shift tactics, sarcastically suggesting they excerpt and republish well-known religious and moralizing works like Father Ripalda's catechism, rather than trying to communicate in the new language of rights.[109] Another pamphlet proclaimed: "The Inquisition was abolished, but its uses remained."[110] This spate of criticism published about the viceregal regime reflected a strategy in which pamphleteers seized upon a handful of press cases as further evidence of tyrannical behavior on the part of officials. That so many critical pamphlets—satirical, oblique, and referential yet clear in their assignment of blame—actually made it into circulation might point contrarily to evidence of viceregal tolerance in the emerging public sphere constructed in print. The fast-changing course of events, however, makes it difficult to assign any overarching coherence to official policy, which was still in formation even as Spanish authority in Mexico began to unravel. Dávila's pamphlet, published in eight installments, mirrored this unraveling, as its *pie de imprenta* (the imprint, which named the place of publication) evolved over successive issues from the "Press of Benavente" (1–3), to the "Press (against Despotism) of Benavente" (4), to the "American Press of Benavente" (5).

In 1821 the viceregal regime collapsed. Merino, whose pamphlet had acted as a key point of departure in broader debates over press freedom, constitutionalism, and viceregal authority, perhaps never embarked for Spain to serve his sentence. Agustín de Iturbide, a creole who had served as colonel in the royal army, enacted his own insubordination in February by defecting and, allied with his former adversary, the holdout insurgent leader Vicente Guerrero, brokered Mexico's independence under the three principles of Catholicism, independence, and unity in August. Valdés, who had first allowed Merino's message to gain a broader audience by failing to oversee his printing shop's activities, stepped easily into the role of Iturbide's imperial printer.

The broader debates surrounding press freedom in 1820 not only addressed the purpose and practice of law in abstract and concrete terms; they also voiced more quotidian concerns about the social and material practices associated with the loosening of restrictions on printing. Thus, while writers like Lizardi developed ideal visions of how best to use this newly acquired right to escape the tyranny of patronage and enlighten the public, printers like Valdés inserted their own claims to power that questioned writers' assumptions about how press freedom would actually work on the ground. In the decades after independence, the printing shop would become a central focus of lawmakers who grappled with how to regulate press freedom in the new nation. Even in 1821, however, the fall of the viceregal government was already reconfiguring long-standing economic relationships between printers and the state. Zúñiga y Ontiveros learned through the grapevine that he had lost an exclusive printing privilege that his father had held since the 1760s.[111] Valdés, on the other hand, capitalized on the change in power to gain new commissions, from designing Iturbide's imperial heraldry to printing paper currency.[112] Valdés gained enough visibility as the imperial printer that he was subject to public mockery in an 1822 broadside complaining that he printed the official news with large type and wide margins so as to overcharge customers.[113] Valdés would soon face competition from an expanded cast of entrepreneurs—including from among the ranks of the insurgency—who began to establish small-scale printing businesses in Mexico City.

Mexico City's world of print production had begun to transform from one in which a handful of actors maintained well-known connections to officials to one populated by a mixture of old and new characters, whose allegiances were far from transparent. As the case of Merino's pamphlet suggests, the protocols for regulating press freedom were far from stable or established, and these practices would continue to evolve after Iturbide's government unraveled and was replaced by a republic. A new era of uncertainty regarding print production had begun, enveloping both printers and their patrons. Lizardi captured this climate in an 1822 pamphlet, *Maldita sea la libertad de imprenta* (Freedom of the press be damned).[114] Prior censorship, his dialogue between the fictional Don Liberato and Don Servilio suggested, was being replaced by subsequent censorship, or punishment after the fact. Because writers could never be sure how their works might be judged under the new legal regime, Don Liberato preferred not to use the term "*freedom* of the press, but rather *danger* of the press."[115] As the following chapter explores, writers, printing shop collaborators, and government officials would have to navigate the increasingly politicized terrain of print production in the early republic.

THREE

Responsibility on Trial

OUTCRY ERUPTED FROM MEXICO'S POLITICAL elite in October 1840, when the Yucatecan senator José María Gutiérrez Estrada published an incendiary pamphlet calling for the establishment of a monarchy ruled by a foreign prince. Republicanism, the text proclaimed, had only produced discord and stalemate since its official adoption in the years after Mexico gained independence from Spain in 1821.[1] In order to achieve material progress and protect the nation's sovereignty from foreign invasion, it reasoned, Mexicans should instead establish a constitutional monarchy, recruiting an outsider to unite the factions that had emerged over the last two decades. The proposal carefully drew analogies from Gutiérrez Estrada's recent four-year tour around the Western Hemisphere and Europe to argue that like France, Mexico should implement a constitutional monarchy better suited to its history. A treatise that engaged central questions of nation building through the lens of comparative politics, the pamphlet also responded in more local and immediate terms to a failed August revolt led against Mexico's centralist government by federalists, which had briefly transformed Mexico City's streets into a battlefield.

Personal experiences also shaped Gutiérrez Estrada's proposal. In 1840 the senator returned to Campeche from his travels abroad, only to discover the region in the throes of a secessionist movement. Relocated to Mexico City, he witnessed the upheaval of the August revolt, in which his own father-in-law had been shot.[2] Evoking memories of the revolt, the pamphlet included a lone lithograph: in a desolate scene, the bombarded facade of Mexico's National Palace crumbles into the foreground as the nation's flag hangs limp and dejected on the ramparts (see figure 13). Playing to emotions, Gutiérrez Estrada hoped to sway a disillusioned public to his cause: to reanimate the

FIGURE 13. *Vista del Palacio Nacional de Méjico, después de la lamentable jornada del 15 al 27 de Julio 1840.* José María Gutiérrez Estrada, *Carta dirigida* (Mexico City: Impresa por I. Cumplido, 1840). Library of Congress.

sagging flag with a plan for national rejuvenation to be established via a constitutional convention. His search for a sympathetic public was met, however, by widespread condemnation from political leaders, military officials, and the press; observer Fanny Calderón de la Barca noted that the pamphlet "seems likely to cause a greater sensation in Mexico than the discovery of the gunpowder plot in England."[3] As denunciations mounted and soldiers were dispatched to make an arrest on charges of sedition, Gutiérrez Estrada went into exile in Europe, aided by his wealthy in-laws, the family of the Conde de la Cortina.[4] The three less fortunate individuals who had published the monarchist pamphlet—the printer Ignacio Cumplido, the former printer Martín Rivera, and the newspaper publisher Francisco Berrospe—on the other hand, were immediately caught and thrown into prison, charged with breaching press laws.

The Gutiérrez Estrada case, which unfolded over months after the senator went into hiding, revealed the challenges of participating in the contentious sphere of printing politics that had taken shape in Mexico in the years since independence. Two decades after national governments had ratified press freedom, publishing remained fraught with uncertainty. Since the founding of a republic in 1824, shifting factions had competed fiercely to define the nature and orientation of Mexico's political system, using printed texts to advance partisan platforms and challenge rivals. Government administrations, though they proclaimed the principles of press freedom, often wielded press laws against political enemies or critics. Official targeting of printing shop communities soon joined the repertoire of early republican political strategies for policing press freedom. Once seen as reliable partners of the state, printers now drew the suspicions of authorities for their role in facilitating controversial texts behind the scenes.

Printers' activities troubled government officials, who struggled to maintain power in a climate marked by political instability and uprisings. The issue of how to regulate printed speech, indeed, became a central thread in debates about the scope of state power, political participation, and rights during the early republican era. In 1835 Antonio López de Santa Anna, the influential general who brokered numerous changes in government in the years after independence, helped end Mexico's first federalist republic, which had decentralized state power and embraced broad male suffrage. Conservative leaders adopted a centralist constitution that restricted citizenship to men of property and pushed legal reforms to strengthen state regulation of printed speech. Most political observers agreed on the need for limits to press freedom, but events like the fallout over Gutiérrez Estrada's pamphlet showed divergence over the power of officials to enforce press laws. At the heart of the matter lay the question of responsibility. Who, lawmakers and government officials asked, could or should be held responsible for texts deemed to have crossed the line? Establishing and enforcing rules about legal responsibility—a category that was related to authorship—connected debates in the halls of national government with the activities unfolding inside Mexico City's printing shops, where artisans and their literary collaborators had learned to exploit the category of the "responsible party" to mitigate the risks of publishing. Centralist efforts to narrow press freedoms by expanding who could be held responsible for texts raised philosophical questions about printers' relationship to the texts they issued, thrusting the working communities of the printing shop to the center of political conversation. Indeed, as debates over responsibility captured the attention of judges, congressmen, executive officials, and journalists alike, printing shop actors gained new opportunities to position themselves in the public eye and become subjects of the political transcript itself.

Centralist reforms of press laws aimed, at least in part, to foreclose federalist and radical challenges to the new system, yet Gutiérrez Estrada's 1840 pamphlet, published as federalist resistance to centralism grew, offered an attack from more conservative quarters by identifying republicanism of all stripes as Mexico's fundamental problem. The centralist government had not only been beleaguered by insurgent federalist uprisings but also faced breakaway rebellions in Texas and the Yucatán and a recent blockade and invasion by French troops at Veracruz. If Mexicans stayed the political course, Gutiérrez Estrada argued, the results would only yield government penury, instability, and assured absorption by the United States. By suggesting that citizens use their constitutional rights to undo republicanism altogether, the senator proposed a still narrower vision of political participation. Although Mexicans had tried and rejected monarchism in a brief imperial experiment headed by Agustín de Iturbide after independence (1821–1823), the pamphlet reopened the conversation, heralding a new "monarchist offensive" that would be armed by an emerging conservative party in successive decades.[5]

When officials in the centralist government responded by jailing the senator's three collaborators, however, they opened space for new arguments that refocused attention on the issue of press freedom and its regulation. As printing-shop deals in which principles and patronage intermingled spilled out into public view, the savvy newcomer Cumplido practiced constructing a new persona—the "printer citizen"—that challenged government efforts to hold him accountable for the promonarchist pamphlet. As this chapter explores, debates over the rules of responsibility not only revealed diverging political attitudes toward printed speech; they also intertwined with printers' attempts to define new roles for themselves in public life and politics.

PRINTING IN A POSTCOLONIAL LANDSCAPE

Political independence brought uneven change to Mexico City's landscape of printing. After governments ratified press freedom laws, Mexico City printing shops flooded the city with ephemeral materials, many of which engaged politics by denouncing officials with indignity or satire, offering counterarguments or dissecting events and actions, or launching rebellious plans (*pronunciamientos*). A burst of pamphleteering, which had started in 1820, continued between 1821 and 1823 as satirists like José Joaquín Fernández de Lizardi and a host of well-heeled and upwardly mobile writers experimented with press freedom and tested markets for political content.[6] Early enthusiasm for the biting, confrontational style of pamphleteering, however, soon gave way to a heterogeneous print production sustained by an opaque mixture of editorial ventures, commercial commissions, church business, state contracts, and political patronage. While the established printing shops with roots in the colonial era still dominated the trade, by 1823 Mexico City's small coterie of printing shops had expanded to twenty-two businesses.[7] Of the new presses, some sought to capitalize on the heightened interest in publishing, while others had been expressly founded with financing from wealthy politicians to incubate emerging partisan platforms.[8] No longer required to import supplies from Spain, printers with access to capital turned to manufacturers and type foundries located in the industrializing North Atlantic, using connections to diplomats and notables living abroad to acquire updated type and iron hand presses from burgeoning printing centers like New York and Philadelphia.[9] Less well-connected businesses operated under tenuous conditions with equipment acquired secondhand from more venerable local presses.

The diverse mix of printing businesses that sprang up in the years after independence navigated shaky postcolonial markets in which print runs of items like newspapers and pamphlets rarely exceeded two thousand copies and hovered closer to five hundred. An 1828 list of one printer's "common prices," for example, structured fees around a baseline of five hundred, with overage charged for each additional hundred copies.[10] These figures reveal the fixed and variable costs of printing—typesetting absorbed a set cost up front while printing expenses fluctuated—while providing a general sense about typical print runs. Higher print runs could generate greater profits, but only if enough buyers could be found to offset the costs of materials. Paper, in nineteenth-century Mexico, cost more than the labor required for printing. The price of a simple pamphlet might equal the entire day's pay of a skilled urban worker, while the cost of commissioning five hundred copies absorbed a full monthly wage.[11]

The end of royal privileges loosened state influence over printing markets after independence, yet government contracts remained a potentially lucrative target pursued by many Mexico City printers. After an effort begun in 1823 to establish a government printing office inside the National Palace failed in 1828, officials turned to a handful of local printers to produce the materials of statecraft: letterhead, ministerial reports, the government gazette, passports, lottery tickets, and the like. Yet while the national government represented a potentially powerful patron, it could not always be relied upon to pay promptly.[12] And while some national administrations directly subsidized local newspapers by buying quantities of subscriptions, buoying a national press through the mechanism of the *subvención*, changes in power could lead to the loss of state patronage as officials retaliated against rivals.[13]

The shifting, often interdependent relationship between the urban printing world and state officials and politicians shaped attitudes toward printers in the early republican era. Government reliance on local printers generated official hand-wringing and complaints about inefficiencies and breaches of confidentiality, reams of paperwork, and occasional scams, like an attempt to defraud customers by producing a fake government gazette.[14] Printers, for their part, faced accusations of deception and partisan bias, leading one newcomer to name his business the Imprenta Imparcial (Impartial Press) in 1833. The printer explained this decision in a broadside that promised to print for all customers regardless of political affiliation, justifying neutrality as a virtuous stance that elevated, rather than undermined, the noble ideal of press freedom.[15] This argument echoed the view, advanced by Lizardi in 1820, that printers should serve customers on a first-come, first-served basis. Yet the 1833 justification revealed a new dimension in debates about publishing: the printer had to defend political impartiality because printing indiscriminately for profit was similarly frowned upon. Printers had become caught uncomfortably between the dual caricatures of partisan hack and moneygrubbing mercenary.

THE POLITICS OF RESPONSIBILITY IN EARLY REPUBLICAN MEXICO CITY

Printers' ambiguous relationship to the political texts they issued made printing shops sites where struggles over specific controversial ideas and the broader framework of press regulations unfolded. At the heart of these struggles lay the question of responsibility for texts, which reemerged whenever controversial publications came to light and officials decided to take action. Identifying who was responsible for texts might seem like a straightforward proposal, but it was not so simple in a world where authors frequently published anonymously, newspaper editorials ran without attribution, and printing shops regularly reprinted material first published elsewhere. The law offered guidance on some of these matters, but the gap between legal protocol and real-world practices generated its own forms of political action. Commentators like Carlos María de Bustamante, the former insurgent and public writer who kept a detailed diary of political events and gossip in Mexico City, offered clues about the politics of responsibility, privately speculating about the "intellectual authors" of controversial printed material and the unceasing intrigues of publishing coordinated between authors and printing shops. Government attempts to put an end to this intrigue gave rise to a repertoire of strategies and counterstrategies through which officials and printing shop actors negotiated the limits of public speech.

Understanding the centrality of responsibility in nineteenth-century printing politics requires a brief overview of press freedom's legal framework and instrumentalization. Political figures in and out of power quickly learned to wield the press laws ratified by Mexico's independent governments. These laws guaranteed the individual's right to publish, provided that texts did not conspire against the state or its religion; incite rebellion, legal disobedience, or disturbance of public peace; violate *buenas costumbres*; or commit libel against a person's private honor or reputation.[16] The broadness of these categories, which had troubled Mexican delegates to the Cortes in 1812, carried the ambiguities of Cádiz's moderate, Catholic vision of tolerated speech forward into the new nation. While individuals and political groups could bring libel charges against texts in order to defend reputations under attack or to outmaneuver rivals, officials in the national government also frequently denounced critical texts on charges of sedition. An appointed press prosecutor or high-ranking official, especially from the Ministry of the Interior (Gobernación), which monitored the press and communicated closely with the president, typically levied charges on behalf of the state.

Press denunciations became a routine component of the official political repertoire as governments with a shaky grasp on power sought to undermine challengers, especially during moments of crisis. In 1827, for example, when tensions rose between the two major political factions organized around competing masonic lodges, the incumbent Yorkinos (populists whose radical wing had begun to push an aggressive campaign to expel Spaniards from Mexico) directed a barrage of defamation charges against *El Sol*, the newspaper associated with the Escocéses (socially conservative liberals).[17] Similarly, in 1832 the press prosecutor aimed a number of sedition accusations at federalist critics of Anastasio Bustamante's more conservative centralist government, a practice repeated again by government officials in 1838 when Bustamante's second administration faced challenges.[18] Powerful individuals also lodged defamation complaints in hopes of uncovering the identities of anonymous enemies or repaying critics perceived to have infringed upon the privileges of status. When the bishop of Yucatán denounced *La Luz* for criticizing his conduct of office, for example, his lawyer urged the presiding judge to punish the culprits more harshly in consideration of his client's holiness.[19]

While politicians of all stripes levied charges against their rivals, the adjudication of press laws generated clearer disagreement among emerging political factions. The original law directed a panel of appointed judges to evaluate press infractions. According to scattered early republican records, Mexico City judges convicted or acquitted defendants in equal measure and dismissed cases with the same frequency.[20] In 1828, however, lawmakers who feared that government officials were using press laws to retaliate against critics established a system of press juries, whereby citizens who met literacy and minimum annual income requirements would judge potential violations of press laws.[21] The press jury afforded this narrower segment of citizens space to weigh in on the acceptable limits of free speech through their deliberations.[22] Yet the new institution returned similar results as in those cases decided by judges who had served before 1828.[23] The press jury, nevertheless, became one issue that distanced politicians with conservative leanings from the more democratic spirit underpinning the 1828 rules. When centralists came to power and began drafting a new constitution in 1835, they eliminated the press jury and reinstated judges as the arbiters of press crimes.[24] A persistent point of dispute, press juries would be reinstated and eliminated periodically throughout the nineteenth century until their final abolition in 1882.

Between officials' bringing charges and issuing a ruling, investigations into press infractions revealed the challenges they faced as they attempted to establish a regulatory framework, which depended on being able to identify a subject who could be held to account. The law designated the author or publisher of a work as its "responsible parties" but tasked printers with keeping track of this responsibility, directing them to retain physical proof in the form of a *responsivo*, a signed copy of the manuscript or original work that attested to an individual's identity. In Mexico City, a *responsivo* might include the name, date, and residence of its signatory, along with a statement such as "I respond before the law of press freedom" for a particular work (see figure 14).[25] The law also required printers to include their names and printing shop information on all printed matter so that responsibility could be traced if an anonymous work faced denunciation. Failure to produce a *responsivo* would make a printer the legally responsible party and subject to fines and jail time.

The responsibility provisions aimed to ensure that no press infraction would go unpunished, yet authors, printers, and their collaborators, savvy

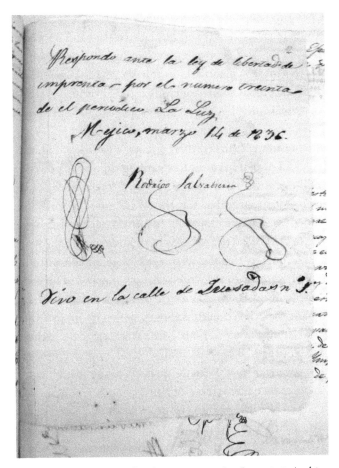

FIGURE 14. *Responsivo* for the newspaper *La Luz*, 1836. Archivo General de la Nación, Mexico City.

about the system, tested a number of work-arounds that exploited this legal category. They acquired general *responsivos* that vouched for all monthly issues of a newspaper, which judges rejected as illegal.[26] They allowed minors to sign *responsivos*, in hopes that their minority status would offer plausible deniability under scrutiny.[27] They reused *responsivos* of editorial staff already serving jail time and paid to use the names of criminals or hospital patients— actors one congressman denounced on the floor of the chamber of deputies as literary pimps (*alcahuetes*)—to mask authorial identities, a practice that was banned in 1835.[28] Another tactic involved simply printing broadsides or pamphlets with no identifying markers, which prompted officials to call on select printers to act as typographical detectives in tracking down the offending printing shop. The experts might canvas the city's shops—visiting the storefronts of their friends and business rivals—and occasionally catch the culprit with jumbled type or incriminating ink printed on the presses' tympans.[29] The most sympathetic expert witnesses could not be wholly trusted to do the job, as some stonewalled the government with technical arguments, explaining that all the city's printing shops used the same imported types, making identification impossible.[30]

After 1835, centralists turned their attention to redefining responsibility in press laws as a next step toward expanding the state's power to regulate speech. In doing so, they confronted Mexico City's complex world of print production. Inside the printing shop, the overlapping and sometimes shifting responsibilities associated with production challenged legislators who struggled to impose categorical definitions that could regulate the field. Printing shop owners frequently doubled as the publishers or editors of newspapers and often collaborated with the writers they commissioned for contributions. Printing shop administrators managed daily operations and answered to owners or made their own decisions about whether or not to accept commissioned work. Compositors (*cajistas*)—the workers who set the individual letters of type into a physical form from which an impression would be taken by pressmen—were at least partially apprised of the textual content of the imprints they produced. Proofreading, furthermore, required reading aloud, allowing texts to circulate within the printing shop. These overlapping and unsystematic relationships came into play in the finger pointing that followed legal action against printed materials, fueling hostile arguments against printers and their establishments. One plaintiff in a defamation case argued that since printing shops earned their bread by publishing libel, "the printer is more criminal than the author, because [the author] is nothing more than a mercenary that lends himself to sign whatever is presented by the printing shop for a miserable quantity, or maybe is not even paid."[31] Although the plaintiff exaggerated printers' autonomy, his complaint advanced the idea that a work was ultimately a material product brought into being in the collaborative, untrustworthy space of the printing shop.

Conservative centralist governments, sharing the plaintiff's attitude, developed a regulatory strategy that approached printing shops as corporate communities. Responding to the evasive strategies of publishing, they drafted measures in 1836, 1839, and 1840 that expanded the definition of "responsibility" to cover everyone involved in print production and distribution, turning the entire printing shop staff into potential criminal accomplices.[32] Such actions did not go uncontested. In 1836, a group of Mexico City and Supreme Court judges challenged a new law that reclassified press crimes as regular criminal offenses, a move that abolished existing press regulations and provided greater leeway to assign responsibility. Arguing that the new law violated press freedom in practice and in spirit, the judges asked, "Would you treat the amanuenses that copied the draft as culprits? The servant who brought it to the printing shop, the printer and his dependents, the vendors of the printed item, those who read it and even those who have news of it and don't denounce it?"[33] Government officials answered affirmatively, explaining that the ultimate goal of the law was to make printers, whom they cast as knowing accomplices to press crimes, more cautious. While dissenting judges argued that the new law turned printers into de facto censors, executive officials explained that it would simply strengthen the "private censorship that printers have always executed" in the course of making judgments about what they would print.[34]

Arguments like these, which engaged the rules of responsibility, reflected competing attitudes toward the emphasis and ultimate ends of press laws: liberals argued that broader laws of responsibility would curb author's freedoms by creating a new form of censorship, while conservatives argued that censorship was a preexisting phenomenon rooted in the economic realities of publishing, which governments could simply exploit to rein in press abuses. These debates continued after 1836, with government advisers insisting that press violations could be tried as ordinary crimes with a wide range of accomplices, and judicial and local officials raising procedural questions that showed their lack of agreement about legal enforcement. That members of Mexico's press freedom commission continued to field questions about how to adjudicate press crimes in 1838 suggests that conservative efforts to completely redefine responsibility—directed behind the scenes by the influential former interior minister Lucas Alamán—had stalled.[35] In 1839, the Supreme Conservative Power (a fourth governmental body established under the centralist constitution) rebuffed another attempt to expand the rules of responsibility when it revoked an executive decree exhorting local officials to crack down on authors and their accomplices.[36]

Parallel to this evolving and contested legal apparatus, printers also faced executive-ordered jail time, official harassment, exile, and occasionally bodily harm for their connection to controversial imprints or the partisan newspapers that emerged from their shops.[37] In the gray areas of enforcement and extralegal action that formed amid disagreements among governing powers, officials might jail the entire printing shop—including writers, workers, and wives—temporarily, or confiscate the printing presses themselves.[38] To navigate their position, printers who owned and operated newspapers acted at least occasionally as guarantors for their staff, helping imprisoned editors who had assumed legal responsibility get out on bail.[39] Such financial support could ameliorate the discomforts of jail time until political fortunes had shifted, and it ensured that presses rarely stopped completely. Printer networks, therefore, sought to manage the risk associated with publication, while government tactics aimed not only to force printers to take more conservative stances toward their publications but also to encourage the formation of clear connections between authors and texts in an era when these relationships could be murky.

THE GUTIÉRREZ ESTRADA PAMPHLET: PUBLISHING POLITICALLY SENSITIVE MATERIALS

Printers chose from an array of strategies when they faced jail time, from mobilizing the press and patronage relationships to blatantly offering their editorial columns for government use in exchange for release.[40] Their responses, however, shared one feature: all denied individual responsibility for their alleged crimes. Even after considerable debate over how to regulate printing, responsibility remained a matter of negotiation, to be pinned on someone or dodged at all costs. Anonymity presented a central challenge confronted by those in charge of regulation, as tracking down authors sometimes proved impossible. But in the most notable episode of its kind—the Gutiérrez Estrada incident in 1840—debates over printing shop responsibility occurred even when the identity of the offending author was ostensibly known to all.

Published on October 18 in a run of two thousand copies, Gutiérrez Estrada's pamphlet used a number of paratextual features to prepare readers for its controversial main proposal, revealing how genre and typographical conventions had shifted in the years since independence. The short, unadorned pamphlets from the early 1820s, whose provocative titles clamored for readers' attention in a visually homogenous field, had fallen out of fashion. Instead, partisan newspapers, published several times a week, funneled political commentary into editorials and letters from readers. Gutiérrez Estrada's pamphlet, too long for any newspaper, took the form of a stand-alone treatise, refusing alliances with any partisan position. To produce a pamphlet of this length, and with a lithographic illustration, involved significantly more resources than a letter to the editor; the object suggested a serious intention. So too did the lengthy title, pitched, in an appeal to power, as a *Letter Directed to the Most Excellent Sr. President of the Republic on the Need to Find in a Convention the Possible Solution for the Evils That Afflict the Republic: And Opinions of the Author Regarding the Same Theme.* The dizzying array of a dozen typefaces that paraded the senator's sober title down a bright blue cover sheet spoke less to the author's message and more to the printer's advertisement of his novelty designs, deployed to catch the viewer's eye (see figure 15). The title page's decorative border, however, featuring illustrations of two eagles and four military drums, alluded to the author's patriotism. Ornaments scattered throughout the text illustrating patriotic themes—"liberty" and "union"—tried to underscore this sentiment in spite of the fact that their slogans appeared in English, evidence of Mexico City printers' links to the US type foundries that manufactured their supplies.[41] On the inner title page, the author's name appeared clearly again, followed by an epigraph from Tacitus, the Roman historian, who proclaimed himself unafraid to incur ill will while serving the public good. The *pie de imprenta* identified Cumplido as the pamphlet's printer and included the printing shop's address, following legal protocol. The text was indeed prefaced by an August letter Gutiérrez Estrada had directed to President Anastasio Bustamante, which called for a constitutional convention but made no mention of monarchy. Perhaps the senator hoped to ease into his argument by reprinting the letter; he had already tested the waters by publishing articles in September and October in the government gazette, taking pains to build his proposition openly while guarding against accusations that he opposed the current administration.

The pamphlet had been promoted with large broadsides posted around the city on October 18, but the text became required reading for the city's political elite after scandal broke days later.[42] The senator himself had collected a majority of the pamphlets from the printing shop, presumably to distribute to targeted members of this community, perhaps with the help of confidants or servants.[43] The printer Cumplido sent just three hundred copies to two local bookstores and a smaller number to Puebla for sale, while the senator exercised considerable control over the bulk of the pamphlet's distribution. Perhaps he hoped to exert greater influence over readers' interpretations through-face-to-face communication or to ensure that each member of

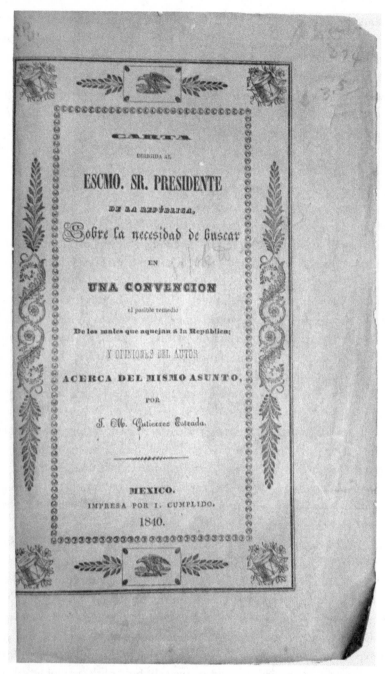

FIGURE 15. Paper cover of Gutiérrez Estrada, *Carta dirigida*, featuring patriotic imagery along with the novelty typefaces commonly seen on pamphlets in the 1840s and 1850s. Library of Congress.

congress and noteworthy government official received a copy. Political observer Carlos María de Bustamante enforced the notion that the pamphlet linked an expanded but still proximate community when he remarked in his diary that the pamphlet "has caused a great sensation as much among those who have read it, as among those who have heard it spoken about."[44]

The Chamber of Deputies denounced the pamphlet two days after its publication, issuing a resolution that called on the Ministry of the Interior to investigate the matter immediately.[45] Before widespread outrage emerged in the press, the ministry initiated action against the pamphlet's publisher. Following procedure, the pamphlet had quickly found its way to the desk of a judge, in this case the *juez de letras* José Gabriel Gómez de la Peña, who deemed it "subversive and seditious in the first degree, tending to incite disobedience against the constituted authorities."[46] But even before the judge issued his communiqué, officials had investigated the matter by paying a visit to Cumplido's printing shop, where they had inquired about the identity of the party responsible for the pamphlet. Although the pamphlet seemed to have been authored by Senator Gutiérrez Estrada—a fact supported by the title page and the senator's careful laying of the groundwork before publication—the signature on file at Cumplido's printing shop revealed a different name: Francisco Berrospe. By the morning of October 21, Berrospe had been rounded up and brought to Cumplido's printing shop, where he confirmed that the signature on file was indeed his.[47] By nightfall, officials returned to arrest Cumplido himself, taking him to the prison of the Ex-Acordada. That day, Berrospe and another printer, Martín Rivera, had also been placed under arrest.

The legal file accompanying the Gutiérrez Estrada affair reveals that the monarchist pamphlet came into being not through the sole actions of Gutiérrez Estrada as author, but rather through his coordinated interactions with this trio of printing world characters: Cumplido, an up-and-coming liberal printer originally from the provinces who in 1840 also enjoyed the distinction of being one of the government's official contract printers; Rivera, a printer who in the 1820s had collaborated with members of the Escocés faction to publish their newspaper *El Sol*; and Berrospe, the editor of one of the longest running Mexico City newspapers, the procentralist *El Mosquito Mexicano*. Berrospe and Rivera, two decades older than Cumplido (they were forty-nine, Cumplido twenty-nine, at the time of the event), were veterans of early republican print politics and had collaborated previously. Both had been imprisoned during moments when political tensions ran high (Berrospe in 1827 and Rivera in 1833), and Rivera had been exiled internally and physically assaulted as a result of his work.[48] When Gutiérrez Estrada judged that even his standing as a senator would not allow him to carry on business as usual and went into hiding, Cumplido, Berrospe, and Rivera were rounded up, jailed, and subjected to questioning about the pamphlet.

The pamphlet's principal author, meanwhile, remained at large, and early reports rumored that he had already fled to avoid capture.[49] Writing three diary entries in one day as the scandal unfolded, the observer Bustamante expressed skepticism that Gutiérrez Estrada would ever be punished for the pamphlet even though it represented his ideas "printed *in fraudem legis.*"[50] He further speculated that French conspirators and powerful local conservative backers (including the senator's wealthy in-laws) must have put Gutiérrez Estrada up to the task, "otherwise he wouldn't have spent 2,500 pesos for the printing of this notebook."[51] In the press, speculation about the senator's actions remained more circumspect, but the fates of the jailed printers quickly came to light. Anticipating the ordeal that would befall the arrested men, *El Cosmopolita* asked, "Should the responsible party by punished as a slanderer?"[52] The article's questioning reference to this narrowly defined term—specifically, the individual who had signed the printing shop paperwork, thus assuming legal responsibility for the published text—suggested that, beyond the narrower world of legal experts who debated press laws, the rules of responsibility were not settled business.

Even after a week had passed, *El Mosquito Mexicano* declared that the pamphlet remained "the sole issue of the day."[53] If reports are to be believed, Mexico City audiences were not satisfied with the brief excerpts that had been reprinted in several newspapers; to buy the original item cost upward of ten pesos, and just to read someone else's copy cost one peso, double a laborer's daily wage.[54] Well-heeled city dwellers came together as they sought out the copies that had made it into circulation, either at two city bookstores or through social networks that intersected with the distribution efforts spearheaded by the pamphlet's author. Low literacy levels and high costs made brightly colored political pamphlets symbolic markers of distinction, but the scandal's depth, driving up the demand for pamphlets and generating discussion, suggests that a wider swath of the city may have come into contact with the debate through urban networks, perhaps catching fragments of public readings or conversations in the streets or workshops. Interpersonal communications thus overlapped with and extended the city's intimate circuits of print distribution.

DODGING RESPONSIBILITY: THE IDEALIST, THE VETERAN, AND THE MECHANIC

As coverage of the Gutiérrez Estrada case developed in the press, the three arrested men gave testimony the day after their detention. As retired militia captains, Berrospe and Rivera enjoyed the privilege of the military's legal exemption or *fuero* and were placed under the jurisdiction of its courts, overseen by a judge advocate.[55] Being a civilian, Cumplido underwent questioning by the judge Gómez de la Peña, who had initially overseen the denunciation of the pamphlet. The three men testified with the hope of escaping punishment, and they deployed a variety of tropes associated with print politics—selfless idealism, mercenary moneygrubbing, patronage politics, and nonpartisan commerce—in different combinations. At the same time, their testimony offers a glimpse into a series of publishing practices and printer relationships that not only crossed political and generational lines but also navigated and challenged the legal mechanisms that sought to clarify print responsibility.

During questioning, editor Berrospe described his involvement with the subversive pamphlet as a matter of unhappy chance. One day, he explained, he had gone to visit his friend Martín Rivera, who told him about a "very brilliant pamphlet" being composed by Gutiérrez Estrada.[56] Knowing that Berrospe had lately criticized Mexico's federalist and centralist systems in his newspaper *El Mosquito Mexicano*, Rivera had invited him to meet with the senator, presumably to discuss publishing the senator's ideas in Berrospe's paper. The two had proceeded to Gutiérrez Estrada's home, where the senator had read passages from the manuscript and explained that he wished to avoid possible challenges to his writings—even though he enjoyed senatorial immunity—by having another individual sign his name, assuming responsibility for the imprint. Berrospe had signed for responsibility in good faith, and he and Rivera had left the house, at which point the latter had informed Berrospe that Gutiérrez Estrada was disposed to pay him for his services.[57] Berrospe had rejected the offer with indignity and returned alone to Gutiérrez Estrada's house to inform him that "if he had signed, it had not been mercenarily, but rather because he believed he did a service to his country."[58] Only later did Berrospe learn the true gist of the pamphlet's contents—the senator had omitted the argument about inviting a foreign prince to govern Mexico in his recitation—which he now claimed repulsed him and violated his principles.

Reporting that he "would rather have been killed than sign such a paper," Berrospe presented himself as a man of ideals. As the editor of a well-known newspaper, he claimed that his personal opinions had long been publicly expressed in its pages, a consistent show of principles that ultimately left him vulnerable to exploitation by the calculating senator. In his telling, Rivera had broached the topic precisely because he knew Berrospe's politics aligned with those professed by Gutiérrez Estrada. This apparent confluence had led Berrospe astray; excited to find a kindred critique of both the federalist and centralist systems that sought a third way through democratic means, he had been duped into supporting a monarchist cause that he loathed. Gutiérrez Estrada, on the other hand, had acted dishonorably by hiding the true nature of his arguments. True, he had read aloud from the pamphlet itself, but he had excerpted egregiously, using the text's specifics to skew its general meaning. In Berrospe's telling, Gutiérrez Estrada had exploited his superior social standing—conveyed by the way he summoned Berrospe to an audience in his sumptuously furnished home—to impress, and was doubly dishonest for using Rivera to offer a payoff once the deal had been sealed, as if Berrospe were a hack for hire.

Berrospe directed responsibility onto Gutiérrez Estrada but also called Rivera's role into doubt. When questioned separately, Rivera confirmed many of the details offered by Berrospe. He had invited—or rather, he corrected himself, informed—Berrospe of Gutiérrez Estrada's concurrent ideas, and the editor had expressed a wish to speak further with the senator on the matter. After the senator's recitation—of a large portion of the manuscript, absent the foreign prince—Berrospe had concurred with the senator's call for a convention for the "political regeneration" of the nation.[59] Hearing Berrospe's favorable response, the senator had been moved to ask him to sign and take responsibility, reasoning that he wanted a companion to help defend the text against naysayers.[60] The manuscript was already printed, he explained, and only needed the signature to begin distribution. Berrospe had then signed, but under the idea that the paper only touched on a political convention and not a foreign prince.

The judge then turned to Rivera's role in the case. Asked how he had found out about Gutiérrez Estrada's manuscript, Rivera explained that on October 13, Cumplido had called him to his printing shop. When he arrived, Rivera had found Cumplido in the act of reading aloud from a sheet of the printed proof—dealing with the point of the political convention—as he corrected the composition. Cumplido had conveyed that the author, Gutiérrez Estrada, wished to find a responsible party, a capable man who could defend his pamphlet if anyone contradicted it. While Rivera himself had declined because "for some time he did not wish to get mixed up in public papers and thus had abandoned even his printing shop," he had suggested Berrospe's name, as he had read similar ideas in Berrospe's *El Mosquito*, and agreed to broach the issue himself.[61] The next day, when Rivera had returned by appointment to Cumplido's printing shop, he had encountered Gutiérrez Estrada, who had repeated the printer's proposal.

Rivera's testimony crafted an image of a man who, while abreast of events, stayed on the sidelines of politics. Highlighting his retirement from printing— which was actually due at least in part to financial troubles unmentioned in the case—Rivera downplayed both his own role as an active agent and his long career of political involvement.[62] He did not deny that he had suggested Berrospe for the job of responsible party, but this was only because he kept up with politics by reading the city's newspapers and knew about Berrospe's perspective. Plus, Cumplido had called him first, a fact that further displaced responsibility onto the pamphlet's printer. Called to the printing shop, Rivera had discovered Cumplido in the compromising position of reading the pamphlet himself (and aloud so all in the vicinity could hear), even if this happened in the course of normal printing shop proofreading duties. If Rivera and Berrospe both denied having full knowledge of the pamphlet's contents, Rivera implied that Cumplido certainly had access to the full picture and had acted in cahoots with Gutiérrez Estrada from the beginning.

While Berrospe and Rivera underwent questioning, Cumplido faced Gómez de la Peña—the man who had first deemed the pamphlet subversive— in a civilian procedure. Unlike the defensive positions staked out by Berrospe and Rivera, Cumplido took a combative stance toward his interviewer. Asked to confirm that he had printed the pamphlet, Cumplido assented, adding perhaps impudently, "because he believed that freedom of the press existed as expressed in the decrees that regulate it."[63] The printer then corrected the judge's line of questioning on typographic procedure aimed at clarifying responsibility. When Gómez de la Peña asked if Cumplido had *corrected* the *form* himself, Cumplido gave a lesson in printing shop protocol: printing shop workers had *composed* the *form* (the physical layout of lead characters, or *planta*), and the author had *corrected* the *proof* (the printed sheet whose impression was taken from the form, or *prueba*), as was customary in all similar cases. Cumplido denied knowledge of the pamphlet's full contents, explaining that he had read fragments of the senator's manuscript as he sent them in piecemeal but left the final revision in the care of his workers.[64] Asked to name these workers, Cumplido refused, even when pressed, to share their identities, stating that he was "disposed that any punishment they might merit should fall upon his person, if, as he said before, freedom of the press does not exist."[65]

The questioning then turned to issues of responsibility. Cumplido carefully delineated his role as a printer when he admitted that he had, in fact, had some knowledge of the pamphlet's contents, which he looked upon with disgust. When Gutiérrez Estrada, "separating him from the role of mechanic," had asked Cumplido for his opinion, the printer had frankly disagreed with his proposed solutions.[66] Berrospe, Cumplido asserted, was legally responsible for the imprint (as his signature on file proved), but only the pamphlet's author had written and edited the text. Gutiérrez Estrada, Cumplido explained, was "responsible for the moral part" of the work, a fact he could prove with a letter, written by the senator, which exculpated Cumplido from any responsibility.[67] But this additional safeguard shouldn't be necessary, Cumplido argued, as he had already produced the responsibility slip and thus proved the illegality of his imprisonment.

Unlike his companions, Cumplido gave remarkably principled testimony. Although he similarly deflected responsibility away from himself and onto the other parties involved, he differed dramatically by exhibiting both defiance and insolence to an authority figure, invoking the right of freedom of the press three times in a way that questioned the judge's own willingness to adhere to the law. Cumplido's closed-door testimony is virtually devoid of honor talk, a vocabulary used to claim citizenship and respectability in republican Mexico and a "center of public life" for the men who purported to represent public opinion in print.[68] While he mentioned his personal and nationalistic repugnance for Gutiérrez Estrada's ideas, Cumplido carefully drew boundaries between his participation as a printer and the content of the productions that emerged from his printing shop. The printer's role should be a disinterested one; he had opinions, but only expressed them when Gutiérrez Estrada pulled him out from his role as "mechanic" to solicit them. Cumplido defined this mechanical role as the one properly assigned to the printer: opining on the productions of others went above and beyond the job description.

By correcting the judge on printing shop terminology, referencing his careful adherence to press legislation, and explaining the customary practices of printing shop production, Cumplido established his expertise in his "mechanical" domain, where he labored under customary practices and the direction of outside patrons. Yet drawing the lines of responsibility was a tricky proposal in a moment when this concept was under debate in the political realm. Cumplido could not deny that his employees were apprised of at least fragments of the textual content of the senator's pamphlet, which they would have learned as they set its type or corrected the proofs. That the senator had given Cumplido a special letter attesting to the printer's innocence looked suspiciously conspiratorial, and the judge was clearly interested in who had possessed prior knowledge of the pamphlet's contents; such individuals might be considered accomplices if he adhered to orders from the executive branch issued in previous years. By highlighting the piecemeal nature of print production, Cumplido hoped to convince the judge that no one had a clear idea of the pamphlet's contents. Of course, type composition, proofreading, and shop gossip virtually ensured that even if no one had had such knowledge from a linear read-through, everyone would have had an idea of the pamphlet's gist in advance. Yet the judge dropped his questioning in the face of Cumplido's protection of his workers' identities. Cumplido's printing shop authority stood, at least regarding his workers.

A "PRINTER CITIZEN" ANALYZES FREEDOM OF THE PRESS

Debates about the pamphlet continued for weeks in the press and involved the full spectrum of local (and some provincial) papers in the cross-referential style common in newspapers of the day. While the government gazette published the strongest denunciations, conservative papers cast the senator's ideas as misguided, rather than outright treasonous, and *El Mosquito Mexicano*, Berrospe's paper, called for moderation.[69] Opposition newspapers, especially *El Cosmopolita*, used the unfolding events to critique the government's handling of the situation, focusing on the plight of the imprisoned men and a likely violation of press laws.[70] While the general consensus disavowed Gutiérrez Estrada's monarchical ideas, none criticized Cumplido's role in facilitating their dissemination. *El Cosmopolita*, instead, warned that his imprisonment heralded the death of press freedom, since holding printers responsible for their publications made them "effectively censors."[71] The editors of the government's *Diario Oficial*, however, denied accusations that the minister of the interior had personally targeted Cumplido.[72]

Cumplido did not sit quietly as his case became a lightning rod for debate over freedom of the press. He quickly seized the opportunity to defend his role in the scandal and, in the process, bolster his emerging reputation. Since establishing his Mexico City printing shop in the early 1830s, Cumplido had published dozens of pamphlets for government patrons and private individuals, often of prominent political standing.[73] His clients included supporters of Santa Anna as well as the current conservative president Anastasio Bustamante, among others.[74] Like other printers of the time, Cumplido produced commissioned work alongside original, ephemeral offerings designed to sell, like his portable yearly almanac, published since 1836, which listed religious observances and prayers alongside scientific facts and curiosities. While little is known about his early career, scattered evidence points to an upwardly mobile individual of provincial origins whose patronage connections seemed to crisscross political affiliations that, in 1840, were fluid and fast changing. Apparently untouched by prior scandals or politically motivated imprisonment (unlike his two collaborators), the printer moved to clarify his role in the publication process for the controversial pamphlet. Within a day of his imprisonment, perhaps while waiting to be questioned, the printer drafted a communiqué, an *Appeal to the Public*, that his own shop printed in the form of a double-sided broadsheet.[75] A week later Cumplido weighed in on his case again with the lengthy *Statement to the Public from the Printer Citizen Ignacio Cumplido*, dated October 31 and published as a pamphlet—similar in form to the monarchist pamphlet and adorned on the title page with the very same printed medallion of liberty—which expanded upon the *Appeal*.[76] Days later, the newspaper *El Cosmopolita* published yet another of the printer's writings, "Defense of the Printer Citizen Ignacio Cumplido," as a special supplement to the issue, doubling its normal page count.[77] *El Mosquito Mexicano* immediately picked up "Defense" in serial form, publishing it in five installments across its front page, with the last fragment appearing in late November.[78] Deploying pamphlets, broadsides, and newspapers, Cumplido had—from his confinement—achieved a multigenre print firestorm of perhaps unprecedented scale.

Cumplido's arguments defined his position in relation to legal status and legal texts. For one, he described himself as a "printer citizen," a designation that highlighted his status as both a skilled artisan and an individual who fulfilled the requirements established by the 1836 centralist constitution defining full political participation. Under the constitution, which had restricted the terms of citizenship established after independence, only adult men possessing incomes of one hundred pesos or more, earned through investments or "industry or personal labor that is honest and useful to society," possessed the right to vote or hold public office.[79] By proclaiming his citizenship alongside his trade affiliation, Cumplido simultaneously asserted membership in an exclusive world of political rights and emphasized the respectable nature of the printer's trade; citizenship itself was contingent upon possession of an "honest mode of living."[80] His first publication, the *Appeal*, also excerpted sections from the current press laws and publicly challenged the government on behalf of his profession: "I demand, as good faith requires, that if there is not freedom of the press, and the decrees that govern it are null, that it be made known, so that in the future those of us who have the honor to dedicate ourselves to the noble art of printing not be victims."[81] As in his testimony, Cumplido mentioned his disgust for Gutiérrez Estrada's pamphlet, which he published "because, as a printer, the laws authorize me to do so."[82]

If the *Appeal* argued that the government's actions violated the law, Cumplido's second pamphlet, the *Statement*, deepened and broadened the narrative. It brazenly deconstructed the judge's actions, alleging them to be contrary to the "genuine sense" of the law and criticizing the Ministry of the Interior for unjust imprisonment (while the "true authors of evil hide under the appearance of external responsibility").[83] "What could be my crime?" Cumplido asked, answering that perhaps he was imprisoned because in his previous *Appeal to the Public* he had admitted that he "understood what Gutiérrez Estrada's writing said."[84] Defending the right to think, Cumplido reasoned that "the law of press freedom does not say that the printer should be an irrational being or incapable of forming an idea of what he reads."[85] Yet freedom of the press only functioned, he suggested, because printers had the intellectual capacity to withhold their personal opinions from the business of printing: "Sacrificing my ideas, because in my profession *I am not a censor*, I admitted a paper for printing, basing this action on the current laws of press freedom."[86] He argued that the fact that he had accepted Gutiérrez Estrada's paper, in spite of disliking its contents, proved that "I work with absolute impartiality in the free exercise of my profession."[87] To bolster this argument, Cumplido listed various items published in his printing shop, including the government's gazette and conservative publications. Thus, Cumplido elaborated a clear separation between the individual—whose private thoughts he might share with any author who asked about them—and the professional printer, who followed a strict code of impartiality.

Cumplido not only made the case for exoneration by describing himself as a law-abiding printer; he also took the opportunity to state his own political platform, itself clearly shaped by the milieu that had produced the

Gutiérrez Estrada pamphlet. Espousing a utilitarian outlook, Cumplido argued for an end to ideology in favor of a pragmatic approach to addressing Mexico's challenges: politicians needed to address the nation's budgetary crises, fixing their attention on income while curtailing expenses, investing in agriculture, establishing a reliable police force, and expanding primary education. Articulating a moderate view, he argued against curtailing special military privileges, which had been a key reform pushed by more radical politicians. Adherence to the law, he emphasized, must trump political division in order to restore the confidence of the demoralized masses.[88]

In short, Cumplido's pamphlet represented the printer citizen's political manifesto, in which he claimed the right of the printer to think. Even as he characterized the printer's role as a disinterested one, he went on to offer informed opinions in the next breath. Although not entirely contradictory, these two positions generated a tension that did nothing to establish what role the real printer had actually played in the affair. Was Cumplido sympathetic to Gutiérrez Estrada's proposal? His moderate political position and future trajectory suggest that the answer is no, but perhaps the vehemence of the backlash had caused Cumplido to redefine his views. In any case, the details of the Gutiérrez Estrada case reveal that Cumplido actively facilitated the production of what he knew would be a controversial pamphlet—precisely the kind of behavior that legislators had recently tried to curtail by expanding the definition of responsibility. Cumplido's public staking out of a political position was an uncomfortable reminder that print production was neither wholly partisan nor entirely contractual. The legal formality of the responsible party, while intended to prevent controversy by holding authors to their word, did little to clarify print world practices that officials wished to discourage. In fact, it opened a space for insiders to circumvent the intention of the law while still invoking its letter in the wake of persecution. Rhetorically, the printer emerged not as one who flouted the law but as its very embodiment: a crusader against injustice perpetrated by perfidious ministers.

Cumplido's arguments, which eschewed the apologetic language and patron-client strategies common in printers' closed-door appeals, linked his specific case to broader debates over the definitions of legal responsibility by drawing upon preexisting arguments against expanding responsibility to include the entire printing shop. When he suggested that holding him responsible for the pamphlet would set a precedent for converting printers into de facto censors, he drew on the 1836 complaint lodged by Mexico City judges against proposed tougher press laws.[89] In his "Defense" published in the press, similarly, Cumplido reprinted an 1839 Supreme Court opinion that revisited the same debate. The opinion argued that printers were artisans whose free exercise of a manual trade would be threatened by a broad legal definition that treated them as somehow responsible for the contents of their imprints. After all, it explained, the question of printing was "purely mechanical," and "mere simple artisans" lacked the abilities to judge the erudite content they produced.[90] "Violations are born of intelligence," it continued, "which cannot be assumed, under any circumstance, in a passive instrument that puts into action the will of an extraneous person, whose operations are of a completely different order than the simple movements of a machine."[91] On the one hand, "the art of printing has nothing to do with the art of thinking, of reflecting, of opining," and by the same token, "the printer, to aptly carry out his trade, does not need to be a man of letters (*letrado*), much less be it to the degree required to assess political doctrines, erroneous or wise opinions in complicated matters of government."[92]

This opinion, which Cumplido reprinted in spite of its clear insult to his honor, was not just useful for his position in the Gutiérrez Estrada case; it also illuminates a central tension underpinning Mexico's limited definition of press freedom. Conservative-leaning governments, emphasizing regulation, had pushed to expand responsibility as a technique for policing print. Liberals' emphasis on the individual's freedom to publish, however, required that printers be conceptualized as if they were machines, who enact the "will of an extraneous person": the author. Yet Mexico's press laws recognized that printers were in fact humans whose decisions shaped the publication process. Indeed, the law depended on printers to establish responsibility in the first place. Liberals confronted this tension by describing printers as "mere simple artisans," men of little consequence without the education to judge the works they produced. While Cumplido's original arguments had reserved the printer's right to think—to have opinions and withhold them in fulfillment of the law—the judicial opinion suggested that the printer cannot possibly think (indeed, the opinion nearly collapses printer and press into a single mechanical object), at least not to the degree required to be thrust into the role of censor. The opinion criticized the government's attempt to classify printers as responsible parties and thus convert them into de facto censors, not only because it impinged on free commerce, but also because it was simply ridiculous to assume a printer could possess the knowledge to judge a work. The opinion's authors raised the specter of a new Inquisition—one staffed by uneducated artisans—to counter conservative attempts to tighten regulations on print.

Cumplido's multipronged defense advanced several positions, all of which contributed not only to the case for his exoneration but more broadly to the creation of the printer as a disinterested public figure. This ideal figure—created with legalistic arguments, emotional appeals, and the opinions of other experts—emerged alongside an equally idealized vision of Mexico's liberal legal order that emphasized press freedom as a positive right. It gained moral force by challenging the government's specific actions as well as its long-term practices toward printers, which fell short of the liberal ideal. Yet in harnessing print to construct his own place in society, Cumplido also assumed the role of a different kind of producer: a "printer citizen" or even an intellectual, who made reasoned arguments based on study, experience, and possession of full political rights. By directly attaching the plight of printers to the upholding of the law, he constructed their image as crusaders for justice, even as he simultaneously advanced the characterization of the printer as a witless reproducer of texts, akin to a machine.

LIBERTY WON, LIBERTY DENIED

Reports from *El Cosmopolita*'s November 25 edition suggest that Cumplido's multipronged tactic to garner support had worked: more than two hundred people attended his hearing before the judges in the Tribunal Superior on November 24.[93] That the hearing attracted significant public attention suggests that interest in press-related cases—perhaps galvanized by liberal indignation—remained strong even in the absence of press juries comprised of citizens. His lawyer's defense lasted for one and a quarter hours; he "spoke very well" and was "heard with satisfaction" by the assembled crowd.[94] After the court issued its decision in the afternoon, Cumplido was cleared of charges. No sooner had he retaken possession of his liberty than he issued another pamphlet, this time to settle scores. Shifting from a defensive strategy based on legal arguments, the printer brazenly challenged the judge who had presided over his arrest, suggesting he thought himself above the law and questioning his honor.[95] Cloaking his quarrel under the guise of a crusader for justice, Cumplido vowed to expose the judge's perfidy by printing a large quantity of his critical pamphlet and advertising it on street corners around the nation.[96] Signing off with this promise of vengeance, Cumplido made another tactical move: printing his own legal testimony from the previous month's ordeal in notarized form. Conforming exactly to the transcript copied in the case file, the testimony made public the exchanges between the judge and the printer. Read in this context, Cumplido's refusal to inform on his employees and defiant invocation of the principles of freedom of the press may have formed part of a carefully orchestrated strategy, much like the publication of Gutiérrez Estrada's pamphlet itself.

Cumplido indeed won justice and pursued vengeance in the Gutiérrez Estrada affair. With professional knowledge of press laws and secondhand understandings of how government officials typically punished printers, he had avoided the regulatory spirit of the law while conforming carefully to its letter. While still in prison, he managed to use the episode to his advantage, wasting no time in creating a media firestorm facilitated by his ownership of a press. Perhaps confidence that his stay in prison would be short gave Cumplido the gall to take a tough stance against government questioning. Principles, combined in equal measure with a desire for self-preservation and glory, surely motivated him as well.

Other actors associated with the episode were caught up in the aftermath of the pamphlet's release. President Bustamante initiated charges against an editorial in *El Mosquito Mexicano*—the newspaper of Berrospe, the editor responsible for the original monarchist pamphlet—that defended aspects of Gutiérrez Estrada's position and argued that no political issue should be taboo in Mexico.[97] Eduardo Novoa, the responsible party behind the editorial and a minor, managed to get out of prison on bail after much finger pointing and claims of ignorance by invoking his father's military *fuero*. Berrospe himself was less fortunate; he languished in jail for months after Cumplido gained his freedom. As the days of his imprisonment dragged on, newspaper articles reprinted the Cumplido verdict and continued to speculate about Gutiérrez Estrada's whereabouts.[98] *El Mosquito* fanned the flames, claiming that a police escort had accompanied the senator in his flight from his suburban retreat at Tacubaya to the port city of Veracruz.[99] Berrospe, trying to redirect press coverage, followed Cumplido's example by issuing his own serialized defense in *El Mosquito*, which ran for two months.[100]

Berrospe's account could not have been more different than Cumplido's. While Cumplido's stuck to the ideals of press freedom and cited the injustice of his position, Berrospe had less opportunity to make a legal or noble argument. He had, after all, signed his name, and the argument that he had been duped was his only recourse. Unable to take the high road, Berrospe's defense delved into the maze of Mexico City's world of print politics; accusations of corruption, collusion, and insider politics; and accounts of his own past heroism as a crusader on issues of national importance. Perhaps his months in custody had embittered the veteran editor, or he believed that a harsh critique might galvanize support for his case. Berrospe seemed to be writing his account in installments that mirrored its publication schedule, because over the course of his two-month public letter, his tone became progressively acidic and accusatory—a position that Cumplido had strategically reserved for the moment *after* his release from jail.

Berrospe's increasingly woeful tale worked to establish his image as an idealist unafraid to risk his personal liberty in the service of his beliefs. He recounted his own activities as a veteran participant in Mexico City print politics, which had resulted in three previous (and, he argued, unjust) imprisonments. Differently from Cumplido's emphasis on impartiality, Berrospe focused on politics as a struggle to achieve a better world, with himself as seasoned fighter—but one who had lost everything in his efforts to bring about change. He recounted his own arrest as a series of bewildering humiliations, using the narrative to critique the legal system. Alleging shock at the pamphlet's contents as it appeared for sale in the Portal de Mercaderes bordering the central *zócalo*, Berrospe soon found himself dragged by officials to the Café de Verolí, where his judge was busy gambling. "Yes, yes, yes, yes," the judge replied, waving away Berrospe's keepers as he turned to resume his customary card game, "arrest him."[101] Building on this negative character assessment, Berrospe later took direct aim at the judge, calling him a "servile agent" of the minister of the interior: a stooge of the executive branch rather than an executor of justice, who was busy toadying up to officials in a bid to keep his job.[102] Disillusioned, betrayed by the system he had tried to improve through his editorial labors, Berrospe signed off his embittered letter, "It isn't madness to say that J. F. Berrospe is a man without a country."[103]

Although he followed Cumplido's example by publishing a public defense, Berrospe proved unable to use the rules of responsibility to his advantage. Behind the scenes, his case had stalled as a succession of judges recused themselves and the seemingly well-meaning but apparently incompetent judge advocate violated protocol by seeking out three separate opinions when he deemed their sentences too harsh.[104] Berrospe's letter also failed to draw significant public interest, not only because his case never came before a court, but also because his tale of woe was simply not convincing, given his status as a veteran of print politics. Like many others before him, the editor regained full liberty, a year after his jailing, when a change in power brokered by Santa Anna offered amnesty to political prisoners.

CONCLUSION: RESPONSIBILITY AS SPRINGBOARD

The Gutiérrez Estrada case vividly reveals the strategies deployed by printers, authors, and printing shop collaborators to produce controversial materials in early republican Mexico City. The depth of the scandal—a result of the senator's shocking monarchist proposal—shined a light on what had become a repertoire of tactics that developed in dialogue with official crackdowns and evolving regulations of freedom of the press. The exact nature of the relationship between Cumplido, Berrospe, Rivera, and the senator remains opaque, but it clearly reflected a coordinated strategy to displace, disperse, and diffuse responsibility. While commonsense notions of responsibility and authorship identified Gutiérrez Estrada as the culprit, the original provisions of liberal law intended to hold authors to their word had paradoxically created loopholes that printing shop collaborators learned to exploit. Although conservative centralist governments tried to close this loophole, Cumplido's exoneration revealed that their efforts to expand and reframe responsibility had stalled for the moment. Debates over whether the charge of sedition was founded or not, meanwhile, gradually faded out of the conversation in light of the monarchist proposal's unpopularity, especially once the rumor spread that Gutiérrez Estrada had fled into exile with the help of the French consul, a move that gave off a whiff of foreign-backed conspiracy.[105]

Meanwhile, Cumplido emerged largely unscathed from the Gutiérrez Estrada incident, suggesting that his performance as a defender of freedom of the press had resonated with a broader public and that government efforts to punish him as a political proxy had failed. Had the printer intentionally probed the limits of Mexico's public sphere, printing monarchist positions as part of a broader liberal strategy to advocate greater freedom of the press? While Cumplido's intentions are difficult to discern, he and other printers would continue to push political boundaries as they faced official crackdowns and changing press laws in the years to come. In 1841, Santa Anna assumed dictatorial powers in Mexico. While he reaffirmed press freedom, like the centralist government he had overthrown, Santa Anna also periodically issued decrees that expanded the rules of responsibility.[106] Stern private warnings from the general, post office stings, and periods of exile failed to curb the activities of printers, however, who resorted to temporarily shutting down their newspapers in public protest, secretly moving printing presses to evade authorities or going into hiding to escape punishment until tempers cooled.[107] The redrafting of press laws would continue after Santa Anna's 1843 ouster and for decades to come, as would targeting of printing shop collaborators.[108] This ensured that responsibility remained a fixture of political disputes throughout the century.

While frequent changes in political power meant that printers and their collaborators rarely faced long jail sentences, the sustained scrutiny of their activities offered opportunities for printers to fashion new identities for themselves. Cumplido led the way by using his predicament to launch a public career. The following year, he won a seat in the Chamber of Deputies and pursued a platform of prison reform inspired by his own spell in the Ex-Acordada jail.[109] Through his writings and testimony, he sketched the outline for a new archetype of the printer, a figure he characterized as simultaneously impartial artisan, faithful servant of the law, and honorable employer. These characterizations sidestepped the obvious question of partisanship, while establishing the printer citizen as a force to be reckoned with in the world of republican debate. Cumplido's decision to represent himself on the printed page coincided with the start of an era in which a handful of Mexico City printers self-consciously reevaluated their relationship to national politics and public opinion. Indeed, Cumplido soon founded the daily newspaper *El Siglo Diez y Nueve* and became a pillar of the emerging faction of moderate liberalism, which he shaped from behind the scenes over a career that would span nearly half a century.[110]

In the coming years, liberals would have to grapple with the dilemma of advocating freedom of expression while increasingly confronted with a monarchist offensive that, if successful, might ultimately curb press freedom.[111] While Cumplido turned political controversy to his advantage, Gutiérrez Estrada continued to push a monarchist option for Mexico from exile in Europe. As fears that the United States would move to annex Texas grew, the former senator's proposal looked increasingly attractive to conservatives, who blamed republicanism and the democratization of politics for the nation's problems. Following the US annexation of Texas in 1845, a small group led by Lucas Alamán plotted with the Spanish foreign minister to create an English-style constitutional monarchy in Mexico.[112] Their plan to convene a constitutional convention that would undo republicanism ultimately fizzled, but it did gain public expression in newspaper polemics sustained by an emerging group of conservative printers, who found cover from a sympathetic government and powerful patrons in 1846.[113] Amid renewed debate over the monarchist option, centralism collapsed, and Santa Anna, returning from exile under the growing clouds of war, helped restore the federal constitution of 1824.

The conflict with the United States proved disastrous for Mexico, resulting in the loss of half of the national territory after the US Army occupied Mexico City. Gutiérrez Estrada, writing from Rome, remarked with horror on General Winfield Scott's proclamations, issued in US-run newspapers printed on Mexican presses.[114] His 1848 pamphlet, *Mexico in 1840 and 1847*, articulated the vision, reproduced not only by political observers but also by much (now discredited) historiography on the US-Mexico war, that political disunity unleashed by republicanism had brought Mexico to its knees. The time was not too late, he argued, to set things right by embracing a political system better suited to the nation's character. The former senator would continue to lobby tirelessly in Europe, searching for a foreign monarch to rule Mexico. His actions came to fruition in a plan that placed the Hapsburg prince Ferdinand Maximilian on the Mexican throne between 1864 and 1867 with the support of French troops. In the postwar disillusionment of 1848, nobody noticed that Gutiérrez Estrada's latest pamphlet was printed by an up-and-coming printer with radical leanings, Vicente García Torres.

FOUR

_____

Selling Scandal

THE MYSTERIES OF THE INQUISITION

IN LATE SUMMER OF 1850, a French novel captured the attentions of prominent religious officials in Mexico City. Set in sixteenth-century Spain, *The Mysteries of the Inquisition*, by V. de Féréal, narrated the plight of a pious young heroine, Dolores, as she resists the ignoble designs of the lustful, murderous Grand Inquisitor of Seville, Pedro Arbués.[1] Dolores receives aid from a cast of colorful characters—criminals with consciences, pious Catholics, even a vengeful woman disguised as a priest—who help her flee the inquisitor's clutches and escape to the Protestant Netherlands to begin a new life together with her betrothed. A translation of the *Mysteries* had circulated in Mexico City with little fanfare in the late 1840s, when Mexico was embroiled in war with the United States. Yet after printer Vicente García Torres began to serialize the novel in his newspaper in 1850, Mexico City's archdiocese took notice. When the printer announced plans to publish a stand-alone volume illustrated with images from the original Paris edition, church officials took action, referring the book to a censor for review.

Leafing through his copy of the novel, a translation published in New Orleans in 1846, the priest assigned to censorship duties would have encountered a series of troubling lithographs. These illustrations, adapted by an American artist from the Paris engravings, brought readers down from tranquil vistas of a lush, exotic Seville into its seamy underbelly of back alleys, taverns, and dens of petty thieves, as well as deeper into the heart of inquisitorial corruption.[2] Graphic images of torture in dungeons (the rack, burned feet, flogged naked bodies, water torture) and sexual coercion in convents and bedchambers depicted priests as members of a secret cabal, hell-bent on destroying innocent lives for pleasure (see figures 16 and 17). The forthcoming Mexican edition, as the censor had likely already learned, would be bursting with an even greater number of illustrations, acquired directly from the Paris publisher thanks to new reproduction technologies and printers' transnational networks.

The *Mysteries* issued a provocation. Its sensationalist representation of the Catholic past, read from Mexico City, assaulted the church's claims to moral authority by depicting institutional religion as a corrupt and dangerous force. Anti-Catholic literature circulated extensively within the nineteenth-century Atlantic world, crisscrossing national borders even as it played a role in consolidating national political imaginaries. In places like the United States, for example, literary representations of a homogeneous, intolerant Catholicism allowed writers to envision a "symbiotic relationship between liberal democracy and Protestantism" and construe the Protestant nation as the sole guarantor of religious pluralism and freedom of conscience.[3] The image of the Inquisition as a symbol of repression and depravity, however, also flourished in the anticlerical discourse of liberal reformers within the Catholic world.[4] Since the eighteenth century, enlightened Catholics in the Spanish Empire had sought to reshape piety into a more individualized, modest affair.[5] Nineteenth-century reformers in Mexico continued this work, advocating freedom of conscience and the curtailment of the corporate power and influence of the church.

Mexico's liberal reformers had already mobilized the specter of the Inquisition to rally support against real or perceived constraints on authors' freedoms. In 1850, however, the negative depiction of the defunct institution in the *Mysteries* resonated with recent events. The previous fall, friars at Mexico City's Colegio de San Pablo had been caught writing obscene graffiti about the nuns who served in the Colegio's hospital.[6] Further investigations revealed that the men had repeatedly harassed and insulted the sisters, and one friar had entered the convent on the pretext of taking confessions only to corner and rape a servant. This affair, which reads like a chapter from the novel itself, prompted the city council, headed by conservatives, to direct a task force against future scandals that threatened to undercut the church's image. In the aftermath of this scandal, the *Mysteries'* fictionalized rendering of ecclesiastical abuse, which threatened the virtue of its sympathetic female protagonist, offered an obvious parallel to contemporary events. By repackaging the novel to better fit Mexico's specific history, printer García Torres urged readers to draw the connections, advancing a broad cultural attack on the church.

García Torres was known for advancing forceful attacks and courting controversy as the publisher of Mexico City's radical daily, *El Monitor*

TORMENTO DEL AGUA.

FIGURE 16. *Tormenta del agua*. V. de Féréal, *Misterios de la inquisición* (Mexico City: Imprenta de V. García Torres, á cargo de L. Vidaurri, 1850).

Republicano, one of three major newspapers that dominated the national press by the late 1840s. Calls to reform the Catholic Church and its relationship to the state had flourished there amid the political crisis provoked by Mexico's devastating defeat by the United States in 1848.[7] After the war moderates, blamed for the war's failure, found themselves beleaguered by both radical republicans, who advocated religious freedom and the expansion of

SOLICITUD DEL INQUISIDOR.

FIGURE 17. *Solicitud del inquisidor.* V. de Féréal, *Misterios de la inquisición* (Mexico City: Imprenta de V. García Torres, á cargo de L. Vidaurri, 1850).

state power over the church, and a newly formed conservative party, which defended the church's autonomy and authority.[8] The three major newspapers, owned by a trio of well-connected printers, helped draw the lines of an energetic postwar debate. Acting as cultural and political provocateurs, they gave shape to partisan differences as writers tangled in polemics that dripped with sarcasm, refracting all the major issues of the day through their constant sparring. The newspapers' anonymous writers sought to humiliate rivals in a tumble of shifting argumentation and puffed-up outrage. A meaty incident or object could be turned over for weeks as an editorial staff pressed its advantage or, when cornered by missteps or cultural mores, changed tactics. Indeed, before readers or censors encountered the actual text of the *Mysteries*, they had been primed by press polemics to understand the salacious novel through the lens of contemporary local politics.

When Mexico City's acting archbishop banned the *Mysteries* and threatened those who read or possessed the volume with excommunication, he exposed tensions with state authorities over the policing of print. Mexico's constitution designated Catholicism as the sole official religion, and press laws granted the church censoring authority over materials related to religious topics. The idea that "public power should be exercised in harmony with the teachings of the Church" had underpinned early efforts to build a liberal, Catholic nation and explained the church's official role as religious censor decades after the abolition of the Inquisition.[9] Politicians of all stripes professed piety and respect for religion, just as religious officials had engaged constitutionalism as they negotiated the church's place in the new nation.[10] The practicalities of this relationship, however, had generated heated debate since independence, especially over the question of whether the new nation-state or the Mexican Church would exercise the Patronato, the appointment of religious officials previously overseen by the king of Spain.[11] Government officials had also moved periodically to assert power over church functions and wealth. The radical administration of Valentín Gómez Farías (1833), for example, prohibited mandatory tithing and attempted to replace religious schools with public education. His administration was soon overthrown, but state officials across the political spectrum pragmatically eyed the church's ample resources as potential solutions to persistent government penury.[12] From the perspective of church officials, novels like the *Mysteries* posed yet another problem, one that recent legal changes seemed unable to solve and government attitudes threatened to exacerbate.

The archbishop's prohibition redoubled efforts to assert the church's role as the nation's moral authority in spectacular fashion, yet it also allowed radicals to press their case against religious power. As printer García Torres had bargained, the church's display depended in part on its ability to commandeer the physical copies of readers, for which it required state support. This dependence had already seriously weakened the church's position. The ensuing struggle over the *Mysteries* drew frustrated religious officials into a behind-the-scenes confrontation with state authorities over legal protocol, one dimension of broader, ongoing negotiations over power sharing. The conflict uncovered competing ideas about the limits of church authority, which radicals argued stopped where the property rights of readers began. Even as he evaded reprisals, García Torres advanced political debates by envisioning a more powerful role for the state as the sole arbiter of print.

REGULATING RELIGIOUS PRINT IN POSTINDEPENDENCE MEXICO

Early efforts to create a Catholic, liberal nation generated a regulatory framework around printing that, at least in theory, involved cooperation and power sharing between church and state. Like other aspects of Mexico's press laws, the idea that authorities of the Catholic Church should precensor manuscripts bearing on religious themes dated back to legislation passed in Cádiz in 1820. Mexican legislators agreed that uncensored commentary about official state religion should fall outside the boundaries of tolerated public speech, ratifying these provisions after independence.[13] While the Inquisition had been suppressed definitively in 1820, the church subsequently formed a *junta eclesiástica de censura*, an ecclesiastical censorship board based in Mexico City (a second was formed in Guadalajara), charged with overseeing religious print.[14] Active throughout the 1830s, the junta's members wrestled with how to fulfill their duties effectively. Not only had the institutional enforcement power of the Inquisition evaporated; the state showed little practical enthusiasm for helping the church defend national religion.[15] In 1831, for example, church officials attempted to reinstate an old ban on works by Voltaire but ran up against the government's rule that each edition required a new censorship process.[16] In 1836, junta officials tried to censor a newspaper article for using a heretical turn of phrase, yet the case petered out in the face of printer evasion and judicial neglect.[17] Further complicating matters, liberals raised the specter of inquisitorial power to push for reforms of press laws. After conservative centralist governments attempted to expand the scope of printers' responsibility in the 1830s, liberals had opposed the measure as an attempt to reinstate "prior censorship," drawing comparisons with the Inquisition to stir outrage. Faced with resistance, the junta began to disintegrate and was disbanded during the tenure of Archbishop Manuel Posada y Garduño (1839–1846).[18]

In the 1840s, however, conversations in the Mexican legislature revealed a growing preoccupation among conservatives that existing press laws were not doing enough to protect state religion from attacks in print. In 1843, after a coalition overthrew a dictatorial regime established by Antonio López de Santa Anna and sent the general into exile, congress began drafting new rules to regulate press freedom. This *reglamento* was supposed to resolve a series of procedural confusions and intragovernmental debates generated since the mid-1830s, when centralists had issued various press restrictions but never drafted their own comprehensive laws. The commission assembled for the task, comprised of three congressmen including the liberal printer Ignacio Cumplido, wrote lengthy rules that they presented to the lower house of congress in January 1845.[19] To the surprise of the commission, which reported on the law's reception in a memo to Interior Ministry officials, religion stood out as one of the principal concerns raised by congressmen in their public discussion of the draft.

In their debates about the proposed law, conservative congressmen forced an in-depth discussion as they worried aloud about how to prevent assaults on Catholicism, described by the commission as "the most sacred object of the nation."[20] The law's first draft, a copy of the original 1820 Spanish regulations, forbade printed texts that directly attacked state religion and required printed materials touching upon religious themes to undergo a process of censorship overseen by the Catholic Church. One liberal representative pointed out the tensions he perceived in the preexisting legislation when he argued that freedom of the press could not coexist with any kind of prior review, since the very definition of press freedom implied the abolition of censorship. Yet other lawmakers argued that policing religious printed materials was essential and requested an expansion of the press law's language. While liberal and conservative voices both described religion as the foundation of Mexican society, conservatives argued that the law should prohibit not only direct attacks on religion but also indirect ones, which were even more dangerous because, as congressman Carlos María de Bustamante put it, it was easy for a Christian to dismiss a text that outright denied the existence of God, "but it is more frightening when satire or other indirect means are used, since [the text] acquires converts and the damage is incalculable and hard to fix."[21] The commission countered that nailing down press abuses was like "counting stars in the sky," an impossible task given the myriad philosophical and pragmatic debates that would result from tasking laypeople serving on press juries with defining indirect attacks on religion. The best way to counter such attacks would be to let them circulate freely, inspiring new champions of Catholicism who would offer even more vigorous and prolific responses. A liberal congressman pointed to the example of England, where, he claimed, the press ran freely and "there isn't a single atheist." In contexts where the press had been controlled, however, like France, atheists and religious critics were numerous, and well practiced to boot.[22]

The congressional debates revealed competing visions of how the law should define the parameters of public expression on religious matters. Liberals and conservatives ultimately reached a compromise that rejected the distinction between direct versus indirect attacks on religion while incorporating conservative concerns about printed texts that undermined piety. When a modified version of the law finally went into effect in November 1846 as the "Lafragua Law," its fourth article extended abuses of press freedom to include "ridicule, satire and invectives" directed against official religion.[23] Yet in spite of detailed provisions sorting press violations into punitive categories and describing adjudication procedures, the new rules made no reference to church authorities. Lawmakers seemed to have tacitly decided that infractions against state religion would be judged by state institutions. Since independence, the practicalities of the collaborative relationship between church and state had remained unresolved. The 1846 press law avoided reference to the question, even as it seemed to widen the scope of civil oversight of printed speech.

PRESS CONSOLIDATION, PRINTER CONFLICT, AND PARTISAN POLITICS IN THE WARTIME ERA

In addition to legal changes, political and technological changes that reshaped Mexico's field of printing politics in the 1840s set the stage for confrontation over the *Mysteries*. A dizzying series of events culminated in Mexico being drawn into war with the United States. The US annexation in 1845 of Texas, which had declared independence from Mexico a decade earlier, raised pressure on Mexican politicians to take action. A military revolt overthrew a moderate, antiwar administration in 1845; a promonarchist faction plotted unsuccessfully to install a European prince who might save Mexico from its northern neighbor. Within a year, Santa Anna returned from exile to lead the war, declaring an end to the centralist republic and reinstating a reformed version of the 1824 federalist constitution before heading off to battle. In the early months of the conflict, the executive first moved to control the press by resurrecting an old decree that held authors, editors, and printers alike responsible for supporting foreign powers or attacking the government in print. Santa Anna himself ordered Mexico City's printers to the National Palace for a threatening lecture, and critical commentators cast the press as a hindrance to national unity and battlefield success.[24]

In the charged environment of war (1846–1848), restrictions on printing nevertheless evolved as the Lafragua Law took effect in November 1846, reversing early wartime policy and bringing several innovations to the evolving debate about press freedom. On paper, the law tightened some of the restrictions on public speech by broadening what counted as press abuse. In addition to forbidding religious satire, the law prohibited attacks on the republican form of government and commentary on private life. These measures reflected political compromise among factions, attempts to fend off monarchists, and elites' social consensus that their private affairs should be insulated from public scrutiny. The law's specific enforcement mechanisms, however, favored liberals' preferences. They reinstated press juries and defined the rules of responsibility for texts in narrow terms. Notably, the law bore the stamp of its co-drafter, Cumplido, in specific provisions bearing on printing. Its final article, for example, explicitly protected printers, emphasizing that "the typographic industry and printing offices are entirely free in their exercise, with no other restrictions than those expressly imposed by the laws."[25] Thus the Lafragua Law, reflecting Cumplido's influence, defined printers' rights as a specific category linked to the broader framework of press freedom.

While the law promised greater protection against official crackdowns, Mexico City's printers took advantage of the political environment, harnessing new technologies to develop more combative, visible public personae. As moderate liberals at the helm of the national government came under fire not only from conservatives but also from radical *puros* who pushed for faster reform, astute printers used their connections to these emerging political factions to become key players in a contentious field of political debate conducted through their newspapers. Polemics had become a defining feature of the consolidated press that emerged in the 1840s as the main printed forum for political commentary, news, and literature. Importing state-of-the-art cylinder presses, like those manufactured by New York–based Richard Hoe & Company, which sped up production, allowed printers with significant capital to further extend their influence (see figure 18). By 1844 Cumplido boasted of his mechanical press in an advertisement for his forthcoming

FIGURE 18. Advertisement for single large cylinder hand printing machine. Cylinder presses like those manufactured by the R. Hoe & Co. sped up production, even if Mexico City printers did not have access to steam power until the 1870s. The advertisement claimed this press could make 800 impressions per hour when operated by hand. R. Hoe & Co. *[Catalogue of] Printing Machines . . .* (New York: R. Hoe & Co., 1873). Courtesy of HathiTrust.

almanac; within a decade, Mexico City printers possessed double, triple, and quadruple cylinder presses.[26] Over the course of the 1840s, newspapers shifted from biweekly to daily production. While four pages remained the standard length, the size of their sheets doubled. Literacy levels remained relatively unchanged (state forays into public education by way of the Lancasterian schooling model returned modest results at best), but the range and tempo of print consumption increased throughout the 1840s, and major newspapers, like Cumplido's moderate *El Siglo Diez y Nueve*, reached readers in urban centers across the nation.[27]

Printers oversaw daily operations of their businesses, which included setting the agenda of the *redacción*, an in-house newspaper editorial staff. Writing in his memoir, writer-statesman Guillermo Prieto (1818-1897) described how Cumplido, employer to some of the finest liberal thinkers on the staff of *El Siglo Diez y Nueve*, "kept each writer in his room, isolated," so he could maintain hawk-eyed vigilance and promote efficiency while blustering around the printing shop seeing to all aspects of the operation.[28] Prieto, who got his first break in Cumplido's employ in the 1840s, described his job as an ideal opportunity but lamented the lack of prestige and autonomy afforded to writers. "For a poor boy, unknown, object of scorn in his school, with a doubtful future, with dreams of glory," he reminisced, "it was a dazzling transformation to see one's name in printing type."[29] Getting into print inaugurated a new, public self for aspiring young writers. Yet Prieto admitted that "in the intellectual aspect there was always servitude and resentment on the writer's part for the small credit given to the trade of living by the pen." Cumplido, on the other hand, expressed certainty about his influence. "You will have seen my opinion externalized in *El Siglo*," he remarked breezily to a friend, construing the newspaper as his personal outlet.[30]

Cumplido had set the model for the politically committed, legally upright printer after founding *El Siglo Diez y Nueve* in 1841, yet his persona vied with other archetypes for public expression. During the war, when he abandoned Mexico to travel in Europe, Cumplido was soon upstaged by García Torres, a radical whose image had a decidedly more roguish cast. García Torres hailed from obscure provincial origins and had learned his trade in England thanks to the largesse of a wealthy patron.[31] By the mid-1840s he had established a printing shop in a former convent, leased from the national government, where he oversaw production of the radical daily *El Monitor Republicano*, which advocated republicanism and popular participation in government, religious tolerance, and the disentailment of church property.[32] A pusher of controversy, García Torres developed a reputation among judges for his habit of "maliciously hiding in anticipation whenever his press releases some subversive imprint."[33] In 1847 he went underground after an angry general threatened him with internal exile, appealing to the Supreme Court for protection and provoking a jurisdictional standoff over his case.[34] He escaped the situation and went on to serve as a lieutenant coronel in the Independencia Battalion, a National Guard unit of citizen soldiers, many of them artisans, who defended Mexico City from US troops.[35] Even as he took up arms against foreign invasion, García Torres defended his right to critique the government, which he blamed for wartime failures.[36] His open criticism of Santa Anna's administration and his performance of a virile patriotism earned García Torres a degree of notoriety among Mexico's political class. Bustamante commented in August 1847 that his press efforts were "more useful in the exterior than amongst us," claiming that US general Winfield Scott said he would not dare to take on Santa Anna were it not for his "support in Mexico," in the form of the printer's divisive tactics.[37] After US troops occupied Mexico City in September, Prieto, García Torres's friend and collaborator, privately counseled him against giving fuel to the invaders by discussing "our army, our politics, our miseries" in *El Monitor* and suggested he drop the aggressive war mongering in favor of a more conciliatory politics that "show a certain resignation with the actual state of things."[38]

While political elites cast the internal disputes sustained by partisans like García Torres as a threat to national security, the superior economic power of the United States in fact played a greater role in Mexico's defeat.[39] The occupation of Mexico City generated fierce resistance from residents across the social spectrum, though local officials, fearing both popular uprising and American looting, ultimately dissuaded civilian attacks.[40] Many wealthy urbanites remained in their homes, dodging bullets and eager for information beyond the scraps conveyed in the newspapers.[41] In a symbolic takeover, the US Army commandeered the presses that normally printed the government gazette and issued instead the *American Star*, whose columns led in English, broadcasting official communiqués and editorials to an increasingly demoralized Spanish-speaking readership.[42] On the very day of US withdrawal from the capital, President José Joaquín Herrera, a moderate who had assumed the office in the wake of Santa Anna's wartime failure, issued a new press rule that prohibited printed attacks on the honor and reputation of individuals, including public functionaries. As Pablo Piccato shows, by construing the personal as off-limits in the public sphere, this law presaged later nineteenth-century expansions of state oversight over public speech.[43] Yet such attacks would continue unabated in the following years, as a vociferous conservative press emerged in 1848.

Mexico's postwar conservative party found its public facilitator in Rafael de Rafael, a former overseer at Cumplido's printing shop. Born in Barcelona in 1817, Rafael had learned the trades of printing and engraving before traveling to New York, where he worked for Spanish publisher and merchant Juan de la Granja, who directed a Spanish-language newspaper with hemispheric circulation. Granja, who also sold printing equipment around the Caribbean basin and established Mexico's first telegraph line, helped Rafael secure employment with Cumplido in Mexico City.[44] Yet while Cumplido was off on his grand tour of Europe, Rafael orchestrated a public split with his former employer in a scathing letter printed in García Torres's *Monitor Republicano*.[45] Rafael attacked Cumplido's honor as a printer and employer, accusing him of "lying like a miserable impostor" by inflating his technological know-how and capital, of contracting him under false pretenses, and of sowing "perpetual enmity" among his employees.[46] Perfectly timed to explain the dissolution of their business collaboration, Rafael's attack on Cumplido advertised a new venture: a state-of-the-art printing shop, which, he did not mention, had been backed by conservative elites to the tune of twenty thousand pesos.[47] Several months later, Rafael launched *El Universal*, the newspaper that most successfully expressed the coalescing conservative line, advocating strong central government, the preservation of traditional privileges (including those of the church), and a plan of limited suffrage.[48]

As the public falling out between Rafael and Cumplido presaged, interpersonal rivalries mapped onto and became intertwined with the partisan conflicts expressed in press polemics and printing politics. The postwar period witnessed a surge of conservative organizing, including the founding of *El Universal*, the creation of a formal conservative party headed by Lucas Alamán, and conservative success in the 1849 Mexico City municipal elections.[49] While conservatives had formed a pact with the radical *puros* to unseat moderates from city government, *puros* found themselves outmaneuvered and excluded from power following the elections.[50] By 1849, political factions were deploying the press and broadsides to discredit their opponents, with bold headlines like "¡DEATH TO D. LUCAS ALAMAN!!" dredging up old allegations that the conservative city council president had masterminded the 1831 execution of the popular insurgent leader and former president Vicente Guerrero.[51] Amid electoral tensions, Alamán sued García Torres for defamation after the latter reprinted an article that labeled the statesman as the "murderer of Guerrero."[52] When García Torres appealed the ruling from behind bars, judges on the Supreme Court found discrepancies between the Lafragua press law of 1846 and new rules issued in 1848.[53] The radical printer gained his freedom in 1850 pending resolution of his case.

The decade of the 1840s witnessed the expansion and consolidation of Mexico City's political press. New cylinder printing presses allowed top printers—some backed by powerful interests—to position themselves as purveyors of modernity while growing their readership beyond the capital. The Lafragua Law had introduced printers' rights into debates about press freedom, yet by 1850 the enforcement of press laws remained as convoluted as ever. The world of printing politics however, was increasingly shot through with tension and distrust, as partisan differences found expression in personal public attacks and relentless polemics.

"The study of the history of the Inquisition today is not purely speculative entertainment, but rather of the highest importance for those peoples who wish to conserve their liberty," proclaimed a prospectus for the Mexico City edition of *The Mysteries of the Inquisition*.[54] Sent to subscribers of Cumplido's newspaper *El Siglo Diez y Nueve* in May 1850 and soon published in its columns, the prospectus condemned the defunct institution as a corrupt tool of absolutist power and charted a march of progress as nations had gradually rid themselves of its tyranny, obtaining "political and civil liberty, [and] liberty of conscience, each aligned with the most holy principles of Christianity."[55] Sliding into sales mode, the prospectus positioned the "seductive form of the novel" as an ideal vehicle for helping readers preserve their God-given rights, which it insinuated were under attack. Adopting the first-person plural pronoun—the "we" used to signal the presence of an anonymous editorial presence hovering behind the text—the prospectus introduced readers to the novel's focus on sixteenth-century Spain and its publisher, the unnamed Ignacio Cumplido, who promised to make the newly translated and amended five-hundred-page work available for just six and a half pesos. The *Mysteries'* prospectus dangled before readers a vision of the modern novel, a category constructed not simply with text written by the ingenious "Monsieur Fereal" but also with French illustrations ("those extremely fine engravings that adorn modern publications") and first-rate imported materials ("printed absolutely with new type, on French paper, with English ink, all first-class materials brought in so that the work unites the greatest beauty with scrupulous copyediting").[56] This cosmopolitan luxury item, the prospectus argued, was an essential tool of liberty.

As its Mexican publisher knew, the *Mysteries'* twisting plot had already entangled readers on both sides of the Atlantic. Written pseudonymously by the French poetess Victorine Germillan and her Spanish, exiled lover Manuel de Cuendías in Paris in 1845, the novel offered a seamy tale of the Catholic past, dressed in the trappings of historical accuracy complete with recognizable real-world characters and footnotes referencing reliable research. Cuendías, who prepared the scholarly apparatus to the fictional work, drew on the history written by Juan Antonio Llorente, a former Spanish Inquisition official and Catholic reformer, to enhance the novel's verisimilitude. The writings of Llorente and other Inquisition critics had been influential in the debates at the Cortes in Cádiz, and their interpretation of the Inquisition as an unwelcome imposition on the Catholic monarchy resonated far into the nineteenth century, as reformers broadened their assault on church power.[57] Llorente's 1817 *Histoire critique de l'Inquisition espagnole*, published while its author was in exile, circulated widely in multiple translations. A few decades later, the *Mysteries* found an even wider international audience through numerous translations and editions issued across Europe and the Americas, each of which contained text edited to suit local purposes. In London, the novel enjoyed commercial success as penny literature, no doubt for its invocation of familiar caricatures of repressive Catholicism, the "Black Legend," which had for centuries featured in English propaganda campaigns against Spain.[58] In majority Catholic societies, however, the novel's negative portrayal of the church hierarchy spoke directly to ongoing efforts to reform church power and reimagine church-state relations.

The Mexico City publisher of the *Mysteries* took pains to highlight the differences between anti-Catholic and anticlerical critique, revealing concerns about a potential backlash. Cumplido's veiled introduction as the mastermind behind the local publication represented a strategic choice in a context wherein the categories of printers and publishers overlapped, and in which claiming public credit carried risks as well as potential for rewards. Partially because of their calculations about routine legal troubles, printers went to great lengths to erect discursive barriers where functional divisions did not exist. They often donned the cap of "publisher" or wrote letters to their own newspapers as a marketing tactic when selling their wares to potential audiences.[59] Cultural capital was also at stake. Publishers, unlike printers, construed in liberal discourse as mute extensions of their presses, might speak freely on a wide range of intellectual topics, offering their opinions and shaping readers' experiences. Publishers could also float above the suspicions and political associations attached to the printing business. Or could they? The publisher of the *Mysteries* clearly anticipated controversy when he assured readers that the novel "in no way attacks religion and piety."[60]

The first challenge to this publishing project came not from critics but from editorial competition, when the printer García Torres scooped Cumplido and issued the first installment of the novel in the June 12 edition of his newspaper, *El Monitor Republicano*. Justifying the move, an introductory article criticized the price of Cumplido's edition and announced plans to publish the text serially in the newspaper, followed by a luxury illustrated edition at half the price of Cumplido's volume.[61] An editorial spat ensued, with both sides highlighting differences in price, aesthetic quality, and textual accuracy.[62] Printers frequently glorified their roles as purveyors of imported literary content, highlighting the material and literary quality of their productions as signs of modernity and progress.[63] These assertions were not just marketing techniques; they also challenged the consolidation of individual authorship as a category associated with social prestige, asking readers to recognize printers' cultural contributions.[64]

The novel's trajectory as a material text, in fact, reveals literary production as an ongoing process of accumulation and reinvention that traversed national borders, far beyond authorial control.[65] In an era before international copyright regimes, García Torres's scooping of the novel was hardly unprecedented. Indeed, the phenomenon of reprinting was widespread across the Americas, a distinctive feature of the hemisphere's early nineteenth-century literary culture.[66] García Torres had lifted the text of the *Mysteries* from an unauthorized translation printed in New Orleans, itself based on the original Paris text. The novel's contents resonated directly with Mexico's own history through the Cádiz influences of its coauthor, Cuendías, yet it had traveled a more circuitous route through the United States, a trading partner with growing influence. In Mexico City, its reprinting in the newspaper—a practice that printers had embraced, serializing texts by popular French authors like Eugène Sue and Alexandre Dumas—offered both economic and political advantages. The shaky market and competition from the European book trade made publishing stand-alone volumes a risky endeavor. Newspapers, however, had a built-in audience, which García Torres exploited strategically in the summer of 1850. *El Monitor Republicano* integrated the novel's text directly into its main columns, as opposed to running it along the bottom edge where it could be cut off and gathered into a small *folletín*. This design decision made the *Mysteries* part of the political transcript, entangling its fate with the habits of the well-heeled readers who consumed the press and blurring the lines between politics and fiction.

The blurring of boundaries between political and literary content only increased when the *Mysteries* became the subject of heated polemic. Three days after its first installment appeared, the conservative daily *El Universal*, owned and overseen by Rafael, attacked the novel in a front-page article, calling its author "impious as well as fantastical and ignorant."[67] Brushing aside any literary merit, the article asserted that "the true object of the work is none other than making Catholicism odious . . . and making apology for and praise of Protestantism."[68] Arguing that scandalous novels had thrown European societies into upheaval since their advent in the eighteenth century, *El Universal* denounced both *El Siglo* and *El Monitor* for bringing similar threats to Mexico. Imported heresies like this, the newspaper suggested, posed grave dangers to local audiences, construed as innocent and insulated from anti-Catholic ideas.

Before long, a three-way polemic overran Mexico City's periodical press, placing the novel at the center of political debate and laying the groundwork for official intervention. Its tumble of argumentation encompassed cosmopolitan appeals and nativist accusations, commentary on undignified editorial practices, and accusations of immorality. The radical and moderate newspapers struggled to maintain focus on the literary and material merits of the text: radical *El Monitor* defended its edition against moderate *El Siglo*'s charges of piracy and inferiority, while *El Siglo* battled conservative *El Universal*'s charge that both newspapers profited by corrupting readers' morals.[69] A game of semantic tit for tat subsumed the debate, as *El Universal* described the newspaper *El Siglo* as the novel's publisher, while *El Siglo* countered that the newspaper had nothing to do with the editorial endeavors unfolding in the same printing shop where the *Mysteries* would soon be published, and accused *El Universal*—because of its owner's Spanish nationality—of pushing a foreign agenda. Technical arguments related to publishing identities that were in reality overlapping and mutable aimed to identify the most prominent target and potential culprit for a press crime in the making. Yet throughout the polemic, *El Monitor* continued publishing installments of the novel in continuous succession, as *El Universal* challenged *El Siglo* to enter the game: "Stain your columns, if you dare, as *El Monitor* has stained its own, with chapters four and five."[70] Chapter five, which *El Universal* found particularly repugnant, introduced readers to the raucous nightlife inside Seville's inquisitorial palace, where bishops and priests held nighttime orgies beneath pornographic murals of Jupiter, Leda, and Venus.[71]

El Universal's moral critique of the titillating text had enough force that it hamstrung the other newspapers' ability to offer a convincing rebuttal. By the end of June, however, Cumplido dropped his plans to publish the *Mysteries* and sold García Torres the printing plates for the French illustrations he had trumpeted months earlier in the novel's prospectus.[72] *El Universal* gloated over its victory, while *El Monitor* dramatically slowed down the novel's daily serialization, recalibrating to prepare for the issue of the book version, whose first installments appeared in July. The promised "fine engravings" turned out to be cheap stereotype reproductions of the Paris originals, metal plates nailed to wood blocks that Cumplido had acquired on his travels in Europe. Yet this technology was precisely what the conservative newspaper had warned against: it brought French ways of seeing to Mexico to corrupt innocent eyes. *El Siglo*, now freed of its commercial stake, disputed *El Universal's* condescending claims. Accusing *El Universal* of advocating censorship and a false piety while steering away from the thorny question of morality, *El Siglo* argued that Mexican audiences "do not need anyone's advice to judge good and bad."[73]

The trajectory and polemic surrounding the *Mysteries* reveal how literature and politics intertwined in the pages of Mexico City's partisan press, thanks to a reprinting culture that linked local debates and transnational currents. The novel's topical content, genealogy, and controversial framing made it well suited, from a liberal perspective, to resonate with contemporary events and inflame readers' outrage. While conservative polemicists refused to discuss the novel's plot, they scrutinized its origins, translation, and materiality in hopes of generating a counterresponse to chasten rival publishers. Far from a rational meeting of dispassionate minds, radicals, moderates, and conservatives battled in a context in which principles and profit seeking overlapped.

DIVINE INTERVENTION: THE *MYSTERIES* GETS CENSORED

Conservative pressure in the press encouraged the *Mysteries'* radical publisher to change tactics as he prepared to release the first installments of the book version. Emphasizing the fact that the Inquisition had been definitively dismantled and thus firmly relegated to a distant past, preparatory articles in *El Monitor* sought to neutralize the novel's obvious contemporary valences and downplay its political connotations, even as it encouraged a broader public to consume the novel. Rather than casting it as a primer for the present, the publisher pitched the *Mysteries* as an innocuous educational tool, useful "so that light-hearted souls might have incentive to study and learn about an epoch of history."[74] While the novel's critics would certainly bridle at the nature of this history lesson, the reframing sought audiences beyond the political press.

Mexico City's capitular vicar, the top administrator and acting archbishop of the capital's archdiocese, José María Barrientos, looked dimly on García

Torres's efforts to teach history through fiction. The next day, he issued an internal circular decrying the spread of immoral materials, especially writings that had already been banned in Europe.[75] While *El Monitor* continued publishing the novel in its columns, the church soon launched a public response that coincided with the release of the first installments of a book version. In 1849, religious officials had restarted the *junta de censura*, which had been dissolved years earlier as ineffective. Now, the revived junta's judgment informed the capitular vicar, who banned the *Mysteries* in September for being immoral, "openly Protestant in its doctrines and tendencies," and libelous against the Catholic Church, its saints, and its ministers.[76] The proclamation threatened any readers or owners of the novel with excommunication.

The capitular vicar's decree culminated lengthy closed-door conversations, which revealed the slow pace of church deliberations that had unfolded in stark contrast to the rapid-fire advance of press polemics. The church had first moved to consider the *Mysteries* in July, nearly two months after debates had started in the press. Religious officials charged the newly reconvened *junta de censura* with evaluating the novel, and the junta tasked a censor to read the novel and report back.[77] Censors typically reviewed manuscripts submitted by authors for prepublication approval, a practice that continued to be observed by devout authors, in accordance with rules established after the abolition of the Inquisition. But since the printer García Torres had not sought prepublication authorization for the *Mysteries*, and as of August it had not been fully published in Mexico, the censor reviewed a copy of the 1846 New Orleans edition—the same text used in the Mexico City edition—which had somehow been acquired locally.[78] Typically, a censor could take anywhere from a week to many months to formulate a response, which would then be approved or modified by the junta.[79] In the case of the *Mysteries*, the censor took one month to prepare his report, apologizing for his delay.[80]

The censor's lengthy report lambasted the novel as "pernicious and full of venom" and argued it "breathed Protestantism all over" in challenging the holiness of Catholic saints like the Inquisitor Pedro Arbués (the novel's villain).[81] Lamenting that such works could erase the "study of centuries" and darken Mexico's uncertain future, he laid the blame squarely on "the implacable determination of certain journalists in propagating such writings," combined with the "acquiescence, or at least weakness of the remaining Mexicans to oppose and hurl [them] with indignation into the filthy mud that these productions deserve!"[82] After ratifying the censor's decision, the junta sent its recommendation to the capitular vicar, who emitted his prohibition.

For the capitular vicar, commanding the consciences of Mexican readers did not go far enough. The following week, he wrote to the nation's minister of justice and ecclesiastical affairs and, appealing to the "Catholic sentiments" of the president, requested that the government "take all the measures within its means, with the object of impeding the introduction of these works in our ports, and their reprinting and circulation within the Republic."[83] This appeal renewed the archbishopric's attempts to influence the realm of cultural production. While lawmakers had deemed attacks on state religion off-limits in the 1846 press regulations, they had remained silent on the enforcement power of the Catholic Church. Laws ratified at independence, however, instructed state officials to assist the church with censorship. Given the relative silence of the *junta de censura* in recent years, the publication of the *Mysteries* offered an ideal opportunity for reasserting the church's role as a moral arbiter. The text had scandalized the local church hierarchy, moving it to take action.

DEBATING THE BOUNDARIES OF RELIGIOUS AUTHORITY

Church officials' overtures to the national government provoked a discussion over their respective powers to oversee printed materials, which had become muddied over numerous constitutions, press laws, and abandoned cases. The publisher of the *Mysteries* participated in these closed-door debates, offering state officials new tools he hoped they would use to sideline religious authorities from regulating print. Getting wind of the capitular vicar's ban, García Torres penned an urgent rebuttal to the government, identifying himself as the owner of the typographical establishment printing the novel (a convoluted formulation designed to dodge his potential responsibility for the text).[84]

The printer advanced a wide-ranging argument that questioned the basis and wisdom of the church ban. First, García Torres argued that the church edict "contains an attack on the current [laws] on press freedom," which could only be overseen by civil authorities.[85] As the 1847 reformed constitution stated, all press crimes, with the exception of defamation, had to be tried by press juries. In order to bring charges, he reasoned, "the ecclesiastical authority must subject itself to the political and civil laws."[86] By ignoring civil procedure, the archbishopric "attacks with its edict the Constitution of the State."[87] Second, García Torres reframed the capitular vicar's ban as a form of theft. "To prohibit the reading and retention of an imprint," he reasoned, "is to attack freedom of the press and the right of property, guaranteed by our laws."[88] Here, the printer framed the novel as a material object, bought and paid for by Mexicans whose property rights trumped church concerns about blasphemy. Finally, the printer leveraged Catholicism in support of his case, theorizing that church bans would only undermine religious authority in the long run. "It is more likely," he predicted, "that the work will continue circulating, that it may be requested more, that it will not be returned by various subscribers." As a result of scandal-driven curiosity, "excommunication will be looked upon with scorn."[89] The novel itself, he claimed, was not the problem. After all, it had circulated freely in several Catholic countries and criticized not religion, but rather "the barbarous and perverse individuals who, profaning it, have aimed to make it a vile instrument of their passions."[90] The real issue, he implied, was the fuss put up by priests.

In his appeal, García Torres argued that the church's spiritual authority depended on its subordination to civil laws determined by the state. These laws detailed procedures for judging press violations, but also secured the property rights of citizens. Conflicts over printed texts, he claimed, would only lead to continued confrontations over individual rights, generating scandals that would make the church appear weak. Yet a weakened church was precisely what García Torres envisioned. "Whatever the work may be," he concluded, "its printing, circulation, and retention is not under the authority of the capitular vicar."[91] Rather than church officials judging works and, by extension, printers, booksellers, and readers, the printer inverted the equation, imagining civil juries as the arbiters of church arguments about piety and morality.

The minister of justice quickly deflected García Torres's request, advising him to direct inquiries to the courts to pursue his rights. He assured the printer, however, that the government would not impede the novel's circulation until the church had demonstrated that "the formulas established by the laws" had been properly followed.[92] The minister, who enjoyed a positive reputation among the clergy, responded on the same day to the capitular vicar, promising him that "like you, the government deplores the progress of immorality and the abuses of freedom of the press, and will endeavor to attack them by means that the laws put into its hands."[93] Forwarding the church's request to the Ministry of the Interior, he asked the capitular vicar whether church officials had indeed observed the legal protocols described by the Cortes in 1813 and elaborated by the archbishop of Toledo in 1821, which, respectively, abolished the Inquisition and established steps for church oversight of religious print. While the printer had cited recent law in support of his arguments, government ministers reached further back to the compromises reached during Spain's liberal revolution.

The capitular vicar replied with a lengthy explanation. Of course, he reasoned, the *junta de censura* was and remained founded on the legal principles cited by the minister of justice. The only aspect of the law the junta had failed to follow involved procedure; namely, it had overlooked the provision that the author or publisher of a censored work deserved a hearing.[94] Justifying this oversight, the capitular vicar first cited practical reasons. Calling together the junta, awaiting the detailed censor's report, and going through a possible appeals process took time. "Meanwhile, the imprint or work [would have] circulated all over, if its contents had not already been forgotten altogether."[95] Complicating matters, "liberal governments and authorities" routinely failed to uphold the basic rules delineated in the 1821 instructions from the archbishop of Toledo, namely, that "no book or treaty on religious matters can be printed without previous license from the ordinary" and that "during censorship trials, the sale of the contracted books shall be suspended, given the great importance of the matter."[96] If the civil government failed to follow these rules because it felt they clashed with "the idol of freedom of the press," he continued, the church could hardly be expected to observe the "extensive procedures of a formal trial, which would make its censorship and prohibition illusory and even ridiculous."[97]

Laying down a tit-for-tat argument of noncompliance, the capitular vicar charted the troubled history of church-state relations on censorship, highlighting tensions that had emerged with independence. The only prohibition ever effected by a Mexican government, he argued, occurred under Emperor Agustín Iturbide (1821–1823). Thus, it was no surprise that the vicar's predecessor, Archbishop Posada y Garduño, had eventually scrapped the *junta de censura* altogether; it was futile to rely on civil authorities that refused to follow their own laws. The newly recreated junta, for its part, had already faced state inaction on several occasions that same year. The flagrant sale of Protestant texts by an American vendor had carried on unabated, while an "impious article" in the *Monitor Republicano* brought to the attention of judicial authorities went ignored and unpunished. "I abstained from dictating its public prohibition," he explained, "considering that since some time had necessarily passed, it would only have served to alarm the publishers of the newspaper, without achieving that the article be collected from subscribers, who perhaps would already have forgotten the news and would refuse to let their edition remain incomplete."[98] Thus, the capitular vicar argued, church efforts to censor immoral works confronted not only state indifference but also active opposition from publishers, low-level officials, and even newspaper readers themselves, who preferred to keep their copies, which they compiled and bound into complete sets at year's end, rather than submit to religious authority by handing over issues containing prohibited texts.

The materiality of controversial texts mattered to the capitular vicar. In invoking readers' newspaper habits, he was not simply spinning an image of a church with its hands tied; he was attempting to cut a deal. In fact, the publication of the *Mysteries* as a stand-alone volume opened an opportunity for him to act without fear of confronting local elites loath to part with their newspapers, those crucial records of the political transcript. Instead, the church claimed it had decided to act when the novel's editors had chosen to "reprint it in a separate luxury edition that would fall into the hands of the most ignorant and incautious," an audience that church officials likely imagined as feminine or uneducated, in contrast to the implied male, bourgeois readership of the newspaper.[99] The novel's characters, after all, might give women readers dangerous ideas. In addition to a protagonist who abandons the Catholic world to preserve her honor, the novel's secondary characters transgress social boundaries yet hold the moral high ground. One turns out to be a young woman living secretly as a priest in order to avenge her brother's murder. She unveils herself and kills the grand inquisitor at the novel's climax, a scene depicted in one of the book's many illustrations (see figure 19). The newspaper edition of the novel, in contrast, featured no images. Arguing that the novel's publisher had interpreted church silence as tacit approval to print the book, the church justified its prohibition and hoped state officials—recognizing themselves as male heads of household who would be unaffected by the proposed strategy and, indeed, might have a stake in policing such texts—would concur. If the junta's actions did not follow civil protocol to the letter, the capitular vicar reasoned, the blame lay squarely with the state, which refused to hold up its end of the bargain. When the government observed the abovementioned articles, he explained, then "the ecclesiastical authority may also restrict itself justly to the civil provisions."[100]

The capitular vicar's letter, at once exculpatory, accusatory, and conciliatory in tone, revealed that church officials faced a similar set of hurdles as their state counterparts, struggling to devise practical controls for materials printed in Mexico City. Yet religious officials also confronted the benign neglect of governments unwilling to enforce church authority. Straining

MUERTE DE PEDRO ARBUES.

FIGURE 19. *Muerte de Pedro Arbués*. V. de Féréal, *Misterios de la inquisición* (Mexico City: Imprenta de V. García Torres, á cargo de L. Vidaurri, 1850).

underneath a shared discourse of respect for Catholicism and abhorrence of immorality, state and church actions worked at cross purposes. Lawmakers had worried in 1845 that pinning down religious infractions of press laws would befuddle press juries, yet the case in question barely touched on the definition of what counted as an attack on religion at all. Instead, it hinged on procedure, prompting the minister of justice to seek outside opinions to resolve the matter. Two days after receiving the capitular vicar's letter, he forwarded the case file to the Supreme Court's prosecutor (*fiscal*) for review.

THE PUBLISHER'S COUNTERCENSORSHIP

As the prosecutor deliberated, García Torres's printing shop ramped up its publicity campaign, releasing a series of writings in *El Monitor* that would later be published as addenda to the book edition of the *Mysteries*. These texts commended the novel's verisimilitude, emphasized its beauty and economy, and lavished anonymous (fabricated) praise on García Torres, who took "a great step in our civilization" by publishing a work that "will figure in all the libraries of curious and enlightened men."[101] Just as religious officials suspected uneducated audiences might be swayed by the novel, its publicity played to the anxieties of upwardly mobile men eager to project social status in their bookshelves. During the entire month of October, *El Monitor* ran *Defense of the Publisher of the Work Entitled "Mysteries of the Inquisition"*, which, despite its title, quickly attacked the church, accusing it of launching a baseless critique, since officials could not refute the novel's historical accuracy and instead cynically cast "enemies of the Inquisition as enemies of faith."[102]

The *Defense*, which scrutinized the original censor's report in excruciating detail, revisited some of the arguments developed by García Torres in his letter to state officials. It, too, argued that the novel violated no principles of faith. Citing evidence from medieval and modern legal codes, classical authors, and scripture, it claimed that church censorship violated "the sacred right of property, and above all else, intellectual liberty."[103] Wading deeper into the debate, the article set out to prove that the Inquisition really was, counter to the claims advanced in the censor's report, a terrible institution bent on suppressing enlightened reason, an interpretation it bolstered with long lists of historical incidents and names of Mexican intellectuals called before its tribunal. While the censor had picked apart the *Mysteries*, the *Defense* countered with a local history of inquisitorial abuse to complement the novel's fictionalized portrait of the Spanish past. Its authors mirrored García Torres's arguments about subjecting church authority to public scrutiny, questioning the censor's own grasp of reading by suggesting he had misinterpreted not only the novel but also his own intellectual touchstones, contained in references to Burke, Voltaire, and Balmes.

At the end of the day, the *Defense* argued, the censor was no better than any other Mexico City reader whose opinions had been influenced by the partisan press. In fact, his mind had already been made up before he had even opened the novel, "since he read . . . the polemic about *The Mysteries of the Inquisition*" first. Of course, the *Defense* argued, he would have absorbed the opinion advanced by the conservative *El Universal*, which "sustains the cause of monarchy and trades in defending theocracy."[104] This the censor chose over the word of the novel's publisher, an "honorable man, good citizen, father of a family, laborious, active and enterprising, who, having learned of the historical and literary merit of the work, consulting with enlightened persons, religious without hypocrisy . . ., attempted to make a reprint that would earn him some profit without any political or religious intentions."[105] By situating the church prohibition against the background of printing politics, the defense painted religious officials not as spiritual authorities but as taking their cues from the conservative press.

Accused of an immoral crime, García Torres defended himself as a money-minded, politically disinterested, and intellectually subservient figure, downplaying his agency as a purveyor of content even as other texts aggrandized his role. The construction of the publisher's honor rested on a whole package of behaviors and attributes—citizenship, piety and conduct as the male head of household, industriousness—in short, an ideal liberal subject who floated above the muck of politics. Given García Torres's history as a partisan activist, this construction was a complete fiction. His ideological messaging, indeed, shone through in the *Defense*'s characterization of religion, explaining that *El Monitor* "defends and has always defended the healthy doctrine of the Savior of the world: *man is free: every man is equal to another: Jesus Christ taught liberty and equality.*"[106] Far from disavowing religion, the article aligned Christian concepts with the liberal emphasis on individualism and equality. This reformulation of Christ's teaching excised the formal institution of the Catholic Church from the picture altogether. Ultimately, the publisher's defense presented an argument not so far removed from that made in the *Mysteries,* which advanced a strongly anticlerical, if not outright anti-Catholic, proposal.

RENEGOTIATING THE STATUS QUO

It took nearly six weeks for national officials to devise a response to the capitular vicar. At first, the prosecutor urged civil authorities to assist the church by seizing copies of the prohibited book. In his view, the *Mysteries* was so "profoundly immoral . . . obscene, [and] conducive to Protestantism" that the law disqualified its author or publisher from the right to a hearing. The church retained jurisdiction over this type of work, he argued, so the state could not bring charges against the publisher but was compelled by law to enforce church authority. Clearly dissatisfied with the prosecutor's opinion, the minister of justice dismissed his recommendation as a misunderstanding and convened a pair of senators to analyze the case. Rather than determine whether or not the state should press charges against the publisher, Francisco M. de Olaguíbel, a radical, and Teodosio Lares, a conservative, should produce a set of guidelines to inform government policy. Although they consulted the same laws examined by the Supreme Court's prosecutor, the senators reached the opposite conclusion. García Torres, they reasoned, did in fact deserve a hearing in the case since he was an interested party, a category that might include authors or publishers, as well as booksellers, printers, or merchants.[107] Because the *junta de censura* had not convened this hearing, it had broken both civil and church law and was thus ineligible for state assistance with seizing the books.[108]

The senators' decision differed markedly from the prosecutor's in its sensibility toward church authority, reflecting a diversity of opinions within the government. While the prosecutor expounded at length on the divine rights invested in church authority and the state's duty to respect and uphold this authority, Lares and Olaguíbel showed greater skepticism. Civil authorities needed a compelling reason to assist the church in exercising an authority they construed as existing primarily over the consciences of believers. Their twenty-one-point memorandum discursively recognized the state's obligations to uphold church authority, yet these new rules did little to clarify government procedure, nor did they address the church's accusations of noncompliance. Instead, they essentially restated portions of law and protocol elaborated elsewhere, postponing resolution for another day. Reflecting this strategy, the government ordered that all documents relative to the case be published in a 138-page pamphlet featuring not only the correspondence between the minister of justice, García Torres, church officials, the prosecutor, and the senators, but also all of the laws and rules cited in their opinions and complaints.

The publication of the facts of the case, while presented as an act of government transparency, advanced a political message. On the surface, the documents offered a guide that officials and publishers could consult to resolve future issues related to religious censorship. The pamphlet also showed the state acting in good faith, since everyone involved had repeatedly stressed the importance of the state's collaborative relationship with the church. Yet the pamphlet also exposed how civil officials had rebuffed the capitular vicar. By dismissing the church's request on technical grounds, government authorities avoided the broader criticism of state noncompliance. The minister of justice's strategy suggests that in 1850, state officials were neither prepared to use the case to provoke outright confrontation with their religious counterparts nor willing to bow to church demands to punish García Torres for publishing the *Mysteries*. Instead, the case allowed them to defuse the situation while showing church officials as supplicants who depended on the state for material enforcement of their spiritual power.

The Lares-Olaguíbel rules published in the wake of the *Mysteries* polemic did little to resolve the broader cultural and institutional tensions reflected in church censorship efforts and uncooperative state responses. They did, however, serve as a guide that religious officials turned to as they attempted to negotiate this relationship. Over the next year, church officials bowed to the government's rules and also displayed open skepticism that censorship could serve as an effective tool for exerting authority. García Torres's radical *El Monitor Republicano* became a frequent target of church ire, but the consensus about how to move forward had frayed. In 1851, one religious official advised the *junta de censura* not only to consult the Lares-Olaguíbel rules carefully before taking action, but also to communicate with the newspaper's publisher in private. It would be better, he reasoned, to persuade García Torres to issue a correction rather than proceed against him publicly. Only if he refused should the church take action.[109] In 1852, a church official advised the archbishop to drop a censorship case against *El Monitor* altogether. A public announcement "would give way to new writings from the impious, which will only increase the scandal for some and further corrupt the morality of others."[110] In the wake of the ruling about the *Mysteries*, church faith in the effectiveness of censorship had weakened.

CONCLUSION: GARCÍA TORRES'S LAST LAUGH?

The capitular vicar's ban on the *Mysteries* remained in effect for those individuals willing to heed its threat of excommunication. Yet religious officials failed to convince the national government to help with enforcement. The novel's serial run in *El Monitor* had finished in mid-October, and the final installments for the book edition had been printed, complete with their provocative illustrations of bare-breasted women flogged in torchlit cells and priests stabbed to death before the altar. The publishers had even added, as an epilogue, a history of the Mexican Inquisition, which readers could consult if they had any doubt of the novel's relevance. In a modest, back-page notice in *El Monitor* in late November, García Torres claimed victory, quietly but forcefully defending his readers' access to this stimulating object. The church might censor the book, but it would get no aid from the authorities without first calling the publisher for a hearing. "In the case that said publisher shows himself reluctant," the article explained, "the vicar will have to lodge his complaint before a popular jury."[111] Thus, the savvy printer positioned himself as the defender of his readers' interests, boasting that "our readers and the numerous subscribers of the *Mysteries* will see that the vicar's achievement of his proposed objective is a remote possibility indeed."[112]

García Torres's arguments spoke to the gradual consolidation of understandings of citizenship linked to individual private property rights, to be protected from religious power by civil law. The printer described books as possessions that, thanks to his mediation, could be protected from seizure. This position clearly challenged religious officials' notions of censorship, which assumed the church's authority to guide Mexicans' reading habits—at least in matters related to religious themes—as essential to the nation's spiritual health. The church itself acknowledged the difficulties of exerting power over material texts even in this more circumscribed sphere of influence when it asked the state to confiscate only the book, rather than the newspaper version of the *Mysteries*. Officials perceived that confrontation with political elites over newspapers might prove counterproductive. The printer, on the other hand, used the case to convince readers that the real issue was not that their souls might be in danger from consuming a novel that had scandalized the church, but that their purchased copies were safe from confiscation by an overreaching power. His vision of the "citizen reader" subject to the secular judgment of peers questioned the interpretive authority claimed by learned church officials even as it pushed debates about press freedom forward. The first press laws in effect in the Spanish Empire granted state authorities power to confiscate not just unsold but also purchased printed copies that violated the rules.[113] By the 1820s, however, this authority was scaled back, and lawmakers in the 1840s further limited officials' latitude to confiscate unsold copies of problematic works.[114] In 1850, García Torres argued that these laws also limited the church's power to interfere with readers' rights of ownership.

A gothic thriller, reprinted through transnational networks and reframed in press polemics, set all of these debates into motion. The arc of the drama about the *Mysteries* uncovered how accusations about profit seeking, property, and morality imbricated opportunistic and ideological positions, expanding beyond the rollicking world of printing politics to entangle powerful institutional actors. While Pablo Mijangos y González has described the incident as primarily an institutional struggle waged over the untenable legal system underpinning Catholic liberalism, the fuller scope of the novel's trajectory reveals that such legal showdowns resulted from political and even interpersonal conflicts and cultural brinkmanship that first gained traction outside the halls of power.[115] Preliminary battle lines over institutional authority were drawn on the shifting, fast-paced terrain of printing, if only at oblique angles that reflected cultural and political constraints. The press polemic surrounding the *Mysteries* revealed that publishers with a stake in a controversial work were reluctant to articulate forceful political proposals directly. García Torres and his editorial staff argued about the interpretation of existing laws, but they never suggested that press freedom should be expanded by abolishing religious censorship altogether. This issue likely circulated behind closed doors, where it was aired in political circles but remained too explosive to broach directly in the press. Instead, the *Mysteries* accomplished this work on its own, triggering a series of reactions that fleshed out the conflict in its cultural and institutional dimensions and showed the growing fault lines over an increasingly unrealistic cooperative relationship between church and state. These tensions would break out into civil war in less than a decade.

In 1852, a more immediate backlash ensued, as Santa Anna returned from exile and, supported by conservative backers, enacted the restrictive press laws that centralist governments had attempted to craft in the 1830s. The 1853 "Ley Lares," named after the senator who had coauthored the *Mysteries* ruling, fulfilled a number of criteria that conservatives had developed over the decades: it abolished press juries; expanded the criteria of press infractions related to religion; and tightened vigilance on printers, requiring them to post signs and pay deposits, which could be drawn down in the case of legal infractions, in order to operate.[116] Conservatives' targeting of printers' bottom lines was an effective strategy, although behind the scenes Santa Anna's administration continued to negotiate. Well-known figures like Cumplido made public statements by closing their newspapers in protest. García Torres found himself facing a familiar adversary, Alamán, the architect of Santa Anna's government and minister of the interior, who moved to repay old scores by targeting the radical printer's lucrative contracts with the national government. Printers' economic relationships to government would become a new source of conflict in the 1850s, as Santa Anna's final administration triggered liberal revolt and initiated a period of sweeping state reforms and civil war, known as La Reforma, which pitted liberals against conservatives and the power of the Catholic Church. Government printing emerged as a field of partisan contestation and heightened concern as officials struggled to forge a viable state in an era shaped by conflict and imperialism.

FIVE

The Business of Nation Building

MEXICO'S INDEPENDENT GOVERNMENTS GENERATED PRODIGIOUS amounts of print. Besides regulating the printing trades through press laws, national and local officials also commissioned and participated in production themselves. The government gazette, laws and decrees, passports, letterhead, stamped paper, internal circulars and ministry reports, even lottery tickets—these utilitarian documents facilitated the state's inner workings while making discursive and symbolic claims to authority. An 1827 *bando* (edict), for example, highlights this multifaceted role. The *bando* itself had a public function. This particular example instructed Spaniards affected by a recent law expelling them from Mexican territory to present themselves to municipal officials for processing.[1] Edicts like this one, following conventions established in the colonial era, would be printed (here in a run of two hundred copies), signed, distributed, and posted in customary places around the city by municipal officials, alerting residents to changes in policy or law. Setting the process into motion, however, required a second document—a *circular* (memo), printed in a run of fifty copies, that instructed local officials to promulgate the *bando* and confirm their receipt of two copies (see figures 20 and 21). These routinized procedures of statecraft involved internal communication and ritualized performances of official power even as they grew state archives behind the scenes. Not only had the *bando's* author ordered the government printing shop to produce twice the number of copies that he apparently intended to distribute; his requests for accountability theoretically also returned a further fifty confirmation letters, to be sewn together by minor functionaries in ever-fattening folios. The archives of the nineteenth-century state are filled not only with confirmation letters—as well as complaints about damaged or missing documents—but also with caches of

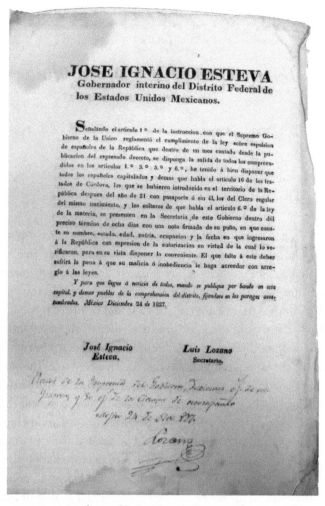

JOSE IGNACIO ESTEVA
Gobernador interino del Distrito Federal de
los Estados Unidos Mexicanos.

Señalando el artículo 1.° de la instrucción con que el Supremo Gobierno de la Union reglamentó el cumplimiento de la ley sobre espulsion de españoles de la República que dentro de un mes contado desde la publicacion del espresado decreto, se disponga la salida de todos los comprendidos en los artículos 1.° 3.° 5.° y 6.°, he tenido á bien disponer que todos los españoles capitulados y demas que habla el artículo 16 de los tratados de Córdova, los que se hubieren introducido en el territorio de la República despues del año de 21 con pasaporte ó sin él, los del Clero regular del mismo nacimiento, y los solteros de que habla el artículo 6.° de la ley de la materia, se presenten en la Secretaría de este Gobierno dentro del preciso término de ocho dias con una nota firmada de su puño, en que conste su nombre, estado, edad, patria, ocupacion y la fecha en que ingresaron á la República con espresion de la autorizacion en virtud de la cual lo verificaron, para en su vista disponer lo conveniente. El que falte á este deber sufrirá la pena á que su malicia ó inobediencia le haga acreedor con arreglo á las leyes.

Y para que llegue á noticia de todos, mando se publique por bando en esta capital, y demas pueblos de la comprehension del distrito, fijandose en los parages acostumbrados. México Diciembre 24 de 1827.

José Ignacio   Luis Lozano
Esteva.   Secretario.

FIGURE 20. *Bando* issued by José Ignacio Esteva, with a marginal note confirming receipt of 200 copies from the printing shop, 1827. Archivo General de la Nación, Mexico City.

undistributed printed matter, unread since printing shop workers gathered it into neat stacks.

The trajectory of state printing in nineteenth-century Mexico reveals the central importance officials attached to printed documents and forms, reflecting state aspirations bound up with paperwork as well as challenges. Government officials had made a grand gesture by founding a press inside the National Palace in 1823, designating state sovereignty over its own printing as a strategic priority. Officials made much use of this resource at first. The press's

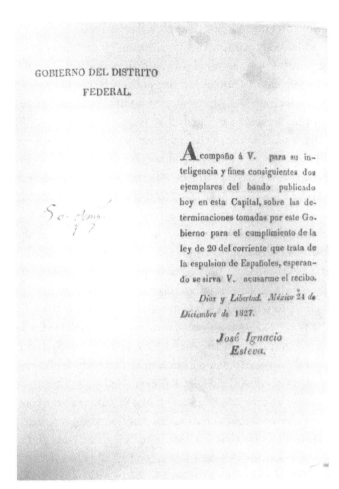

GOBIERNO DEL DISTRITO
FEDERAL.

A compaño á V. para su inteligencia y fines consiguientes dos
ejemplares del bando publicado
hoy en esta Capital, sobre las de-
terminaciones tomadas por este Gobierno para el cumplimiento de la
ley de 20 del corriente que trata de
la espulsion de Españoles, esperan-
do se sirva V. acusarme el recibo.

Dios y Libertad. México 24 de
Diciembre de 1827.

José Ignacio
Esteva.

FIGURE 21. *Circular* issued by José Ignacio Esteva, with a marginal
note confirming receipt of 50 copies, 1827. Archivo General de la
Nación, Mexico City.

director reported that in 1824 its workers had printed 742 different jobs, total-
ing nearly 1.5 million copies.[2] Faced with the expense of printing, however, the
national government soon turned to Mexico City contractors to produce the
essential materials of statecraft. The contracting process returned lucrative
results for a handful of reliable printers whose reputations and networks with-
stood the frequent changes in administration of the early republican era.
Indeed, the rise of the contract system helped support broader printing markets by generating new sources of income for which local printers competed in

public auctions. Yet outsourcing preoccupied officials, who feared that misinformation and shoddy printing might undermine government stability.

Official printing also illuminates another dimension of the state's participation in Mexico City's world of printing politics. By the 1850s, politicians in the national government had abandoned a fairly stable set of contracting relationships for a patronage system that assigned contracts on the basis of partisan affiliation. The rise of clientelistic practices in government printing paralleled growing political tensions that eventually boiled over in the years following the US-Mexico war. In 1853, Antonio López de Santa Anna rose to power from the ashes of his military defeat, allied with conservative supporters who argued that only a strong leader could rescue Mexico from crisis. The general's attempts to consolidate power, his administration's corruption, and his unpopular negotiation of the Gadsden Purchase provoked resistance from liberal politicians and provincial leaders, who revolted in 1854 under the Plan de Ayutla. A slate of radical liberals swept into power and began a concerted effort to reform Mexico's political institutions. The early years of La Reforma produced a series of legal measures that abolished religious and military privileges; decreed the mandatory sale of church and corporate properties; and convoked a new constituent assembly that culminated in the passage of an 1857 constitution, which expanded press freedom and proclaimed the state sovereign in religious affairs. Within the year, conservatives backed by the church staged a coup against the liberal government, plunging the nation into a bloody civil war that lasted for three years and mobilized Mexican society. During this decade of often radical political shifts and protracted conflict, Mexico City printers with partisan connections navigated circumstances that swung between favorable and dangerous as they engaged the politics of print clientelism, sustaining the government's printing needs and self-representation, which were periodically interrupted altogether by lack of funds and war.

In the 1860s, a centralized vision of official printing reemerged, this time as the product of an occupying foreign power eager to consolidate its mandate. Although liberals emerged victorious from the Wars of Reform, Mexico almost immediately faced invasion by French forces after president Benito Juárez stopped servicing Mexico's foreign debts and Napoleon III attempted to reassert European influence in the Western Hemisphere. During French occupation, the emperor—along with a delegation of Mexican conservatives—invited Ferdinand Maximilian, the archduke of Austria, to rule in Mexico as Maximilian I. Juárez maintained an itinerant government in opposition to

Maximilian, but the emperor established his administration in Mexico City, where he reenvisioned the state's printing policy from the central core. Reconfiguring production as an aspect of governance that should be carefully monitored from above, he established a government printing shop, the Imprenta del Gabinete Civil, in 1865.

Even as the Imprenta del Gabinete took shape, ties between government administrations and partisan local printing shops endured, a transition captured in the story of one of the most infamous documents produced under Maximilian's rule. This document, the so-called *decreto negro* (black decree), issued in October 1865, proclaimed that any opponent of the empire could be summarily tried and executed upon capture. The harshness of its terms would influence Benito Juárez's decision to execute Maximilian two years later. The decree's text and materiality, including its typography, size, and exceptionally high print run, projected the image of a powerful state. Yet its unusual production and deployment underscored state weakness. Its printing by a local contractor, after all, flew in the face of the emperor's own pretensions to establish a functional printing works, modeled on French precedent.

The second opening of the government printing shop, though tentative and modest in scope, heralded an ultimately enduring shift in the dynamics of Mexico City's printing landscape, as the state's politicized approach to production gave way to state consolidation. After the defeat and execution of Maximilian in 1867, the liberal governments of the Restored Republic (under Juárez and later Sebastián Lerdo de Tejada) built upon the model of the Imprenta del Gabinete Civil, never to return on the same scale to the contractual relationships that had defined printer-government business dealings at the height of political conflict. As the national government reentered the business of printing, it enlisted bureaucrats and laborers alike to expand the scope of official printing, incubating a new vision of modern statecraft linked not simply to forms, decrees, and internal memos, but also to intellectual production about the nation itself, designed for the post-Reforma era and underwritten by the liberal state.

PROJECTING THE STATE'S SOVEREIGNTY: THE IMPRENTA NACIONAL, 1823–1828

After independence, government officials immediately moved to bring print production under direct control. Colonial rulers had been troubled by insurgent decrees that threatened their monopoly over official documents. Now, national authorities adopted policies that mirrored those implemented by the Bourbons in Spain. These policies, in turn, had been modeled on French precedents, specifically Louis XIII's founding of the Imprimerie Nationale to support the expansion of the state in the seventeenth century. Mexican officials, too, prioritized state sovereignty over printing—the government's direct oversight of printing in order to represent itself and consolidate its authority in the nation-in-formation. Turning away from the long-term colonial practice of entrusting a local printer with commissions, they founded the National Printing Shop of the Supreme Government of Mexico. Plans for the press were launched less than a month after Mexico's brief experiment as an independent empire gave way to the construction of a new republic in 1823. Underscoring the importance assigned to print as both symbol and tool of governance, the press would be installed inside the National Palace itself. To accomplish the task, Joaquín de Miramón, a former cavalry captain and printer appointed as the printing shop's director, took up residence in the room once used as Emperor Iturbide's private kitchen.[3] From there, he oversaw the installation of the new printing shop on the palace's ground floor. Dedicating his efforts to the good of the nation, Miramón worked without salary, drawing on his war pension as he set about his task.[4]

In spite of officials' support, the director's regular reports revealed the challenges of getting into the printing business. Half of the shop's type had been pied—jumbled into an unusable heap—and needed to be laboriously sorted out piece by piece. Its various rooms, located at street level, lacked windowpanes, and thus the shop was exposed to constant theft of supplies and documents. With many integral pieces of equipment missing, a carpenter enjoyed a steady stream of work.[5] Yet over the course of the year, as he proudly demonstrated in a printed report presented to his superiors, the director improved the shop's ad hoc conditions.[6] Mexico's finance minister, drawing on merchant contacts, acquired two new printing presses from the United States, raising the total number of hand presses to nine.[7] The director organized workflow into two divisions, one serving congress, the other the executive branch. Each division had a staff of compositors and apprentices working in two composition rooms and a number of *tiradores* (press operators) and *tintadores* (inkers) printing in two press rooms. Quarters were tight, and bookbinders responsible for folding newspapers and stitching ministerial reports had to carry out their labor in the street, presumably in full view of city residents and at risk of afternoon downpours.

The new government printing shop, though designed to serve the state, also presented a challenge to Mexico City's broader printing community. It immediately absorbed many of the state commissions once enjoyed by colonial contractors like Alejandro Valdés. On a smaller scale, too, it cut into the market for private commissions, since in order to cover shortfalls in the state budget for operating expenses, the shop accepted job work for such unofficial items as marriage announcements, poetry, labels for wine and liquor bottles, and perfume advertisements.[8] Other local institutions, like the Catholic Church, civic militias, and tollbooth operators, to name a few, patronized the government printing shop for sundry documents, especially printed forms, which quickly became a house specialty. One church, for example, placed an order for sheets of *cédulas de confesión y comunión*, which would be cut up into little slips and distributed to parishioners as proof of their mandatory yearly confession (see figure 22).[9] These chits, in use since at least the seventeenth century, would later be collected by a religious official, who logged them in sacramental registers to keep tabs on the community's piety. Though resistance to the religious surveillance grew in the late eighteenth century, the forms endured, now joined by a proliferating set of secular accounting devices embraced by the state and printed on the same presses.[10] The government commissioned a flurry of forms in the wake of independence: military orders, employment forms for staffing the bureaucracy, forms listing newly elected local officials, forms for paying soldiers' pensions from the independence wars, tax forms, and more. These new documents marked a departure from the colonial regime by naming new bureaucratic entities, visualizing state functions and promises in tables and statistics, and promulgating the new national seal of the eagle and cactus.

The government printing shop enjoyed such high demand in its early years that during times of peak activity it was unable to keep up with the state's needs, let alone private commissions. Over the course of 1824, its director outsourced work to at least six local printing shops.[11] Especially when the production of the 1824 federal constitution caused a backlog starting in October, workers transported heavy galleys full of type through the city streets to nearby shops for printing.[12] The physical logistics of outsourcing meant that the government's official business occasionally spilled into the public space. In one episode, type for an issue of the government gazette had to be painstakingly picked up from the streets and re-composed after being dropped by a servant en route to another press.[13] The state's early printing experiments, spanning genres and clientele, also revealed its position within

FIGURE 22. *Cedulas de confesión y comunión*, [1828]. Archivo General de la Nación, Mexico City.

urban craft networks that blurred the boundaries between private and government spheres.

OUTSOURCING AND INFORMATION POLICY AMID GOVERNMENT PENURY, 1828–1851

The enthusiasm surrounding the government printing shop had dissipated in less than a decade, as willingness and ability to sustain an operating budget declined. In 1828 officials shuttered the press and auctioned off its equipment at a discount.[14] This decision inaugurated an extended period during which the national government outsourced its official communications to local printers through a system of contracts aimed at saving on costs. The shift to contracting marked a modified return to the older practice whereby the colonial government had designated local printers to produce official materials through licensing and privileges. Yet much had changed since independence, especially the emergence of a vibrant local network of printers who cultivated affiliations with political factions. Printers were no longer the trusted collaborators of a familiar and long-lived regime; as previous chapters have explored, they were instead perceived as disruptive, unpredictable, and generally up to no good.

Officials confronted the challenges of controlling information in the landscape of printing politics. In 1844, for example, the Ministry of the Interior complained that newspapers would often publish congressional debates that instead of "including the opinions presented by both parties, only present those spoken in favor of the ideas that the newspaper supports."[15] To counter politicized inaccuracies, the minister decreed that no private newspaper could publish official news until it had first been printed in the government gazette. This both targeted skewed information and aimed to give the *Diario Oficial*, and the government in power, a minor tactical advantage in the press. In reality, little differentiated the government gazette from its private counterparts. Both led with official news, followed by editorials. State officials, too, hired a *redactor* to defend government actions and refute critics in the editorial section. Behind the scenes, furthermore, the lines between state and private spheres also blurred. Governments frequently took out bulk subscriptions or supported the private press with subsidies. Payments to newspaper staffs were not systematic, but the Ministry of the Interior sometimes underwrote production costs in monthly sums exceeding hundreds of pesos and attempted to consolidate this practice at midcentury under the rubric of *fomento de periódicos*. The state's own persistent penury, however, undermined sustained efforts to manage coverage through financial support of newspapers. Officials were just as likely to be cutting their subscriptions and support for the press as allocating funds to partisan allies.[16] And the government could not always manage its own newspaper. At least once, officials jailed the *Diario Oficial*'s own editor for an alleged press crime.[17] While efforts to protect the integrity of official news showed the state's self-understanding as a privileged participant in the arena of public opinion, its power to influence the broader field of printing politics remained uneven.

Given attitudes toward the politicized printing world, government officials turned to a trusted source to manage much of the state's paper presence after they shuttered the government printing shop in 1828. The buyers of the government's presses, Juan Gómez de Navarrete and his wife Luisa Cacho de Navarrete, had firsthand knowledge of the history of printing politics and the legal context of press freedom. Gómez de Navarrete had served as a judge and member of the Supreme Court. In 1820, before independence, he had presided over the investigation into the controversial pamphlet *El liberal a los bajos escritores*, discussed in chapter 2. Taking a hands-off approach, the couple entrusted management of their printing shop, the Imprenta del Aguila, to a skilled administrator who also managed contracts with the national government.[18]

The Imprenta del Aguila was not the only state contractor in the early republican era, but it held the longest tenure.[19] Over twenty years, its administrator coordinated regularly with the Ministry of the Interior to produce the government gazette and other forms of official printing. Their relationship survived numerous changes in administrations, constitutional overhauls, and complaints, with periodic renegotiations carried out with little fanfare[20] The arrangement served the national government well. True, outsourcing printing generated considerable paperwork and bureaucratic anxieties. The printing shop administrator and the editor of the government gazette had to swear to follow strict secrecy protocols so that no information would slip out inopportunely. They also deflected frequent admonishments to speed up production and post the gazette on time from ministry officials. State-level governments around the country routinely grumbled that their copies of the official gazette arrived late or mangled, and ministry officials in Mexico City pressured postal workers who in turn blamed the printing shop staff for delays.[21] Yet in spite of these everyday disputes, the contract relationship endured.

The Imprenta del Aguila tolerated the challenges of working for a government that rarely paid its bills on time. Though promised a weekly outlay of three hundred pesos, reams of paper, and eventual payment on overage, the press often ended up financing the state's printing costs. These could accrue to substantial sums over months before accounts were gradually settled, but the state also represented one of the largest clients in town and a source of regular income.[22] Perhaps the Imprenta del Aguila's owners viewed underwriting the state's press as a patriotic contribution. Yet by the late 1840s, after US forces had commandeered the press for their own purposes, its owners' relationship with the national government and the press's financial position began to falter. The press rebranded itself with a new name after the occupation, but its capable administrator, José Jimeno, had retired, and Gómez de Navarrete died in

1849. Amid complaints about quality control, government officials canceled the contract, prompting the new administrator to submit a bitter complaint. The printing shop, he explained, had subsidized the government's printing needs for decades, operating at a loss and often failing to pay workers, who occasionally rose up in protest. Now "in the very sad state of being unable to serve the public, for having worn out its very abundant type in the service of the Supreme Government," the printing shop had been abandoned to its fate with the government still owing more than seven thousand pesos.[23]

Before long the Imprenta del Aguila was shuttered as Luisa Cacho de Navarrete settled her husband's debts, a process that lifted the curtain on the organizational and technological realities of operating a printing press whose fortunes had waxed and waned. The press's machinery and supplies were a mix of old and newer technologies, a common feature of midcentury printing shops, in which costly new equipment would be acquired gradually and older technologies remained useful for certain kinds of jobs. Four wooden handpresses—probably those that had once served as the government's presses in the 1820s—had been supplemented with three mechanical presses over the years.[24] Five tons of lead type had accumulated over time, along with various ornaments and an assortment of stereotyped printing plates for illustrations. The financial assessment of the press's equipment matched its administrator's lament that the Imprenta del Aguila had worn itself out in the service of the government; another business sold two years earlier with a similar array of equipment had fetched nearly six times the price.[25] The press's owner had also failed to pay workers' salaries in its final months, leading her to transfer the press to them as compensation for back pay. Far from being a windfall, the arrangement was a burden. The value of even this worn-out equipment far exceeded their delinquent wages. Without enough capital to invest in the press, workers had to resell the equipment to another printer with greater resources so they could extract their wages from the deal.

Meanwhile, other presses in the city flourished, especially those that published major newspapers, which outstripped the government gazette's popularity with more exciting fare, like *The Mysteries of the Inquisition*. Indeed, after officials canceled the Imprenta del Aguila's contract in 1851, they rewarded the *Mysteries*' publisher Vicente García Torres with the lion's share of the state's printing business on terms that seemed to tilt in his favor.[26] Before long, government authorities were questioning whether the printer was overcharging them for bills, which he submitted in cursory requests scrawled hastily across half-slips of paper. García Torres clashed with treasury officials in the administration of Mariano Arista (1851-1853), who struggled to overcome the nation's postwar financial crisis by reforming government spending. One sizable bill for over twenty thousand pesos prompted an extended inquiry, and within a year the Ministry of the Interior had drafted a formal set of rules to govern official printing. In addition to centralizing the state's oversight of production, the guidelines explained that printers should bill the government with detailed receipts.[27] The relatively stable, long-term relationship with the Imprenta del Aguila never completely assuaged the bureaucratic anxieties caused by the state's reliance on contract printers. By the 1850s, these anxieties would contribute to the overt politicization of outsourcing.

PRINT PATRONAGE AMID THE PENDULUM SWINGS OF THE REFORMA ERA, 1853–1863

Political patronage in the form of government printing contracts became the norm amid the radical pendulum swings of the Reforma years, when liberals pushed their reform agenda and conservatives coalesced into a defined opposition force. When Santa Anna came to power in 1853, he did not just increase controls over printing with novel tactics like mandatory printers' deposits and confiscation of presses.[28] His administration also used state contracts to encourage and punish local printers. This type of print clientelism had existed in various forms during the early republican era. Officials might subsidize the printing costs of authors with whom they had political ties, for example. Most major printers cultivated ties with patrons who could gain them government business beyond the main contract for national printing. After briefly working as the state's contract printer, for instance, Ignacio Cumplido used connections to his friend and patron, Mariano Riva Palacio, to gain commissions when the latter held posts in national and state-level administrations.[29] Political bonds overlapped with close friendships. Cumplido was good friends with Mariano Otero, another prominent liberal politician who worked on the editorial staff of *El Siglo Diez y Nueve*. When the young Otero died during a cholera epidemic, Cumplido and Riva Palacio exchanged expressions of grief as they worked to secure financial support for Otero's widow.[30] Printers' networks emerged organically out of shared ideological affinity, mutual need, and the fraternal bonds of newspaper work.[31] Beginning with Santa Anna's assumption of the presidency, however, administrations pursued an openly partisan agenda toward official printing, treating the contract as spoils handed down from above.

The variable fortunes of García Torres, a former critic of Santa Anna from the days of the US-Mexico war, illustrate the shift toward partisan patronage. In 1853 García Torres found his government contract summarily canceled and distributed to printers with ties to the new conservative regime. Fuming in a letter of protest, García Torres described the development as "an act of Power, naked of all form, destitute of all legality," and with calculated incredulity accused the government of being worse than a monarchy.[32] The printer bemoaned the lengths he had gone to in serving official printing needs as the state's contractor: he had amassed a large stock of paper of many sizes and qualities, acquired additional printing presses, and contracted extra workers. Because the government never paid on time, the printer claimed, "I have had to defray enormous expenses, compromise my credit, contract debts, and expose myself to the dangers of bankruptcy."[33] García Torres had also fallen afoul of an old political rival, conservative statesman Lucas Alamán, who had assumed the post of interior minister precisely as the printer's paperwork arrived for review. Alamán, who had unsuccessfully sued García Torres for defamation in 1849, surely took pleasure in flatly denying the printer's appeal when it crossed his desk several years later.[34] In a copy of the new contract, his office crossed out García Torres's name, reassigning it the publisher of Alamán's recent magnum opus, the *Historia de Méjico*, along with two other conservative printers.[35]

Alamán's cancellation of García Torres's contract was more than a substantial financial blow; it also marked a turning point in the evolving relationship between government officials and Mexico City's world of printing, as partisan politics conditioned official attitudes. When liberals regained power after the Revolution of Ayutla, they reversed Santa Anna's press laws, replacing the restrictive Ley Lares with a revised version of the 1846 law, which, though it restored protections for printers, suppressed the press jury and prohibited anonymous publications.[36] These legal changes were framed as a provisional compromise until political stability could be achieved, but the liberal government chose expediency when it also undid the prior government's contracts with local printers. Conservative printers who had cultivated close ties with the regime lost this source of income and encountered a hostile political climate as liberals initiated a process to draft a new constitution. The printer Rafael de Rafael, once the main facilitator of conservatism and rewarded by Santa Anna for his work with the commission of the national consul in New Orleans and New York, quit Mexico altogether. Remaining abroad, he sold his Mexico City printing business, renounced his consulship, and made off with fifteen thousand pesos from the treasury, which he claimed as payment for services rendered.[37] Rafael established himself in Cuba, still part of the Spanish Empire, where, besides making an unsuccessful attempt to filibuster at Veracruz in the 1860s, he ran a conservative newspaper until his death.[38]

Meanwhile, liberal printers returned to action, and García Torres worked doggedly to recover the printing contracts canceled by Santa Anna. In 1856 he managed to reclaim printing contracts with Mexico City's municipal government. Reinstating his contract with the national government proved more difficult, as officials were preoccupied with preparations for the constitutional convention. In 1857 the printer pressed the minister of the interior for restitution, but the minister replied apologetically that the president "could not decide anything regarding this matter until the treasury department is arranged."[39] When the treasury sent out a new call for bids for the government printing contract later that month, García Torres quickly reminded it of his pending contract, and the treasury suspended the bidding process until the matter could be settled.[40] Unfortunately for the printer, before the contract could be renegotiated, civil war had broken out, and conservative forces soon took over the government in Mexico City.

The Three Years' War pitted conservatives, who occupied Mexico City, against liberals, who moved their headquarters around the territory, contesting their opponents' legitimacy. In the capital, García Torres predictably lost his municipal printing contract in 1858, a casualty of the change of government.[41] Officials split the national contract between two partisans in April 1858. The practice of distributing work to multiple individuals kept printers on their toes, generating competition alongside occasional complaints.[42] In the parallel liberal government led by Juárez, on the other hand, authorities hired local printers on an ad hoc basis as they established operations outside of the capital. In Veracruz, their base for a time, liberals relied on a revolving series of printers to produce a parallel government gazette and official decrees.[43] When they triumphed over conservatives in 1861 and returned to Mexico City, they reshuffled contracts again, but they lacked the resources to establish a regular printing apparatus at all; the government gazette went unpublished during the second half of 1861 due to government penury.[44] Conservatives had run up a hefty war debt, and when Juárez suspended payments to foreign creditors, French troops invaded Mexico on the orders of

Napoleon III. While García Torres had regained his municipal printing contract for the second time after the Three Years' War, he lost it yet again in 1863, as French forces, allied with conservatives and the clergy, occupied Mexico City.[45] The printers of the former conservative regime reassumed their posts as key contractors for the newly formed imperial government, headed by Maximilian I.

Between 1850 and 1863, a handful of printers served as contractors for a warring political class increasingly divided by irreconcilable differences, differences printers themselves had stoked in their newspapers. Pursuing government contracts, especially given the degree of polarization and the fact of war, involved losing out as often as reaping the rewards. When conservatives controlled Mexico City in wartime, for example, the radical printer García Torres barely published at all.[46] That he and his conservative counterparts were able to weather the political climate spoke to the possession of other resources—accumulated capital, other income sources, or assistance from patrons out of power—on which they could draw until the pendulum swung back.

MAXIMILIAN'S PRINTING POLICIES AND THE IMPRENTA DEL GABINETE, 1863–1867

The imperial officials and local collaborators who established a government in Mexico City beginning in 1863 inherited their predecessors' struggles to set clear parameters around public speech and oversee the state's printing. While some of the strategies they deployed continued historic practices, administrators in Maximilian's regime also displayed new attitudes, visible in their efforts to further centralize oversight of printing and expand the state's use of print as a tool of governance. From the outset, interim officials found themselves managing the old contracting system, juggling numerous relationships and fielding requests and complaints as they continued to rely on local printers. At first the influx of European administrators—Maximilian's coterie was described derisively as a "tower of babel" by one Mexican diplomat—multiplied difficulties in establishing clear protocols.[47] In the transition, contracts were accidentally signed in duplicate, forcing ministry officials to pay double, and printers like García Torres pressed the regime to assume the debts of the liberal government it had recently displaced.[48] A seemingly helpful offer by the senior statesman Basilio Arrillaga to continue compiling and publishing Mexico's legislation—a task he had undertaken since 1830—turned into a bureaucratic nightmare once officials realized that the aging Arrillaga's project was not as financially self-sustaining as the former senator had claimed.[49]

Soon, however, authorities established working relationships with two local printers who had contracted with conservative governments in previous years, and by 1865 the government had founded a new Imprenta del Gabinete, which brought official printing inside the walls of the National Palace once again. To head this effort, the regime contracted four Europeans as the printing shop's core staff, including its director. Most of the workers were hired from Mexico City, however, and the director was soon replaced by an up-and-coming local printer, Francisco Díaz de León, who possessed managerial experience, greater knowledge of the city's printing networks and practices, and the right connections. He had started his career as an apprentice for conservative printer Rafael, learning the trade at age thirteen after his father's death sent him in search of work.[50] By age seventeen he had taken over management of the shop, by then under the co-ownership of printer Felipe Escalante and bookseller José María Andrade, who bought Rafael's business after he absconded to Cuba. Escalante printed for Maximilian's government and probably recommended Díaz de León for the position, further cementing his economic ties to the regime and gaining a contact inside the palace itself.

The creation of the imperial printing shop represented one part of a broader strategy to use and regulate printed speech, reflecting the imperial administration's preoccupations and anxieties. Maximilian's regime initially imposed a strict censorship system, requiring individuals to solicit prior authorization to publish any newspapers that touched on political themes. The most significant liberal and radical newspapers, including those run by Cumplido and García Torres, opposed these rules and ceased publication in protest against the occupation. Those who continued to publish were expected to submit their plans to administrators for review, a process the emperor personally oversaw, approving most printers' and editors' initial requests.[51] Known critics and provocative titles, like "A visit to *tierra adentro,* or Don Benito Juárez and the June 1863 emigres from Mexico City," which referenced liberal opposition to Maximilian's regime, garnered extra attention, prompting officials to call printers to the ministry for in-person consultations.[52] Those who continued to publish faced an evolving legal landscape, as Maximilian's administration gradually lifted restrictions on the press, assimilating its policies to more closely resemble the laws in place before the French intervention and reflecting the emperor's reformist sensibilities, to the chagrin of his conservative supporters.[53] By 1865, prior censorship and authorization had been formally eliminated and a warning system enacted, under which newspapers faced three strikes before they could be suspended permanently.[54]

Like his predecessors in Mexico's republican governments who feared political criticism in print, Maximilian actively monitored the Mexico City press. In 1864, administrators established a central press directorate to systematize this oversight. The emperor received daily digests of the capital press alongside key articles, which officials clipped and pasted into albums for his consultation.[55] Empress Carlota also remained abreast of the news; her complaint that *La Sociedad* had reprinted a confidential letter of Maximilian's first published in a foreign paper inspired a decree in 1865 forbidding Mexican newspapers from printing any official information not first published in the government gazette.[56] Other policies attempted to consolidate the emperor's authority beyond the capital, building on the 1865 reorganization of Mexico's states into prefectures. Prefecture employees and offices, for example, were expected to subscribe to the government gazette. The regime also supported the creation of government printing offices and newspapers, envisioning them as outposts of empire that could reproduce official news "as well as standardize public opinion and defend the general interests of the district."[57]

Maximilian viewed the creation of an efficient bureaucratic state as a key precondition for winning Mexicans' political loyalties.[58] Yet efforts to vertically integrate official information and expand the state's presence through print met with uneven success. Employees often failed to cover their subscriptions to the government gazette, leading central authorities in Mexico City to press prefectures for payments, which ran into the thousands of pesos.[59] The ministry of the interior approved plans for state printing offices that could publish official newspapers in smaller urban centers like León, Tulancingo, and Tehuantepec. Municipalities, however, also vied with prefectures for central government funds. In Guanajuato, for example, prefecture officials canceled the León government's newspaper to save costs. León officials complained to imperial administrators in Mexico City, who chastised the Guanajuato prefecture for circumventing the emperor's information policy, since he had personally approved León's newspaper. Facing their own economic difficulties, Guanajuato officials dragged their heels, refusing to pay for the printing costs and editorial salary of the León newspaper, attempting to force the central authorities to cover the expense and eventually gaining their own official news subsidy to boot.[60] Regional authorities smartly played on the central government's interest in official news to extract resources. When Guadalajara officials solicited advice on their official printing contracts from the emperor, for example, they also managed to obtain a monthly earmark of five hundred pesos to run the press.[61]

Because of his outsider status, Maximilian showed a deep concern over political legitimacy and spent heavily on projects that made symbolic claims to power.[62] The Imprenta del Gabinete thus bridged the twin goals of creating an efficient bureaucratic state and projecting an image of state efficiency to the nation. Yet the disjuncture between the imperial administration's investments in printing and its authority emerged in its most notorious document, a decree printed in October 1865 as French troops battled republican forces led by Juárez. Despite the French army's efforts, republican resistance to Maximilian continued throughout his rule, though in 1865, his anti-imperial struggle at a low point, Juárez had retreated to Chihuahua, where he attempted to regroup along Mexico's northern border. Maximilian seized the opportunity to press his advantage, issuing a direct address to the nation, which led in capital letters: "MEXICANOS" (see figure 23). The broadside proclaimed: "The cause that D. Benito Juárez sustained with such valor and constancy had already succumbed, not just to the national will, but also before the very law that this *caudillo* invoked in support of his titles."[63] According to the emperor, Juárez had delegitimized his cause by withdrawing from Mexican soil, crossing into the United States for safety and thus abandoning his claims. Reframing the conflict between occupying French troops and Mexican republican forces, the emperor proclaimed, "From today forward, the struggle will only pit honorable men of the Nation against gangs of criminals and bandits." The decree that followed Maximilian's address, ratified by the emperor's cabinet but allegedly drafted by General François Bazaine, head of the French army battling for full control of Mexican territory, ordered that all Mexicans caught participating in unauthorized "gangs" would be subject to court martial. If found guilty, they would be executed within twenty-four hours. Taking a hard line against Juárez supporters, the decree also imposed stiff penalties on any individuals who aided the resistance.

Draconian in its provisions, the decree was equally atypical in its material form. For one thing, the printed text used unusual typography. Departing from standard practice, the typographers used an ornamental, blackletter-inspired typeface—called Alemana (German) in Mexico—which they may have associated with the emperor's Austro-Hungarian extraction, to reproduce his name. The document was also printed on a sheet of paper twice the

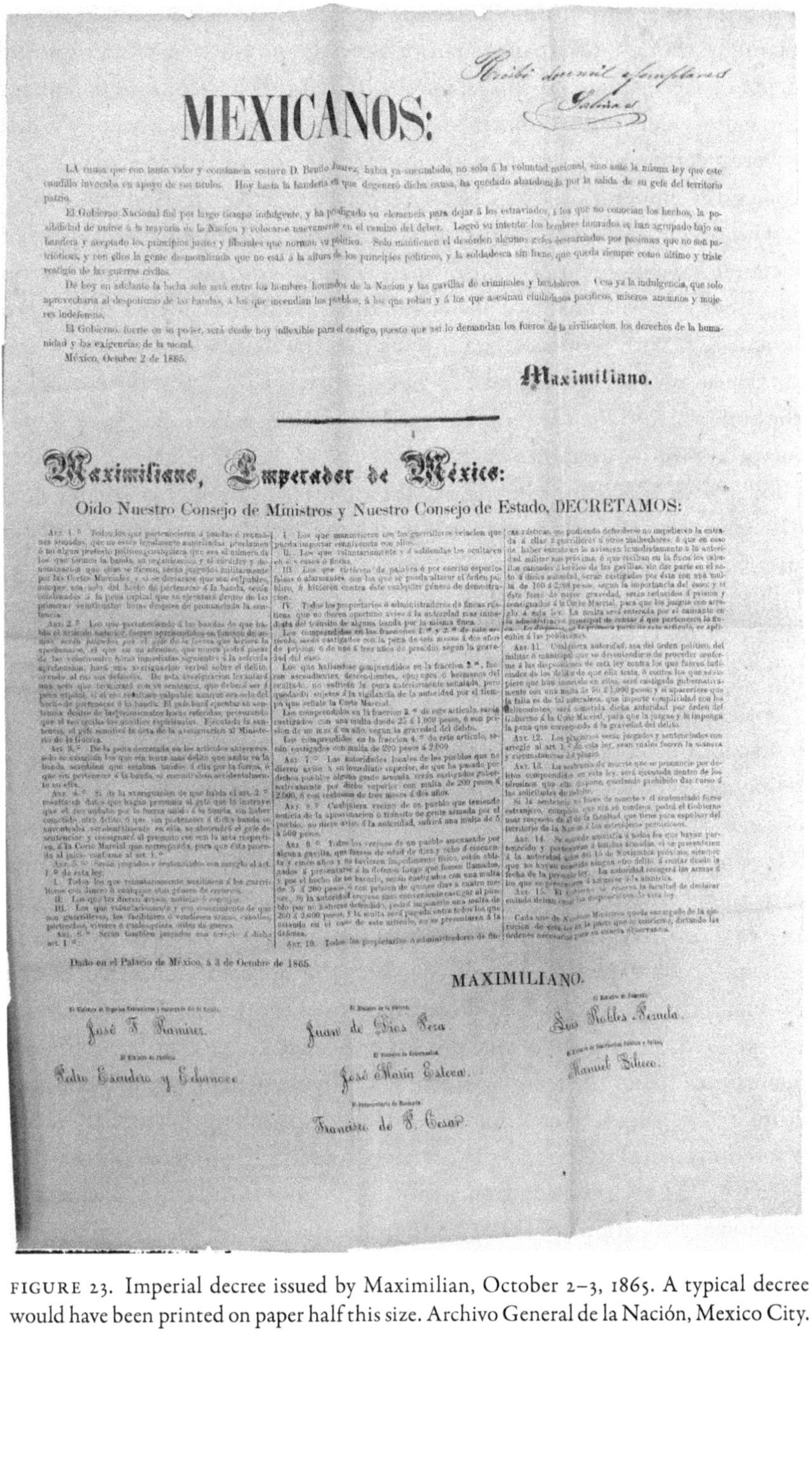

FIGURE 23. Imperial decree issued by Maximilian, October 2–3, 1865. A typical decree would have been printed on paper half this size. Archivo General de la Nación, Mexico City.

size of a typical government decree, eighteen by twenty-six inches. Most surprisingly, though, the government ordered the production of an unprecedented sixteen thousand copies, making the so-called *decreto negro* perhaps the most widely printed official decree in Mexico up to that time.[64] While government decrees were normally printed in runs of two to five hundred copies, the emperor's advisers clearly viewed a massive printing effort as an essential demonstration of the imperial state's due diligence in wielding what it claimed as a monopoly over legitimate violence. In an accompanying cover sheet, printed in a quantity of five hundred, ministers ordered prefects to "circulate it with profusion in all the cities, towns, workers' quarters, and rural farms in your Department."[65] Local officials should post the decree "in the busiest streets, on the walls of churches, on the doors of theaters, prisons, inns and taverns, and, ultimately, in any place where it might receive most publicity," including by bringing it to the attention of republican "dissidents." This decree would pass through official channels, but its dissemination stretched far beyond the customary practices of promulgation. Instead, in the midst of conflict, its drafters imagined it posted on every corner in every village across the nation, alerting ordinary people to the dangers of supporting the republican resistance.

Following a unique practice that reflected the emperor's overtures to indigenous communities, the administration also translated and printed a bilingual Nahuatl-Spanish version of the decree.[66] "Mexicaye," its address began in the right column, where text indigenized Maximilian as the "Huei Tlatoani Mexico (great ruler of Mexico)." The Nahuatl text was peppered throughout with parenthetical insertions of Spanish intended to emphasize key concepts flagged by the translators ("gobierno," "bandas," "jefe de la fuerza," "pena capital"). Strung together, the Spanish embedded in the Nahuatl text almost conveyed the main point of the decree, as if the translator doubted the efficacy of his mission or wanted to reassure monolingual Spanish readers of the translation's fidelity: "from here forward . . . the government . . . gangs . . . commander-in-chief . . . capital punishment." Such printed overtures were virtually unprecedented in the nineteenth century, reflecting the exclusionary frameworks through which central authorities envisioned the nation's political community. Indeed, the last government to address Nahuatl-speaking audiences in print was the colonial regime, which, in a moment of desperation, had issued a decree in 1810 to dissuade indigenous leaders from joining the Hidalgo Revolt.[67] Printing in indigenous languages, once a key component in early colonization and evangelization efforts, had long been abandoned as the technology intertwined with the creation of a creole and later national intellectual culture conducted largely in Spanish.[68] Maximilian's *indigenista* policy, underpinned by paternalism and exoticism, imagined integrating indigenous communities into the nation through a top-down project of assimilation and whitening, a move that also involved symbolic overtures like the decree's translation.[69]

The *decreto negro*, the product of a virtually unprecedented multilingual printing campaign, showed state weakness as much as it projected state power. Its comparatively large quantities sought to reach a wide audience, but the decree's effectiveness depended on the government's ability to enforce its claims. Maximilian's failure to subdue opposition surely shaped how such a document would have been received, if it ever arrived at its intended destinations. Furthermore, the decree had been printed by a contractor, in spite of the emperor's plans to use the Imprenta del Gabinete as a centerpiece of state information. The government printing office remained a work in progress and never developed the capacity to meet the state's demands, even as Maximilian's rule unraveled. While the Imprenta del Gabinete and printing efforts like the *decreto negro* departed from recent state practice, his administration also maintained key continuities with previous governments, including in the way its commitment to press freedom coexisted with periodic crackdowns on journalists and editors, which only accelerated after 1866 when Napoleon III withdrew his troops and the empire began to collapse. The regime's policies toward official information and frequent attempts to corral public speech—Laurence Coudart identifies twenty-six press-related orders emitted over four years—reveal the importance its officials attached to print as a medium that could shore up its flagging fortunes, as well as the enduring challenges of bringing printing under state control.

LIBERALS' REVENGE: THE IMPRENTA DEL GOBIERNO SUPREMO

The emperor's *decreto negro*, which Juárez referenced in a victory speech given in Mexico City, played a major role in the logic behind his decision to court martial and execute Maximilian by firing squad in 1867.[70] The emperor's printing shop, on the other hand, would be occupied and rededicated as the Imprenta del Gobierno Supremo (later the Imprenta del Gobierno Federal) in 1867. Like its imperial predecessor, the new press remained in the National

Palace. In 1870 it was located on the ground floor, where its nine rooms, each corresponding to various printing shop tasks, faced onto the patios in the palace's northern sector.[71]

Liberals' takeover of the imperial presses unfolded even as the new government settled scores against printers who had worked with Maximilian's regime. For example, Escalante, who had printed the imperial gazette, had his printing shop occupied by order of General Porfirio Díaz when liberal forces reentered Mexico City in June 1867. Díaz confiscated the shop's contents and sent them to the National Palace, where the first director of the government printing shop divided up the spoils.[72] Escalante's business partner, the bookseller and noted bibliophile Andrade, went into exile, as did the valuable collection he had recently sold to Maximilian to form the core of an imperial library. After Maximilian's execution, an agent packed the library off to Europe for sale at auction, where American collector Hubert Howe Bancroft purchased much of the collection.[73]

The liberal government used confiscated presses to develop vivid, ideological renderings of the immediate past, asserting the state's authority to frame the nation's political history in print. Among its first publications, the new republican government issued a small printed book titled *Los traidores pintados por sí mismos* (roughly, The traitors: A self-portrait).[74] Printed with the certification of the chief clerk of the Ministry of External and Internal Affairs, who testified to the text's veracity, the work promised to reproduce "the secret book of Maximilian, containing his impressions of his servants." An introductory text explained that readers were about to encounter a book recently discovered among the private papers of the dead emperor. Maximilian's book, described carefully in the introduction, sounded altogether ordinary. The object would have been a familiar part of Mexico City's world of writing and scribal accoutrements: a blank book, handwritten across one hundred sheets of paper bound economically *a la holandesa* (in quarter leather) and purchased at a local bindery for two pesos.[75] Guarding against accusations of forgery, the introduction invited skeptics to visit the ministry offices, where they could consult the executed emperor's paper trail firsthand. Yet if the book looked mundane on the outside, its text was sensational. Written in French allegedly by Maximilian's adviser Félix Eloin, the text amounted to crib notes for the emperor about the various Mexicans who had collaborated with or opposed his rule. Short biographical blurbs were organized alphabetically, many offering highly unflattering character assessments, describing shortcomings like incompetence, mediocrity, or alcoholism.

Translated into Spanish, the text presented a once secret tool of statecraft to public scrutiny.

Los traidores heralded the establishment of the national printing shop as a liberal triumph, shaming those who had collaborated during the French intervention. While Maximilian had worked to centralize and streamline government bureaucracy to build state power, liberal victors rummaged through his archives for evidence to publicly settle scores. In doing so, they turned up a second document, which they appended to the emperor's secret book: a biography of Archbishop of Mexico Pelagio Antonio de Labastida y Dávalos, a member of the committee that had invited Maximilian to rule Mexico and who now, in 1867, fled to exile in Rome. This short biography had been written especially for Maximilian by a Confederate naval commander, Matthew Maury, who had fled to Mexico after the US Civil War and who, like other Confederates, sought favor at the imperial court.[76] Maury probably wrote the text to ingratiate himself into Maximilian's service, and it painted the archbishop in a deeply unflattering light, describing him as corrupt, avaricious, and manipulative, while suggesting that Labastida had schemed to bring Maximilian to Mexico as a puppet who would help him restore church power.[77] The original politics and accuracy of the biography aside, in the context of the empire's defeat it fit a liberal narrative about the treachery of a clergy that had pursued personal profit and the glory of Rome over the sovereignty of the nation. The publication of *Los traidores* deployed a familiar technique of printing politics—the sensational exposé, sharing features with the 1850 *Mysteries of the Inquisition*—to drum up outrage and consolidate support for the task of liberal nation building that lay ahead.

Beyond humiliating losers and distributing spoils, the government printing shop played a critical role in the development and consolidation of the new liberal-controlled state in two ways. Fulfilling the vision of the nation's founders and Maximilian himself, it successfully brought a sizable portion of the government's official printing under centralized control. This eliminated the need to negotiate with city printers, who, in addition to being unpredictable political actors, also submitted unpredictable bills and complained frequently about payment. The new printing shop replaced outside contractors with an internal staff of administrators who answered directly to ministry officials and operated according to a set of rules and a predetermined budget, set by the legislature. Legislators emphasized the point of cutting off external ties, explaining in the 1873 set of rules that "the administrator of the printing shop of the supreme government may not be employed in another office, nor have his own press, nor be a partner in business of this nature, including typography, bookselling, lithography, editing, manufacture of related goods, etc."[78]

Although the genres of official documents and communications did not dramatically change, the process became streamlined; functionaries of the government ministries located in various wings of the National Palace could compose informational memos and send them across the building to be converted into loose-leaf circulars or decrees, printed in runs of one to six hundred copies.[79] The government gazette, the *Diario Oficial*, continued to serve its old function but would finally gain a consistent title, instead of one that changed with each administration. Standardization did not necessarily correlate with increased circulation, however; in 1877, the government printing shop produced two thousand copies of the government gazette, which far exceeded the gazette's readership. After copies had been distributed to the various government functionaries and subscribers, the remaining five hundred copies were deposited in the archives, where the archivist complained, "They nearly fill one of the largest rooms in this establishment and if they continue in this proportion, soon there won't be anywhere to put them."[80]

Second, and perhaps more important, the government printing shop became a key site of production for government-sponsored publications that worked to make the nation intelligible through print. Scholars who have studied the ways in which political elites mapped and visualized the nation rightly draw attention to the Restored Republic, the period after Maximilian's defeat, as an important turning point in the state's capacity to represent itself and its plans for the nation.[81] These efforts were inextricably linked to the success of the government printing shop, which soon published not only detailed guidelines for government sectors, foreign trade treaties, and plans for commercial and infrastructure projects, but also scholarly and educational works on geography, political economy, medicine and public health, military tactics, and law.[82] The development of projects to describe, measure, and define Mexico corresponds with what Oz Frankel has termed "print statism," the historical emergence of a state that constructs its population as a "target of observation and scrutiny" through a field of printed communication between the state and its constituencies.[83] As in the US and British contexts that Frankel studies, Mexico's "print statism" represented a gesture toward an ideal that did not directly translate into hegemonic power. Nevertheless, it marked a real change in the government's ability to establish an identity as an authority figure in the realm of knowledge production, a change reflected in printed materials themselves, as their imprint information became gradually standardized and anonymous, effacing the role of printers in producing state documents. While government decrees and official ephemera had nearly always been printed without any attribution, larger works (like *reglamentos*, reports, legal compilations, or diplomatic treaties) published before the Restored Republic bore the stamp of the contracted private printer—material evidence of the state's dependence on these figures (and, ironically, made visible by the government's own press laws mandating this mark of origin). The evolution of the relationship between printer and state authorship can be traced in the first decade of the government printing shop, when directors customarily included their own names alongside the Imprenta del Gobierno imprint. This practice faded around 1880, and the government printing shop alone claimed institutional credit.

CONCLUSION: A NEW HUB IN THE CITY'S WORLD OF PRINTING

The consolidation of the government printing office reorganized the relationship between urban printers, including prominent figures like García Torres and Escalante, and the national government by effectively ending the long-term practice of contracting out printing jobs, at least at the national level. Regional studies may amend or challenge the timeline of government printing to offer a fuller account of the relationship between printing and state formation; for example, Guadalajara possessed a state printing shop before Maximilian's initiative, but it fell apart in 1862.[84] At least in Mexico City, while certain ministries did occasionally commission local printers for specific jobs, the era of competition for national government printing contracts, linked to politics and personal relationships, ended. Furthermore, legislators emphasized that cronyism had no place within the new printing shop; anyone wishing to have their items printed on the government's presses would have to pay market rates.[85] Politics and personal relationships, of course, continued to play a role in government printing, since ministry officials in the executive oversaw the printing budget and sometimes subsidized printing costs for favored individuals and organizations.[86] And the printing office connected the liberal state to the city's expanding and industrializing printing world. As a new entrant into the business of printing, the government patronized the same merchant houses, paper manufacturers, and type suppliers as local printers.[87]

Since Mexico's independence, official printing had been a "state fixation," a formulation Raymond Craib developed, following anthropologist James Scott, to describe state cartographic projects, but which could also be applied to the way government printing materialized claims over law, administration, and eventually, historical and scientific inquiry.[88] Printed documents had offered tangible, if fragile, representation of the state's presence and claims to governance over the often-contested national territory. The formal and symbolic connections between the printed decree, for example, and the assertion of power and legitimacy explain why those who raised arms against the state printed up their own plans of grievances whenever possible, with visual styles that mimicked official communiqués. Given Mexican governments' ongoing struggles to achieve sovereignty and centralize power in the decades after independence, the state's paper presence materialized, if only in aspirational form, its very claim to exist, yet government penury and reliance on contractors threatened to undermine this claim. The reestablishment of a government printing office in the Restored Republic signaled a new phase in state efforts to represent itself and mark out the parameters of the nation, its history, and its future.

The government's printing shop was an early site in the development of a state bureaucracy governed by a philosophy of administration over politics, which would characterize the tenure of Díaz, the general who greatly expanded the Mexican state's power in the late nineteenth century. It also quickly became one of the most important hubs in state-sponsored cultural and intellectual initiatives. As a place where educational projects and state aspirations came together, the national printing shop was a space where workers, bureaucrats, and intellectuals labored alongside each other in the service of official knowledge production. As such, it represented a key point of contact between the state and the urban workers who gave its various projects material printed form. If 1879 census figures are any indication, at least 20 percent of the city's population of printers had passed through the national printing shop's doors.[89] High turnover and part-time working conditions, furthermore, suggest that these same printers worked in other shops around the city, perhaps simultaneously with their tenure in the National Palace. The following chapter situates this space of contact within a broader world of printing shop culture, structured by internal hierarchies yet crisscrossed by horizontal networks of intellectual exchange that characterized the collaborative endeavor of printing under Mexico's triumphant liberal regime.

SIX

Workers of Thought

REPURPOSED FROM THE ASHES of Maximilian's failed empire, Mexico's national printing shop became a preeminent site at which triumphant republican governments began to consolidate liberalism as a hegemonic political ideology after 1867. Conservatives had been defeated and discredited for their support of the occupying regime. The actual, contentious work of implementing the Reforma platform lay ahead, but officials turned immediately to printed texts as they began the process of making liberalism the lingua franca of national discourse. After its refounding in the late 1860s, the government printing shop began to release didactic and utilitarian volumes, the vanguard of the state's educational plans, intended to mold the nation's cultural outlook, promote liberal citizenship and patriotic history, and encourage economic development. Liberal governments published not just anti-conservative texts like *Los traidores pintados por sí mismos*, but also textbooks, periodicals for children, the journal of the Society of Geography and Statistics, works of history, Latin grammars, and medical bulletins.

Renowned journalist, poet, and liberal statesman Guillermo Prieto published one such work in 1871, *Elementary Lessons in Political Economy*, based on lectures he had given at Mexico's law school. Reflecting liberalism's central preoccupations, the first lesson discussed property and property rights, defining their "essential characteristics as: inviolable, individual, unequal and transmissible."[1] Lesson three defined *work* as "the application of intelligence and force towards production," describing it in gendered terms as the source of man's dignity ("se siente hombre trabajando") and man's aspirations as containing the "seeds of capital accumulation, the engine of improvement."[2] Referencing Mexico's historic and contemporary labor context, Prieto excoriated Mexico's colonial guild tradition as monopolistic and tyrannical; refuted socialism for attempting to impose freedom and security upon the individual by force; and warned against the dangers of even voluntary worker associations, which could do harm unless formed by the right people, namely, honorable men with access to capital.[3]

Disseminating his lectures beyond the relatively privileged halls of the law school with state support, would Prieto have imagined printing shop workers as an audience for his ideas? Behind the scenes, the government's compositors had systematically replicated his manuscript in lead type, letter by letter, paid for each line of text they set into place. Would these compositors have seen themselves represented in his text? "*Piece work*," explained the venerable statesman, "is generally superior to the *day's wage*; the artisans who work by the piece ... advance more than those who are remunerated by salary."[4] Prieto certainly had great familiarity with compositors as a subsector of print workers. Having started his own career under Ignacio Cumplido, he had firsthand knowledge of the inner workings of the printing shop, though by 1871 he had risen to lofty heights and probably spent little time in these gritty working spaces.

Compositors, for their part, developed creative, craft-inflected responses to the ideas put forth by prominent intellectuals like Prieto, influenced by liberalism but also seizing on socialist and anarchist ideas that circulated among the urban artisan class. These responses flourished in the years of the Restored Republic (1867–1876) and the first presidential term of Porfirio Díaz (1876–1880), when triumphant liberalism brought a degree of reprieve to the printing industry and the press began to regain its cacophonous voice. In 1875, for instance, an anonymous article entitled "El cajista" (The compositor) reformulated the meaning of work by considering the unique role of the compositor. "If we consider the *cajista* only as the printing shop employee who collects and orders type to compose what is given to him," the article mused, "the *cajista* is nothing more than the worker who reduces a work of intelligence to material labor." Yet the article encouraged readers to reframe their perceptions of printing shop work by seeing "the man who spends two-thirds of his life arranging the thoughts of others, looking over and justifying the proofs in order to make the words of so many writers, article makers, advertisers, editors and chroniclers decipherable."[5] The sometimes tongue-in-cheek essay portrayed the compositor as an overlooked figure who, puzzling out the unintelligible scribbling of educated *letrados*, "transforms material work into works of intelligence." In playful form, the author riffed on liberal definitions of work, splitting Prieto's combination of "intelligence and force" into components that seemed to chase each other around the printing shop, illuminating and challenging the social hierarchies that accompanied intellectual production in the process. Published in the worker newspaper *El Socialista*, the essay threatened to pull the rug out from under the idea of the lone author, arguing for a greater appreciation of printing shop workers' contributions to literate culture.

The article proposed a collaborative vision of authorship precisely at the moment when authorship was being consolidated as an individualized category in Mexican law. Intellectual property laws that granted rights to authors had existed since independence yet had received relatively little attention except as a thread in broader debates about press freedom. Officials, lawmakers, and political commentators cared much more about hammering out issues of authorial responsibility as they related to press laws than about assuring the property rights of individuals over their printed works. Debates about authorship flourished as a subset of debates about press freedom, in part because there was not much money to be made in publishing, and also because officials had condoned the practice of republishing international works for local markets against the complaints of foreign authors.[6] Thus, it was a new set of press regulations, drafted under Benito Juárez and his successor, Sebastián Lerdo de Tejada, that narrowed definitions of authorship with the 1868 reissue of the Ley Zarco, which had been written and briefly instated in 1861 before the French invasion. The law required authors to publish their names with their printed texts, foregrounding authorial responsibility and prohibiting anonymity. Affirming once again that "the typographic industry, printing offices and their annexes are completely free," the law also eliminated most of the specific rules that had until then identified printers and other "responsible parties" as potential culprits for the texts they produced. The old rules of responsibility, intended to police the boundaries of press freedom, had produced a cat-and-mouse game between officials and printing shops, as chapter 3 showed. Under the new law, however, individual authors alone would be responsible for their writings. While Francisco Zarco, the law's architect, credited the ban on anonymous publishing with raising the stature and respectability of Mexico's public writers by holding them to their word, printers immediately seized upon the provision to increase their own autonomy.[7] The printing shop owner Cumplido, for example, brushed aside an 1869 summons over a recently denounced article in *El Siglo Diez y Nueve*, telling the authorities that "since all of the [articles] are duly signed by their authors, you should speak with them directly."[8] While the state continued to police printed speech, its attentions shifted away from the printing shop as another institution, the press jury, took on greater significance as a regulatory mechanism.[9]

The strengthening of individual authorship reduced scrutiny of the printing shop precisely at the moment when printing shop workers began to step into the public arena to claim authorship for themselves. During the 1870s, urban artisans began to publish their own weekly newspapers, complementing an emerging labor movement that coalesced around mutualism, a form of voluntary association in which workers pooled financial resources to aid members and mitigate their economically precarious conditions.[10] In the pages of this artisan press, workers discussed the challenges that they faced as workers—for example, vagrancy laws that targeted the underemployed and could result in the loss of citizenship. Influenced by socialism, they grappled with the "social question," parsing the relationship among workers, employers, and the state and debating the best course of action for improving workers' conditions.[11] They also argued over internal mutualist politics and published poetry in praise of beauty, love, and heroes. These writings reveal workers, like their bourgeois counterparts, to be *a particular category of intellectuals* engaged in self-conscious acts of representation as they participated in literate production.[12]

What did it mean to be a worker-intellectual in liberal Mexico? Print workers, overrepresented in the ranks that wrote for long-running artisan newspapers like *El Hijo del Trabajo* and *El Socialista*, engaged with this question in their own writings, as the author of "El cajista" did. The essay encouraged workers to stretch beyond the tasks of the shop floor to engage in intellectual activities, describing the ideal compositor as "a man who from time to time puts down the composing stick to make use of the writer's pen."[13] Writing, in turn, could lead to social advancement. "The compositor, in short," finished the article, "is a man who, starting with manipulating type, the brush and the proofing cylinder, can manage to become a newspaper editor, writer, etc."[14] Thus, printing could offer escape to a future free from manual labor altogether. In its ambivalence toward dirty work, "El cajista" suggested that it was not noble labor and capital accumulation, as liberals like Prieto claimed, but rather intellectual expression and freedom from work that paved the way for the worker's social transformation.

Printers engaged their medium in sometimes surprising ways as they navigated their in-between status and intellectual aspirations under Mexico's triumphant but contested liberal regime, contributing in the process to the mythologization of liberalism as well as to an emerging critique of its shortcomings. A unique type specimen booklet prepared by compositors in the government printing shop in 1877, in particular, shows how printers wove narration of Mexico's liberal victory into their workplace negotiations. At a moment when industrialization, economic growth, and labor radicalism increasingly preoccupied elites engaged in liberal state building, printers developed their own creative responses that reframed these issues from the printing shop floor. These expressions were influenced at once by the realities of work; the lack of dignity afforded by elites; individual and collective aspirations for recognition and transformation; and the literate culture of the printing shop, which permeated printers' imaginations. As largely self-taught intellectuals, their analyses were sometimes contradictory, betraying what Pierre Bourdieu describes as the "arbitrariness of [the autodidact's] classifications and therefore of his knowledge—a collection of unstrung pearls, accumulated in the course of an uncharted exploration."[15] Yet printers' writings represent some of the few surviving examples of popular intellectual production, reflecting lives spent laboring within the lettered city as well as a desire to participate in the drafting of its myths.

PRINTING SHOP WORK AND CULTURE

Mexico City's printing world—both state and privately sponsored—flourished in the Restored Republic and played an important role in the elaboration of liberalism as a hegemonic political discourse. Prominent liberal boosters like Cumplido and Vicente García Torres restarted their newspapers in the postwar era, reaping the rewards of their status as veteran supporters of the liberal cause (newspaper publisher Ireneo Paz noted that not only did every household in Mexico read *El Monitor Republicano*, but its owner, García Torres, had profited handsomely from the state's auctioning off of church property after Maximilian's defeat).[16] An outpouring of printed texts framed Mexico's history through the lens of liberal victory, casting conservatives as traitorous monarchist zealots who had hindered the nation's material and moral progress. Works like the richly illustrated and sensationalist *El libro rojo, 1520–1867*, for example, implicated the church in its blood-soaked depiction of Mexico's colonial past, evoking the anticlerical critique launched in *The Mysteries of the Inquisition*.[17] Much of the conservative press fell silent after Maximilian's defeat, though conservative printers found new work in the Catholic press, which emerged in the 1870s as conservatives sought new ways to organize.[18] Liberal publications, however, proliferated as new newspapers, reflecting multiplying liberal factions, gained traction alongside a satirical illustrated press that deployed the increasingly available technology of lithography as its weapon.[19]

Foremost among the places where liberal ideas and narratives crystalized in official discourse was Mexico's national government printing office, a space that brought together men from different social backgrounds around shared literary projects underwritten by the state. The printing shop's records—some of the only surviving documents that archive the laboring landscape of printing in nineteenth-century Mexico City—shed light on the work rhythms, crosscutting social interactions, and shop floor politics that intersected with state printing. These meticulous accounting documents, kept by the printing shop's first director, José María Sandoval, show an operation functioning like a well-oiled machine. The view, however, looked somewhat different from the shop floor. Even as printing shop workers interacted with the celebratory rhetoric of the liberal state, they recognized the internal hierarchies that distinguished collaborators by job type, education level, skill, and favoritism.

The spatial organization of the printing shop established clear divisions and a hierarchy among the various subspecializations that powered production in the semi-industrial workplace. Unlike in private printing shops, where owners often oversaw both technical and editorial production, the state established two directors—one for general operations and another for the government gazette—splitting manual from literary expertise. Each of the directors had his own private office, which clients and workers could enter for consultations.[20] In the back of the house, compositors worked in the shop's four composition rooms, all of which featured windows to provide natural light but possessed just one three-legged stool to discourage workers from idling. Compositors worked standing, ideally, according to one printing manual, with straight legs and smooth gestures that economized movement and increased accuracy as they plucked individual letters from the type case.[21] They gathered in the first composition room, which acted as a central meeting place, with sixteen hooks where jackets could be hung at the start of the workday; many cabinets that stored metal type; and the shop's proofing press, used to take quick, preliminary impressions for proofreading. The other composition rooms contained various combinations of tools—more type cabinets, worktables, racks to store galleys of standing type—which ensured that compositors would move back and forth within these rooms

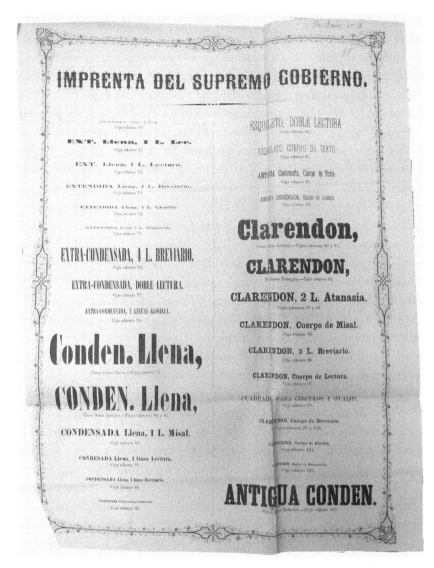

FIGURE 24. *Muestrario* created at the government printing shop, 1870. One of four made to display the shop's type collection. Archivo General de la Nación, Mexico City.

over the course of the day. On the wall in one of the composition rooms hung four large sample sheets of the shop's type collection (see figure 24). Meticulously prepared and carefully printed, these documents could be consulted for stylistic inspiration when planning out a printed composition. In addition to reproducing the name of the corresponding typeface, the sample sheets also had handy reference numbers so compositors could locate the type in its designated drawer in the type cabinet.

The printing shop had a unique sensory environment, mixing mechanical, organic, human, and animal elements. In the room reserved for proofreading, an assistant would read copy aloud as the proofreader scanned the printed document for mistakes. Proofreaders enjoyed greater luxury in the printing shop; their room was furnished with a number of chairs, lamps to augment natural light, and even an old beat-up couch for reclining while reading or waiting for proofs. Down the hall in the pressroom, the sensory environment was more intense. The pressroom was filled with four mechanical presses—all from the US manufacturer Hoe & Company, in various sizes—that could be attached to a mule-powered motor. Three other presses were operated by hand or foot power for specialized jobs, and the pressroom contained all manner of equipment for operating and maintaining the presses, from metal chases where type would be secured for printing to cylinder molds for casting new inking rollers. Suffused with animal and chemical smells and punctuated by the clopping of mule hooves and the "monotonous noise of the press, that sounded at regular intervals," the pressroom was also the most dangerous place to work, as fingers or arms could be crushed in the presses.[22] Vats for dampening paper, along with racks to dry finished prints, stood near a satin press, used to remove the buckles from freshly printed sheets. During production in the shop's pressrooms, ink was supposed to stay on the type and not migrate onto the hands of the workers who fed and removed paper from the press, where it could be transferred as smudged fingerprints onto the clean sheets, spoiling the illusion of an unmarked page and interrupting readers' attention.

In the composition rooms, inky residue from frequently used type or the proofing process would end up on compositors' hands as a matter of course, to be scrubbed off as best as possible in a basin at the end of the day, when compositors would don their jackets and head out into the city streets. Keeping ink in its proper place preoccupied not only administrators, who emphasized the importance of scrupulous cleanliness, but also compositors, whose ink-stained fingernails marked them as workers. Central to the craft and individual reputations cultivated by printers, cleanliness often depended on women's poorly remunerated labor. The only woman employed at the printing shop in 1870 worked as a full-time servant, moving through the shop's permeable spaces, sweeping up dust, scrubbing type, washing the workers' aprons, and collecting mule waste.[23]

Divisions and circuits within the printing shop revealed a working space shaped as much by its collaborative rhythms as by its internal hierarchies. On the one hand, printing shop departments were porous, and workers had plenty of opportunity to transit though the space, carrying supplies or stacks of paper from place to place, coordinating with other departments, giving or receiving orders, catching snippets of a proof's reading along the way, or overhearing the official business of the directorial team. After all, the director of the *Diario Oficial* shared his office with the workers who folded the newspapers on an oilcloth-covered table in the corner. And the printing shop director kept the shop's copy of the dictionary in his office, so compositors and proofreaders would have to enter whenever they had spelling questions. While compositors were supposed to work in silence, they were infamous for breaking the rules. Anyone's printing shop business was everyone's business. Yet spatial organization also marked lines of division. The directors' offices erected a barrier between visitors from government offices and the working spaces of the printing shop, blocking the clattering sounds of mechanical presses and perhaps stifling the wafting smell of manure from the four mules who lived on-site in an adjacent windowless stable. And the printing shop's divisions, porous as they were, corresponded to different work rhythms and pay scales, generating hierarchies as well as mythologies based on skill and job type. Many of the shop's employees received a fixed weekly salary, though the amount varied among positions (see table 1). At the top of the scale, the director of the government gazette earned significantly more than the director of the printing shop, even though the latter oversaw a much larger staff. Further down the scale, however, skilled laborers like pressmen earned more than literary workers like the assistant proofreader. The shop's lone female employee earned less than half of the next-highest-paid worker.

Printing shop compositors complicated the overarching economic bias that tilted in favor of literary production and the editorial staff. Unlike the other shop workers, they earned their pay through piecework, which produced salaries that could fluctuate radically from week to week. Though required to report to the office each morning to receive daily assignments, compositors could not anticipate steady employment.[24] Instead, their wages depended on work availability, the distribution of tasks, and the amount of labor competition at any given time. Managers played an important role in distributing tasks and (with the exception of the government gazette) preferred to assign individual *cajistas* to complete individual projects rather than breaking large composition jobs into component parts that could be completed more quickly by multiple men.[25] While some compositors might work a full day setting type for the government gazette or on a long ministerial report, others might spend just an hour or two

TABLE 1. Monthly Wages, Mexico's National
Government Printing Shop, 1870

Job Title	Monthly Wage (Pesos)
Editor of *Diario Oficial*	200
Director of printing shop	125
Editor's assistant	80
Press director	70
Proofreader	60
First pressman	40
Second pressman	36
Proofing assistant	35
Newspaper imposition	30
Translator	30
Compositor	20–700*
Workers for newspaper press	16
Press "turners"	15
Workers for the small press	15
Shop cleaner	8

SOURCES: "Impresiones: Se pide a la Tesorería General," January 1870, AGN, Gobernación, leg. 1305, caja 2, exp. 1; "Impresiones: Se pide noticia de la distribución," March 1870, AGN, Gobernación, leg. 1305, caja 2, exp. 2; and Order to Hacienda, 8 July 1870, AGN, Gobernación, leg. 1305, caja 2, exp. 2.

* Monthly estimates based on minimum and maximum weekly wages.

composing one-page circulars or decrees, which paid at a better rate but produced less overall income at the end of the day. One printers' trade journal caricatured the episodic rhythms of composition work as following the relaxed whims of the editorial staff: the *cajista* "arrives to the printing shop at 7 a.m.," respecting the rigid time discipline expected of workers, but then "goes for a stroll, smokes, and talks until ten or eleven in the morning, when the editors show up: they work an hour or less: they go back to strolling and talking, because the *original* still isn't ready."[26] For workers paid by the piece, depending on the leisurely pace of salaried writers surely provoked grumbling on smoke breaks. Yet the prospect of better work assignments also had to be factored in. At the government printing shop, where commissions fluctuated according to the state's needs, *cajistas* could outearn everyone in the printing shop when the opportunity arose. While they tended to average setting two to three hundred lines of text in a day and earned a median weekly income between five and twenty pesos, the fastest typesetters, given the work, could quintuple this output.[27] Over the course of three days, for example, one *cajista* set 2,444 lines of type, earning seventeen pesos.[28] Assigned to a particularly lengthy text, star *cajista* Manuel Aburto earned 184 pesos in a week, roughly six times the printing shop director's weekly pay and twice the yearly salary of the servant.[29]

Skill and favoritism both factored into how tasks were distributed among the compositors. There was usually one compositor in the shop who consistently set the smallest type the fastest, or perhaps enjoyed the partiality of management, and consequently received the most work. In 1875, this honor was held by José María Sierra, who on top of his frequent assignments to set 8-point type, also received a fixed salary as the *formador* who prepared the newspaper's type for press. This plum position earned him an extra 350 pesos per year plus 1 peso per week for tracking the labor and calculating the wages of his fellow compositors. When Sierra died, the news spread quickly among Mexico City's compositors, and numerous candidates applied for his job.[30] Sierra's replacement, however, was an inside hire chosen by the director of the gazette, who went on to earn some of the highest wages on the shop floor.[31]

The unpredictable work rhythms of type composition made this sector of the printing shop particularly mobile within Mexico City's broader world of print production. Worker turnover in the government printing shop was high, especially among the compositors, who came and went, dropping in to pick up occasional work or leaving for better opportunities. Indeed, of the forty-four *cajista* names listed in wage data in 1870, 1872, and 1875, only three individuals appear on the rolls in all three years.[32] The contingencies of compositor labor meant that an individual might work in fits and bursts, which offered free time for other occupations or movement in search of work opportunities. *Cajistas*, consequently, would need to be well connected if they wanted steady work. Unpredictable work rhythms also gave rise to stereotypes about "bad" *cajistas* who preferred to work the bare minimum to support a lifestyle that critics imagined as unfolding in the city's *pulquerías* and taverns. Rules at the national printing shop included prescriptions in favor of "cleanliness, order, and morality" to counter printers' perceived vices.[33] Printers were also forbidden to fraternize with potential clients, and workers could be dismissed for committing any of a number of infractions, including talking to outsiders and bringing alcohol or gambling accoutrements to work. When the printing shop director learned that one of his employees had appealed to the Ministry of the Interior for compensation after breaking an arm in a government press, he countered that the worker had already healed while receiving a partial salary, yet "only occupied himself in going to the *pulquerías* and strolling about, according to members of his own family."[34] Drawing on stereotypes of the job shirker, the director cast the worker—who described himself as a "poor artisan" recovering "from the injuries occasioned by my laborious work"—as an arrogant individual who hid under the furniture in order to evade his duties.

Unpredictable working hours and the diverse social composition of the printing shop undoubtedly stimulated the cultural projects compositors pursued off the job. When not moving through the city's various printing shops in pursuit of work, they participated actively in the organizing activities and publication program of mutualism. Without an established local guild tradition of their own, unlike many of Mexico City's artisans, printers had first met as a trade in the 1850s, founding, with lofty, republican verve, the Typographical Brotherhood Artistic Association.[35] They gained steam in the 1870s with mutualist groups like the Mexican Typography Society and Printers' Mutual Aid Society and contributed to the founding of worker conglomerates like the Gran Círculo de Obreros (Great Workers' Circle).[36] Printers' organizing efforts did not yield substantial material gains—their associations quickly fell prey to internal conflicts, and mutualism began to decline in the 1880s—but they did generate opportunities to socialize in meeting halls, celebrate at banquets, recite poetry at anniversary galas, and fulminate in the newspapers that were always a crucial first step in any organization's quest for recognition. Here, printers' workplace connections proved especially useful. Their ties to journalists and writers could be leveraged in the service of mutualist publishing projects. The newspaper *La Firmeza*, the arm of the Printers' Mutual Aid Society, for example, featured contributions from writers who also worked at the government printing office. Compositors had enlisted Andrés Clemente Vazquez, a chess master exiled from colonial Cuba who worked on Mexico's government gazette, to write for *La Firmeza*, where he contributed summaries of the association's activities and published a regular chess column on the back page.[37] In 1873, printers represented less than 3 percent of Mexico City's artisans, yet they cropped up repeatedly on the directorial boards and social calendars of mutual societies across various trades. Their access to technology may even help explain printers' ubiquity in the flurry of worker organizing during the Restored Republic—each group needed time on a printing press to publish its platform.[38] It is perhaps in their literary productions, rather than in their organizing efforts as workers, that printers' destabilizing potential was greatest.

As spaces of sociability where intellectual exchange and collaboration cut across status hierarchies and divisions of labor, printing shops featured prominently in Mexico's nineteenth-century literary imaginary. José Joaquín Fernández de Lizardi had grumbled in 1820 about writers who hung out in printing shops, describing this activity as indecorous. By the late nineteenth century, however, few journalists would imagine launching their careers in any other way. In his memoir, for instance, the writer turned diplomat Federico Gamboa (1864-1939) described his first job in a printing shop with nostalgia, highlighting the late nights, low pay, and cross-class friendships he developed on the job. Gamboa viewed his experience through rose-tinted lenses, yet printers might have found themselves depicted in a less-than-flattering light. Describing his new workplace and the bonds of fraternal camaraderie he developed there, Gamboa recounted coming to love the printing shop's compositors, "in spite of the fact that they are—in all parts of the world—the most vice-ridden workers despite their continuous brush with elevated theories, [and] humanitarian and progressive ideas."[39] Undercutting caricatures such as these emerged in teasing observations about printing shop life published by upwardly mobile journalists unsure of their own social status, resonating with older attitudes of distrust toward printers as destabilizing figures within the world of politics. Compositors in particular had become something of a literary and political trope in the press, blamed in innumerable articles whenever an error had been printed (errata often read "the *cajista* made us say . . .") or invoked to undermine the soundness of a rival's line of argumentation.[40]

The most famous caricature of a printer appeared in the 1854 *costumbrista* work *Los mexicanos pintados por sí mismos*, a commercially successful collection of social types modeled on European precedents and published during Antonio López de Santa Anna's final dictatorship.[41] The collection projected an urban, liberal vision of society, marginalizing rural, indigenous, and female characters in its imagined community while excluding religious figures altogether.[42] Individual vignettes, furthermore, used satire to examine social relations and advance reformist messages. The lithographic illustration from the vignette *El cajista* shows a compositor absentmindedly setting type while smoking and, quite ridiculously, wearing a top hat on the job (see figure 25). In the image, he appears to ape the fashions of his social superior, the editor or proofreader, who works at the back of the scene beneath a series of broadsides advertising the *cajista's* poor performance: "Opera El Fiasco," and the misspelled "Los Mexc."

The *cajista's* working-class dandyism, threatening to bourgeois masculinity, is underscored not only by his formfitting trousers but also by the accompanying text, which highlights his activities as a gossip, paramour, and social climber. Cutting him down a peg, the vignette describes the *cajista* as not an *hombre letrado* but an *hombre de letras*, casting his connection to words as a function of his physical manipulation of lead type. Most memorably, the *cajista* is so distracted on the job by his daydreams that he creates typos that transform a social announcement into a funeral notice, literally bringing about the downfall of respectable society with poor composition. The vignette smartly plays with the idea of the *cajista's* power over intellectual production by inserting a "real" compositor into the storyline, who edits out a passage of text that describes his amorous affair with a married woman, censoring the vignette's narrator by replacing his description with … (an ellipsis). Produced for bourgeois audiences, the caricature showed the *cajista* as a destabilizing figure whose ambitions threatened to undercut social order and authorial intent.

Beginning in the 1870s, printers began to contest these familiar caricatures in the newspapers that flourished alongside mutualism, and in which they, with privileged access to the press and steeped in literate culture, figured prominently. These newspapers, issued weekly and directed at urban artisans, who represented over a third of the city's workforce, acted as a forum for workers' concerns, analyzing politics; the economy; and pressing issues like the strike, nascent industrialization, or women's participation in the workforce.[43] These articles—written by a mix of workers and invited journalists—incorporated a variety of political perspectives, reflecting the heterogeneous intellectual mix that flourished in the late nineteenth century. The artisan press was also filled with poetry, character sketches, and serial novels that evidenced workers' literary aspirations, mythologies, and playfulness. Indeed, the content of the artisan press was as much about analyzing and formulating solutions to the problems facing Mexico's urban workers as it was about engaging the sphere of literate production itself. Within this context, printers were particularly concerned with rehabilitating their image not simply as respectable artisans worthy of citizenship, but also as individual and collective subjects recognized for their literary talents and contributions to intellectual life.

As autodidacts, printers betrayed their anxieties by venerating formally educated collaborators in their newspapers. They frequently highlighted their connections to literary figures with name recognition, and invited journalists and politicians to participate in activities that might raise the stature of mutualism and their newspapers. Cultural luminaries like writer and

FIGURE 25. *El Cajista. Los Mexicanos pintados por sí mismos* (Mexico City: Imprenta de M. Murguía y Comp., 1854). The Nettie Lee Benson Latin American Collection, University of Texas Libraries, University of Texas at Austin.

statesman Ignacio Altamirano (1834–1893) and exiled Cuban journalist José Martí (1853–1895) participated in the programming of the Printers' Mutual Aid Society and received recognition in the pages of *La Firmeza*.[44] Yet printers' respect for literary experts sometimes generated dissonant perspectives in the pages of their own newspapers. For example, *La Firmeza* featured a bland article by a journalist who praised mutualist organizing and the fraternal bonds it generated outside of the workshop. "All of this contributes powerfully to the enlightenment of the worker," the author explained, who is on track to one day labor "on par with workers from the most civilized countries."[45] This vision, optimistic about Mexico's prospects in relation to its European counterparts, naturalized social differences within the nation, foreclosing the possibility of Mexican workers' repositioning within local structures.

When printers addressed the theme of progress, they did so in writings colored by trade-specific mythologies about the legacy of Gutenberg and the power of print as a tool not only of enlightenment but also of social transformation. They, too, grappled with their status in a world where talk of progress increasingly dominated intellectual and political debate, especially as positivism took hold in Mexican intellectual circles in the 1870s. As autodidacts, they displayed an impressive diversity in their formulation of and answer to the "social question" facing Mexico City workers, and printers in particular. Their writings drew from the classical liberal emphasis on the individual's potential and socialist and anarchist ideas of communitarian spirit and self-reliance, filtered through the prism of the printing shop. In 1875, for example, Mexico City's most renowned and respected compositor, Juan N. Serrano, argued that printers desperately needed to change their social position. "What future awaits the unfortunate *cajista*," he asked, "who, standing all day in front of a type cabinet, exhausting his physical and moral forces, can only discern a dark and miserable future, since his difficult labor leads, just like the press operator's, to chest illness, loss of vision, moral decay, nothingness?"[46] Not only were compositors' labors vulnerable to changes in politics and the fortunes of the state; their condition was made worse by the particularities of their work. "How often does the exercise of our profession suggest ideas of progress to us," he exclaimed. "How often also, does the same enlightenment that we receive from the art only serve to make us see our unfortunate destiny as more inhumane, crueler, more tyrannical!" Compositors, Serrano argued, should take pride in being, "with our abnegation and our corporeal and intellectual work, the ones chosen to display progress to the world, given that without us the genius of illustrious men would shatter impotently."

Serrano's diagnosis offered an inversion of Gamboa's assertion that compositors were vice ridden in spite of their contact with "humanitarian and progressive ideas." Instead, he argued that they were psychologically stymied by their heightened awareness of being left behind by "progress." Serrano seemed to perceive this hurdle as part of a broader structural problem, linked to the denial of compositors' "corporeal and intellectual" contributions to literate culture. Yet his diagnosis ultimately blamed compositors, whom he charged with engaging in self-destructive behavior, including lack of esprit de corps and notorious absenteeism, especially on "Monday," the day reserved for suffering Sunday's hangover. Serrano wanted printers to become "the apostles of social progress," yet restoring their honor required upholding their end of the principle of "legal contract, without restriction, of capital and labor."[47] Whether Serrano's critique contained a kernel of truth or showed his internalization of elite attitudes toward workers, his suggestions for advancement reproduced broader discourses of mutualism that idealized harmony between capital and labor as a route to progress for workers, albeit with a distinctive printer's twist. Others echoed Serrano's interpretation. The compositor Jesús Laguna labeled *cajistas* "interpreters of thought" and "children of Guttenberg [*sic*]" and called on his fellows to manifest their status as a vanguard in the "regeneration of the worker."[48]

Printers' claims to being a special, even superior kind of artisan found expression in paeans to Gutenberg and to themselves. The young compositor Luis Alva argued in his article "Workers of the Light" that printers were the most important workers, being "sculptors of thought and ideas, carried by the ministry of their hands to far-away distances and remote generations."[49] The anonymous acrostic poem "Lira Tipográfica" echoed this characterization in its third stanza (the final acrostic of three reading GUTTENBERG, LA IMPRENTA, EL IMPRESOR):

He is the instrument of progress,
Farmer that pays it tribute;
Intelligent and invisible
Miner [illeg.] of thought;
From his type case to the wind
Speeds the fecund idea
Spreads its light that streams
Over time and mankind!

Worker, your name is obscure,
Your task, redemptive!

Es del progreso instrumento,
Labrador que le da culto;
Inteligente y oculto
Minero [illeg.] del pensamiento;
Por él de su caja al viento
Rauda la fecunda idea
Esparce su luz que ondea
Sobre los tiempos y el hombre!
Obrero, oscuro es tu nombre,
Redentora tu tarea!

Comparing compositors at their type cases to farmers casting seeds, the poem decenters the author by establishing the printer as the heroic spreader of ideas. Yet it acknowledges the printer's underappreciated status (presumably in contrast to the author's) by describing him as anonymous and unrecognized. This hidden quality of the labor of printing, the poem suggests, offers humanistic redemption to those who practice it. Others echoed this perspective with more direct arguments, describing printers as the "hidden workers and unknown collaborators of the intellectual progress of the country" and calling on them to associate to improve their education and social capital.[50]

Although printers took up the same concerns over and over again, their self-analysis produced competing assessments of the printer's social position. While some commentators described the anguish of being a literate worker unable to capitalize on this valuable skill, others decried printers' illiteracy in spite of their daily contact with words.[51] Some blamed greedy capitalists for the printer's material stagnation; others pointed to the trade's own lack of moral fiber as the source. Although many commentaries offered synchronic surveys of Mexico City's industry, others constructed (often mythical) narrative histories with opposing trajectories, either decline from a glorious past or improvement from dark days.[52] These swings in analysis—often expressed in different articles within a single newspaper edition—spoke to a multiplicity of opinion generated by printers' diverse experiences, informal education, and political goals, but evidenced a general dissatisfaction among the compositors who surveyed the field. They also revealed the difficulties in resolving the tensions embodied by printers' labor status, which led them to value intellectual recognition as much as material improvement.

PRINTING AS PERFORMANCE IN THE 1877
GOVERNMENT PRINTING SHOP

While the artisan press shows how printers expressed their aspirations to a community of likeminded readers, the shop floor represented another site where these ideas were put into action. An unusual type specimen booklet produced in 1877 offers remarkable testimony to how printers contested their situation on the job. Given their self-characterization as "workers of light" and "sculptors of thought," it is perhaps unsurprising that the printers' challenge appeared in textual form, submitted by compositors to their superiors as a printed document. Unlike most printed texts, however, this item seems to have been unique—that is, produced as a single copy, or at least in an extremely small quantity. As such, it subverts normative expectations about what printing is good for while underscoring its symbolic and performative dimensions.

The source in question emerged from the government printing shop, which in late 1876 was upended for the first time since its founding by a change in political power. General Díaz, a hero of the struggle against the French occupation, seized power after successfully overthrowing Sebastián Lerdo de Tejada during the Tuxtepec Rebellion. Winning elections that solidified his legitimacy as president, Díaz began to organize his administration. Within days of Díaz's arrival at the National Palace, the directorial slate of the government printing shop was wiped clean, and its original director, Sandoval, was replaced. The impeccable order Sandoval had demanded became a casualty of his dismissal. In the following months, under the supervision of the interior minister, the printing shop experienced constant reshuffling, with various high- and mid-level appointments and resignations.[53] Printing shop workers might have used the commotion of turnover to their advantage, quietly pilfering type and equipment and relaxing the work rhythms maintained by Sandoval. This was the appraisal given by Filomeno Mata, an inexperienced administrator who was thrust into the position of printing shop director in mid-December after his predecessor quit in the shuffle. After just a week on the job, Mata's salary doubled as he transformed from being a staffer on the government gazette to a top official. Within a month, his supervisor, himself a newly minted interior minister, requested the inevitable accounting of the state of the printing shop.

Mata knew he had to present his best face to his supervisors. As a young, ambitious man from San Luis Potosí with shallow roots in the capital, he was aware that maintaining his position, obtained through patronage, required rising to the occasion—making good on the personal connections he had already forged, first in journalism and then on the battlefield. Mata, the son of a tenant farmer-muleteer, had left a career in teaching when he struck out for Mexico City to make his fortune. He cut his teeth working for Ireneo Paz, a newspaper editor who published the anti-Lerdo satirical periodical *Padre Cobos*. Like Paz, Mata joined Díaz's Tuxtepec Rebellion, serving as a general's secretary in the Tlaxcala campaign and later receiving his appointment on the staff of the government gazette.[54] Given his tenuous position within a nascent regime, Mata had good reason to prepare his director's report with care. As a newcomer to the world of printing administration, he had little sense of how to proceed with his task and a narrow time window in which to complete it.

Mata leaned heavily on his printing shop subordinates—some of whom had remained during the government switch—to orient himself to the shop's inner workings as he prepared to draft his report.[55] Choosing his words carefully, Mata composed a narrative summary containing his evaluation and suggestions for improvement. When compared to a detailed inventory and report prepared by Sandoval in 1870, Mata's cursory description betrayed his inexperience. While Sandoval, a printer by trade, had mastery over protocols like forming inventories (a practice generally conducted for monetary evaluation that involved sorting and weighing type and describing machinery with careful precision), Mata's familiarity with printing came from having worked as a journalist in the employ of experienced printing shop owners. In an unusual twist, once the draft of his narrative was complete, Mata handed over his copy to the composition department. Deploying printing shop labor to prepare an internal memo, Mata chose to present his superiors with a printed document. The usual laborious or slapdash scripts of routine bureaucratic correspondence were replaced in this instance with the neat, regular forms of a script typeface, which itself mimicked, ironically, human handwriting (see figure 26).

Imagine what the compositor assigned to the job would have thought as he absorbed Mata's report in the process of transforming the handwritten document into print, probably for the wage of one peso. The text was far from complimentary, although most of the harshest criticisms were aimed at the former director, who was no longer in the picture. Mata first targeted the composition department, kingdom of the *cajistas*, which he explained had "suffered much due to its state of abandonment."[56] Mata blamed printing shop employees for this lamentable state. "The final days of life of the past administration were fatal for this office," he wrote, "as the workers, on pretext that the personnel was going to change, after printing several forms, did

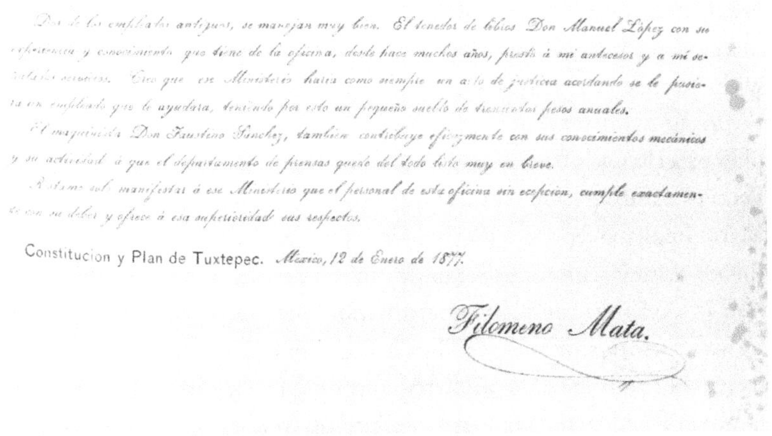

Dos de los empleados antiguos, se manejan muy bien. El tenedor de libros Don Manuel López con su experiencia y conocimiento que tiene de la oficina, desde hace muchos años, prestó á mi antecesor y a mí señalados servicios. Creo que ese Ministerio hará como siempre un acto de justicia acordando se le proporcione un empleado que le ayudara, teniendo por esto un pequeño sueldo de trescientos pesos anuales.

El maquinista Don Faustino Sánchez, tambien contribuye eficazmente con sus conocimientos mecánicos y su actividad á que el departamento de prensas quede del todo listo muy en breve.

Réstame solo manifestar á ese Ministerio que el personal de esta oficina sin ecepcion, cumple exactamente con su deber y ofrece á esa superioridad sus respectos.

Constitucion y Plan de Tuxtepec. Mexico, 12 de Enero de 1877.

Filomeno Mata.

FIGURE 26. Detail of report prepared by Filomeno Mata and printed with his signature using a script typeface, 1877. Archivo General de la Nación, Mexico City.

not proceed to distribute them, causing by this a jumble of different types" and requiring the exclusive labor of two men to clean up this "most complete disarray." Mata also referenced a set of examples of all the typefaces contained within the printshop, which he submitted as proof positive of poor printing shop conditions: "The types in general, as you will see in the examples (*muestras*) that I attach, are very abused." The pressroom did not escape Mata's critical eye either, receiving citation for "excessive abandonment" due to a combination of worker laxity and directorial mismanagement.

Mata's report, in sum, depicted the printing shop as a place in need of reform and positioned him as the man for the job. Yet by choosing to have it set in type and printed, Mata revealed its contents to the entire printing shop—not just to a handful of superiors in the Ministry of the Interior. This journalist turned bureaucrat obviously believed that printing his report would lend his words an authoritative air or augment his prestige. Why else would he waste government resources to produce a report intended for an extremely narrow audience? Although new to the job, he surely understood that the shop would quickly become aware of his somewhat unflattering depiction. News of the content of Mata's report must have spread quickly from the composition room. Perhaps workers accused Mata of exaggerating the state of the printing shop to bolster his own image in the eyes of his superiors. Workers were surely not flattered by Mata's suggestion that they had failed in their duties but would have supported his request for funds to replace worn-out equipment. Although the report portrayed workers' actions negatively, it ultimately exculpated their behavior by laying the final blame firmly on the previous director. Mata's closing words left no doubt about his intentions to work with—rather than against—his subordinates: "It remains only for me to convey to the Ministry that the personnel of this office, without exception, complies exactly with their duties and sends their respects to their superiors."[57] Perhaps printing shop workers weighed the positive and negative aspects of Mata's finalized report in shop conversations as they moved about the space in their routine circuits or broke for the midday meal. Was Mata offering protection in exchange for their subordination and cooperation? Did he have to tarnish their reputations as skilled artisans in order to make his demands for increased funding to the ministry, and were his insults to their professional honor justified by the pursuit of better shop conditions for all?

When Mata instructed his employees to produce an accounting of the printing shop's typefaces to accompany his report, he gave them the opportunity to offer their own commentary. While he may have given some direction on the document he envisioned, Mata likely relied on the compositors' professional know-how as he familiarized himself with his new responsibilities. Perhaps he delegated the task to a *cajista* who knew his way around, or maybe to a newcomer who might have felt beholden to the new director. Perhaps, unaccustomed to the typical practice of assigning one job to one individual, he set several compositors to work on the same item to speed up the process. One wonders whether the display posters, produced in 1870 under Sandoval's experienced eye, still hung on the wall of the composition room as guides to the shop's type collections (figure 24). Had the sheets been stashed away, torn and irrelevant? Did any compositors remain in the shop from the group that had produced the earlier version? Undoubtedly some had seen the type catalogs produced in Mexico City printing shops or sent from the United States by the New York–based Bruce & Co. type foundry, which, unlike the utilitarian examples made during Sandoval's tenure, played with the genre of the type specimen to delightful effect.[58]

The document ultimately produced at the government printing shop in 1877 bore a stylistic affinity with the genre of the type specimen, a professional reference work produced by type foundries, printing shops, and distributors to display and identify typefaces. In Mexico City, major printers—Manuel Antonio Valdés, Mariano Galván Rivera, Ignacio Cumplido, Rafael de Rafael, and José Mariano Fernández de Lara—had already produced specimens of their type stock.[59] While utilitarian and commercial in nature, these specimens also used graphic and textual features to craft a printer's image: the

FIGURE 27. *Muestra de los carácteres de la imprenta de Don José M. Lara* (Mexico City: Imprenta de Don José M. Lara, 1855). Newberry Library, Chicago.

liberal Cumplido used international news headlines, factoids, and important liberal milestones to present his eye-catching typefaces; the conservative Fernández de Lara excerpted religious texts and reprinted his own name ad nauseam in a show of professional bravado (see figure 27); and Rafael exhibited his impressive multicolored presswork.[60] In addition to showcasing the stylistic qualities of multiple typefaces, a typical nineteenth-century type specimen also denoted their names, along with reference numbers, which indexed a particular typeface's physical components or location. The 1877 example, which Mata referred to as a *muestra* (sample), contained no naming or numbering system, making it a professionally useless document and arguably not a true type specimen. After all, why include a numbering system for a document that would be sent to the bosses, clueless paper pushers who might not recognize a type specimen if they saw one?

Nevertheless, the *muestra* opens a window onto the intellectual world of the printing shop, reproducing, as it undoubtedly does, textual content cooked up by the shop's compositors. Perhaps the *cajistas* decided to have a little fun; without a fastidious director like Sandoval to hold them accountable, they could experiment with the form and content of their type specimen and not be overly concerned with producing the kind of rigid, uncreative document embodied in the perfectly printed 1870 posters (figure 24). When they composed the 1877 *muestra*, printing shop workers seized the opportunity of bureaucratic accounting to address their superiors in line after line of erudite references, witty slogans, and thinly veiled demands. These demands, presented in worn-out and damaged type, underscored and amplified Mata's own calls for greater printing shop resources. In this sense, the document was less about worker resistance than about appropriation and agreement. But the *muestra* also communicated a message that tested the limits of acceptable genre conventions to claim and convey mastery over a cultural capital not normally ascribed by elites to practitioners of the skilled and manual trades. Such a privilege, after all, was generally reserved for men like Mata, who through his use of writing and printing had the opportunity to compose and convey lengthy narratives to bureaucratic superiors and as a result potentially change working conditions that would affect employees. Thus, when the *cajistas* stepped out from their assigned role as mindless reproducers of texts, they claimed status as "the intellectual *producers* who elaborate (rather than merely transmitting) ideological messages"—as rightful members of the lettered city itself, fully entitled to map out its contours and determine who (and what) else deserved admission and esteem.[61]

A TYPE SPECIMEN AS TREATISE: MEXICO'S POLITICAL DRAMA WRITTEN FROM BELOW

The *muestra* indeed forms a textual map scattered across its eleven unsystematically designed and composed pages, in which an educated reader finds the names of hundreds of recognizable places, important historical figures, political leaders, and cultural luminaries. Even at a casual glance, the names of illustrious individuals—almost exclusively men—jump off the pages (see figure 28).

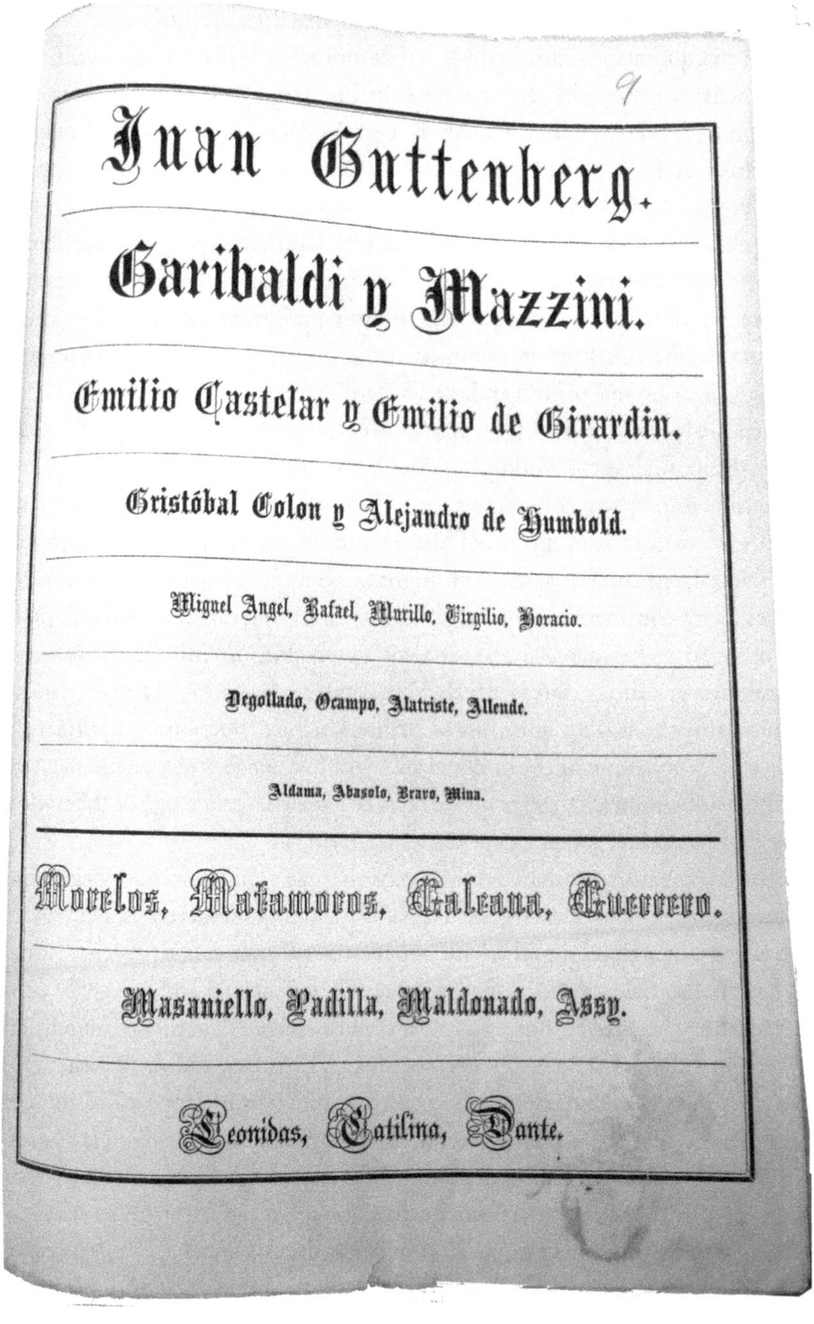

FIGURE 28. *Muestra* created at the government printing shop, 1877. Archivo General de la Nación, Mexico City.

A second examination reveals passages of texts—brief phrases that contain aphorisms, quotations, and factoids—that more closely resembled the kinds of specimens produced in the private printing shops of Galván Rivera and Cumplido. Under systematic analysis, certain contours emerge that help us read this map for its broader message.[62] The *muestra*'s central themes are politics, geography, and the humanities and sciences, expressed in wide-ranging references linked with particular historical moments, people, and places. Allusions to Mexico's recent history (approximately a third of the textual references) share space with references to contemporary events unfolding internationally: the ongoing processes of Italian unification, for instance, and industrialization in England and the United States. Contemporary references, in turn, are interspersed with the names of historical figures dating back to the Greco-Roman classical world. The document's nonlinear juxtapositions collapse time and space, converging the living and the dead in a manner that reveals its creators' conceptions of history and the political stakes of historical narration. In genre terms, the text might be thought of as a search for origin stories about the liberal nation, specifically stories that could amplify its makers' own claims for material and intellectual recognition. Indeed, the *muestra* contains several direct statements that break out of the narrative frame in order to proclaim the unique position of printers within liberalism's civilization project. Keenly aware of the political stakes of history making, particularly in the midst of regime change, print workers composed a genealogy of the nation that expressed their social and political aspirations.

The compositors constructed their genealogy as a pantheon of political and cultural heroes. With the largest share of its references reserved for Mexicans, the *muestra* contributed to the "cult of personality" that accompanied a "surge in nationalist themes and topics in various publications and imagery" produced after the French defeat as liberal elites reconstituted and redefined national pride in volumes devoted to Mexico's history and achievements.[63] The document's secondary attention to geographical and geopolitical themes echoed the vision advanced by preeminent mapmaker Antonio García Cubas, whose influential geography textbook *Curso elemental de geografía universal* had been printed at the government printing shop in 1869. The *muestra*'s creators were perhaps more cosmopolitan in their orientation, eager to place the nation in a broader regional and international context. For example, they nodded to a shared hemispheric history in the descending juxtaposition of "Simon Bolívar, Jorge Washington, and Benjamin Franklin," who appear under the prominent headline of newly elected president Díaz (see figure 29).

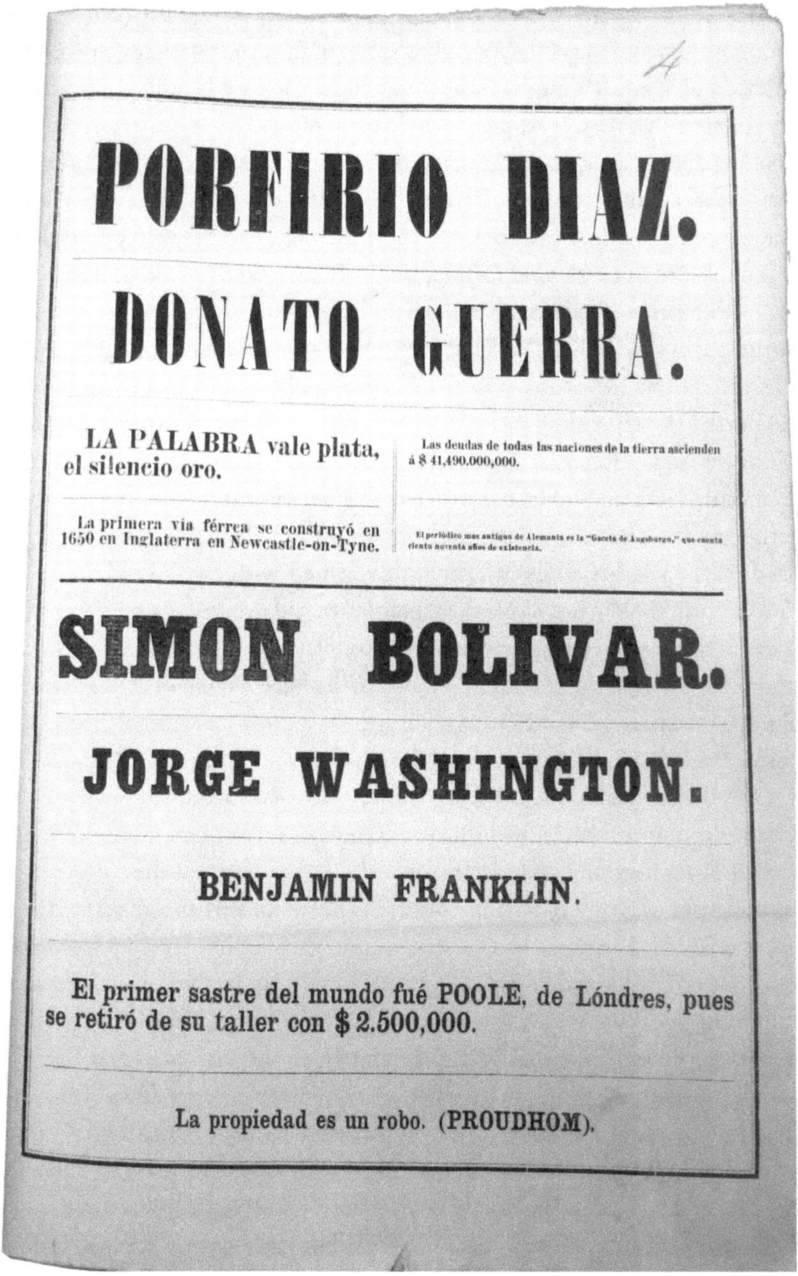

PORFIRIO DIAZ.

DONATO GUERRA.

LA PALABRA vale plata, el silencio oro.

Las deudas de todas las naciones de la tierra ascienden á $ 41,490.000,000.

La primera via férrea se construyó en 1650 en Inglaterra en Newcastle-on-Tyne.

El periódico mas antiguo de Alemania es la "Gaceta de Augsburgo," que cuenta ciento noventa años de existencia.

SIMON BOLIVAR.

JORGE WASHINGTON.

BENJAMIN FRANKLIN.

El primer sastre del mundo fué POOLE, de Lóndres, pues se retiró de su taller con $ 2.500,000.

La propiedad es un robo. (PROUDHOM).

FIGURE 29. *Muestra* created at the government printing shop, 1877. Archivo General de la Nación, Mexico City.

In political matters, the document articulated urgent links between Mexico's recent history and the struggles and successes of European nations, especially in France and Spain. Throughout the nineteenth century, Mexican political elites and intellectuals developed their ideas in dialogue with European liberal thinkers and political struggles. Avid students of comparative politics, they consumed the weekly column of former Spanish president Emilio Castelar (referenced in the *muestra*), which shaped Mexico's political debate over the thirty years that it was published in *El Monitor Republicano*.[64] The *muestra*, too, showed compositors' awareness of the republican experiments unfolding across the Atlantic, citing Spain's recently failed First Republic (1873–1874) and France's nascent Third Republic (1870–1940) in references to politicians and journalists who supported the republican cause. Mentions of the French journalist Émile de Girardin and politicians Louis Blanc, Adolphe Thiers, and Alphonse de Lamartine, among others, constructed an international community under a rather capacious republican political tent, strong in its liberal leanings but sprinkled with socialists and anarchists (represented with the Proudhon quote, "Property is Theft"). Just as Mexican politicians had debated the merits of these ideas in the Mexico City press before the country had descended into civil war and occupation in the 1850s, the *muestra* articulated a bond of solidarity with European counterparts still struggling against the self-proclaimed reactionary forces of monarchy.[65] Mexico, after all, had secured its republican victory.

The document's political story showed Mexico in the vanguard of the liberal republican world. Its numerous references to writers, composers, artists, philosophers, and scientists posited this achievement as the culmination of centuries of intellectual and cultural expression. Perhaps unsurprisingly, these references betrayed the Western canonical bent of the *muestra*'s world, which privileged ancient Greece and Rome along with the Romance language–speaking regions that would become France, Spain, and Italy as sources of literary and artistic inspiration. Thus, classical poets and Spanish Golden Age dramaturges share space with French philosophes and Mexican and Italian opera composers and interpreters. In fact, Rossini and Verdi, whose operas were extremely popular in Mexico City's theaters, are the only references repeated in the document. Perhaps one of the *cajistas* had caught a performance in the Gran Teatro Nacional or the Teatro Principal, venues that attracted a diverse patronage eager to hear international music stars like Ángela Peralta and Adelina Patti, who also featured in the *muestra*.[66]

The *muestra*'s absences provoke questions about the assumptions and biases of its creators. Industry and technology, however large they would come to loom in late-century notions of secular progress, barely appear in the document. The railway, for example, makes just one understated appearance, in spite of the recent inauguration of the Mexico City–Veracruz line in 1873. References to commercial and technological innovation—particularly directed toward the United States and England—do convey a sense of burgeoning industry, but only beyond Mexico's borders. Were the compositors trying to downplay Mexico's underperformance, was progress mania still a largely elite affair, or did its elision suggest a deeper ambivalence toward technological change rooted in fears of being displaced by automated typesetting machines that seemed poised to burst onto the market?

Other conspicuous absences reveal that compositors imagined their community of world-shaping heroes in gendered and socially exclusionary terms. The paucity of women (with the exception of Roman goddesses; only four real women are represented: Dolores Guerrero, a Mexican poet; opera stars Patti and Peralta; and Marie Antoinette, the *muestra*'s only antihero) casts the compositors' historical pantheon as a reflection of the printing shop's homosocial imaginary. Even if women were increasingly entering the industrial workforce in Mexico City (making up 32% in an 1879 census), the printing trades were predominantly (even exclusively, according to the same census) male, and the *muestra*, relying as it does on extolling the virtues of public men, affords little room for women in the story.[67] Male heroism, indeed, forms the intellectual and emotive base of the compositors' history.[68]

The *muestra*'s exclusions emerged out of a professional habitus steeped in the veneration of Western literate culture but insecure about its position vis-à-vis other social groups. Virtually no pre-Columbian heroes appear in the document, departing from the elite practice of rendering Mexico's indigenous past as a preamble to national history in patriotic discourse (only Nezahualcoyotl, the Mexica poet-philosopher ruler, appears).[69] The document does not celebrate the history of the conquest; no conquistadors appear in its references, though Christopher Columbus is recast, paired with Alexander von Humboldt, as a scientist-explorer. Neither Hispanist nor indigenist in orientation, it ignores most of Mexico's complex "prehistory" altogether, eschewing the space-time continuities commonly constructed by nation builders. Instead, it selectively appropriates European history for Mexico. The *muestra* does not necessarily hold Europe as a model for the future; instead, it implies that liberalism's spirit found its fullest expression and greatest political success after it jumped the Atlantic and took hold in Mexico, where republicanism flourished.[70] Consequently, this story contains its own prejudicial elisions, especially in its silence on enduring racial inequalities, the legacies of colonialism, and the place of indigenous communities within the nation-state. The compositors' silence on race and claiming of a mythologized European history as the basis for the liberal political project likely reflects one or several factors: printers' habitus and the urban prejudices that viewed indigenous communities as unproductive and backward, uneasiness about their own socio-racial status, or their construction of liberalism as promising race- and caste-blind justice.[71]

If the *muestra* is largely silent on race, it explicitly intervenes in a long-running conversation about the value of formal education and its links to social advancement. To counter the assumption of *cajista* ignorance, its creators compiled and prepared what amounted to a display of common knowledge, expressing a desire for respect or recognition within the exclusive world being depicted. To leverage this claim, the compositors interspersed moralizing phrases, aphorisms, and direct statements that established a clearer tone for the *muestra*'s immediate purpose, which underscored and moved beyond the printing shop director Mata's own aims in ordering the preparation of this document. Indeed, unlike workers who in other historical circumstances might have used a "distinctive working class voice" to critique and transform the social order, the compositors generally reproduced the elite discourse that was used to deny them full participation.[72] Yet their selections and fragmentary statements contain inconsistencies that hint at discontent with, or at least discussion of, the status quo and reveal the emerging contours of a liberal intellectualism with a popular bent: an alternative to the positivist ideas and fascination with progress crystallizing among elites and influencing journalism and university curricula in Mexico City in the 1870s. On the one hand, the *muestra* suggests—in classic liberal parlance that identifies education as a remedy for social inequality—that "if legislators are interested in the prosperity of the people, the worker's absolute independence would be their second task: mass instruction would be the first." On the other, the document defines and defends printers' status as informally educated individuals. "Talent is worth more than instruction," it proclaims, recalling the moniker of the *hombre de talento*, an honorific commonly reserved among journalists for the best public writers, who received recognition for their individual merits rather than inherited privileges.[73] Here, the compositors seize the title for themselves, valorizing informal know-how and natural ability over institutionally acquired knowledge. The sequence reads like an internal dialogue being hashed out by a *cajista* as he works through various themes of liberal discourse, playing with their creative appropriation to contest social prejudice.

For all its broader claim making, the *muestra* shows its creators' awareness of the political stakes of storytelling, even in its scattershot form. Though the document is full of Mexican liberal heroes—of the independence era, the Reforma wars, and the Tuxtepec Rebellion—it conspicuously omits Juárez, the liberal president credited with dogged resistance to French occupation and salvation of the Mexican republic.[74] Conservative political figures are categorically excluded from the document, but neither Juárez nor his presidential successor, Lerdo de Tejada, appears. Instead, the recently triumphant Díaz (and his interim president Juan N. Méndez) is feted as the inheritor of Mexico's liberal tradition, while Juárez's absence hovers around the document like the negative space surrounding the printed letters, throwing the *muestra*'s partisan and strategic allegiances into sharp relief.

The *cajistas* pressed their claims most expertly on the *muestra*'s penultimate page, whose posterior placement suggests that even they were uncomfortable with their own wit. Although the document contains a fair amount of subtle politicking, embedded in the strategic juxtaposition of names, comments, and aphorisms, the compositors staged their boldest demands on page 10, where the name of the interim president, Juan N. Méndez, appears in boldface, authoritative letters (see figure 30). Directly below, the name of Protasio P. Tagle, the minister of the interior and the government printing shop's direct supervisor, is printed in a novelty display typeface. Next, a clearly legible roman script—stylistically out of place on a page dominated largely by decorative display faces—proclaims: "The printing shop of the Federal Government finds itself in a lamentable state." Next, the smaller typeface reading, "Talent is worth more than instruction," appears, followed by an even smaller phrase, "Liberty is a common cause." In flowery print, the names of three figures associated with the Protestant Reformation and resistance to Catholic orthodoxy—Luther, Calvin, and Savonarola—appear. And, in a popular nineteenth-century typeface that mimics logs of wood, "Printing is Light."

With one of several direct statements that break from the narrative frame to comment directly on the state of the real government printing shop, the compositors reproduced the complaints leveled in their director Mata's report, which decried the poor condition of the shop's type. Their broader claim, which they achieve through a particularly pointed linkage between the printing shop, its overseeing superiors, and the very possibility of enlightened thought, is clear. When the compositors choose talent over instruction, grasp at freedom, and herald printing as the embodiment of enlightenment, they cast themselves as the heroes in their own story. They almost seem to

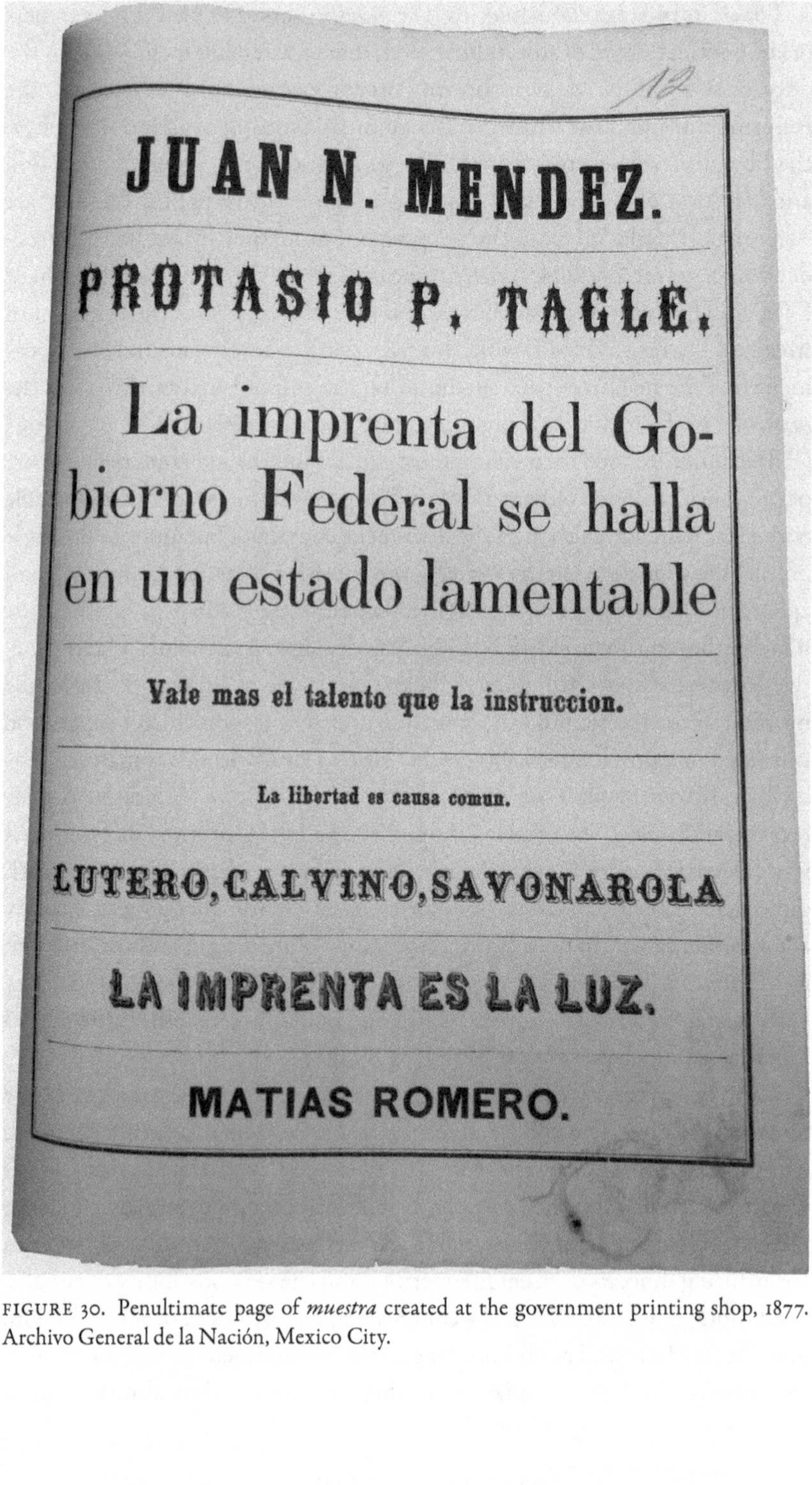

12

JUAN N. MENDEZ.

PROTASIO P. TAGLE.

La imprenta del Gobierno Federal se halla en un estado lamentable

Vale mas el talento que la instruccion.

La libertad es causa comun.

LUTERO, CALVINO, SAVONAROLA

LA IMPRENTA ES LA LUZ.

MATIAS ROMERO.

FIGURE 30. Penultimate page of *muestra* created at the government printing shop, 1877. Archivo General de la Nación, Mexico City.

equate their efforts with those of Luther, Calvin and Savonarola; their crusade, ostensibly one of reform against intolerable conditions, in fact seeks recognition within the exclusive world they so thoroughly inhabited through their work behind the scenes.

CONCLUSION: COMPOSING VERSE AT THE COMPOSITION STICK

The *muestra* offers a rare view of how *cajistas* communicated their worth to superiors within Mexico's world of intellectual production after the triumph of liberalism. Complementing compositors' arguments in the artisan press, the document's creators challenged their second-class status, describing themselves as essential to the broader project of literate culture. Emerging out of compositors' experiences at the intersection of manual and intellectual worlds, the document advanced an alternative vision of authority and creativity based not on formal education or individual genius, but around collaborative production and scrappy self-reliance.

Unfortunately for the staff of the government printing shop, however, these claims went unheeded during the Tuxtepec transition. Before long the leadership of the government printing office had been shuffled again, and compositors clashed with its new director, going on strike to protest his proposal to lower their wages.[75] In an exposé letter in the artisan press, a compositor accused the new director, himself a printer, of violating the egalitarian ethic of the shop floor. Since he had ascended to power, the writer argued, he had begun treating former friends "in sultanic fashion" and referred to the compositors with the insulting term *operarios* instead of *artesanos*.[76] The *cajistas* framed their strike as a struggle for dignity and respect. This respect had been denied by a fellow printer who, in his promotion to management, had apparently violated the displays of fraternal camaraderie *cajistas* demanded on the job. While the strike ended and printers blamed the director for lowering wages, shop records revealed that compositors' fee structure remained stable after the incident.[77] This was, perhaps, cold comfort considering that wages remained unchanged for the next twenty years, translating into a loss of earnings over time.[78] The director, however, targeted compositors in an 1880 proposal for new shop rules, ordering them to "observe in all their acts the best decency and composure, avoid treating their companions with scorn or insolence, [and] avoid provoking quarrels, which will be reprimanded with the greatest severity."[79] The director rightly viewed *cajistas'* demands for respect, founded in their social aspirations and literate status, as challenges to his authority.

Even as a growing sector of compositors lost earning power across the span of Díaz's tenure, the expansion of government printing during his rule opened new opportunities for those able to capitalize on connections forged on the shop floor. Luis Rubin, for example, rose from *cajista* to direct the printing shop of the Ministry of Public Works (Fomento), which was founded in 1883.[80] When not overseeing daily operations at the press or preparing reports, Rubin gave recitations of his poetry at mutualist meetings around the city, receiving acclaim for his sentimental readings. Rubin not only published regularly in artisan newspapers; he also used the ministry's presses to release entire volumes of his own poetry.[81]

Networks and relationships forged in government printing shops facilitated printers' careers in the private sector and fueled their literary ambitions. Mata, who briefly directed the national printing shop under Díaz, soon started his own business, where he applied his experience to publish *El Diario del Hogar*, a bourgeois daily that took a surprising turn to become one of Díaz's most outspoken and tenacious critics. Mata brought Aurelio Garay, also a former *cajista* at the government printing shop, along with him, and Garay capitalized on his literary talents to become a proofreader for *El Diario del Hogar*. On the side, Garay wrote an urban underworld thriller called *The Hydra: Memoir of a Suicide*, which he published pseudonymously in the artisan press before the lure of fame became irresistible and he claimed public credit after six months of serialization. Inspired by the work of French luminaries like Victor Hugo and Eugène Sue, Garay pitched *The Hydra* as a social novel that would expose, for working-class audiences, the seven secular sins of ignorance, fanaticism, opulence, usury, prostitution, drunkenness, and gambling in Mexico City.[82] Its byzantine plot of urban intrigue, reflecting the author's anti-conservative politics, unfolds in the aftermath of the French intervention, as a depraved former collaborator tries to seduce a poor, innocent girl. Alongside love triangles, scheming relatives, and a catastrophic ending in which the story's villain kills himself after devastating revelations about a former lover, the real printing shops of liberal luminaries Cumplido and García Torres make cameos in the novel as sites for working-class education and transformation. While one young character had started out in the printing shop as a barefoot illiterate, "now," according to an approving street vendor whose folksy dialect marks her uneducated status, "he says he makes those 'ditorials (hora dizque hace esos ditoriales)" and has the "proves to show for it (le ha enseñado las prebas)."[83] Here, Garay nods to an insider audience of printer-readers, since the ignorant street vendor is unaware of the ambiguities of the young man's position: is he a writer or, more probably, a type compositor, proudly showing the printers' proofs from the newspaper as evidence of his success?

In Garay's novel, as in his own life, printing shops served as potential sites of working-class transformation, though the process was not an easy one. Garay was working on his novel even as he mentored the young journalist Gamboa, who was also employed by Mata on *El Diario del Hogar*'s culture beat. Gamboa, who developed a friendship with and admiration for Garay, lovingly yet humiliatingly described Garay's social struggles in his memoir, which he published at the age of twenty-eight. "To prevent the editors from looking down on him," Gamboa related, "he chose a sort of *tapanco* or attic in the back of the printing shop, closer to the roof than the floor; he read and studied unceasingly to prevent his letters from scorning him."[84] Gamboa's chronicle subtly undercut Garay, even as it recognized his achievement, by exposing struggles to earn respect that he had clearly hoped to hide. Yet Gamboa admitted that the former *cajista* had offered useful advice. Garay's suggestion, made during some late-night revelry, to "write like you speak," perhaps inspired Gamboa as he wrote his own novels after leaving the printing shop behind to join the ranks of the Porfirian administration.[85] The dense printing networks that crisscrossed the city's private sector and expanding state institutions provided avenues for individuals able to navigate job performance, political patronage, and personal connections, but printers' ability to transform these experiences into transcendent cultural examples faced an uphill battle.

The everyday conflicts that unfolded inside the printing shop and found expression not only in printers' texts but also in memoirs and novels written by formally educated intellectuals reveal the expanded significance of the printing shop as a contested sociocultural space in the Mexican liberal and literary imagination. As printing flourished during the Restored Republic and early tenure of Díaz, its communities had more opportunities to represent its working spaces as something other than a site of inky subterfuge and instability. Negative characterizations endured, to be sure, but the printing shop also appeared—and even served, in some cases—as a place where ambition and talent could find an outlet in a society organized as a liberal republic.

Even as printers' literary endeavors reached a high point, a new generation of intellectuals was beginning to reframe liberalism, arguing that traditional political action should be displaced by "scientific politics" based on facts and observation.[86] Proponents of this "new liberalism" rejected the democratic valences and combative republican spirit of the Reforma era in favor of social order in the service of economic growth. Díaz, who began to consolidate a more powerful national state during his second presidency, absorbed these reformers into the ranks of his administration, embracing "order and progress" as central themes. Yet some of the most tenacious political challenges to a regime that would endure for nearly thirty years emerged out of the original Tuxtepec conjuncture, encapsulated in the resistance of former printing shop administrator Mata. Once the recipient of political patronage, Mata broke with the regime, offering a counterproposal that drew upon Mexico's classical liberal tradition to criticize General Díaz's policies. Mata's appropriation of the liberal printing shop tradition to formulate his politics of opposition highlighted the legacies of previous generations as printing politics transformed in the face of an increasingly powerful state.

SEVEN

———————

Criminalizing the Printing Press

IN 1906, THE DIRECTOR OF MEXICO CITY'S correctional school for boys asked the city's governor for permission to use two printing presses stored in the school's warehouse. Due to the dampness of the storage area, these presses, along with cases of metal type, had begun to oxidize and deteriorate.[1] Wouldn't it be better, the director proposed, to get them back into working order, so that they could be used in the printing shop of the correctional school? After all, it had been years since government officials had confiscated the presses from their previous owners, Daniel Cabrera and Juana Belén Gutiérrez de Mendoza (1875–1942). These critics of the regime of Porfirio Díaz, in power since 1884, had lost presses once used to publish opposition newspapers in legal battles adjudicated by an unsympathetic state. Now, the reform school's director hoped he could harness confiscated technology to transform poor adolescent offenders into productive workers. The director met with an unsatisfactory response. According to a local judge, the paperwork for the cases had been lost, so no determination on the equipment could be made. By 1910, however, the presses may well have been brought out from storage, their time served and ready for new life. An image published in a printers' trade magazine, part of a feature story on government printing, offered a glimpse of Mexico City's correctional school, where incarcerated youths posed with the presses (see figure 31).[2] Could these be the same machines seized a decade earlier? Under the watchful eye of two instructors, the boys and the presses underwent a mutual process of rehabilitation, their movements and output oriented toward officially sanctioned ends.

The example of confiscated presses being repurposed by the state to train incarcerated youths encapsulates broader shifts in official thinking about printing in relation to law, politics, and society in late nineteenth-century

FIGURE 31. *Departamento de prensas de la Escuela Correcional de Tlalpam* [*sic*], *D.F.* "Las imprentas del gobierno en México," *El Arte Tipográfico*, July 1910. The Rare Book & Manuscript Library, Columbia University.

Mexico. Once mythologized by liberals as a bulwark against tyranny, the printing press gained new associations, during the thirty-year tenure of Díaz, with the creation of a productive, efficient, and orderly nation. Díaz consolidated his position in Mexican politics while expanding the power of the state. Looking abroad to reestablish Mexico's credit and find investors for infrastructure and industrialization projects, Porfirian administrators strengthened private property protections to pave the way for economic growth. While policy makers emphasized law and order, ordinary people experienced a reign that combined formal emphasis on the rule of law with instances of brutal repression, often carried out at the hands of powerful *jefes políticos* (regional political leaders).[3] Room for negotiating over political speech, furthermore, narrowed as Díaz's tenure wore on.

Though the regime borrowed many well-worn tactics from the early republican era to manage criticism in print, it also capitalized on a changed sociopolitical climate to exert greater influence. Many of Díaz's bourgeois supporters had turned away from the democratic valences and promises of social transformation highlighted in popular iterations of liberalism. Intellectuals and officials instead advocated a new form of "scientific politics" that rejected political confrontation in favor of administrative policy making.[4] The boisterous public sphere that had flourished in the 1870s increasingly looked like an unruly hindrance to progress. Having mastered the state's own printing apparatus, officials set their sights on Mexico City's world of production, aided by legal changes that recast press infractions as crimes. For criminologists in Porfirian Mexico, punishment served as a tool of social conditioning, capable of changing undesirable behaviors that reformers argued were determined by environmental or hereditary factors.[5] More than just a tactic to silence journalists or punish dissent, the Díaz regime's new legal approach sought to reshape printing in the service of progress.

The state's criminalization of printing, which construed printers as potential agents of disorder, drew from familiar formulations that cast printing shops as disruptive and politically suspicious spaces. At the same time, it claimed expanded power to intervene in production by reclassifying printing presses as weapons whose improper use threatened to undermine political stability and economic growth. Consequently, vocational programs like the one at the correctional school aimed to introduce poor urban youths to printing in a controlled environment, devoid of the political commitments and social ferment that historically flourished on Mexico City's shop floors. Rather than receiving a workplace education informed as much by artisanal training as by literate culture and print-world sociability, young delinquents were supposed to be molded into a compliant workforce, ready to serve the expanding needs of an industrializing economy.[6] While the actual success of these training programs was modest at best, trade schools, which flourished under state auspices and also in a range of private settings, broadened the scope of efforts to direct and channel print production from above, adding new dimensions to familiar government strategies that sought to police and mold the public sphere.[7]

A broader set of processes aided state efforts to channel printing during the late nineteenth century. During Díaz's tenure, Mexico City's printing world was transformed, shaped not only by coercive or violent political pressure but also by economic, technological, and cultural changes associated with urbanization and industrialization. Once linked inextricably with politics, the printing sector developed a more heterogeneous set of business strategies and commitments as economic growth brought new opportunities for specialization. More printers found success doing job work, producing commissioned materials like forms, letterhead, preprinted ledgers, and invoices that served Mexico's expanding commercial sector.[8] Niche presses like the one operated by publisher Antonio Vanegas Arroyo sprang up to produce cheap popular ephemera, targeting a growing working class and recently arrived rural migrants. The penny press, which flourished at the turn of the century, used satire and gentle self-mockery to reform working-class sensibilities while asserting the importance of artisans and workers within the nation.[9] Catholic publishing ventures, too, expanded as activists used printing to reengage politics and envision a more socially committed church in the wake of conservative defeat.[10] With the financial support of the government, a commercial press that explicitly disavowed politics and shifted toward a news- and information-based model emerged for the first time, equipped with state-of-the-art printing facilities and capable of churning out large runs of newspapers, to be sold for a cent. Despite the assertions of entrepreneurs like Rafael Reyes Spíndola, who pioneered this style of journalism in *El Universal* (1888) and *El Imparcial* (1896), the commercial press implicitly and explicitly supported the Díaz regime.[11] Reyes Spíndola was a member of Díaz's inner circle of advisers, a group that in 1892 was dubbed the *científicos* for advocating a nonpartisan, "scientific" outlook on government administration. By the turn of the century, the commercial press had displaced a broader field of political commentary, having consolidated its presence in newspaper production with state support.[12]

The rise of job printing and the commercial press pushed printing toward serving as a disciplined and disciplinary arm of the Porfirian state's project of order and progress, to be achieved through cutting-edge technologies. At midcentury, only a handful of the city's largest printing shops incorporated mechanical presses powered by humans or animals. By the last decades of the nineteenth century, however, mechanization had become more common, and presses could be attached to steam- and later electric-powered motors that sped up production.[13] New "jobbing" presses that automated ink distribution and economized labor accelerated the creation of ephemera in the pressroom, even if type composition remained unchanged until the early twentieth century, demanding an expanding workforce of *cajistas*. Beyond the pages of the progovernment press, printing helped reinforce the valorization of material progress, especially through commercial illustration processes that proliferated celebratory images of trains, steamships, and factories as emblems of modernity, emblazoned across all manner of commercial ephemera.[14] Trade magazines published in the United States and aimed at Latin American practitioners urged printers to see themselves not as members of a storied trade with roots in political struggle, but as businessmen forging a path toward growing prosperity.

The printing shops that maintained explicit commitments to political debate in the late nineteenth century ran counter to these trends. In these often scrappy, unevenly industrialized shops in Mexico City, printers and their collaborators cultivated the image of romantic print crusaders, casting themselves as the true inheritors of Mexico's liberal tradition, which they defined, looking backward to a glorious past, in relation to the 1857 constitution. For these underdogs in an age of disciplined print—like opposition cartoonist Cabrera and newspaper publisher Filomeno Mata—technology represented both a challenge and an opportunity for negotiating fraught relations with the Porfirian government. Whereas lawmakers had once debated whether printers were extensions of their presses or calculating textual accomplices who needed to be held responsible for their actions, Porfirian officials shifted the conversation by treating printing presses as agents in an assemblage of material evidence that, viewed holistically, produced a crime. As the twentieth century dawned, efforts to control printing evolved into struggles over the meanings and materiality of the press itself.

TECHNOLOGY AND THE NEW POLITICS OF PRINTING

A report from Mexico's secretary of fomento (public works) encapsulated late nineteenth-century state attitudes toward printing, describing the press as "that indispensable instrument" which, by "stimulating mental labor alongside material labor," could lead Mexico down the path to "material progress."[15] The secretary envisioned an "active publicity campaign" that could use texts to transform Mexico's image abroad and reshape the knowledge and labor of even the humblest peasants and workers. The contrast between this official vision and the one advanced by the government forty years earlier is clear. For midcentury liberals, the press was a "marvelous invention of the human spirit," an emblem of "liberty that, hour by hour, has fought, over centuries, against all manner of tyranny."[16] While both official formulations described printing's transformative potential, by the late nineteenth century, rhetoric about freedom had been replaced with visions of progress.

Nonstate actors, especially merchants and printers themselves, played an important role in realigning printing's symbolic meanings with material progress throughout the late nineteenth century. Beginning in the mid-1870s, everyday awareness about printing technologies increased, especially among urban newspaper readers who, with little effort, could have acquired at least a passing familiarity with some of the inner workings of a printing shop. Not only did journalists and publishers sprinkle references to type compositors' labors throughout their columns; images advertising state-of-the-art presses and equipment ran frequently across the pages of Mexico City's most widely circulated newspapers. The back cover of a single 1874 edition of *El Siglo Diez y Nueve*, for example, featured four different ads for printing equipment, all from New York–based manufacturers.[17] While well-positioned intermediaries like *El Siglo's* publisher initially profited from their transnational connections when the trade first began to expand in the 1870s, hardware retailers and general stores like Ellis Read and G. Lohse y Compañía soon displaced them as local equipment distributors, selling presses with the wide range of imported machines that poured into Mexico from the industrialized North Atlantic.[18] In specialty catalogues and on the back pages of newspapers, stock images of jobbing and cylinder presses proliferated alongside power saws, boilers, and sewing machines (see figure 32).[19] Reprinted repeatedly as advertising occupied more space in the press, these accumulating images forged new symbolic associations among printing technology, Mexico's burgeoning modernization—manifest not only through railroads and streetcars but also through a proliferation of machines, tools, and consumer goods—and material progress.[20]

Not all observers viewed printing's commercial expansion with enthusiasm. Catholic officials, quoting papal encyclicals, criticized how excessive press freedom had "prostituted the noble art of printing," and urged devout readers to shun proliferating "immoral and impious newspapers."[21] Liberal victory had constrained the church's public power in 1867, prompting lay activists to form new organizations that could revitalize its presence in society. While Catholic social organizations debated whether to engage the political sphere or not, all embraced printing as an arm of religious activism.[22] The Sociedad Católica, for example, formed a special publishing committee to develop moralizing newspapers and print material, while *La Voz de México* and *El Tiempo*, though not officially sanctioned by the clergy, ran for decades as Catholic political newspapers.[23] Francisco Abadiano, heir to Mexico's most active Catholic printer, collaborated with the Sociedad, even as new

FIGURE 32. *Prensas de pie columbianas. Gran depósito de útiles para imprenta* (Mexico City: G. Lohse y Comp., Sucs, 1885). Newberry Library, Chicago.

publishing venues specializing in Catholic literature sprang up.[24] These publishers issued familiar materials like devotional pamphlets and prayers, as well as treatises written by militant activists who envisioned restoring religious piety against the advances of liberalism.[25] Catholic publishing and other forms of social activism, like philanthropy, benefited from the rapprochement between church and state that took place during Díaz's presidency.[26] Yet church officials openly embraced the idea that mass printing efforts could reinvigorate Catholic piety only in the final years of the nineteenth century, when they urged the faithful to subscribe to and support the Catholic press, which, they admitted, often struggled financially.[27] For Mexican archbishops like Pedro Loza, the "noble art of printing" could be harnessed to create "good newspapers" written "in defense of the Catholic cause and to counteract and impede ... the immense harm caused in all senses by bad newspapers."[28] Religious officials, like their government counterparts, eventually embraced the idea of mass publishing campaigns. The contrast between church and state emphases on printing in the service of a resurgence of faith versus material progress, however, revealed how broader outlooks and objectives framed institutional understandings of technology.

For the city's expanding ranks of print workers, new technology generated fascination and suspicion. According to imperfect statistics, Mexico City's printer ranks quadrupled from 330 in 1879 to 1,219 in 1890, as the nation's economy began to grow after decades of stagnation.[29] These workers labored in increasingly varied environments, from the state-of-the-art print works established inside Ernesto Pugibet's El Buen Tono cigarette manufacturing company—one of the first large firms to produce in-house packaging and publicity on an industrial scale—to small jobbing shops with just one or two presses acquired secondhand.[30] Despite the diversity of these laboring experiences and their technological scenarios, printers kept abreast of trade developments through interpersonal networks that overlapped with the publishing program of the working-class press.[31] Workers' newspapers reported on the latest international inventions and their adoption in Mexico, offering behind-the-scenes tours of the government's printing shops or clarifying who had first applied new processes locally.[32] While articles imagined that new technology might bring "perfection and rest for the worker," they also worried whether, in the hands of capital, it would ultimately produce new forms of exploitation or obsolescence. The much-anticipated automation of type composition, an effort in the works for decades in the North Atlantic world, loomed as a "sword of Damocles" in printers' imaginations, reflecting ambivalence about technological change.[33]

Among job printers and commercial publishers, in contrast, celebrations of technology actively downplayed workers' concerns about displacement and positioned new printing processes as bringing salutary reforms to Mexico's artisans. "The machine will educate the worker," proclaimed an 1899 cover story in the state-subsidized newspaper El Imparcial, announcing the arrival of linotype machines in its printing facilities.[34] These state-of-the-art machines, which, using a keyboard, a series of movable matrices, and a pot of molten lead, could cast type on demand, threatened to put compositors, whose ranks had grown over the last two decades, out of work. Yet El Imparcial argued that the new technology would actually benefit Mexico City printers by forcing them to develop new skills. The main benefit of linotype, the article argued disingenuously, was the way it merged various printing shop roles into one. In the old system, the article alleged, "the typographic worker only needed a partial grasp of reading, or even just to recognize the letters to be able to order them according the original [copy.]" Then a copy editor and corrector would fix the typos created by semiliterate *cajistas*. Good linotype operators, in contrast, composed, proofed, and corrected type all at once. The technology itself required greater attention to words, the article claimed, since it cast individual letters into a solid bar of "hot metal" text that could not be altered after the fact.[35] While hand composition errors could be fixed by swapping individual letters of type, linotype mistakes required recasting an entire line of type. In order to avoid getting bogged down in corrections, reasoned the article, "the typographer needs general knowledge, grammar, a bit of everything." Recurring to familiar caricatures of type compositors as ignorant, the article repackaged a technology designed to reduce labor needs as a new form of worker education. Yet in contrast to the more optimistic type compositors, who imagined knowledge acquired on the job leading to the worker's social transformation, the education described by *El Imparcial* ultimately served the goal of greater workplace efficiency.

In the expanding discourse on commercial printing, the relationship between presses and printers attracted new attention, with machines educating and shaping printers into a disciplined workforce. Emerging reproduction technologies like the halftone, which made it possible to convert photographic negatives into relief plates for printing, allowed commercial printers to advance this idea by inviting viewers into model modern workshops outfitted with cutting-edge machinery and streamlined by effective managerial strategies. This can be seen in early twentieth-century images of the Müller Brothers firm, which had started as a two-press operation around 1900 and expanded over a decade to feature dozens of presses and a large bindery department staffed by women workers.[36] In one image of the press room, for instance, each printer stands at the ready, poised to feed a new sheet of paper into the platen jobbing press (see figure 33).[37] A belt, connected to a power source under the shop floor, powered the printing presses and controlled the speed of their movements. The power source determined the regimented position of the printing presses, yet the workers' placement in relation to their presses for the photograph conveys a sense of productive potential made possible by the fusion of man and machine. A far cry from literary depictions of the printing shop as a space of smoking, chatting, daydreaming, and social confraternity, where the racket of the press forms a backdrop to the action, in the Müller Brothers' job shop, the efficient printer-press production unit is the subject of representation. An overseer hovers

FIGURE 33. *Departamento de prensas de platina en el establecimiento de los Sres. Müller Hnos., en México.* "Un establecimiento tipográfico modelo," *El Arte Tipográfico*, October 1909. The Rare Book & Manuscript Library, Columbia University.

behind the overall-clad workers, pocket watch at the ready to manage time on the shop floor and curtail distractions.

Discourses about printing as a modern business—rather than an artisanal trade shaped by political commitments and social aspirations—flourished in state-sponsored outlets like *El Imparcial* and through the promotional efforts of US-based manufacturers.[38] Indeed, the Müller Brothers' workshop featured in the glossy trade magazine *El Arte Tipográfico*, which represented the New York–based National Paper and Type Company, an arm of the behemoth conglomerate American Type Founders (ATF), which dominated type production following its consolidation in 1892. This impressively printed magazine, ATF's overture toward Latin American buyers, contained advertisements for printing supplies, demonstrations of new printing techniques and paper stock, and feature stories about successful printing shops located around the region. Carefully selected spots depicted orderly shop floors like those of the Müller Brothers, well-stocked shelves, and industry captains and government bureaucrats, whom article writers showered with praise for helping advance the art of printing in the Americas. Advertisements and advice columns, which were blurred together, also positioned US suppliers and practitioners as a technological vanguard eager to connect Latin America's modern printers with the latest tools and knowledge. Linked to sales, on the one hand, these discourses also modeled class relations through their depictions of printing shop owners, workers, and machines. The expertise of suit-wearing managers, seated behind desks, appears both different from and essential to the smooth operation of the manual labor unfolding on the shop floor.[39] Construing craft practices and solidarity as a hindrance to progress, these discourses pushed printers to seek respectability, prestige, and prosperity among "industrial and commercial groups."[40]

Despite the rhetoric that cast printing as an apolitical, commercial arm of progress, state intervention shaped printers' ability to access new technologies and markets. Indeed, Porfirian officials, in concert with prominent business allies, had engineered the commercial press by outfitting the modern printing facilities of *El Imparcial*, with its high-capacity rotary press, to the tune of hundreds of thousands of pesos in 1896.[41] *El Imparcial* famously published its daily print run on the front cover of every edition, right under the masthead. Besides appealing to advertisers, this was an act of braggadocio, since few had access to such technological capacity. Now, the constant focus on numbers positioned mass media technologies as sweeping away an old world of artisanal printing. Rather than the familiar journalistic style that took "the route of scandal" in order to sell copies, *El Imparcial* promised to meet the needs of a "public [that] now prefers a decent newspaper."[42] Dismissing the journalistic tactic of publicizing one's prison sentences as badges of honor, *El Imparcial* mocked the opposition press for its constant use of "the sacramental phrase, 'the prison of our Director.'"[43] Rather than heroic martyrs, such journalists were merely delinquents, who reproduced the same trite headlines to elicit public sympathy, covering over shameless violations of the law.

El Imparcial positioned itself as the paper of law and order by criticizing opposition journalism, even as its constant focus on production figures advanced new arguments about the value of print in Mexican society. By suggesting that quantity mattered most and that *El Imparcial* was the first newspaper to achieve something like mass circulation and affordability, the editors recast Mexico's long-term issues with newspaper readership not as reflections of economic penury or social inequality, but as a problem of underproduction, to be overcome by more efficient printing technologies.

Critics expressed skepticism about the newspaper's circulation figures, casting El Imparcial's claims as dubious publicity stunts. The newspaper, however, addressed doubters by hiring a notary, who attested to the veracity of the print run on the front page.[44] While El Imparcial's discourse about mass production depended on the continued legitimacy of the venerable legal institution of the notary, competitors raised doubts by reminding readers that the commercial press could only print prodigious quantities thanks to its political connections.

Opposition newspapers reformulated the growing emphasis on technology in the service of progress in their own political criticism of the Díaz regime. When opposition newspaper El Hijo del Ahuizote acquired new type in 1894, for example, its publisher joked in a column that, while repressive government policies "prevent me from using clarity in language, I have substituted clarity in typography."[45] El Diario del Hogar, whose director frequently faced jail time over conflicts with the Díaz government, routinely ran advertisements for old printing equipment that jabbed at the state (see figure 34).[46] When the newspapers' presses had been confiscated by a judge, the ad explained, sympathetic printers had rushed to supply old presses for El Diario's use. Now the publisher was happy to pass this used machinery on to customers in Mexico's provinces. Thus, the newspaper wove anecdotes about political repression into its resale business, inviting regional buyers to see technology transfer as an act of solidarity.

Rejecting the image of the disciplined printing shop striving to maximize efficiency, opposition publishers cultivated counterimages of the printing shop as a site of political struggle and social confraternity. An image of El Ahuizote's printing shop, for example, presented a romanticized vision of shop floor life that contrasted with the regimented portrait projected by commercial typography studios.[47] In the photograph, a cross-section of the printing shop poses alongside the machinery which, due to the artisanal scale of the business, shares space in a single room (see figure 35). The composition suggests that the shop's activity has been interrupted, as if the photographer had stumbled upon the cluttered scene while exploring the streets of Mexico City. Rather than working in a space of military-like discipline, the shop's inhabitants seem to move about their tasks with a degree of autonomy; a cajista even leans casually against the wall in the background. In a second shot, workers huddle around a copy of the newspaper, inspecting their efforts and pausing for a bit of communal reading. Of course the shot is carefully orchestrated. Someone even took the time to print up a series of placards

FIGURE 34. "Prensas mecánicas de venta," *El Diario del Hogar,* January 17, 1908. The Nettie Lee Benson Latin American Collection, University of Texas Libraries, University of Texas at Austin.

bearing the name of the newspaper and tack them onto the walls. This, plus the centered stacks of newspapers atop the table, emphasizes the ties between workers' efforts and the editorial line of the finished product. The image's "invitation" into the printing shop places the collaborative efforts of the community in the service of political debate on full display, suggesting that although the shop might not be the picture of order, its staff has nothing to hide. The title of the accompanying article, furthermore, does not attribute the "Success of our Weekly" to the latest technological innovations but

FIGURE 35. Printing shop staff posing with machinery. "El éxito de nuestro semanario: un resultado de la libertad de pensar," *El Ahuizote*, September 30, 1911. The Nettie Lee Benson Latin American Collection, University of Texas Libraries, University of Texas at Austin.

rather, mobilizing the language of rights, describes it as "a product of freedom of thought."

Marginalized by the commercial emphasis on circulation, profit seeking, and capital-intensive technologies, opposition printers crafted public images as Porfirian underdogs, whose political commitments flourished in the undisciplined spaces of Mexico City's unevenly industrialized printing shops. These underdog publishers did not advocate a return to premechanical printing practices; rather, by framing printing as political struggle, they mythologized themselves and their craft as maintaining integrity against seemingly insurmountable odds and the impersonality of the commercial press. Figures like Mata, who published *El Diario del Hogar*, and Cabrera, from the satirical weekly *El Hijo del Ahuizote*, represented the archetype of the underdog publisher. Both of these men were products of the post-Reforma era, and both had benefited from Porfirian patronage and participation in state institutions. Mata had briefly directed the government printing office, while Cabrera had trained as a lithographer at the Escuela Nacional de Artes y Oficios, a state-sponsored trade school.[48] By 1886 Cabrera's journal had run afoul of the Díaz regime, and in 1888 Mata publicly broke with the president over his decision to seek reelection for a second time. Their alignment with constitutionalists, who claimed the mantle of liberalism and rallied around the 1857 constitution, put these underdogs at odds with peers in the press who embraced the intellectual shift toward positivism and scientific politics. While fellow print-world actors like journalists Justo Sierra and Federico Gamboa joined the ranks of the Porfirian administration, Mata and Cabrera found themselves in the mixed company of the staff of *El Tiempo*, a Catholic newspaper that became a long-term critic of Díaz, and aging radicals like Vicente García Torres, whose *Monitor Republicano* continued to be published until its founder's death in the mid-1890s.[49] García Torres might have provided inspiration for Mata and Cabrera's own public personae, but most of the former's contentious career had unfolded in a different historical context.[50] By the turn of the twentieth century, Mata and Cabrera faced a more powerful state with greater capacity to intervene in the everyday practices of printing. A fixation on technology and progress narrowed Porfirian officials' attentions toward the printing press itself, as the state sought to shape what it perceived as the unruly behavior of opposition publishers.

THE PRINTING PRESS RECONFIGURED IN LAW

An 1893 political cartoon depicted a recent crackdown on freedom of expression as an assault on printing presses. Published in the satirical weekly *El Hijo del Ahuizote* and likely drawn by the journal's printer-cartoonist Cabrera, the image showed a raging serpent, eyes wide and spitting with indignation, in the process of strangling a mechanical press (see figure 36). Having already upended the inkwell of "journalistic honor" with its tail, the snake attempts to silence the free press—in tatters as its last copies float off the press—by seizing material production. The snake represented the increasingly powerful regime of Díaz, and its label of "psychology" referenced a well-known legal theory developed by government lawyers to justify crackdowns on the press. The *doctrina psicológica*, an argument elaborated by Díaz's advisers, posited that the designation of a crime "happened only in the mind of the judge and was not subject, therefore, to discussion by others," giving criminal judges greater authority to pursue accusations against the press.[51] In the cartoon, as the snake of psychology constricts, type cases and composition sticks tip over in the background, showering lead onto the printing shop floor and suggesting

FIGURE 36. *Actualidades*. *El Hijo del Ahuizote*, May 7, 1893. The Nettie Lee Benson Latin American Collection, University of Texas Libraries, University of Texas at Austin.

that it will take a concerted effort to put the endeavor of independent journalism back into working order.

The cartoonist's decision to depict the printing press as a victim of the Porfirian regime was more than a facile exercise in allegory. Indeed, as Díaz consolidated his power at the national level, his administration increasingly used technology seizures as part of its strategy for policing printed speech. The 1882 reform of article 7 of the constitution, carried out during the presidency of Manuel González, paved the way for the criminalization of certain kinds of printing. This reform of press freedom rules abolished the press jury as a mechanism for trying cases and abrogated the Ley Zarco, the midcentury legislation that had declared printing shops free in the exercise of their activities. Shifting the law's emphasis to the protection of an individual's reputation (what Pablo Piccato calls the construction of "reputation as a juridical good"), reformers reframed debates over press freedom around the issue of honor, garnering willing support from legislators who agreed that private life should be definitively off limits in the public sphere.[52] Underscoring the state's role in protecting individual reputations from libel and slander, the regime narrowed the institutional framework for adjudicating press crimes and abandoned midcentury provisions that had explicitly protected printers' labors. Going forward, accusations would be judged by executive-appointed justices in accordance with the general criminal code, which had been drafted in 1871.[53]

Under the criminal code, press seizures gained new legitimacy as a strategy for punishing political critics, especially after Díaz, who had been elected for a second nonconsecutive term in 1884, convinced congress to change the constitution, allowing for his subsequent reelection in 1888. In response to outcry over election changes, the administration honed the tactic of charging writers and newspaper publishers with *ultraje* (attacks) against public officials and counseled regional authorities on similar tactics. Defamation charges launched by officials and individuals provided judges with opportunities to crack down strategically on the press. All of these tactics had roots in the early republican era, but the criminalization of press infractions brought new dimensions to a familiar political repertoire. After a judge, using the *doctrina psicológica*, had determined that a crime had been committed, he would then investigate the crime by discerning its *cuerpo del delito* (corpus delicti), a legal concept verifying that a crime had occurred and identifying a causal link to its perpetrator. Reconstructing the *cuerpo del delito* required identifying the assemblage of actions, objects, and evidence associated with a crime's commission. In addition to detaining potential criminal suspects, judges also began to confiscate printing presses and other printing shop supplies as part of routine criminal inquiries.

The government-forced closing of printing shops and confiscation of presses had precedents in the early republican era. They had occurred sporadically throughout the nineteenth century, always during moments of acute instability or when the ruling party felt its mandate slipping away, and usually, though not exclusively, at the hands of conservatives.[54] Seizure of a printing press could also come as a form of political payback, as occurred in 1867, when a young General Díaz himself had confiscated Felipe Escalante's printing press and added it to the inventory of the government printing shop, punishment for Escalante's collaboration with Maximilian's regime.[55] Printers' petitions to get back their presses reveal that they understood press confiscations as temporary political actions that could be reversed when the crisis ended, or when tempers had cooled, through back-channel negotiations.[56] Of course, appealing to officials rarely paid off if a printer's press had been sacked altogether, as had happened in sporadic violent incidents—often directed against conservative printing shops by liberal opponents willing to mobilize popular violence—since the 1820s.[57] Though political factions tacitly condoned and sponsored overt violence against printing shops during moments of crisis or victory, observers seemed to understand the seizure or sacking of printing shops as an extralegal measure used by factions to settle scores against their enemies.

The criminalization of press infractions assimilated such seizures into routine judicial practice, changing established precedent and putting new pressures on printers. While early republican press laws had required printers to maintain proof of individual responsibility for printed texts in the form of a *responsivo*, decades of negotiations had brought reprieve in the form of laws that explicitly protected printing shops from state intervention. When the criminal code replaced press laws in 1882, however, printers and printing shops disappeared from the legal language altogether. Only article 660 offered specific instructions on how to investigate a press crime, providing for the confiscation of any "writings, prints, pictures, or any other thing that has served as a medium for injury, defamation, or calumny."[58] In the absence of detailed instructions, Mexico City judges quickly developed their own adaptations of the general provisions of criminal law to fit the world of print production. In addition to citing article 660 in their decisions, they invoked article 106 of the Criminal Code and article 83 of the 1891 Criminal Procedures Manual to justify press seizures. Each of these articles described procedures for handling material evidence in criminal cases, essential for establishing the *cuerpo del delito*: the facts of the case and proof that a crime had been committed. Article 106 stated that any instrument used illegally in a crime should be decommissioned, while article 83 described the procedures for analyzing "the material object of the crime" in great detail, part of a process of "description" used to demonstrate the links between a criminal action and its relationship to the physical world.[59] Used in combination with article 660, these provisions presented judges with ample tools to target a range of actors associated with print production, as well as the materials of printing shops themselves, configured legally as criminal evidence.

The criminal code thus entangled printing presses in a web of responsibility for texts that encompassed not simply writers but also printers and machines. Printers faced this reality and its challenge to their livelihoods when they ran afoul of the authorities. When Cabrera faced charges of defamation for a negative portrayal of Spanish merchants published in a 1900 edition of *El Hijo del Ahuizote*, for instance, a district judge ordered him sent to prison and seized his presses.[60] Subject to questioning, Cabrera carefully lay the groundwork for his case by painting a detailed picture of responsibility inside the printing shop. First he described the specific job duties of each of his collaborators, explaining who had worked on *El Hijo del Ahuizote* and who had been occupied with other tasks. Then he enumerated the activities of his two printing presses, a small Golding jobbing press used for printing the problematic newspaper and a second press used only to print books. While he claimed personal responsibility for the newspaper in order to shield his workers, Cabrera also sought to mitigate the effects of the judge's seizure of his equipment. If he could convince officials that at least one of his printing presses held no association with criminal activity, perhaps it might be released from state custody.

Press confiscations, operating alongside a range of other tactics, revealed how Porfirian officials established a legal regime aimed at disciplining printers into using technology for state-sanctioned ends. For example, stiff sentencing, applied unevenly and unpredictably, sent the message that the regime was prepared to jail offenders for a year or more if they crossed the line. At the same time, the regime expanded subsidies to newspaper businesses, extending or withdrawing support to influence the press and blunt criticism.[61] And while Díaz tolerated public criticism, his administration encouraged moderation by scapegoating key opposition publishers like Cabrera and Mata with a punitive approach. As Fausta Gantús shows, officials allowed Cabrera to leave prison for family meals or to conduct editorial business. Cabrera's mobility, however, also encouraged rival newspapers to sow doubts about his integrity, undercutting his image as a principled Porfirian critic.[62] Faced with petitions on behalf of imprisoned journalists or publishers, meanwhile, Díaz emphasized his compliance with the law as his guiding principle. In 1888, for example, Mata wrote to Díaz to ask for assistance with his imprisonment. Díaz responded politely, but explained that "my intervention would be undue and ineffective," since a judge was already overseeing the case.[63] When members of Mexico's relatively new Associated Press protested another one of Mata's imprisonments in an open letter in 1892, Díaz argued that his intervention in the case would be "a lamentable misunderstanding of our primary institutions," brushing aside the journalists' complaints by proclaiming respect for the balance of powers.[64]

Behind the scenes, judges could stall cases indefinitely, gaining a bargaining chip against future infractions and undermining printers' finances by tying up their presses. This strategy worked even in cases where printers secured a reprieve from higher courts. Cabrera confronted the slow pace of

Porfirian justice after successfully petitioning the Supreme Court to reopen his printing shop in 1900.[65] Despite the order, Cabrera's Gordon press remained in government custody six years later, warehoused at Mexico's Correctional School for Boys like a problem child.[66] Printers attempted to mitigate the effects of press seizures by spreading around ownership of their presses to other individuals, who petitioned authorities to release their equipment.[67] Officials viewed such petitions with suspicion, however, highlighting the likelihood of guilt by association. The staying power of the Porfirian regime presented hurdles for those without the capacity to find new equipment. By 1903, Cabrera had retired from business after nearly two decades of on-and-off incarceration. While he had leveraged these periodic imprisonments to cultivate his public image, press confiscations upped the economic stakes of political criticism.

THE PRINTING PRESS AS *CUERPO DEL DELITO*: EVIDENCE OR ICONOCLASM?

Late Porfirian judges' reinterpretations of responsibility for printed texts assimilated the technologies of printing into the provisions of criminal law. These interpretations stretched prior legal understandings of authorship, once strongly associated with individual textual production, to incorporate machinery and equipment into the rubric of responsibility. Earlier in the century, experts had debated which human actors should be the object of state regulations, with liberals likening printers to machines in order to free them from responsibility and conservatives highlighting their agency as facilitators of texts. The actual press, in both lines of argumentation, was a passive object through which ideas or human agency flowed. The criminalization of printing, however, construed the press as an integral piece in the web of action that comprised a case's *cuerpo del delito*. A series of cases between 1900 and 1910 show how lower court judges, in particular, seized printing presses under the argument that they provided evidence that a crime of *ultraje* or defamation had been committed. Yet what kind of evidence could the printing press provide in the process of connecting a crime to its perpetrator? In earlier decades, investigations into press crimes might involve searching for type, proofing sheets, or impressions on a tympan that linked a particular printing shop to an unlawful text. Yet late Porfirian judges went further by construing the whole technological apparatus of printing as if it were a bloody knife deployed in a stabbing. Commentators in the press took issue with classifying printing presses as part of the *cuerpo del delito*, developing counterarguments that pushed back against the soundness of this legal argument. A case from 1907, involving Mata, reveals how printing press confiscations became a focal point for discussing the terms of press freedom and justice in late Porfirian Mexico.

Mata's trajectory reflected the evolution of political affiliations in late nineteenth-century Mexico as well as the endurance of a classical liberal tradition organized around the 1857 constitution. He had initially founded the Tipografía Literaria in the late 1870s as a Díaz supporter and had benefited periodically from the president's patronage.[68] A bourgeois lifestyle periodical, *El Diario del Hogar*, became a vehicle for criticism after 1888, however, when Mata broke with Díaz over the president's reelection plans.[69] In subsequent years, Mata gained renown and notoriety for his frequent terms in Belén prison, aided by sympathetic commentators in the press, who chronicled and caricatured his conflicts with the Porfirian regime. As Ana María Serna notes, Mata has received relatively little scholarly attention despite his long career as an opposition journalist and publisher.[70] Yet his activism probably explains why the younger, better studied journalists Jesús Flores Magón, Ricardo Flores Magón, and Antonio Horcasitas—who as students had met with violent repression while protesting Díaz's 1892 reelection—turned to him to print *Regeneración*, a periodical famous for its brazen challenges to Díaz.[71] *Regeneración* featured a *denuncia*-style of journalism, holding the administration up against its own discourse of law and order by denouncing instances of corruption and hypocrisy.[72] Mata temporarily lost his press for publishing *Regeneración* and for participating in liberal organizing against Díaz's mandate in 1901.[73] Yet while press seizures prodded opposition cartoonist Cabrera into retirement and political pressure pushed the Flores Magón brothers into exile, Mata regained his press and managed to keep his publishing business afloat.

In late October 1907, Mata faced his first imprisonment since his collaboration with the Flores Magón brothers had unraveled in 1901. Two officials from Mata's home state of San Luis Potosí accused *El Diario del Hogar* of defamation for publishing anonymous letters denouncing their behavior.[74] After Mata refused to divulge the identity of the letter writer, a criminal judge remanded him to custody and closed his press, the Tipografía Literaria, on November 1. His newspaper quietly mentioned the case in a small notice on the second page, explaining that Mata's bail had been denied and that he had been sent to Belén to await trial.[75] Mata's son, Luis, who had taken over the newspaper in his father's absence, quickly found a sympathetic printing shop where he could issue *El Diario del Hogar* despite the closure of the press, and production carried on at the undisclosed location of the Tipografía Literaria Número 2.[76] Mexico City newspapers soon picked up the story and issued comments on Mata's case, which *El Diario del Hogar* in turn reproduced, amplifying the coverage.[77]

Meanwhile, Mata's lawyer petitioned a district court to release his client and return his press. Not only had the publisher lacked malicious intent in publishing the controversial letters, the lawyer argued; there was no actual offended party in the crime, since the letter itself did not name anyone directly in its text, and no crime had even occurred, since Mata had respected the boundaries of press freedom, whose only limitation was "respect for private life, morality, and public peace."[78] The lawyer also requested the return of Mata's printing shop, including the press that had produced *El Diario del Hogar*, five other presses, type, and equipment that had been confiscated by the police.[79] The criminal judge's application of the provision of *cuerpo del delito* to printing presses was an irrational proposition, he argued. These objects, rather than criminal elements, were actually Mata's property, and had been expropriated illegally by the judge, violating Mata's constitutional rights. By positioning printing presses as private property, Mata's lawyer contested the criminal judge's actions as state overreach.

From Belén prison, Mata anxiously awaited news of his printing shop's fortunes. He learned from visitors that the police, acting on orders of the criminal judge, had been overseeing the systematic dismantling of his presses, using prison labor to accomplish the task.[80] As they readied the machinery for transport to the correctional school, the prisoners clumsily pied the type into an unusable jumble. While the prisoners dismantled Mata's shop, printing shop workers apparently idled in the doorway, cursing the judge who had put them out of work.[81] Complementing the lawyer's arguments about the press as a form of property, Mata's disgruntled employees framed the closure of the Tipografía Literaria as an attack on their labor. Before two weeks had passed, a district judge denied Mata's petition for bail but approved the request to return his press.

As his lawyer launched a petition to the Supreme Court, coverage of Mata's jailing multiplied across Mexico, appearing in newspapers from the city of Guadalajara to the small town of Linares in Nuevo León. The spread of coverage reflected the dissemination of printing technologies and the expansion of newspapers across the national territory during the Porfiriato. The editors at *El Diario* reprinted all of this coverage, using the provincial press not only to demonstrate widespread support for its director but also to continually reestablish the facts of the case, since provincial newspapers also reprinted original *Diario* coverage, which *El Diario* re-reprinted in kind. Thus, *El Diario* amplified its own original interpretation of Mata's situation while presenting sympathetic perspectives that widened the scope of the arguments. Letters about Mata frequently struck an optimistic tone, suggesting that the publisher and his press would probably be freed very soon, a move likely designed to appeal to officials' liberality without directly challenging judicial rulings.[82] Back page appeals in Mata's name asked regional readers to pay their subscriptions promptly to help offset the financial strain.

As journalists discussed Mata's predicament, they advanced a range of interpretations about the illegitimacy of the court proceedings, focusing on Mata himself but devoting a good portion of their arguments to the confiscation of his press. One commentator argued that closing down the printing press would endanger its owner's family and employees, casting Mata as a responsible businessman and paterfamilias being undermined by an interventionist state.[83] Others highlighted the judge's unreasonable application of the criminal code. How absurd it was, observed one writer, that the judge had ordered the confiscation of various small printing presses from Mata's typographical studio, since only a large press would have been capable of producing *El Diario del Hogar*.[84] The other presses could hardly be responsible for crimes associated with a particular kind of technology. *El Correo de Jalisco* brought new information to the table, explaining that the judge was willfully contradicting the Supreme Court, which had just recently "issued a judgment indicating that printing presses cannot be considered instruments that figure as *cuerpo del delito*."[85] Several days later a second article echoed the idea that treating printing presses as evidence violated settled legal precedent, which had apparently been decided in a case involving *La Revista de Tabasco*.[86] If the judge had any knowledge of his field, he should never have confiscated Mata's presses in the first place. Regional newspapers, even more vulnerable to the actions of local political leaders, took a keen interest in the printing struggles unfolding in the capital and also had important information to share with their Mexico City counterparts. If the example of *La Revista de Tabasco* offered any lessons, Mata's case represented a flagrant violation of settled precedent.

The reprinted regional commentary on Mata's case allowed *El Diario* to continue its indirect coverage despite the fact that a district judge had, in fact, already ordered the return of his printing equipment. While this decision had seemed to be a victory, as Mata waited for a Supreme Court ruling on his own release, it became clear that the criminal judge was dragging his heels on returning the presses. When Mata complained, the district court called the criminal judge to account for the delay. He explained that, while he had received the order from the district judge to release Mata's printing supplies from custody, all of the equipment had already been moved into storage at the correctional school.[87] The matter, the judge claimed, was now out of his hands and would have to be taken up with executive branch authorities who managed the school. Mata's presses had been caught up in the Porfirian bureaucracy.

When it became clear that Mata's printing presses might never be retrieved, commentators in the press shifted their focus to the judge's rationale for confiscating the equipment in the first place.[88] Writers at *El País* argued angrily that the lower court judge had broken protocol and demanded to see his original order to confiscate the press. "Under what premise would the señor Judge have founded his order to occupy the printing shop of the *Diario del Hogar?*," the article asked incredulously in capital letters, since "A PRESS OR THE IMPLEMENTS OF A PRINTING SHOP ARE NOT NOR CAN BE *CUERPOS DEL DELITO* IN A PRESS [CRIME]."[89] Linking the protection of political speech with the safeguarding of printing shops, the article argued that the press needed "to have its rights protected in a practical way against persecutions."

Commentators also puzzled over the legal and epistemological rationale for treating printing presses as criminal evidence, challenging the Porfirian regime's strategy as confounding protocol and logic itself. Monterrey's *Renacimiento* mocked the judge for "order[ing] the decommission, as *cuerpo de delito* of defamation—that's right, as *cuerpo de delito*—of the press and other tools of the press of said newspaper, which unfortunately supposes a superior ignorance of penal law."[90] *El Tiempo*—the Catholic paper that had suffered similar persecution as Mata's *Diario*—criticized the judge's poor interpretation of the penal code and applauded the fact that he had been ordered to pay for the return of Mata's equipment by a higher court.[91] Another newspaper cast the confiscation of "the press, and not the denounced issue or newspaper" as "anachronous and unfounded" actions proper to places like Russia and Portugal, where governments struggled against revolution, and not to a nation like Mexico, "in the zenith of its prestige."[92] The writers at *El Trueno,* in Linares, Nuevo León, drew on their experience on a small-town paper vulnerable to political retaliation to cast the judge's confiscation as a surprising relic of another time, when "the Syrians, contemporaries of Alexander and the savage tribes of remote antiquity destroyed the towns and smashed to pieces the temples and gods of the conquered."[93] Comparing the seizure of printing presses to an act of iconoclasm, the writers argued that "the act of punishing inanimate objects is not proper to civilized men." Instead, the printing press should be viewed as a harbinger of civilization that "has made it so that men today don't have the same stupid ideas as their ancestors, excepting those who order the decommissioning of presses."[94]

Under what rationale had the criminal judge confiscated Mata's printing shop? When he answered to higher authorities, he explained that he had acted according to article 660 of the penal code, which provided for the confiscation of printed materials in the case of a crime of defamation. When the Supreme Court finally reviewed the case months later, it issued a strong rebuke of the lower court judge, who had incorrectly applied the penal code to the case. "It is indisputable," read the 1908 decision, "that the text and spirit of this legal precept is to collect and disable the writing, print, or thing that has served as a means for defamation, and not the printing press, workshop, or establishment that emits prints or things used as a means to commit defamation."[95] Here, the judges classified printed objects as the primary evidence of a crime, while the tools of production were viewed as neutral technologies outside the bounds of agency or evidence. Applying the article as the judge had was an "absurd and monstrous" act that invested agency in an inanimate object. Thus, the Supreme Court rebuked a lower court official while extending its protection over Mata's possessions. Though months would pass between Mata's initial imprisonment and the Supreme Court's ultimate granting of protection over his case, the publisher had already regained his freedom and printing shop, greeted by a shower of congratulations from the press.

CONCLUSIONS: THE REVOLUTION'S RETURN

Porfirian efforts to reconfigure printing presses as criminal evidence spoke to new ways in which officials attempted to expand the state's role as an arbiter of print, extending regulatory power beyond authors and printers to encompass not just citizens but also their tools. New cultural conceptions and official discourses about printing as an essential technology of progress fueled the urgency of state interventions in areas of material production. Those whose unruly use of printing threatened to undermine this particular vision would, thanks to press seizures, be excluded from reaping the benefits of material progress themselves. Press seizures also reflected late nineteenth-century thinking about the interconnected relationship between workers and machines, in which printer and press fused together for productive ends. Observers asserted that machines, when used properly, could exert disciplinary force on their operators and thus become tools of reform. Officials hoped that removing presses from the hands of problematic printers would encourage the entire trade to adopt a similar vision. Despite the successful legal appeals of opposition printers like Mata and Cabrera, the Supreme Court's practice of overruling lower court judges provided only incomplete or temporary respite. Mata suffered several subsequent imprisonments, for example, including two sentences in 1910, when his presses were again confiscated.[96]

While Mexico City printers navigated the scrutiny of the national government during the late nineteenth and early twentieth centuries, regional printing expanded alongside access to technologies like the mechanized jobbing press and the linotype machine, which sped up small-scale production and dramatically reduced the need for compositor labor in the printing shop. Proliferating beyond the traditional stronghold of Mexico City, modest printing outfits multiplied opportunities to sustain critical perspectives within the national territory, sprouting up in small cities beyond regional capitals. As Mata's 1907 imprisonment revealed, commentary from provincial and local newspapers helped prolong discussion of controversial events like press seizures. Reprinting practices extended the cycle of debate and fueled discontent among political communities like those centered in liberal political clubs, once support vehicles for Díaz that became loci of anti-reelectionist organizing against the aging dictator.

The decentralization of printing and spread of photomechanical technologies played an important role in the revolution that broke out in 1910. While disgruntlement within Mexico's elite ended Díaz's presidency, politics quickly evolved into the upheaval of an all-consuming revolution that would overturn the state, refocusing attention on classical liberal principles like liberty and constitutionalism alongside new social demands for land. Printers commodified the conflict on an unprecedented scale in postcards, on broadsides, and through the urban press. Each faction traveled with an embedded photographer, whose negatives could be transformed into halftone printing plates and used to reproduce strategic visions of the unfolding conflict for urban consumers.[97] Revolutionary leaders engaged the media and communication technologies flourishing around them, echoing historical precedent.

Emiliano Zapata, for instance, kept tabs on his own printing operations, overseen by sympathetic urban intellectuals, via telegraph, and used railroad lines to distribute printed materials across Mexican territory.[98] In 1914 and 1915, his collaborators were busy hauling sequestered presses across haciendas and commandeering government printing shops in Morelos to issue reprints of the Plan de Ayala, which urged dispossessed peasants to occupy lands.[99] Although the revolutionaries struggled to find typographers to fix the presses when they broke down, Zapata's publishing apparatus chugged along, even as Mexico City's industrial presses churned out representations of the peasant leader posing with his rifle.[100]

Mata barely lived to see the revolution. Perhaps weakened by his recent stay in prison, he died in 1911, just months after Díaz renounced power and fled the country, and soon after the old press used to print *El Diario del Hogar* gave out.[101] Posthumous appreciations poured into the offices of *El Diario del Hogar* from across Mexico as newspapers and anti-reelectionist clubs telegraphed their condolences. Francisco Madero, Díaz's principle challenger, had recently praised Mata as "a veteran of our cause."[102] Now supporters commemorated the publisher as an "old gladiator," "one of the liberal community's most persistent defenders," and the "prophet of the democratic revolution when everyone called it an illusion."[103] *El Diario del Hogar*, framed with black borders in a gesture of mourning, reported that thousands of visitors had attended the publisher's wake and described Mata as a martyr of Porfirian persecution with the headline, "Victims Wounded by the Dictatorship Continue to Fall."[104] Yet despite the outpouring of anti-Porfirian catharsis, Mata's newspaper would fold the following year amid growing polarization over the policies of President Madero. Unraveling without its charismatic leader, the newspaper's abrupt end underscored the fragility of printing endeavors and their political commitments as revolution spread.

Mata did achieve a posthumous symbolic victory in the revolutionary constitution of 1917, which reevaluated Porfirian policies bearing on printing and the press. By the time of its drafting, the popular, regional movements of peasants and workers that had burst forth in 1911 to demand access to land, resources, and the political sphere were being channeled and sidelined from power by liberal elites. Yet the constitution incorporated numerous radical demands for social rights in its final text. Written by delegates from a variety of revolutionary factions, the constitution redressed Porfirian policies that had favored large landowners and capital, especially in articles that provided for land reform, labor codes, and subsoil rights for the nation. The new article 7, the provision on freedom of the press, responded to Porfirian tactics still fresh in the memories of its drafters. "In no case," reads article 7, adding new language to text lifted from the 1857 constitution, "can a printing press be seized as an instrument of a crime." The article also proclaimed a commitment to the laboring world of the printing shop when it dictated that a set of regulations would henceforth serve to "avoid the imprisonment, under pretext of press denunciations, of the vendors, 'papeleros,' workers, and other employees of the establishment where a denounced writing is released, unless their responsibility has been previously demonstrated."[105] This language directly countered the Porfirian government's strategies for regulating printed speech and recognized that print workers, too, often became targets in the process.

In writing article 7 in this way, lawmakers not only responded to the predicament faced by Mata and other printers in Porfirian Mexico; they also resolved a century-old conversation about the regulation of public speech and its relationship to the rights of printers and the nature of printing. For one thing, the article's language identified the printing press itself as a fundamental component of press freedom, underscoring the material dimensions that underpinned abstract notions of "the press." The special mention of presses, too, echoed liberal efforts to cast the technology as private property and thus off limits to state seizure. Mata and his lawyers had developed this argument in their petitions before the Supreme Court, and revolutionary framers agreed that the individual's ownership of a printing press was worth more than the state's desire to discipline press infractions. The proposition that citizens had the right to own a press and use it freely as a source of income, however, had a much older genealogy. Printer Alejandro Valdés had made the point in 1820 when he tangled with José Joaquín Fernández de Lizardi, and liberal judges developed it more fully in 1839. Thus, liberal arguments about printers' property rights framed the horizons of the revolutionary constitution. At the same time, the document also conveyed social rights when it identified print workers as a special group in need of further legal protection, upgrading legal language drafted by Ignacio Cumplido in 1845 with an eye toward the working-class inhabitants of Mexico's printing shops.

Even as article 7's drafters affirmed that printers' rights (to their tools and labor) were integral to press freedom, they ensured that the printing shop would continue to be an important site where the limits of public speech would be policed by embedding the double-edged sword of "responsibility"—that familiar and thorny category used in liberal press regulations of the pre-Reforma era—into the constitution itself, magnifying its importance. As the text stated, printers would remain free "unless their responsibility has been previously demonstrated." This phrasing placed the burden on the state to define and demonstrate responsibility, and lawmakers followed suit by drafting a new set of press regulations in 1917.[106] The new regulations, in turn, resurrected many of the same policies laid out in Mexico's original press laws, drafted a century earlier, showing the extent to which revolutionary lawmakers looked back to the liberal past for inspiration, with striking specificity. Original copies of a work were supposed to be signed and retained in the printing shop, resurrecting the mechanism of the *responsivo*. Not only were authors or responsible parties required to print their names on all materials; printing shops were again mandated to print their location and the date of publication. In the absence of any of these items, the work would be considered "clandestine," a new legal category, which would allow authorities to confiscate copies and fine the owners of the printing shop. If the clandestine publication violated press laws, the stakes were higher. In the event an author could not be identified, the printing shop overseer or, in his absence, the owner, would face punishment under the law. And printing shop workers, too, along with distributors of printed materials, could be held responsible if they were authors, editors, or directors in their own right, or in the absence of an overseer or owner to take the fall.

Though the 1917 regulations resurrected many older policies, they also revealed how evolving media practices expanded lawmakers' notions of what counted as "the press." The press law presented a catalog of Mexico's world of communication, extending its purview beyond the printing press to encompass not only "writings, pamphlets, imprints, songs, engravings, books, images, announcements, cards or other papers or figures, paintings, drawings, or lithographs" created via technologies like "manuscripts, or the press, drawing, lithography, photography, cinematography, [and] engraving," but also oral communications like "speeches, shouts, songs, threats," or "malicious expressions made verbally or by signs in the presence of one or more people." Known technologies of distribution such as "mail, telegraph, telephone, [and] radiotelegraphy" were cataloged alongside unknown innovations, expressed in wording that covered "any other manner that exposes or circulates [illegal messages] to the public." The law also expanded the list of potential responsible agents and scenarios, including not just the standard list of authors, editors, and printers but also pseudonymous authors, printing shop overseers, printing shop workers, journalists, newspaper directors, newspapers that had been sold to new owners, responsible parties located outside of Mexico, distributors, and importers.

As lawmakers attested, Mexico's world of communication had expanded and transformed, encompassing emerging technologies like photography and film alongside familiar ones like writing, the press, and lithography. Furthermore, the popular upwelling of the revolution had brought illiterate and semiliterate communities to the center of political life. Lawmakers, anxious to clarify regulatory pathways that encompassed the revolutionary social body, ended up becoming media theorists and ethnographers, observing and cataloging emerging technological practices while reevaluating the old and familiar. Ultimately, the nets of regulation expanded even as they purported to contract, since the law now made specific provisions for any number of media forms previously unaccounted for in liberal press laws (like oral communications and singing). The detailed pathways of responsibility, furthermore, offered a handy blueprint to help savvy authors, publishers, or other print-world actors evade the spirit of the law, letting the buck stop with the printing shop's most vulnerable workers. Thus, printers gained special protected status in the constitution precisely as lawmakers reinscribed rules that could undermine this protection in practice and reopened pathways to circumvent the law. Printing had been decriminalized, but the revolution ensured that the terrain of production would remain a central arena of debate for future generations of media makers.

Conclusion

WRITING FROM PRISON IN 1849, Vicente García Torres argued to a judge, "I am not a printer, nor an author, nor an editor." Rejecting responsibility, García Torres elaborated a vision of the printer as a conduit with no active role in textual production, deflecting charges that blamed him as the architect of a scandalous libel. In claiming, with the use of an old dictionary and knowledge of the law, "I am not responsible," he was not just shrugging his shoulders behind the scenes in an attempt to secure immediate release.[1] He was also intervening in a long-running debate over the policing of printed speech to advocate greater autonomy for printers.

As this book has shown, debates about the power and responsibility of printers were central to negotiations over press freedom and public speech throughout the nineteenth century. Efforts to define and regulate printers' relationship to texts were multifaceted, illuminating much about Mexico's postindependence urban political culture and tenuous process of state formation. They encompassed discursive, legal, and symbolic dimensions that were inseparable from political, material, and social concerns. The printed broadsides, pamphlets, books, and decrees that animated a rollicking world of political debate, after all, were not disembodied texts but textual objects produced and circulated in urban space. Sorting out the practical and philosophical ramifications of printing politics thus engaged a wide swath of urban society—from powerful politicians to humble type compositors—who grappled with the entanglement between texts and the context of their production.

By attending to the messiness of these debates as they unfolded on the ground, this book has underscored how efforts to prescribe, transcend, or reimagine social categories animated Mexico's nineteenth-century printing politics. Indeed, approaching politics through the printing shop reveals how elites' attempts to create a particular kind of public sphere, in which individuals could debate freely and rationally in print, involved marginalizing printers from public life. The many laws and official actions that struggled to channel and contain printed speech after independence attest to this historical project. Officials and intellectuals expressed shared anxieties about the power of untrammeled press freedom to sow political chaos, dissolve social order, and erode piety. These concerns, coupled with the knowledge that rivals would use printing to try to capture power or undermine legitimacy, inflected state efforts to regulate printers' activities and establish workable limits around press freedom. Frustration with printers' aspirations, which challenged elite visions of public opinion as properly shaped by educated *hombres de bien*, fueled state scrutiny of printing shops. And the national government's own reliance on urban printers to manage its official image between 1828 and 1865 deepened this frustration.

Printers, for their part, sought rhetorical and political independence from state and religious authorities, fueling official anxieties over public speech. At the outset of this story, during the late colonial era, printers trumpeted their loyalty to these patrons, upon whose good will they depended for survival. After independence, patronage remained a feature of printers' business models, yet they increasingly sought their own paths, negotiating a fraught relationship to the state while pursuing an opaque mix of profit seeking and partisan activism in a climate of political instability. Being a mouthpiece for government interests lost its allure as republicanism advanced and the treasury remained empty. Economic precariousness, indeed, helps explain why printers often turned to controversy as part of their business strategy. An official response to a provocative text, after all, confirmed the relevance of printers' activities and, as polemicists loved to point out, only increased sales. It also gave printers the opportunity to develop recognizable public personae by leveraging hardships and hassles. Over time, printers elaborated more autonomous discourses, proclaiming their independence from officials and revealing the printing shop as a space wherein urban working communities talked back to power.

As state and religious officials struggled to regulate printed speech throughout the nineteenth century, their shared concerns and anxieties fragmented over the pragmatic issues of how to deal with the challenges posed by printers' autonomy. The printing shop and its regulation, as this book shows, thus became an issue over which ideological differences took shape. Early republican conservative governments sought to engineer a more cautious public sphere by pressuring printers and their employees, including them in a broad legal definition that made them responsible for texts. In the conservative construction, printing shops were corporate communities that could be conscripted into policing textual content in partnership with the state. Conservative lawmakers thus proposed a different regulatory solution than church officials, who claimed the right to review religious manuscripts in advance and whose regulatory efforts proved comparatively weaker. Liberals, on the other hand, eventually embraced the idea that a functional press system depended on securing printers' freedom from government intervention. Otherwise, they argued, governments would turn printers into a new inquisitorial censor that impeded authors' rights to publish. To counter conservative realpolitik, liberals conceptualized printers at once as artisans whose rights to ply their trade should be guaranteed by the state and as machines or neutral conduits through which the will of the author must freely flow.

Liberal lawmakers' theorizations and regulatory efforts formed part of a political and intellectual project to counter conservative controls while simultaneously strengthening authorship as an individual legal category. In advocating printers' freedoms, liberals were not so much championing their interests as seeking a way to free authors while also holding them to account by other means. Liberals, after all, embraced limits on press freedom just as conservatives did. But the liberal counterconstruction of the printer—as artisan or machine—endeavored to safeguard authors from conservative controls by wresting power away from printers. The specter of the printer as censor, echoing complaints once launched by writers like José Joaquín Fernández de Lizardi, who in 1820 felt stymied by printers' unexpected gatekeeping powers, tapped into elite concerns that uneducated artisans would, under conservative rules, be empowered to judge the works of their social betters. Authors' words should be evaluated not by ink-stained printers operating in back rooms, liberals argued, but by juries of their peers, selected by income and deliberating in the public eye. As liberals gained power, their press laws would free printers while tightening legal responsibility for texts around authors alone, strengthening authorship's individual character in the process. In Mexico, where weak markets for print raised few questions about intellectual property rights (often understood as an area through which individual notions of authorship historically emerged), the proposition that authorship was an individual legal category thus cohered around press laws. Liberals' efforts to engineer a public sphere free from printers' political influence and judgment reveal the exclusionary logics underpinning the free-flowing yet well-regulated world of intellectual exchange they imagined.

For nineteenth-century printers, the search for greater autonomy from state and religious officials dovetailed with and diverged from liberal efforts to free the printing press. On the one hand, many printers performed essential work as partisan activists. When they ran afoul of authorities, activists like Ignacio Cumplido or García Torres mapped pathways for loosening conservative and church controls by linking press freedom and freedom of conscience to the state's role as a guarantor of property rights and individual liberties. Their contention that printing had little to do with politics and ideas and everything to do with economic contracts and rights helped them weave a public image as nonpartisan (and thus legitimate) champions of press freedom, even as it served liberal strategy. Yet printers' ongoing activism nevertheless reflected demands to be taken seriously as political actors and thinkers, in direct contradiction to liberal lawmakers' efforts to effectively silence printers (by construing them as passive machines) so that authors could speak. Despite downplaying their agency, printers' writing and activism—from public denouncements of persecution to poetry in the worker press—asserted their role as co-creators of politics and ideas. *Hombres de bien* valorized cultural capital, especially formal education, as a condition for full membership in the nineteenth-century lettered city. Yet in criticizing official interventions, printers crafted their public image not as passive conduits but as active defenders of press freedom.

Mexico's printers did benefit from the liberal party's victory over conservatives in 1867, including through laws that explicitly freed them from textual responsibility. Viewed from the perspective of the printing shop, therefore, the Restored Republic and first term of Porfirio Díaz marked an important inflection point in Mexico's nineteenth-century trajectory, offering relative autonomy and political continuity that allowed printers' activities to flourish. This victory proved fleeting, however, since the late nineteenth-century process of state consolidation under Díaz allowed the government to intervene more forcefully as both underwriter and arbiter of printed speech and property. By the 1880s, the state had abandoned even its rhetorical commitment to printers' freedoms, once central to liberal ideology. Yet the Porfirian government also magnified historic tensions between liberal theory and practice, since it institutionalized repressive tactics that had long existed within the liberal camp (and indeed, among all of Mexico's factions), in the form of seizure and destruction of printing presses. As a young general riding the wave of liberal victory in 1867, after all, Díaz himself had overseen the confiscation of conservative presses, despite his party's high-minded rhetoric.

Iconoclastic events underscored how printing, a technology used to proclaim and contest power, remained central to the performative, public choreography of political ritual throughout the nineteenth century. If governments used printing to issue official directives, to promulgate laws, and as symbols of legitimacy, those with grievances appropriated the same symbols when they issued printed plans during violent uprisings against the state, forming a through line from Miguel Hidalgo and Agustín de Iturbide to Francisco Madero and Emiliano Zapata.[2] Some printed genres came to occupy greater space in the political imaginary than others. Late nineteenth-century political cartoons attest to this uneven symbolic repertoire, filled as they are with drawings of constitutions (shredded, trodden upon, punctured by literal heads of state), public decrees posted to city walls, and newspapers.[3] The everyday social contexts in which certain genres circulated also informed political strategy. This explains why religious officials had tried to stop the publication of the book version of *The Mysteries of the Inquisition*, for instance, while leaving the newspaper version alone so as to avoid conflict with elite heads of household. Political actors' broader investments in the rituals of publishing, regardless of their institutional or partisan affiliation, nevertheless, nourished print's status despite disagreement over the medium's symbolic meanings. Indeed, shifting competition to define print's ultimate purpose in Mexican society ensured that access to and control of the printing press would remain a key element of political struggle throughout the nineteenth century.

For the printers whose professional lives were intertwined with these struggles, political affiliations mattered. Liberal and radical printers arguably played a more visible role in advancing debates about print and press freedom, since they pushed the boundaries of tolerated content and even courted scandal in order to advance their cause. Cumplido's printing of the monarchist pamphlet in 1840, García Torres's issuing of the salacious *Mysteries of the Inquisition* in 1850, and the liberal government's release of the 1867 exposé *Los traidores pintados por sí mismos* are examples of how liberals stoked outrage even as lawmakers emphasized rational accountability. Conservative printers and those who worked for the church certainly articulated ideological positions through their publications. Rafael de Rafael, for example, urged the church to action with fiery polemics against liberals, whom he accused of introducing anti-Catholic smut to innocent Mexican audiences. Thus, printers across factions participated in the heated meta-commentary that helped engineer publishing controversies as such, articulating competing notions of what purpose print should serve.[4] Perhaps because printing remained so entangled with politics and ideology, however, printing shop owners never articulated a unified front, except around the issue of paper tariffs, which they opposed.[5] Those who printed for the church could hardly have been expected to defend colleagues like García Torres, who courted the opprobrium of religious officials in order to advance the liberal cause. And while late nineteenth-century policies encouraged the formation of new political alliances among liberal and Catholic printers, the increased economic power of the state and the rise of job printing undermined solidarity.

Beyond the ranks of the outsized personalities who dominated printing politics, however, shared affinities among printing shop workers reveal how craft inflected political worldviews. Ordinary print workers questioned top-down efforts to sideline them from the public sphere for possessing insufficient cultural capital and for their association with gritty work. The printing shop, indeed, incubated enlightened ideas about the complementary relationship between manual and intellectual labor and explorations of the creative aspects of work itself. The composition of a simple poem, organized laboriously into the delicate petals of a flower, for instance, displayed a printer's mastery of craft and language. An acrostic filled with puns playing on the dual meanings of printing shop equipment similarly showed how the work of textual production generated new ways of thinking about texts.[6] Especially as the Restored Republic promised to inaugurate greater freedoms for printers and spurred an expansion of printing, the sector's workers increasingly claimed their medium for themselves. Type compositors' popular discourse reimagined print workers as architects of the vast archive of politics and ideas that underpinned Mexico's liberal victory. Distinct from romantic notions of authorship as grounded in the individual's creative genius, printers conceptualized this category as inherently collaborative by highlighting the behind-the-scenes processes of composing, correcting, and designing that gave the writer's words "form and life."[7]

While printers' arguments about their unrecognized contributions to literate culture pushed to democratize the lettered city, they simultaneously reinforced social hierarchies associated with literacy and print. Printing shop communities, indeed, depended on the distinction between literate and other modes of expression to distinguish themselves from other working groups. Yet in other ways, printing shops undermined rigid hierarchies, since their inhabitants blurred the boundaries between manual and intellectual labors and proved that social mobility via the written word was possible even for those without formal educations or powerful patrons. Mexico City's urban working communities celebrated figures like the autodidact compositor-turned-novelist Aurelio Garay precisely because they upended expectations about the life pathways prescribed for the worker.

The Mexican Revolution culminated a century of debate about the role of printers in politics and textual production, with printers emerging as both its winners and its losers. The 1917 constitution prohibited the seizure of print-ing presses and reaffirmed printers' freedom from state interference, promis-ing new security for property and labor. Yet a new press law, tellingly, exposed enduring state anxieties about public speech by resurrecting an ambiguous—and familiar—framework for its regulation, which remains in effect to this day. The law expanded its definition of both responsibility and "the press" to encompass an increasingly diverse world of communications. Listing a wide array of potential "responsible parties" for press infractions, lawmakers acknowledged that the liberal project to configure authorship as an individ-ual legal category had failed. Instead, a constellation of textual collaborators could be called upon to stand trial, evoking an older set of press rules that, while potentially detrimental to printers, also recognized their agency in literate production. Printers' success at inserting themselves into the political conversation ensured that future media makers would also have to navigate the thorny category of responsibility for texts.[8]

Other key features associated with nineteenth-century printing politics continued well into the twentieth century. Mexican lawmakers observed a world of proliferating media production driven by consumerism, yet literacy rates grew gradually: in 1940, only 42 percent of adults were literate, and not until 1970 did that rate increase to 76 percent.[9] The sensationalist *nota roja* press—focused on crime and critical of the justice system—engaged numer-ous readers in the postrevolutionary period, but state support remained criti-cal for keeping a commercial press afloat into the 1980s.[10] To keep newspapers in business during the difficult economic climate of the Great Depression era (1930s), revolutionary governments established and later expanded the Producer and Importer of Paper (Productora e Importadora de Papel, PIPSA), a monopoly on newsprint imports that subsidized paper costs.[11] Printers had complained about the high cost of paper since at least 1844, but state officials favored tariffs on paper imports to help construct a domestic paper industry, which they viewed as important for economic development and national security.[12] A century later, printers and newspaper publishers got relief, but the state also gained new leverage through its control of the paper supply, which it could withhold to dampen press criticism and encourage favorable coverage. Still, economic compromise did not prevent journalists from publishing critical coverage, especially by leveraging scandal.[13] Rather, material concerns would remain an issue around which media producers negotiated as the revolution turned toward one-party rule.

Mexico City's printers seemed to shrink from political center stage in the postrevolutionary era, eclipsed by new actors like publishers and newspaper editors, who spent less time on the printing shop floor. The trade continued to become more specialized, decentralized, and diversified. Linotype reduced the need for type compositors and the purchase of large quantities of type, since new type could be cast on demand and repeatedly remelted into a pot of molten lead attached to the linotype machine. Linotype operators, proud of their association with this cutting-edge technology, even debated excluding type compositors from their Union Linotipográfica in 1909, since they believed compositors "abandoned work to give themselves over to vice" and thus might "become a heavy burden and discredit us."[14] In 1925, a feature story in the weekly magazine *Revista de Revistas* introduced readers to "Mexico's Most Ancient Typographers," depicted in photographs with downcast eyes and dour expressions. The printing shop, in the magazine's coverage, had become a curious relic, out of step with modernity and a throwback to the political battles of yesteryear, which the revolution had resolved.[15]

Though the gritty spaces of the printing shop receded from public discourse, printers became the subject of unprecedented mythmaking in the postrevolutionary era, used by revolutionary governments, artists, and intellectuals to distance themselves from the Porfirian regime. The state celebrated Filomeno Mata as a martyr of the revolution by renaming a street after him in the center of Mexico City. Artists like Dr. Atl and Diego Rivera reconfigured popular illustrator José Guadalupe Posada and his publisher Antonio Vanegas Arroyo as revolutionary precursors and folk sources of inspiration.[16] Printmaking, with its craft associations, strengthened revolutionary artists' self-identification as workers, while the rediscovery of nineteenth-century practitioners like Posada inspired artists and intellectuals to address the masses with affordable prints.[17] For officials eager to draw contrasts with the Porfirian regime, print media and printers themselves provided a useful tool. Publishing projects—mobile counterparts to the muralist movement—reenvisioned the revolutionary social body.[18] And by celebrating individuals like Mata and Posada as revolutionary martyrs or precursors, the state positioned itself as sweeping away Díaz's repressive, illiberal, and elitist policies.

Other celebratory treatments of printing history took a different path, one linked to scholarly and antiquarian inquiry. In the early twentieth century, bibliophiles and bibliographers published monumental studies of Mexico's printing trades, compiling archival sources and critical appraisals of the colonial and postcolonial output of urban printing houses.[19] In contrast to the revolutionary celebration of popular printing or opposition journalism, bibliographers often valorized printed materials as monuments to Hispanic civilizational or national progress, advancing a more conservative counterpart with a tinge of disdain for mass printing.[20] The prologue of Chilean bibliographer José Toribio Medina's still unsurpassed, 1912 eight-volume *La imprenta en México* shows a familiar ambivalence about printers' labor in relation to the task of intellectual production. Explaining that he had set up his own press for the explicit purpose of creating the work, which he issued in a limited run of 250 copies, Toribio Medina apologized for any shortcomings that resulted from "being at once authors, editors, and printers.... In another press with better implements than ours, the book would have been better printed, but we would not have been able to supervise the work," which might have turned out less accurate as a result.[21] In his paean to the printing press, Toribio Medina sacrificed quality to maintain intellectual control—in other words, to avoid dealing with real, living printers, whom he distrusted to handle the task of reproducing their own history.

Rather than leave the last word with Toribio Medina, whose scholarship has underpinned a century of research on the printing trades, I turn to the Mexico City printing shop that, in 1919, published an illustrated broadside recasting the meanings of printers' relationship to the world of politics and ideas. The broadside, titled *Calavera de la Prensa*, satirizes the space from which it came in celebration of the popular Catholic holiday Day of the Dead (see figure 37).[22] At the center of the broadside, an old, repurposed engraving by artist Posada depicts his frequent collaborator, the Mexico City publisher "Toncho" Vanegas Arroyo, as a skeleton outfitted in a bowler hat and nattily dressed: the socially destabilizing dandy even in death. Reaching into his pocket, Toncho grasps a fistful of bills, implying that his business has rewarded him handsomely. Meanwhile, a host of skeletal minions scurry underfoot as they set type, work the presses, correct proofs, and hawk the broadsides. A pistol lying atop a heap of papers suggests that the editor is not above defending his words with actions.

The broadside forms part of a genre, commercialized around the turn of the twentieth century, that used the skeleton to offer social commentary on

FIGURE 37. *Calavera de la prensa* (Mexico City: Tip. de la Test. de Antonio Vanegas Arroyo, 1919). Courtesy of the Colección Andrés Blaisten, Fondo Francisco Díaz de León, México.

urban Mexico's obsession with the trappings of modernity. Though this genre drew on the older Catholic visual tradition of the memento mori or vanitas painting—reminding viewers of the futility of earthly pleasures and the inevitability of death—it interwove a classical liberal critique aimed at the progress mania of the Porfirian age and its emphasis on material accumulation.[23] The broadside's text applies this act of social leveling to the spaces its creators knew best, reimagining the hierarchies of intellectual production in the process. Its witty rhyming poem unspools in the voice of Vanegas Arroyo, who died in 1917 yet addresses readers from beyond the grave. Toncho first hails the illustrious newspapers of Mexico City before turning his attention to the various characters of the printing shop, whom he proceeds to skewer each in turn from a shifting perspective. From the speedy compositors, desperate to outpace their linotypist competitors, to the cursed linotypists (may their d*mned livers cook in a pot of molten lead), to the lazy correctors who show up late, to the pretentious imposition men who steal credit from the compositors, to the uptight journalists—the whole cast of characters will meet at the cemetery, where, Toncho explains, they will end up as "dried-up skulls" composed of various typefaces and point sizes.

The broadside presents a tension between the publisher's poetic reminder that social hierarchies evaporate in death and his swaggering masculine persona, who looms larger than life as the epitome of printing shop success. The tension encapsulates the broader dynamics that made the printing shop a space of social and intellectual ferment throughout Mexico's first century of liberal experimentation and transformation. Even as the broadside's creators advanced a social critique, drawing on the democratic valences of liberalism to question inequality, they cast themselves as the heroic protagonists of the lettered city. The broadside's retelling, which envisions the history of the press as a story about printing shops, shows how printers endeavored to scrub the ink from under their fingernails to gain recognition as the creators, not just silent mechanical reproducers, of political and intellectual life. Rejecting categorical definitions imposed from above, they redefined these working spaces as sites of education, collaboration, and transformation. For printers, their work opened the door to new horizons via literate production. Their aspirations can be seen at the feet of the publisher, where heaps of printed papers lie strewn about, waiting to shape the stories of future generations.

ACKNOWLEDGMENTS

Many people shaped this book. It began as a doctoral dissertation at Duke University, yet the book's origins date further back to creative and intellectual experiences at the Center for Book Arts and Wesleyan University, where I had the good fortune to stumble into the worlds of letterpress printing and Latin American studies. I am grateful to the printers, bookbinders, artists and curators at the center—especially Ana Cordeiro, Barbara Henry, Roni Gross, and Sarah Nicholls—from whom I learned in a postapprentice world. I also appreciate the capacious thinking of my teachers at Wesleyan—Fernando Degiovanni, James McGuire, and especially Ann Wightman and the late David Schorr—who encouraged me to explore the links between bookmaking and Latin American history.

At Duke, I had the immense privilege to learn from incredible mentors committed deeply to ideas and education. Jocelyn Olcott guided me through the process of researching and writing, offering insightful feedback, indispensable advice, and encouragement along the way. She remains a cherished adviser, role model, and friend. John D. French helped me hone many of the book's insights and arguments with much-appreciated enthusiasm. Pete Sigal and Sumathi Ramaswamy encouraged me to see the project from different angles, while Kathryn Burns inspired and cheered my explorations. I am deeply grateful for the generosity and warmth of my mentors in the Triangle, who created a truly generative intellectual community.

Since then, many colleagues have offered helpful feedback and good cheer. At Georgia Southern University, I have benefited from the history department's congenial environment. Kathleeen Comerford, Brian Feltman, Carol Herringer, Cathy Skidmore-Hess, and Jon Bryant offered advice and encouragement. I am especially grateful to Robert Batchelor and Felicity Turner for reading portions of the manuscript and for our stimulating intellectual exchanges.

A postdoctoral fellowship at Emory University's Fox Center for Humanistic Inquiry provided time to complete the manuscript. I am grateful to Walter Melion, Keith Anthony, Colette Barlow, and Amy Erbil for making the residency a fruitful experience. The other fellows formed an ideal, engaged interdisciplinary community for rethinking the work. I thank Yanna Yannakakis, Amín Pérez, Ángeles Picone, Falguni Sheth, Lizzy LeRud, Michael Peletz, Jenny Wang Medina, Anna Nelson, Suyun Choi, Ingrid Meintjes, Miriam Udel, and Rosemary Magee for sharing their ideas and camaraderie. Deepika Bahri warmly welcomed me into her Atlanta home. A short-term fellowship at the John Carter Brown Library allowed me to finish research. I'm grateful to Neil Safier, Tara Kingsley, Valerie Andrews, and Kimberly Nusco for facilitating the program and providing helpful guidance. I thank Stijn Van Rossem for sharing his knowledge of early modern book history.

Many scholars generously furthered my research and provided feedback on writing and the publishing process at various stages. I am grateful to Laura Suárez de la Torre, María Esther Pérez Salas, Marina Garone Gravier, Manuel Suárez Rivera, Kenya Bello, Javier Rodríguez Piña, Mercedes Salomón Salazar, Olivia Moreno Gamboa, and many others who welcomed me into the vibrant community of scholars working on print culture and bibliography in Mexico. Emilio de Antuñano, Daniela Bleichmar, Susan Deans-Smith, Caroline Garriott, Florence Hsia, and Javier Villa-Flores graciously read and commented on specific chapters. Ken Ward, Pablo Mijangos y González, Aaron Hyman, Linda Arnold, Kate Moran, Ritika Prasad, Celso Castilho, Felipe Martínez Pinzón, Jesse Hoffnung-Garskof, and Mey-Yen Moriuchi provided invaluable advice on key sources and problems. Adriana Chira, Teresa Davis, and Pablo Palomino sparked my imagination with their insightful discussion during my fellowship year in Atlanta. The Georgia Atlantic, Latin American, and Caribbean Studies Initiative (GALACSI!) offered a welcome forum for sharing early writing, and I thank Julia Gaffield, who organized the group, as well as Pablo Palomino, Lia Bascomb, J. T. Way, Jennifer Palmer, Teresa Davis, Germán Vergara, Tom Rogers, Yanna Yannakakis, Alex Wisnowski, and Adriana Chira for their insights. Alejandro Velasco, Drew Konove, and David Sartorius offered helpful advice on publishing.

I am grateful to the participants in the 2017 "Paper Technologies" conference at Wesleyan and Yale Universities, who provided helpful comments on chapter 3. Gary Shaw helped make the conference possible and encouraged me when I taught at Wesleyan as a visiting professor. I thank Robert Conn, Jim McGuire, and Ann Wightman for their warmth and mentorship. John Kuhn, Diana Schwartz, and Luis Francisco became cherished friends.

Thanks especially go to Edward Wright-Rios, Margaret Chowning, and the anonymous reviewer whose thoughtful and generous engagements with this manuscript helped me shape its final version. Pamela Voekel also provided invaluable feedback, as did the participants at a book manuscript reading organized by Jolie Olcott at Duke University. I extend my sincerest thanks to Kate Moran, Jessica Delgado, Nora Jaffary, John French, Pete Sigal, Ben Fallaw, Jaime Pensado, Faren Yero, Gray Kidd, Robert Franco, Stephen J. Andes, Saúl Espino Armendáriz, Martha Liliana

Espinosa, Sydney Marshall, Natalie Gasparowicz, and L. J. Brandli for their helpful suggestions.

Colleagues and friends have nurtured my fascination with print and engagement with Latin America. Since entering academia as a graduate student I have learned from and alongside fellow travelers Carlos Abreu Mendoza, Daniel Bessner, Justin Blanton, Angélica Castillo, Aaron Colston, Christina Davidson, Ashley Elrod, Robert Franco, Jon Free, Vanessa Freije, Stephanie Friede, Caroline Garriott, Mandy Hughett, Lance Ingwersen, Gray Kidd, Ameem Lutfi, Bryan Pitts, Ryan Poe, Logan Puck, Yuridia Ramírez, Ben Reed, Rochelle Rojas, Elizabeth Shesko, Farren Yero, Serkan Yoloçan, Ashley Young, and many others. I am fortunate to have met Santiago Muñoz Arbeláez, Rachel Stein, Hwisang Cho, Alex Hidalgo, and Nick Wilding at the Rare Book School and to have benefited from our collaborations. The Mellon Society of Fellows in Critical Bibliography introduced me to a warm and eclectic community of scholars whose wide-ranging interests inflected this work.

Caroline Garriott, Gabriela Goldin, Paula Park, and Vanessa Freije have been constant interlocutors, generous readers, and dear friends. Paula and I exchanged lots of early drafts, and she and Ulli Bach offered much-appreciated encouragement. Vanessa has been a cherished reader, confidant, and travel buddy over the years. I thank also dear friends Ana Cordeiro, Angélica Castillo, Dan Fox, Nathan Nagy, Carmen Rivera, Nico Udu-gama, and Eva Seidelman for keeping me laughing across decades and long distances, and my beloved cousin Reuben Tomar for research assistance, and for always coming along for the ride. I thank my extended family, especially Renée Green, Cathy and Tom Riley, Jeanne and John Forester, the Dabbs family, the Begali-Tutone family, and the Leso family, for their love and encouragement.

Material support brought the project to fruition. I am profoundly grateful to the American Council of Learned Societies, the American Printing History Association, the Bibliographical Society of America, Duke University and the Duke Center for Latin American and Caribbean Studies, Emory University's Fox Center for Humanistic Inquiry, Georgia Southern University, the John Carter Brown Library, the National Endowment for the Humanities, and the Social Science Research Council for funding research and writing fellowships.

I appreciate the archivists, librarians, and staff of the many institutions I visited while researching this book. In Mexico, the professional staff at the Archivo General de la Nación, the Archivo Histórico de la Ciudad de México, the Archivo Histórico de Notarías, the Archivo Histórico de la Suprema Corte de Justicia, the Biblioteca and Hemeroteca Nacional, the Biblioteca Clavigero of the Universidad Iberoamericana, the Archivo Histórico de Jalisco, and the Archivo de la Real y Literaria Universidad de Guadalajara all provided courteous and efficient support, as did staff at the Archivo General de Indias in Seville. In the United States, I am grateful to the librarians at the Sutro Library, the Bancroft Library, the Nettie Lee Benson Library at the University of Texas, Austin, the Newberry Library, the Rare

Books & Manuscript Library at Columbia University, the Historic New Orleans Collection, and the Henderson Library at Georgia Southern, who all provided helpful assistance. I especially thank Christopher Palazzolo, head of collections at Emory University's Woodruff Library, who obtained and helped me analyze a dataset of Mexico City publications from WorldCat. Carlos Uzcanga Gaona of the Fundación Andrés Blaisten and Lilliam Pimentel Bernal and Pedro Morales Pérez of the AGN generously helped with image permissions.

Thanks especially to Kate Marshall at UC Press for embracing this project with enthusiasm, and to Enrique Ochoa-Kaup, who shepherded the manuscript through production in the middle of a pandemic with professionalism and care. I thank production editor Jessica Moll, Claudia Smelser for her wonderful cover design, Sharon Langworthy for her meticulous copyediting, Jon Dertien for attentive project management, and the printers and production team at Books International for making it real. An earlier version of chapter three appeared as "Defining Responsibility: Printers, Politics, and the Law in Early Republican Mexico City," *Hispanic American Historical Review* 98, no. 2 (2018): 189–222. Portions appear here with the permission of Duke University Press.

This book is dedicated to the memory of my grandfathers, Robert Haas and Izzy Zeltsman, whose very different but equally fascinating lives as twentieth-century printers inspired me as I researched and wrote it. Although I believe that I came to printing of my own accord, I know I was preconditioned toward curiosity by the books, objects, and anecdotes that crowded my childhood. More than anyone, I thank my parents, Miriam Haas and Jon Zeltsman, for nurturing these interests and for teaching me to see the world from the perspective of the artist and craftsperson. And thank you, Mattia, for your unwavering companionship, curiosity, and impish wit.

NOTES

Following are abbreviations and acronyms/initialisms used in notes that list archival sources.

AGI	Archivo General de Indias
AGN	Archivo General de la Nación
AHAM	Archivo Histórico del Arzobispado de México
AHCM	Archivo Histórico de la Ciudad de México
AHJ	Archivo Histórico de Jalisco
AHN	Archivo Histórico de Notarías
AHSCJN	Archivo Histórico de la Suprema Corte de Justicia de la Nación
ARANG	Archivo de la Real Audiencia de la Nueva Galicia
art.	artículo
BLAC	Nettie Lee Benson Latin American Collection, University of Texas at Austin
caja	box
doc.	documento
exp., exps.	expediente/expedientes (file/s)
f., fs.	foja/fojas (sheet/s)
FEZ	Fondo Emiliano Zapata, AGN
HD	Juan E. Hernández y Dávalos Manuscript Collection, BLAC
leg.	legajo (dossier)
MRP	Mariano Riva Palacio Collection, BLAC
ND	no date

no.	número
RBML	Columbia University Rare Book and Manuscript Library
s/n	sin número (without numeration)
s/s	sin sección (without section)
Sutro Library	California State Library, Sutro Branch
TSJDF	Tribunal Superior de Justicia del Distrito Federal, AGN
v.	verso
vol., vols.	volume(s)

INTRODUCTION

1. "La Prefect. remite un pasquín que se encontró fijado en las esquínas de esta corte," 9 January 1865, Archivo General de la Nación (AGN), Gobernación, leg. 1046, exp. 3.

2. Marta Eugenia García Ugarte, *Poder político y religioso: México siglo XIX* (Mexico City: Universidad Nacional Autónoma de México, Instituto de Investigaciones Sociales / M. A. Porrúa, 2010), 2:1138.

3. Pablo Mijangos y González, *The Lawyer of the Church: Bishop Clemente de Jesús Munguía and the Clerical Response to the Mexican Liberal Reforma* (Lincoln: University of Nebraska Press, 2015), 387.

4. David M. Henkin, *City Reading: Written Words and Public Spaces in Antebellum New York* (New York: Columbia University Press, 1998).

5. "El Gobernador del Distrito acompañando un impreso contra la ocupación de los Bienes Ecc.os y refiriendo haberlo engañado el impresor," 1847, AGN, Gobernación, leg. 176, exp. 7, no. 69.

6. "La Prefect. remite."

7. Magdalena Chocano Mena, "Colonial Printing and Metropolitan Books: Printed Texts and the Shaping of Scholarly Culture in New Spain, 1539–1700," *Colonial Latin American Historical Review* 6, no. 1 (1997); Magdalena Chocano Mena, *La fortaleza docta: Elite letrada y dominación social en México colonial (siglos XVI–XVII)* (Barcelona: Ediciones Bellaterra, 2000); and Marina Garone Gravier, *Historia de la tipografía colonial para lenguas indígenas* (Mexico City: CIESAS / Universidad Veracruzana, 2014).

8. This process looked different in places like Río de la Plata and Venezuela, where local printing cultures were not established until the late eighteenth or early nineteenth centuries.

9. William G. Acree Jr., *Everyday Reading: Print Culture and Collective Identity in the Río de la Plata, 1780–1910* (Nashville, TN: Vanderbilt University Press, 2011), 6; and Ronald Briggs, *The Moral Electricity of Print: Transatlantic Education and the Lima Women's Circuit, 1876–1910* (Nashville, TN: Vanderbilt University Press, 2017), 9.

10. *Legislación mejicana, o sea colección completa de las leyes, decretos y circulares que se han expedido desde la consumación de la independencia* (Mexico City: Imprenta de Juan R. Navarro, 1855), 647.

11. Briggs, *Moral Electricity of Print*; and Víctor Goldgel, *Cuando lo nuevo conquistó América: Prensa, moda y literatura en el siglo XIX* (Buenos Aires: Siglo Veintiuno Editores, 2013).

12. Ecuadorian statesman Vicente Rocafuerte, quoted in Javier Fernández Sebastián, "From the 'Voice of the People' to the Freedom of the Press: The Birth of Public Opinion," in *The Spanish Enlightenment Revisited*, ed. Jesús Astigarraga (Oxford: Voltaire Foundation, 2015), 231.

13. *A History of the Book in America*, ed. Scott Casper, Jeffrey D. Groves, Stephen W. Nissenbaum, and Michael Winship, vol. 3, *The Industrial Book, 1840–1880* (Chapel Hill: University of North Carolina Press, 2007).

14. 1895 statistics defined literacy as the ability to read and write. Mary Kay Vaughan, "Primary Education and Literacy in Nineteenth-Century Mexico: Research Trends, 1968–1988," *Latin American Research Review* 25, no. 1 (1990): 43.

15. Joaquín García Icazbalceta, "Tipografía Mexicana," in *Diccionario universal de historia y de geografía*, ed. Lucas Alamán (Mexico City: Imp. de F. Escalente y Ca.; Librería de Andrade, 1854), 5: 974.

16. Ángel Rama, *The Lettered City*, trans. John Chasteen (Durham, NC: Duke University Press, 1996).

17. Michael P. Costeloe, *The Central Republic in Mexico, 1835–1846: Hombres de Bien in the Age of Santa Anna* (New York: Cambridge University Press, 1993).

18. Printer Vicente García Torres, for example, defended the rights of the ambulatory vendors of Mexico City's Baratillo market both as a newspaper publisher and during a brief stint as a representative on the city council in the 1870s. Andrew Konove, *Black Market Capital: Urban Politics and the Shadow Economy in Mexico City* (Oakland: University of California Press, 2018), 126.

19. "Incidente de la causa que se instruye en el Juzgado 20 de lo Civil por el Lic. P. de Lebrija contra D. Vicente G. Torres como responsable de un art.o publicado en el Monitor," 1849, AGN, Tribunal Superior de Justicia del Distrito Federal (TSJDF), caja 262, exp. s/n.

20. Richard Sennett, *The Craftsman* (New Haven, CT: Yale University Press, 2008), ch. 3; and Kelly Donahue-Wallace, *Jerónimo Antonio Gil and the Idea of the Spanish Enlightenment* (Albuquerque: University of New Mexico Press, 2017).

21. Sonia Pérez Toledo, *Los hijos del trabajo: Los artesanos de la ciudad de México, 1780–1853* (Mexico City: El Colegio de México / Universidad Autónoma Metropolitana-Iztapalapa, 1996); Sarah C. Chambers, *From Subjects to Citizens: Honor, Gender, and Politics in Arequipa, Peru, 1780–1854* (University Park: Pennsylvania State University Press, 1999); and Iñigo L. García-Bryce, *Crafting the Republic: Lima's Artisans and Nation Building in Peru, 1821–1879* (Albuquerque: University of New Mexico Press, 2004).

22. José Joaquín Fernández de Lizardi, *Maldita sea la libertad de imprenta* (Mexico City: Oficina de Betancourt, 1820).

23. Charles A. Hale, *Mexican Liberalism in the Age of Mora, 1821–1853* (New Haven, CT: Yale University Press, 1968); Emília Viotti da Costa, *The Brazilian Empire: Myths and Histories* (Chicago: University of Chicago Press, 1985); Brian F. Connaughton, *Clerical Ideology in a Revolutionary Age: The Guadalajara Church and the Idea of the Mexican Nation, 1788–1853*, trans. Mark Alan Healey (Calgary, AB: University of Calgary Press, 2002); Pamela Voekel, *Alone before God: The Religious Origins of Modernity in Mexico* (Durham, NC: Duke University Press, 2002); and Elías José Palti, *La invención de una legitimidad: Razón y retórica en el pensamiento mexicano del siglo XIX (un estudio sobre las formas del discurso político)* (Mexico City: Fondo de Cultura Económica, 2005).

24. Guy P. C. Thomson, "Popular Aspects of Liberalism in Mexico, 1848–1888," *Bulletin of Latin American Research* 10, no. 3 (1991); Florencia E. Mallon, *Peasant and Nation: The Making of Postcolonial Mexico and Peru* (Berkeley: University of California Press, 1995); Michael T. Ducey, "Liberal Theory and Peasant Practice: Land and Power in Northern Veracruz, Mexico, 1826–1900," in *Liberals, the Church, and Indian Peasants: Corporate Lands and the Challenge of Reform in Nineteenth-Century Spanish America*, ed. Robert H. Jackson (Albuquerque: University of New Mexico Press, 1997); Peter Guardino, *The Time of Liberty: Popular Political Culture in Oaxaca, 1750–1850* (Durham, NC: Duke University Press, 2005); Rosalina Ríos Zúñiga, *Formar ciudadanos: Sociedad civil y movilización popular en Zacatecas, 1821–1853* (Mexico City: ESU Plaza y Valdés, 2005); Karen Deborah Caplan, *Indigenous Citizens: Local Liberalism in Early National Oaxaca and Yucatán* (Stanford, CA: Stanford University Press, 2010); Benjamin T. Smith, *The Roots of Conservatism in Mexico: Catholicism, Society, and Politics in the Mixteca Baja, 1750–1962* (Albuquerque: University of New Mexico Press, 2012); and Timo H. Schaefer, *Liberalism as Utopia: The Rise and Fall of Legal Rule in Post-Colonial Mexico, 1820–1900* (New York: Cambridge University Press, 2017).

25. Hilda Sabato, *Republics of the New World: The Revolutionary Political Experiment in Nineteenth-Century Latin America* (Princeton, NJ: Princeton University Press, 2018), 149.

26. Pablo Piccato, "Jurados de imprenta en México: El honor en la construcción de la esfera pública, 1821–1882," in *Construcciones impresas: Panfletos, diarios y revistas en la formación de los estados nacionales en América Latina, 1820–1920*, ed. Paula Alonso and José Antonio Aguilar Rivera (Mexico City: Fondo de Cultura Económica, 2004); Elba Chávez Lomelí, *Lo público y lo privado en los impresos decimonónicos: Libertad de imprenta, 1810–1882* (Mexico City: Universidad Nacional Autónoma de México / Facultad de Estudios Superiores Aragón / M. A. Porrúa, 2009); Pablo Piccato, *The Tyranny of Opinion: Honor in the Construction of the Mexican Public Sphere* (Durham, NC: Duke University Press, 2010); Laurence Coudart, "La regulación de la libertad de prensa (1863–1867)," *Historia Mexicana* 65, no. 2 (2015); and Fausta Gantús, "La libertad de imprenta en el siglo XIX: Vaivenes de su regulación. Presentación," *Historia Mexicana* 69, no. 1 (2019).

27. Jürgen Habermas, *The Structural Transformation of the Public Sphere: An Inquiry into a Category of Bourgeois Society* (Cambridge, MA: MIT Press, 1995).

28. Benedict Anderson, *Imagined Communities*, rev. ed. (London: Verso, 1991). For critical perspectives on Anderson, see Trish Loughran, *The Republic in Print: Print Culture in the Age of U.S. Nation Building, 1770–1870* (New York: Columbia University Press, 2007); and Sara Castro Klarén and John Chasteen, eds., *Beyond Imagined Communities: Reading and Writing the Nation in Nineteenth-Century Latin America* (Baltimore, MD: Johns Hopkins University Press, 2003).

29. Adrian Johns, *The Nature of the Book: Print and Knowledge in the Making* (Chicago: University of Chicago Press, 1998); Miles Ogborn, *Indian Ink: Script and Print in the Making of the English East India Company* (Chicago: University of Chicago Press, 2007); Derek R. Peterson, Emma Hunter, and Stephanie Newell, eds., *African Print Cultures: Newspapers and Their Publics in the Twentieth Century* (Ann Arbor: University of Michigan Press, 2016); Kathryn A. Schwartz, "The Political Economy of Private Printing in Cairo as Told from a Commissioning Deal Turned Sour, 1871," *International Journal of Middle East Studies* 49, no. 1 (2017).

30. Advertising revenue and newspaper sales seem to have played a somewhat larger role in printers' business strategies in the late colonial and early republican United States than in Mexico. Joseph M. Adelman, *Revolutionary Networks: The Business and Politics of Printing the News, 1763–1789* (Baltimore, MD: Johns Hopkins University Press, 2019), 4–7.

31. Christine Haynes, *Lost Illusions: The Politics of Publishing in Nineteenth-Century France* (Cambridge, MA: Harvard University Press, 2010).

32. Edward Wright-Rios, *Searching for Madre Matiana: Prophecy and Popular Culture in Modern Mexico* (Albuquerque: University of New Mexico Press, 2014).

33. These general observations reflect quantitative analysis of records in WorldCat, the world's largest bibliographical database. I counted all titles (excluding periodicals) printed in Mexico City at ten-year intervals from 1780 to 1910 and discovered that the number of titles printed in each sampled year dipped and rose in relation to political conditions and economic downturns related to politics (especially war), before assuming a more stable upward trend after the 1860s. The number of total pages printed over the nineteenth century followed a similar path, as did the median number of pages in each printed volume, which increased tenfold between the late eighteenth and early twentieth centuries. Newspapers frequently folded within months or even weeks, making quantification of titles less illuminating as an exercise.

34. Cristina Soriano, *Tides of Revolution: Information, Insurgencies, and the Crisis of Colonial Rule in Venezuela* (Albuquerque: University of New Mexico Press, 2018), 6–7; and Rebecca Earle, "Information and Disinformation in Late Colonial New Granada," *The Americas* 54, no. 2 (1997).

35. Here, I draw on Claudio Lomnitz's argument that national belonging in Mexico emerged not through broadly shared horizontal affiliation but through vertical "bonds of dependence" linking a small nucleus of full citizens to a broader community of "weak, embryonic or partial citizens." Claudio Lomnitz, "Nationalism as a Practical System: Benedict Anderson's Theory of Nationalism from the Vantage Point of Spanish America," in *The Other Mirror: Grand Theory through the*

Lens of Latin America, ed. Miguel Angel Centeno and Fernando López-Alves (Princeton, NJ: Princeton University Press, 2001), 337–38.

36. On the links between literacy, orality, and ritual see Joanne Rappaport and Tom Cummins, *Beyond the Lettered City: Indigenous Literacies in the Andes* (Durham, NC: Duke University Press, 2012), 119; and William E. French, "The Conjunction of the Lettered City and the Lettered Countryside in 19th-Century Mexico," in *Oxford Research Encyclopedia of Latin American History* (May 9, 2016), https://oxfordre.com/latinamericanhistory/view/10.1093/acrefore/9780199366439.001.0001/acrefore-9780199366439-e-10, 14. Leah Price highlights the symbolic valences of books in relation to social difference in *How to Do Things with Books in Victorian Britain* (Princeton, NJ: Princeton University Press, 2012).

37. Felipe Martínez Pinzón and Mey-Yen Moriuchi, email messages to author January 2020.

38. María José Patricia Rojas Rendón, "Los impresos poblanos efímeros: Una mirada a 'Tertulia de pulquería', de José A. Arrieta, 1851," *Inmediaciones de la Comunicación* 12, no. 2 (2017); and Mey-Yen Moriuchi, *Mexican Costumbrismo: Race, Society, and Identity in Nineteenth-Century Art* (University Park: Pennsylvania State University Press, 2018).

39. Marina Garone Gravier, *La tipografía en México: Ensayos históricos (siglos XVI al XIX)* (Mexico City: Universidad Nacional Autónoma de México, 2012), 103.

40. Piccato, *Tyranny of Opinion*, ch. 2.

41. Emilio Rabasa, *La gran ciencia; El cuarto poder* (Tuxtla Gutiérrez, Chiapas: Consejo Estatal para la Cultura y las Artes de Chiapas, 2000), 210.

42. Laura Suárez de la Torre and Miguel Ángel Castro, eds., *Empresa y cultura en tinta y papel: 1800–1860* (Mexico City: Instituto de Investigaciones Dr. José María Luis Mora / Universidad Nacional Autónoma de México, 2001); Miguel Ángel Castro, ed., *Tipos y caracteres: La prensa mexicana, 1822–1855* (Mexico City: Universidad Nacional Autónoma de México, 2001); and Laura Suárez de la Torre, ed., *Constructores de un cambio cultural: Impresores-editores y libreros en la ciudad de México, 1830–1855* (Mexico City: Instituto de Investigaciones Dr. José María Luis Mora, 2003).

43. Jesse Hoffnung-Garskof, "To Abolish the Law of Castes: Merit, Manhood and the Problem of Colour in the Puerto Rican Liberal Movement, 1873–92," *Social History* 36, no. 3 (2011); and Robert Buffington, *A Sentimental Education for the Working Man: The Mexico City Penny Press, 1900–1910* (Durham, NC: Duke University Press, 2015).

44. Jesús Laguna, "El cajista," *El Desheredado*, February 14, 1875.

45. This tradition linked printers and printing enthusiasts across time and space. Elizabeth L. Eisenstein, *Divine Art, Infernal Machine: The Reception of Printing in the West from First Impressions to the Sense of an Ending* (Philadelphia: University of Pennsylvania Press, 2011), 194–95; Jesse Hoffnung-Garskof, *Racial Migrations: New York City and the Revolutionary Politics of the Spanish Caribbean* (Princeton, NJ: Princeton University Press, 2019), 43.

46. Ignacio Cumplido, *Impresiones de viaje* (Mexico City: Tip. de I. Cumplido, 1884), 32–33.

47. Jacques Rancière, *Proletarian Nights: The Workers' Dream in Nineteenth-Century France* (London: Verso Books, 2012), 5, 8.

48. Lisa Maruca describes this collection of textual and embodied practice as "text work." Lisa Maruca, *The Work of Print: Authorship and the English Text Trades, 1660–1760* (Seattle: University of Washington Press, 2007), 4.

49. Gérard Genette, *Paratexts: Thresholds of Interpretation* (New York: Cambridge University Press, 1997).

50. Roger Chartier, "Laborers and Voyagers: From the Text to the Reader," *Diacritics* 22, no. 2 (1992): 50.

51. Víctor Goldgel-Carballo, "'High-Speed Enlightenment': Latin American Literature and the New Medium of Periodicals," *Media History* 18, no. 2 (2012): 2.

52. Emmanuel Velayos, "Painting Words, Drawing Republics: Embodied Arts and New Beginnings in Simón Rodríguez," *Hispanic Review* 87, no. 2 (2019): 137–138.

CHAPTER ONE. THE POLITICS OF LOYALTY

1. Manuel Antonio Valdés, preliminaries, *La Gazeta de México*, 1802–1803.

2. Gabriel B. Paquette, *Enlightenment, Governance, and Reform in Spain and its Empire 1759–1808* (Basingstoke, UK: Palgrave Macmillan, 2008), 57–58.

3. David Sartorius, *Ever Faithful: Race, Loyalty, and the Ends of Empire in Spanish Cuba* (Durham, NC: Duke University Press, 2013), 2.

4. Comparative studies will surely deepen our knowledge of the variegated mechanics of colonial print censorship. According to Mónica Ricketts, members of the university of Lima, for instance, could publish without official permission until 1786. Mónica Ricketts, *Who Should Rule? Men of Arms, the Republic of Letters, and the Fall of the Spanish Empire* (New York: Oxford University Press, 2017), 89.

5. Joseph M. Adelman, *Revolutionary Networks: The Business and Politics of Printing the News, 1763–1789* (Baltimore, MD: Johns Hopkins University Press, 2019), 81.

6. Olivia Moreno Gamboa, "La imprenta y los autores novohispanos: La transformación de una cultura impresa colonial bajo el régimen borbónico (1701–1821)" (PhD diss., Universidad Nacional Autónoma de México, 2013), 190.

7. Kelly Donahue-Wallace, *Jerónimo Antonio Gil and the Idea of the Spanish Enlightenment* (Albuquerque: University of New Mexico Press, 2017), 8; and Paquette, *Enlightenment, Governance, and Reform*, 5.

8. Ricketts, *Who Should Rule?*, 35–39.

9. Bianca Premo, *The Enlightenment on Trial: Ordinary Litigants and Colonialism in the Spanish Empire* (New York: Oxford University Press, 2017), 226.

10. Kenneth C. Ward, "'Mexico, Where They Coin Money and Print Books': The Calderón Dynasty and the Mexican Book Trade, 1630–1730" (PhD diss., University of Texas at Austin, 2013), 75. On the preproduction censorship process in the early colonial era, see Albert A. Palacios, "Preventing 'Heresy': Censorship and

Privilege in Mexican Publishing, 1590–1612," *Book History* 17 (2014). On eighteenth-century licensing, see Marcela Zúñiga Saldaña, "Licencias para imprimir libros en la Nueva España, 1748–1770," in *Del autor al lector: Libros y libreros en la historia*, ed. Carmen Castañeda García (Mexico City: Centro de Investigaciones y Estudios Superiores en Antropología Social, 2002), 163–78. On book censorship in colonial Peru, see Pedro Guibovich Pérez, *Censura, libros e inquisición en el Perú colonial, 1570–1754* (Seville: Consejo Superior de Investigaciones Científicas / Universidad de Sevilla / Diputación de Sevilla, 2003).

11. For a social portrait of viceregal authors, see Moreno Gamboa, "La imprenta y los autores novohispanos," 90, 99.

12. AGN, Inquisición, vol. 1103, exp. 4, fs. 61–62; vol. 1196, exp. 22, f. 264; vol. 1312, exp. s/n, fs. 256–57. AGN, Indiferente Virreinal, General de Parte, caja 0245, exp. 003.

13. Martha Ellen Whittaker, "La cultura impresa en la ciudad de México, 1700–1800: Las imprentas, las librerías y las bibliotecas," in *Historia de la literatura mexicana: Desde sus orígenes hasta nuestros días*, ed. Nancy Vogeley and Manuel Ramos Medina (Mexico City: Siglo XXI / Universidad Nacional Autónoma de México, Facultad de Filosofía y Letras, 2011), 42.

14. Ward, "'Mexico, Where They Coin Money,'" 239; and Juan José de Eguiara y Eguren, *Prólogos a la Biblioteca mexicana*, 2nd ed., trans. Agustín Millares Carlo (Mexico City: Fondo de Cultura Económica, 1944), 223.

15. Marina Garone Gravier, *El Arte de ymprenta de don Alejandro Valdés (1819): Estudio y paleografía de un tratado de tipografía inédito* (Toluca de Lerdo, Mexico: Fondo Editorial Estado de México, 2015), 108–10; and Manuel Suárez Rivera, *Dinastía de tinta y papel: Los Zúñiga Ontiveros en la cultura novohispana (1756–1825)* (Mexico City: Instituto de Investigaciones Bibliográficas, Universidad Nacional Autónoma de México, 2019), 173, 212.

16. Moreno Gamboa, "La imprenta y los autores novohispanos," 64. In Lima, the other hub of publishing in the Spanish Americas, printers similarly served local markets. Pedro Guibovich Pérez, *Imprimir en Lima durante la colonia: Historia y documentos, 1584–1750* (Madrid: Iberoamericana / Vervuert, 2019), 12.

17. Privileges structured printer-official relations in Puebla, too, the secondary publishing center in New Spain. Marina Garone Gravier, *Historia de la imprenta y la tipografía colonial en Puebla de los Ángeles, 1642–1821* (Mexico City: Instituto de Investigaciones Bibliográficas, Universidad Nacional Autónoma de México, 2014), 542–43.

18. Ken Ward reconstructs the Calderón family's business in "'Mexico, Where They Coin Money.'"

19. Ward, "'Mexico, Where They Coin Money,'" 204. On the Jáuregui family that inherited Ribera's privileges, see Ana Cecilia Montiel Ontiveros, *En la esquina de Tacuba y Santo Domingo: La imprenta de María Fernández de Jáuregui, testigo y protagonista de la cultura impresa 1801–1817* (Mexico City: Coalición de Libreros / Sísifo Ediciones, 2015).

20. Martha Ellen Whittaker, "Jesuit Printing in Bourbon Mexico City: The Press of the Colegio de San Ildefonso, 1748–1767" (PhD diss., University of California, Berkeley, 1998), 67.

21. Suárez Rivera, *Dinastía de tinta y papel*, 108–12; and Felipe Zúñiga y Ontiveros, *Efemérides*, marginal annotations from March 1763 and February 1770, Sutro Library.

22. Felipe Zúñiga y Ontiveros, *Efemérides*, marginal annotations from May 1770, Sutro Library.

23. Javier Villa-Flores, "Reframing a 'Dark Passion': Bourbon Morality, Gambling, and the Royal Lottery in New Spain," in *Emotions and Daily Life in Colonial Mexico*, ed. Javier Villa-Flores and Sonya Lipsett-Rivera (Albuquerque: University of New Mexico Press, 2014), 162.

24. On early colonial printing shop organization, see María Isabel Grañén Porrúa, "El ambito socio-laboral de las imprentas novohispanas: Siglo XVI," *Anuario de Estudios Americanos* 48 (1991).

25. Ward, "'Mexico, Where They Coin Money,'" 129, 183, 224. In early colonial Lima, printer Antonio Ricardo seems to have financed his business by transferring several enslaved men and women as loan collateral. Guibovich Pérez, *Imprimir en Lima durante la colonia*.

26. Ward, "'Mexico, Where They Coin Money,'" 26; Kelly Donahue-Wallace, "Publishing Prints in Eighteenth-Century Mexico City," *Print Quarterly* 23, no. 2 (2006): 140.

27. Adelman, *Revolutionary Networks*, 49.

28. In one 1731 notice, printers referenced Saint John as a protector. Donahue-Wallace, "Publishing Prints," 141.

29. For a history and typographical analysis of the specimen, the oldest known type specimen found for Mexico, see Marina Garone Gravier, "El comercio tipográfico matritense en México durante el siglo XVIII," *Secuencia* 88 (enero–abril 2014).

30. Kelly Donahue-Wallace, *Art and Architecture of Viceregal Latin America, 1521–1821* (Albuquerque: University of New Mexico Press, 2008), ch. 6; and Pamela Voekel, *Alone before God: The Religious Origins of Modernity in Mexico* (Durham, NC: Duke University Press, 2002), 24–27.

31. "Todos los individuos que se hallan empleados en esta oficina, felicitan los días a su amado Patron el Señor Don Alejandro Valdes, en el siguiente soneto" [1815–1820?], Sutro Library, SMBC7, Miscellanea.

32. William H. Sewell, *Work and Revolution in France: the Language of Labor from the Old Regime to 1848* (New York: Cambridge University Press, 1980), 61.

33. Martin Austin Nesvig, "'Heretical Plagues' and Censorship Cordons: Colonial Mexico and the Transatlantic Book Trade," *Church History* 75, no. 1 (2006).

34. Pablo González Casanova, *La literatura perseguida en la crisis de la Colonia* (Mexico City: Colegio de México, 1958), 83–103. On the satirical *pasquines* that circulated as handwritten artifacts, see Gabriel Torres Puga, *Opinión pública y censura en Nueva España: Indicios de un silencio imposible (1767–1794)* (Mexico City: El

Colegio de México, 2010), 323–26. Torres Puga also discusses the underground best seller *Fray Gerundio* in "Inquisición y literatura clandestina en el siglo XVIII," in *Historia de la literatura mexicana: Desde sus orígenes hasta nuestros días*, ed. Nancy Vogeley and Manuel Ramos Medina (Mexico City: Siglo XXI / Universidad Nacional Autónoma de México, Facultad de Filosofía y Letras, 2011).

35. Cristina Gómez Álvarez and Guillermo Tovar de Teresa, *Censura y revolución: Libros prohibidos por la Inquisición de México (1790–1819)* (Madrid: Trama Editorial / Consejo de la Crónica de la Ciudad de México, 2009), 42, 53.

36. Torres Puga, *Opinión pública y censura*, 534, 545.

37. Torres Puga, *Opinión pública y censura*, 235.

38. Donahue-Wallace, "Publishing Prints," 153. For an extensive reconstruction of printmaking in Mexico, see Donahue-Wallace, "Prints and Printmakers in Viceregal Mexico City, 1600–1800" (PhD diss., University of New Mexico, 2000).

39. William B. Taylor, *Theater of a Thousand Wonders: A History of Miraculous Images and Shrines in New Spain* (New York: Cambridge University Press, 2016), 410, 417.

40. Donahue-Wallace, *Jerónimo Antonio Gil*, 8.

41. Quoted in Donahue-Wallace, *Jerónimo Antonio Gil*, 8.

42. Pedro Rodríguez de Campomanes, *Discurso sobre la educación popular de los artesanos y su fomento* (Madrid: Impr. de D. A. de Sancha, 1775), 44.

43. On economic and religious reform, see Susan Deans-Smith, *Bureaucrats, Planters, and Workers: The Making of the Tobacco Monopoly in Bourbon Mexico* (Austin: University of Texas Press, 1992); Voekel, *Alone before God*; and Brian R. Larkin, *The Very Nature of God: Baroque Catholicism and Religious Reform in Bourbon Mexico City* (Albuquerque: University of New Mexico Press, 2010).

44. Susan Deans-Smith, "'A Natural and Voluntary Dependence': The Royal Academy of San Carlos and the Cultural Politics of Art Education in Mexico City, 1786–1797," *Bulletin of Latin American Research* 29, no. 3 (2010).

45. Albert Corbeto, "Tipografía y patrocinio real: La intervención del gobierno en la importación de tipos de imprenta en España," in *Imprenta Real: Fuentes de la tipografía española*, ed. José María Ribagorda (Madrid: Ministerio de Asuntos Exteriores y de Cooperación / AECID, 2009), 38.

46. For a detailed introduction to the technical processes of printing in the early modern era, consult Philip Gaskell, *A New Introduction to Bibliography* (1995; repr., New Castle, DE: Oak Knoll Press / St. Paul's Bibliographies, 2012).

47. Corbeto, "Tipografía y patrocinio real," 30, 37–42.

48. Marina Garone Gravier, "La influencia de la Imprenta Real en América: El caso de México," in *Imprenta Real: Fuentes de la tipografía española*, ed. José María Ribagorda (Madrid: Ministerio de Asuntos Exteriores y de Cooperación / AECID, 2009), 94–96. On Felipe Zúñiga y Ontiveros's purchase of matrices designed by Jerónimo Antonio Gil, see José Toribio Medina, *La imprenta en México (1539–1821)* (Santiago, Chile: Impreso en casa del autor, 1912), 1:CCLIX; and Garone Gravier, "El comercio tipográfico matritense," 12.

49. Corbeto, "Tipografía y patrocinio real," 40. On the internal conflicts between Gil and directors of the academy, who saw engraving as an inferior art, see Deans-Smith, " Natural and Voluntary Dependence,'" 278–95.

50. Donahue-Wallace, *Jerónimo Antonio Gil*, 300.

51. Marina Garone Gravier, *La tipografía en México: Ensayos históricos (siglos XVI al XIX)* (Mexico City: Universidad Nacional Autónoma de México, 2012), 157.

52. Garone Gravier, *Historia de la imprenta*, 400.

53. Voekel, *Alone before God*, 47–49.

54. Torres Puga, *Opinión pública y censura*, 359.

55. Quoted in Carmen Castañeda, "Periodismo en la ciudad de México: Siglo XVIII," in *Historia de la literatura mexicana: desde sus orígenes hasta nuestros días*, ed. Nancy Vogeley and Manuel Ramos Medina (Mexico City: Siglo XXI / UNAM, Facultad de Filosofía y Letras, 2011), 138.

56. Matías de Gálvez Edict, 4 December 1783, AGN, Indiferente Virreinal, Impresos Oficiales, caja 6062, exp. 22.

57. Quoted in Castañeda, "Periodismo en la ciudad de México," 138.

58. Daniela Bleichmar, *Visible Empire: Botanical Expeditions and Visual Culture in the Hispanic Enlightenment* (Chicago: University of Chicago Press, 2012).

59. "A L. P. de V. Exca. Su mas obligado súbdito Manuel Antonio Valdés," *La Gazeta de México*, January 2, 1784.

60. "Prólogo," *La Gazeta de México*, January 2, 1784.

61. "Prólogo," *La Gazeta de México*, January 2, 1784.

62. *La Gazeta de México,* June 30, 1784.

63. Manuel Antonio Valdés, preliminaries, *La Gazeta de México*, May 4, 1789.

64. Manuel Antonio Valdés and Juan López Cancelada to Viceroy Pedro Garibay, 27 June 1809, "Expediente sobre pretensión de establecer imprenta en México," Archivo General de Indias (AGI), Gobierno, Audiencia de México, exp. 2792.

65. Manuel Suárez Rivera, "El periodismo en construcción: Estrategias comerciales de la *Gazeta de México*, 1784–1785," *Relaciones* 143 (verano 2015): 217.

66. While other periodicals, like Alzate y Ramírez's second *Gazeta Literaria*, received approval for publication, they were prohibited from publishing news. Dalia Valdez Garza, *Libros y lectores en la Gazeta de literatura de México (1788–1795) de José Antonio Alzate* (Mexico City: Bonilla Artigas Editores / Instituto Tecnológico y de Estudios Superiores de Monterrey / Iberoamericana, 2014), 28.

67. Raúl Coronado, *A World Not to Come: A History of Latino Writing and Print Culture* (Cambridge, MA: Harvard University Press, 2013), 1.

68. Gabriel Torres Puga, "La transformación de la *Gazeta de México*, 1805–1808," in *Guerra, política y cultura en las independencias hispanoamericanas*, ed. Marco Antonio Landavazo and Moisés Guzmán (Morelia: Universidad Michoacana / El Colegio de Jalisco, 2013), 24.

69. *Suplemento a la Gazeta de México*, August 6, 1793.

70. Laurence Coudart, "El 'Diario de México' y la era de la 'Actualidad,'" in *Bicentenario del Diario de México: Los albores de la cultura letrada en el México*

independiente, 1805–2005, ed. Esther Martínez Luna (Mexico City: Universidad Nacional Autónoma de México, 2009), 200.

71. *El Diario de México*, October 1, 1805.

72. Susana María Delgado Carranco, *Libertad de imprenta, política y educación: Su planteamiento y discusión en el Diario de México, 1810–1817* (Mexico City: Instituto de Investigaciones Dr. José María Luis Mora, 2006), 47. For content overview and analysis of *El Diario*'s connection to the literary circle of the *Arcadia Mexicana* see Ruth Wold, *El Diario de México: Primer cotidiano de Nueva España* (Madrid: Editorial Gredos, 1970).

73. Timothy E. Anna, *The Fall of the Royal Government in Mexico City* (Lincoln: University of Nebraska Press, 1978), 36.

74. For a detailed reconstruction of the reprinting of news from Spain in *La Gazeta* and the political uncertainty it generated, see Torres Puga, "La transformación de la *Gazeta de México*," 37–45.

75. *Suplemento a la Gazeta de México*, August 3, 1808.

76. Torres Puga, "La transformación de la *Gazeta de México*," 49.

77. *El Diario de México*, August 11, 1808; and *La Gazeta de México*, October 1, 1808, and February 15, 1809.

78. *La Gazeta de México*, September 17, 1802, and October 29, 1802.

79. Delgado Carranco, *Libertad de imprenta*, 28.

80. The Royal College of Lawyers denounced Cancelada for reprinting Juan López Cancelada, *Decreto de Napoleón, emperador de los franceses sobre los judíos residentes en Francia, y deliberaciones que tomaron estos en su cumplimiento, con un resúmen de otros sucesos interesantes* (Mexico City: En la oficina de Don Mariano de Zúñiga y Ontiveros, calle del Espíritu Santo, 1807).

81. "El S. Inquisitor Fiscal de este Sto Oficio contra Dn Juan López Cancelada, Editor de la Gazeta de esta N. E. por Proposiciones," 15 July 1808, AGN, Inquisición, vol. 1441, exp. 28, f. 272.

82. Juan López Cancelada to Viceroy Pedro Garibay, 2 November 1808, "Expediente sobre pretensión de establecer imprenta en México," AGI, Gobierno, Audiencia de México, exp. 2792.

83. Archbishop Lizana y Beaumont to Manuel Antonio Valdés, 26 June 1809, "Expediente sobre pretensión de establecer imprenta en México."

84. Manuel Antonio Valdés and Juan López Cancelada to Viceroy Pedro Garibay, 27 June 1809, "Expediente sobre pretension de establer imprenta en México."

85. Opinion of *Fiscal* Ambrosio Sagarzurieta, 30 August 1809, "Expediente sobre pretensión de establecer imprenta en México."

86. Francisco José de Noriega to Viceroy Lizana y Beaumont(?), [Sept./Oct. 1809], "Expediente sobre pretensión de establecer imprenta en México."

87. Manuel Antonio Valdés to Viceroy Lizana y Beaumont, 8 November 1809, "Expediente sobre pretensión de establecer imprenta en México."

88. Opinion of *Oidor* Melchor José de Foncerrada, 6 December 1809, "Expediente sobre pretensión de establecer imprenta en México."

89. Manuel Antonio Valdés to Junta Suprema Central(?), 30 December 1809, "Expediente sobre pretensión de establecer imprenta en México."

90. "Advertencia del autor de esta gazeta," *La Gazeta de México*, December 30, 1809.

91. Anna, *Fall of the Royal Government*, 61.

92. Lizana y Beaumont to Junta Suprema Central, 6 February 1810, "Expediente sobre pretensión de establecer imprenta en México."

93. Anna, *Fall of the Royal Government*, 61.

94. Domingo Antonio de Llanos to Secretaría de Estado de España y de sus Indias, 30 December 1809, "Expediente sobre pretensión de establecer imprenta en México." Llanos was probably an employee who worked on the *Gazeta*. Manuel Suárez Rivera, "Se buscan lectores: El modelo de suscripción en los impresos novohispanos a finales del siglo XVIII," in *Libros y lectores en las sociedades hispanas: España y Nueva España (Siglos XVI–XVIII)*, ed. Francisco Javier Cervantes Bello (Puebla, Mexico: Benemérita Universidad Autónoma de Puebla; Educación y Cultura, 2016), 379.

95. Juan López Cancelada, *La verdad sabida y buena fé guardada: Orígen de la espantosa revolución de Nueva España comenzada en 15 de setiembre de 1810* (Cádiz: Imprenta de D. Manuel Santiago de Quintana, 1811), vi.

96. J. E. Hernández y Dávalos, *Coleccion de documentos para la historia de la guerra de independencia de Mexico de 1808 a 1821* (Mexico City: J. M. Sandoval, impresor, 1877), 1:278. Referenced in Anna, *Fall of the Royal Government*, 57.

97. Manuel de Torres to Antonio Castro Manuel, 27 December 1812, "Expediente sobre pretensión de establecer imprenta en México."

98. José Servando Teresa de Mier Noriega y Guerra, *Historia de la revolución de Nueva España antiguamente Anáhuac, ó Verdadero origen y causas de ella, con la relación de sus progresos hasta el presente año de 1813*, 2 vols. (London: Impr. de G. Glindon, 1813). On the importance of Philadelphia for Spanish-American exiles, see Rodrigo Lazo, *Letters from Filadelfia: Early Latino Literature and the Trans-American Elite* (Charlottesville: University of Virginia Press, 2020).

99. Juan López Cancelada, *Sucesos de Nueva España hasta la coronación de Iturbide* (Mexico City: Instituto Mora, 2008).

100. Tomás Pérez Vejo and Marta Yolanda Quezada, *De novohispanos a mexicanos: Retratos e identidad colectiva en una sociedad en transición* (Mexico City: Instituto Nacional de Antropología e Historia, 2009), 16.

101. Pérez Vejo and Quezada, *De novohispanos a mexicanos*, 154.

102. Donahue-Wallace, *Jerónimo Antonio Gil*, 1.

CHAPTER TWO. NEGOTIATING FREEDOM

1. "Señores curas de este arzobispado," 1813, AGN, Operaciones de Guerra, vol. 939, exp. 129, f. 194.

2. On the role of print in the Age of Revolution, see Bernard Bailyn, *The Ideological Origins of the American Revolution* (Cambridge, MA: Belknap Press of Harvard University Press, 1967); Jeremy D. Popkin, *Revolutionary News: The Press in France, 1789–1799* (Durham, NC: Duke University Press, 1990), 4; David P. Geggus, "Print Culture and the Haitian Revolution: The Written and the Spoken Word," *Proceedings of the American Antiquarian Society* 116, no. 2 (2006); Cristina Soriano, "'A True Vassal of the King': Pardo Literacy and Political Identity in Venezuela during the Age of Revolutions," *Atlantic Studies* 14, no. 3 (2017); Richard S. Newman, "Liberation Technology: Black Printed Protest in the Age of Franklin," *Early American Studies: An Interdisciplinary Journal* 8, no. 1 (2010); and Jeremy D. Popkin, "A Colonial Media Revolution: The Press in Saint-Domingue, 1789–1793," *The Americas* 75, no. 1 (2018). For a skeptical appraisal see Rebecca Earle, "The Role of Print in the Spanish Wars of Independence," in *The Political Power of the Word: Press and Oratory in Nineteenth-Century Latin America*, ed. Iván Jaksic (London: Institute of Latin American Studies, University of London, 2002).

3. Anna Macías, "Cómo fue publicada la Constitución de Apatzingán," *Historia Mexicana* 19, no. 1 (1969): 20.

4. François-Xavier Guerra, *Modernidad e independencias: Ensayos sobre las revoluciones hispánicas*, 2nd ed. (Mexico City: Editorial MAPFRE / Fondo de Cultura Económica, 1993), 302; and Cristina Soriano, *Tides of Revolution: Information, Insurgencies, and the Crisis of Colonial Rule in Venezuela* (Albuquerque: University of New Mexico Press, 2018), 50.

5. See Rebecca Earle's discussion of Martin Lienhard's arguments about the "fetishisation of writing" within the context of independence-era New Granada in Rebecca Earle, "Information and Disinformation in Late Colonial New Granada," *The Americas* 54, no. 2 (1997): 184.

6. For a useful extended discussion of the pitfalls of causal argumentation about print and revolution, including a weighing of different approaches to the question, see Robert Darnton, "Do Books Cause Revolutions?," in *The Forbidden Best-Sellers of Pre-revolutionary France* (New York: W. W. Norton, 1995), pt. 3.

7. On the intellectual sources and broader political effects of the liberal revolution, see Roberto Breña, "The Cádiz Liberal Revolution and Spanish American Independence," in *New Countries: Capitalism, Revolutions, and Nations in the Americas, 1750–1870*, ed. John Tutino (Durham, NC: Duke University Press, 2016). For an interpretation of how creoles mobilized citizenship practices after 1808, see Tamar Herzog, *Defining Nations: Immigrants and Citizens in Early Modern Spain and Spanish America* (New Haven, CT: Yale University Press, 2003), ch. 7.

8. Eric Van Young, "Islands in the Storm: Quiet Cities and Violent Countrysides in the Mexican Independence Era," *Past and Present* 118, no. 1 (1988).

9. "Expediente formado con el edicto publicado por este Tribunal de la Inquisición de México en 24 de Junio de 1789," AGN, Inquisición, vol. 1240, exp. 4, fs. 19–177.

10. "Edicto publicado en este Capital el 24 de Enero de 73 prohibiendo diferentes estampas, inscripciones, y escritos satíricos e injuriosos al Rey Nuestro Señor y su Gobierno," AGN, Inquisición, vol. 1038, exp. 3, fs. 177–246.

11. On the role of documents in mediating colonial authority, see Miles Ogborn, *Indian Ink: Script and Print in the Making of the English East India Company* (Chicago: University of Chicago Press, 2007); and Sylvia Sellers-García, *Distance and Documents at the Spanish Empire's Periphery* (Stanford, CA: Stanford University Press, 2014).

12. Hugh M. Hamill, *The Hidalgo Revolt: Prelude to Mexican Independence* (Gainesville: University of Florida Press, 1966), 124.

13. Eric Van Young, "Agrarian Rebellion and Defense of Community: Meaning and Collective Violence in Late Colonial and Independence-Era Mexico," *Journal of Social History* 27, no. 2 (1993); Peter Guardino, "The War of Independence in Guerrero, New Spain, 1808–1821," in *The Wars of Independence in Spanish America*, ed. Christon I. Archer (Wilmington, DE: Scholarly Resources, 2000).

14. On *papel sellado* see Bianca Premo, "Legal Writing, Civil Litigation, and Agents in the 18th-Century Spanish Imperial World," in *Oxford Research Encyclopedia of Latin American History* (February 27, 2017), https://oxfordre.com/latinamericanhistory/view/10.1093/acrefore/9780199366439.001.0001/acrefore-9780199366439-e-247.

15. Testimony of José Trinidad Buitron, February 1811, Archivo de la Real Audiencia de la Nueva Galicia (ARANG), Ramo Criminal, caja 174, exp. 11, progresivo 2715.

16. "Oficio reservado del virrey sobre indio capturado," February 1811, AGN, Operaciones de Guerra, vol. 810, exps. 25–27, fs. 86–89.

17. Macías, "Cómo fue publicada la Constitución de Apatzingán," 15; and Carlos María de Bustamante, *Cuadro histórico de la revolución mexicana, comenzada en 15 de septiembre de 1810 por el ciudadano Miguel Hidalgo y Costilla* (Mexico City: Impr. de J. M. Lara, 1843), 1:407.

18. Ignacio Rayón to José María Liceaga, 14 December 1812, AGN, Operaciones de Guerra, vol. 939, exp. 21, f. 31.

19. Macías, "Cómo fue publicada la Constitución de Apatzingán," 17.

20. On efforts to recruit papermakers rumored to be working in the town of Yurira, see "Junta Subalterna, Año de 1815, Contestaciones de Govierno," Benson Latin American Collection (BLAC), Juan E. Hernández y Dávalos Manuscript Collection (HD), 831, 8.651.116; and "Junta Subalterna, De Hacienda," 6 December 1815, BLAC, HD, 855, 9-3.874.

21. "Junta Sabalterna, Año de 1816, Libro Comun de Cargo y Data de Caudales Nacionales," BLAC, HD, 882, 25.5170–5213.

22. Francisco Xavier Venegas Decree, 21 March 1812, AGN, Operaciones de Guerra, vol. 353, f. 411; and Ignacio Rayón Decree, 7 April 1813, AGN, Operaciones de Guerra, vol. 345, exp. 2.

23. Lucas Alamán, *Historia de Méjico desde los primeros momentos que prepararon su independencia en el año de 1808 hasta la época presente* (Mexico City: Imprenta de J. M. Lara, calle de la Palma num 4, 1850), 3:appendix 51.

24. Hugh M. Hamill, "Royalist Propaganda and 'La Porción Humilde del Pueblo' during Mexican Independence," *The Americas* 36, no. 4 (1980): 442.

25. Eric Van Young, *The Other Rebellion: Popular Violence, Ideology, and the Mexican Struggle for Independence, 1810–1821* (Stanford, CA: Stanford University Press, 2001), 348–49.

26. Hamill, "Royalist Propaganda," 428. Propagandists also dehumanized insurgents by comparing them to animals. Marco Antonio Landavazo, "Guerra, discurso y terror en la independencia de México," in *Creación de estados de opinión en el proceso de independencia mexicano (1808–1823)*, ed. Laura Suárez de la Torre (Mexico City: Instituto de Investigaciones Dr. José María Luis Mora, 2010), 105–6. On the viceroy's appeal to propagandists and their profiles, see Víctor Gayol, "Escritores cortesanos y rebelión: La breve respuesta de los letrados a los sucesos de 1810 en México," in *Las guerras de independencia en la América española*, ed. Marta Terán and José Antonio Serrano Ortega (Mexico City: Colegio de Michoacán / Universidad Michoacana de San Nicolás de Hidalgo / Instituto Nacional de Antropología e Historia, 2002).

27. "Se repartieron los convites, dentro y fuera de esta capital," 3 July 1812, AGN, Operaciones de Guerra, vol. 730, exp. 8, f. 24.

28. Agustín Pomposo Fernández de San Salvador, *Convite a los verdaderos amantes de la religion católica y de la patria* (Mexico City: En la oficina de Ontiveros, 1812), 5.

29. Fernández de San Salvador, *Convite a los verdaderos amantes de la religion católica*, 7–8.

30. Agustín Pomposo Fernández de San Salvador to Félix Calleja, 5 August 1814, AGN, Operaciones de Guerra, vol. 760, exp. 18, fs. 101–6.

31. Félix Calleja to Agustín Pomposo Fernández de San Salvador, 9 August 1814, AGN, Operaciones de Guerra, vol. 760, exp. 18, f. 109.

32. Puebla official to Félix Calleja, 14 January 1815, AGN, Operaciones de Guerra, vol. 760, exp. 20, f. 121.

33. François-Xavier Guerra, "'Voces del pueblo': Redes de comunicación y orígenes de la opinión en el mundo hispánico (1808–1814)," *Revista de Indias* 62, no. 225 (2002): 360; and Elías José Palti, *La invención de una legitimidad: Razón y retórica en el pensamiento mexicano del siglo XIX (un estudio sobre las formas del discurso político)* (Mexico City: Fondo de Cultura Económica, 2005), 69–71.

34. Clarice Neal, "Freedom of the Press in New Spain, 1810–1820," in *Mexico and the Spanish Cortes, 1810–1822: Eight Essays*, ed. Nettie Lee Benson (Austin: University of Texas Press, Institute of Latin American Studies, 1966), 98.

35. "Decreto de 10 de noviembre de 1810: Libertad política de imprenta," in Manuel Dublán and José María Lozano, *Legislación mexicana ó: Colección completa de las disposiciones legislativas expedidas desde la independencia de la República* (Mexico City: Imprenta del Comercio de E. Dublán y Comp., 1876), 1:337.

36. Neal, "Freedom of the Press," 92.

37. Timothy E. Anna, *The Fall of the Royal Government in Mexico City* (Lincoln: University of Nebraska Press, 1978), 109.

38. David L. Frye, "Translator's Note," in José Joaquín Fernández de Lizardi, *The Mangy Parrot: The Life and Times of Periquillo Sarniento; Written by Himself for His Children* (Indianapolis, IN: Hackett Publishing, 2004), xxxvii.

39. "Reales órdenes comunicadas al Exmo. Sr. Virey," *Gaceta del Gobierno de México*, July 18, 1820.

40. *Sobre el abuso de la libertad de imprenta* (Mexico City: En la oficina de D. Alejandro Valdes, 1820), 2.

41. *Sobre el abuso de la libertad de imprenta*, 4.

42. Jean Franco, "En espera de una burgesía: La formación de la inteligencia mexicana en la época de la Independencia," in *Actas del VIII Congreso de la Asociación Internacional de Hispanistas*, ed. David Kosoff et al. (Madrid: Istmo, 1986), 21.

43. Rafael Rojas, "Una maldición silenciada: El panfleto político en el México independiente," *Historia Mexicana* 47, no. 1 (1997): 38.

44. José Gregorio de Torres Palacios, *Al que le venga el saco que se lo ponga: Por varios rumbos y distintos modos que se cumpla la ley queremos todos* (Mexico City: Oficina de D.J.M. Benavente y Socios, 1820), 7.

45. Richard A. Warren, *Vagrants and Citizens: Politics and the Masses in Mexico City from Colony to Republic* (Wilmington, DE: SR Books, 2001), 52.

46. *Diálogo entre D. Ruperto y el Impresor: Traslado al Observador del Observador J. y suplemento al Noticioso General num 751* (Mexico City: Impreso en la oficina de D.J.M. Benavente y Socios, 1820).

47. Juan Ruíz de Apodaca Decree, *Gaceta Extraordinaria del Gobierno de México*, June 19, 1820.

48. "Reales órdenes comunicadas al Exmo. Sr. Virey," *Gaceta del Gobierno de México*, July 18, 1820.

49. Neal, "Freedom of the Press," 91.

50. Neal, "Freedom of the Press," 107.

51. The junta would serve as the main legal mechanism for judging press violations, even after a new set of rules, ratified in October in Spain, specified a slightly different protocol for enforcing the laws. The Spanish law made provisions for a junta for the protection of freedom of the press, to serve as an advocate for press freedom, and replaced the *junta de censura* with a panel of judges. Mexico continued to follow 1813 protocol. Neal, "Freedom of the Press," 108.

52. Notifications, July 1820, Archivo Histórico de la Ciudad de México (AHCM), Ayuntamiento, Justicia, Jurados de Imprenta, vol. 2739, exp. 3.

53. "Decreto del 22 de octubre de 1820," in *Colección de los decretos y ordenes de las Cortes de España, que se reputan vigentes en la república de los Estados-Unidos Mexicanos* (Mexico City: Imprenta de Galvan á cargo de Mariano Arévalo, 1829), 152.

54. "Decreto del 22 de octubre de 1820," 153.

55. "Decreto del 22 de octubre de 1820," 153.

56. José Ignacio Espinoza resignation, 1 September 1820, AHCM, Ayuntamiento, Justicia, Jurados de Imprenta, vol. 2739, exp. 3.

57. The press was auctioned off for fifty-two pesos. Viceroy Apodaca to Ministers of the Treasury, 16 September 1820, AGN, Indiferente Virreinal, Hacienda, caja 5576, exp. 8.

58. José Calapís Matos, 23 October 1820, AHCM, Ayuntamiento, Justicia, Jurados de Imprenta, vol. 2739, exp. 3.

59. José Joaquín Fernández de Lizardi, *The Mangy Parrot: The Life and Times of Periquillo Sarniento; Written by Himself for His Children*, trans. David L. Frye (Indianapolis, IN: Hackett, 2004), 5, 8.

60. Dorothy Tanck Estrada, *La educación ilustrada, 1786–1836: Educación primaria en la ciudad de México*, 2nd ed. (Mexico City: El Colegio de México, 1984); and Franco, "En espera de una burguesía."

61. Nancy J. Vogeley, "Las vicisitudes editoriales de 'La Quijotita y su prima,'" *Legajos: Boletín del Archivo General de la Nación*, no. 18 (2013): 135–93.

62. "Nota," *El Conductor Eléctrico*, no. 18 (1820): 156 (misprinted as 195).

63. The author's identity, José Gregorio de Torres Palacios, may have been familiar to some readers. J. G. T. P., "Comunicado," *El Conductor Eléctrico*, no. 18 (1820): 154.

64. J. G. T. P., "Comunicado," 155.

65. Alejandro Valdés, *La prensa libre* (Mexico City: En su oficina, 1820), 2.

66. Valdés, *La prensa libre*, 1.

67. Valdés, *La prensa libre*, 3.

68. José Joaquín Fernández de Lizardi, "Reflecciones interesantes," *El Conductor Eléctrico*, no. 19 (1820): 161.

69. Fernández de Lizardi, "Reflecciones interesantes," 161.

70. Customs officer Manuel Reyes similarly described Mexico City bookshops as "the rendezvous for disputations" several years later. Nancy J. Vogeley, *The Bookrunner: A History of Inter-American Relations—Print, Politics, and Commerce in the United States and Mexico, 1800–1830* (Philadelphia, PA: American Philosophical Society, 2011), 117.

71. Joaquín Fernández de Lizardi, *Sociedad Pública de Lectura: Por el Pensador Mexicano* (Mexico City: En la oficina de D. Juan Bautista de Arizpe, 1820).

72. Mariana Ozuna Castañeda and María Esther Guzmán Gutiérrez, "Para que todos lean: La Sociedad Pública de Lectura de El Pensador Mexicano," in *Empresa y cultura en tinta y papel: 1800–1860*, ed. Laura Suárez de la Torre and Miguel Ángel Castro (Mexico City: Instituto de Investigaciones Dr. José María Luis Mora / Universidad Nacional Autónoma de México, 2001), 283.

73. "Aviso al público sobre despotismo de imprentas," in José Joaquín Fernández de Lizardi, *Obras, IV: Periódicos* (Mexico City: Universidad Nacional Autónoma de México, 1970), 405–6.

74. "Aviso al público sobre despotismo de imprentas."

75. "Rociada de el Pensador a sus débiles rivales," in José Joaquín Fernández de Lizardi, *Obras, X: Folletos (1811–1820)* (Mexico City: Universidad Nacional Autónoma de México, 1981), 330.

76. "Rociada de el Pensador a sus débiles rivales."

77. F. M. [Félix Merino], *El liberal a los bajos escritores* (Puebla: Oficina del Gobierno, 1820). The episode is briefly treated through analysis of the pamphlet's text in Jesús Reyes Heroles, *Los orígenes*, vol. 1 of *El liberalismo mexicano* (Mexico City: Universidad Nacional de México, Facultad de Derecho, 1957), 44–49.

78. "Sumaria contra el teniente Félix Merino por libelo titulado 'El liberal a los bajos escritores,'" 1820, AGN, Indiferente de Guerra, vol. 290A.

79. "Sumaria contra el teniente Félix Merino," f. 47.

80. "Sumaria contra el teniente Félix Merino," f. 47.

81. "Sumaria contra el teniente Félix Merino," f. 47.

82. "Sumaria contra el teniente Félix Merino," f. 47v.

83. "Sumaria contra el teniente Félix Merino," f. 47v.

84. "Sumaria contra el teniente Félix Merino," f. 48v.

85. "Sumaria contra el teniente Félix Merino," f. 48v.

86. Anna, *Fall of the Royal Government*, 195.

87. "Sumaria contra el teniente Félix Merino," f. 49.

88. Alejandro Valdés, "El impresor al respetable público," epigram to Mariano Barazábal, *Mordaza al liberal que se dice* (Mexico City: Alejandro Valdés, en su oficina, calle de Sto. Domingo, 1820), 4.

89. *Suplemento a la Gazeta del Gobierno de México*, October 7, 1820.

90. Manuel Galán, *Prisión en la ciudadela del teniente Galan* (Mexico City: Imprenta de D. J. M. de Benavente y Socios, 1820).

91. Galán, *Prisión en la ciudadela*, 3.

92. The titles translate roughly as *On the Puebla Paper "El Liberal a los bajos escritores"*; *The Sincere American in Defense of the Most Excellent Viceroy, Count of Venadito, offended by the Paper titled "El liberal a los bajos escritores"*; *Another Liberal to Low Scribblers*; and *The Third Liberal to Low Scribblers*.

93. "Sea una pluma *liberal* o sea una pluma *servil*, de nadie ha de escribir mal y con nadie ha de ser vil." El Licenciado Cachaza, *Cortadillos de imprenta (*) de coco y almendra* (Mexico City: En la imprenta de D. Juan Bautista de Arizpe, 1820).

94. Lucas Alamán described Merino as a distinguished officer, "although of rash character." Lucas Alamán, *Historia de Méjico*, 4:171n8. His father, Manuel Merino, remained loyal to the crown throughout the wars of independence. Carlos Juárez Nieto, "El intendente Manuel Merino y la insurgencia en Valladolid de Michoacán, 1810–1821," in *Las guerras de independencia en la América española*, ed. Marta Terán and José Antonio Serrano Ortega (Mexico City: Colegio de Michoacán / Universidad Michoacana de San Nicolás de Hidalgo / Instituto Nacional de Antropología e Historia, 2002), 202.

95. "Sumaria contra el teniente Félix Merino," f. 58v.

96. For a list of owners, see "Sumaria contra el teniente Félix Merino," f. 59.

97. "Sumaria contra el teniente Félix Merino," f. 57v. "Pobre de tí tata, renuncia por que te quitan pero brevecito. A Dios."

98. "Sumaria contra el teniente Félix Merino," f. 72.

99. Felix Merino, *El liberal al público* (Puebla, Mexico: Imprenta Liberal, 1820).

100. Merino, *El liberal al público*, 4.

101. "Sumaria contra el teniente Félix Merino," f. 71.

102. "Sumaria contra el teniente Félix Merino," f. 73.

103. "Sumaria contra el teniente Félix Merino," f. 76v.

104. Alamán, *Historia de Méjico*, 4:41. Also quoted in Reyes Heroles, *Los orígenes*, 39.

105. J. N., *Predicar en desierto sermon perdido* (Mexico City: Impreso en la Oficina de D. J. M. Benavente y Socios, 1820), 4.

106. "Avisos," *Gaceta del Gobierno de Mexico*, November 18, 1820.

107. Rafael Dávila, *La verdad amarga, pero es preciso decirla* (Mexico City: Imprenta de J. M. de Benavente y Socios, 1820).

108. *Solicitud de un ciudadano por la libertad de Davila* (Mexico City: Imprenta de Ontiveros, 1820).

109. J. N., *Predicar en desierto*, 3.

110. El Observador J. V., *La Inquisición se quitó pero sus usos quedaron* (Mexico City: Imprenta de Ontiveros, 1820).

111. "D. Mariano de Zuñiga y Ontiveros reclama la impresión de la guía de forasteros que se ha mandado hacer en la oficina de D. Alejandro Valdés," December 1821, AGN, Gobernación, sin sección, caja 10 (old numbering system), exp. 1.

112. "D. Alejandro Valdés sobre a cual de los Escudos de Armas que presume debe arreglarse," 30 January 1822, BLAC, HD, 16-8.3677. Valdés seems to have participated in a short-lived project for producing paper money, and his press issued an anonymous pamphlet in favor of paper notes in 1823. *El papel moneda se quita* (Mexico City: En la Imprenta Imperial de Sr. D. Alexandro Valdés, 1823). On the failed paper money project, see José Antonio Bátiz Vázquez and José Enrique Covarrubias, *La moneda en México, 1750–1920* (Mexico City: Instituto Mora / El Colegio de Michoacán / El Colegio de México / Instituto de Investigaciones Históricas, UNAM, 1998), 189-91.

113. La Observadora, *La libertad de imprenta todo lo cuenta* (Mexico City: Oficina de Betancourt, 1822).

114. José Joaquín Fernández de Lizardi, *Maldita sea la libertad de imprenta* (Mexico City: Oficina de Betancourt, 1820).

115. Fernández de Lizardi, *Maldita sea la libertad de imprenta*, 11.

CHAPTER THREE. RESPONSIBILITY ON TRIAL

1. José María Gutiérrez Estrada, *Carta dirigida al Escmo. Sr. Presidente de la República, sobre la necesidad de buscar en una convención el posible remedio de los males que aquejan á la República: Y opiniones del autor acerca del mismo asunto* (Mexico City: Impresa por I. Cumplido, 1840).

2. Michael P. Costeloe, *The Central Republic in Mexico, 1835–1846: Hombres de Bien in the Age of Santa Anna* (New York: Cambridge University Press, 1993), 161, 171.

3. Frances Calderón de la Barca, *Life in Mexico* (Berkeley: University of California Press, 1982), 282.

4. Frank J. Sanders, "Jose María Gutiérrez Estrada: Monarchist Pamphleteer," *The Americas* 27, no. 1 (1970): 56; and Costeloe, *Central Republic in Mexico*, 283.

5. Edmundo O'Gorman, *La supervivencia política novo-hispana: Reflexiones sobre el monarquismo mexicano*, 2nd ed. (Mexico City: Fundación Cultural de Condumex, Centro de Estudios de Historia de México, 1969), 28. On the initiation of a more radical phase of conservativism see Elías José Palti, *La política del disenso: La "polémica en torno al monarquismo" (México, 1848–1850) . . . y las aporías del liberalismo* (Mexico City: Fondo de Cultura Económica, 1998), 16. For a helpful overview of liberal historiography's treatment of monarchism, see Erika Pani, "Monarchism and Liberalism in Mexico's Nineteenth Century" (working paper presented at the "Liberalism, Monarchy and Empire: Ambiguous Relationships" conference, School of Advanced Study, University of London, 2012).

6. Laurence Coudart, "En torno al correo de lectores de *El Sol* (1823–1832): Espacio periodístico y 'opinión pública,'" in *Transición y cultura política: De la colonia al México independiente*, ed. Cristina Gómez Álvarez and Miguel Soto (Mexico City: Facultad de Filosofía y Letras, Universidad Nacional Autónoma de México, 2004), 96.

7. Laura Suárez de la Torre, "Editores para el cambio: Expresión de una nueva cultura política, 1808–1855," in *Transición y cultura política: De la colonia al México independiente*, ed. Cristina Gómez Álvarez and Miguel Soto (Mexico City: Facultad de Filosofía y Letras, Universidad Nacional Autónoma de México, 2004), 48.

8. The printing shops that published early republican rival newspapers, *El Águila* and *El Sol*, are two well-known examples.

9. "Cuenta de diferentes gastos extraordinarios . . . de febrero de 1824," 10 March 1824, AGN, Imprenta del Gobierno, vol. 1; and "Copia de la memoria de letra y adornos que se pidió a los Estados Unidos día 28 de Dbre de 1824," Mexican Manuscript Collection, California State Library, Sutro Branch (Sutro Library), SMMS HG 1, folder 1.

10. José Jimeno, "Nota de precios corrientes de imprenta," 31 March 1828, in "Sobre arreglo del Registro Oficial," AGN, Gobernación, leg. 139, exp. 11.

11. Jimeno, "Nota de precios corrientes de imprenta." The price list quotes the cost of printing five hundred copies of a single sheet (eight pages when folded) as between 7 and 14 pesos, depending on the size of the type. Each additional one hundred copies cost 1 peso. Extra fees applied for jobs printed overnight and on holidays. Combined with paper costs, the total would easily equal monthly wages for skilled workers paid .5–1 peso/day and exceed unskilled workers' wages of .25–.5 peso/day. Mark Wasserman, *Everyday Life and Politics in Nineteenth Century Mexico: Men, Women, and War* (Albuquerque: University of New Mexico Press, 2000), 40.

12. José Ximeno to José María Bocanegra in "El contrastista de las impresiones," 29 September 1829, AGN, Gobernación, leg. 82, exp. 1; and José Ximeno to Lucas Alamán in "El contratista de las impresiones . . . . .," 24 July 1830, AGN, Gobernación, leg. 140, exp. 5.

13. On press subsidies see, for example, "Impresiones del Gobierno," 1833, AGN, Gobernación, leg. 140, exp. 2; and "Fomento de periódicos," 1849, AGN, Gobernación, leg. 248, exp. 1.

14. "Sobre que se exija al Antonio Valdés el producto de las impresiones del Boletín Oficial," January 30, 1830, AGN, Gobernación, leg. 140, exp. 5.

15. "Impreso por G. Ignacio Avila sobre la Imprenta Imparcial," 1833, AGN, Gobernacion Sin Sección (s/s), caja 165, exp. 11. Brazilian publisher Francisco de Paula Brito similarly renamed his press the Tipografia Imparcial to protect himself from political retaliation. Rodrigo Camargo de Godoi, *Francisco de Paula Brito: A Black Publisher in Imperial Brazil,* trans. H. Sabrina Gledill (Nashville, TN: Vanderbilt University Press, 2020), 72.

16. *Colección de los decretos y ordenes de las Cortes de España, que se reputan vigentes en la república de los Estados-Unidos Mexicanos* (Mexico City: Imprenta de Galván á cargo de Mariano Arévalo, 1829), 152–53.

17. See, for example, "Expediente formado sobre denuncia del no. 1611 del periódico del *Sol*," 1827, AGN, TSJDF, caja 25, exp. 68. On splits between Escocéses and Yorkinos and between moderate and radical Yorkinos, see Richard A. Warren, *Vagrants and Citizens: Politics and the Masses in Mexico City from Colony to Republic* (Wilmington, DE: SR Books, 2001), ch. 4.

18. "Denuncio del Impreso titulado el *Fénix de la Libertad* no. 45," May 1832, AGN, TSJDF, caja 72, exp. 68; "Denuncio del Impreso titulado el *Fénix de la Libertad* no. 48," May 1832, AGN, TSJDF, caja 72, exp. 52; "Denuncio del impreso titulado *Oiga el vice-presidente la sentencia de su muerte*," July 1832, AGN, TSJDF, caja 72, exp. 51; "Denuncio del impreso titulado *La Columna de la Constitución Federal de la República Mejicana*," September 1832, AGN, TSJDF, caja 72, exp. 84; "El Gobierno del Departamento de México acompaña copia del ocurso que hizo el presbítero Alpuche," 24 October 1838, AGN, Justicia, vol. 135, exp. 5; and "Orden al gobernador del depto. para que proceda al arresto del impresor del barrio de San Sebastián," November 1838, AGN, Justicia, vol. 135, exp. 9.

19. "El Licdo. Don José Basilio Guerra, a nombre del Ilmo. Sor. Dn. José María Guerra Obispo de Yucatán," March 1836, AGN, TSJDF, caja 109, exp. s/n.

20. I base this statement on analysis of press crime case files from Mexico City's Tribunal Superior de Justicia from 1827. See AGN, TSJDF, caja 25, exps. 68, 69, 70, 73, and 74.

21. Pablo Piccato, *The Tyranny of Opinion: Honor in the Construction of the Mexican Public Sphere* (Durham, NC: Duke University Press, 2010), 35–36. While Piccato's study presents the most comprehensive overview of press legislation, more targeted studies of the early republican era include Alejandra Sánchez Archundia, "Legislación de imprenta y voceo de papeles en las calles de la Ciudad de México, 1821–1834," in *Miradas y acercamientos a la prensa decimonónica*, ed. Adriana Pineda Soto and Fausta Gantús (Mexico City: Universidad Michoacana de San Nicolás de Hidalgo / Red de Historiadores de la Prensa y el Periodismo en Iberoamérica, 2013); and Reynaldo Sordo Cedeño, "La libertad de prensa en la construcción del estado laico: 1810–1857," in *El Estado laico y los derechos humanos en México: 1810–2010*, ed. Margarita Moreno Bonett and Rosa María Álvarez de Lara (Mexico City: Universidad Nacional Autónoma de México, 2012).

22. Piccato, *Tyranny of Opinion*, 61.

23. I base this statement on analysis of press crime case files from Mexico City's Tribunal Superior de Justicia. See AGN, TSJDF, 1829, caja 45, exp. 47; 1832, caja 72,

exps. 52, 68, and 84; 1836, caja 109, exp. s/n; 1840, caja 151, exp. s/n; and 1845 (misfiled in 1849), caja 261, exp. s/n.

24. Carlos María de Bustamante happily noted the elimination of the press jury during constitutional deliberations in Carlos María de Bustamante, *Diario histórico de México, 1822–1848*, ed. Josefina Zoraida Vázquez and Héctor Cuauhtémoc Hernández Silva (Mexico City: El Colegio de México / Centro de Investigaciones y Estudios Superiores en Antropología Social, 2001), November 9, 1835.

25. "El Licdo. Don José Basilio Guerra, a nombre del Ilmo. Sor. Dn. José María Guerra Obispo de Yucatán," AGN, TSJDF, 1836, caja 109, exp. s/n, f. 12.

26. "Denuncio hecho por el Sindico del Exmo. Ayuntamiento al *Sol* número 1613," November 1827, AGN, TSJDF, caja 25, exp. 74; and Declaración, 21 and 24 March 1830, Archivo Histórico de Notarías (AHN), Tirso Rodríguez Loaria, #597.

27. "Contra impreso de Eduardo Novoa en el *Mosquito Mexicano*," 7 November 1840, AGN, TSJDF, caja 151, exp. s/n.

28. "Denuncio del impreso titulado *El Fénix de la Libertad* no. 45," May 1832, AGN, TSJDF, caja 72, exp. 68; Bustamante, *Diario histórico*, July 11, 1845. The practice is described in Piccato, *Tyranny of Opinion*, 37, and for Brazil, in César Braga-Pinto, "Journalists, Capoeiras, and the Duel in Nineteenth-Century Rio de Janeiro," *Hispanic American Historical Review* 94, no. 4 (2014): 593.

29. "El Gobierno del Departamento de Puebla remitiendo dos pliegos," August 1843, AGN, Gobernación, leg. 176, exp. 3, no. 16; and "El Gobierno de México comunicando haber encontrado en la esquina de Cadena el impreso titulado Santa Anna traidor y astuto," August 1843, AGN, Gobernación, leg. 176, exp. 3, no. 20.

30. "Sobre averiguación de los que imprimieron un Plan de conspiración," June 1836, AGN, Gobernacíon, Justicia, vol. 150, exp. 34.

31. "El Licdo. Don José Basilio Guerra, a nombre del Ilmo. Sor. Dn. José María Guerra Obispo de Yucatán," March 1836, AGN, TSJDF, caja 109, exp. s/n.

32. "Sobre las dudas ocurridas a los Jueces de letras de México a cerca del modo de conocer de los delitos de imprenta," June 1836, AGN, Justicia, vol. 132, exp. 22; Piccato, *Tyranny of Opinion*, 38; and Sordo Cedeño, "La libertad de prensa," 140.

33. "Sobre las dudas," June 1836, AGN, Justicia, vol. 132, exp. 22, f. 296.

34. "Sobre las dudas," f. 306.

35. When officials raised procedural questions about enforcing press laws in 1838, Alamán, member of a commission on press freedom, provided the response that reiterated the position established in 1836. "Sobre las dudas," 8 October 1838, f. 328.

36. Costeloe, *Central Republic in Mexico*, 155. For the decree and its revocation see Manuel Dublán and José María Lozano, *Legislación mexicana ó: Colección completa de las disposiciones legislativas expedidas desde la independencia de la República* (Mexico City: Imprenta del Comercio, a cargo de Dublán y Lozano, Hijos, 1876), 3:617, 645. An 1840 project proposed by minister Juan de Dios Cañedo similarly failed. Sordo Cedeño, "La libertad de prensa," 139–40.

37. Violent actions against printing shops preceded the centralist turn of 1836 and continued throughout the nineteenth century. See descriptions of printing shop

violence, exile, and imprisonments in Bustamante, *Diario histórico*, August 14, 1828; June 12, 1833; October 30, 1833; June 24, 1836; April 17, 1838; and October 29, 1838.

38. "El Gobierno del Departamento de México acompaña copia del ocurso que hizo el presbítero Alpuche," 24 October 1838, AGN, Justicia, vol. 135, exp. 5.

39. "Expediente formado sobre denuncio de un artículo editorial," May 1827, AGN, TSJDF, caja 25, exps. 69 and 73; and "Denuncia del periódico no. 394 conocido por 'El Universal,'" December 1849, AGN, TSJDF, caja 260, exp. s/n.

40. "Orden al gobernador del depto. para que proceda al arresto del impresor del barrio de San Sebastían," November 1838, AGN, Justicia, vol. 135, exp. 9; and "Orden al gobernador del depto. para que inmediatamente haga detener al impresor Manuel Gallo," December 1838, AGN, Justicia, vol. 135, exp. 10.

41. Cumplido had traveled to the United States and purchased type in 1839. Ignacio Cumplido, "Al público mexicano," in *Cuarto calendario portátil de I. Cumplido, para el año de 1839: Arreglado al meridiano de México* (Mexico City: Impreso por el Propietario, en la oficina de la calle de los Rebeldes Num. 2, 1839).

42. *El Cosmopolita*, October 24, 1840, 4.

43. "Sumaria instruida contra los Capitanes D. Francisco Berrospe y D. Martín Rivera," 1840, AGN, Archivo de Guerra, vol. 766, exp. s/n, fs. 82–83.

44. Bustamante, *Diario histórico*, October 21, 1840.

45. *Diario del Gobierno*, October 21, 1840, 1.

46. "Sumaria instruida," f. 1.

47. Ignacio Cumplido, *Manifestación al público del impresor ciudadano Ignacio Cumplido, con motivo de su prisión, verificada el 21 de octubre de 1840* (Mexico City: Imprenta de Cumplido, 1840), 3–4n.

48. In 1827, Berrospe had acted as the responsible party for Rivera's paper *El Sol*. "Expediente formado sobre denuncia del no. 1611 del periódico del *Sol*," 1827, AGN, TSJDF, caja 25, exp. 68. On Rivera's imprisonment, see Chávez Lomelí, *Lo público y lo privado*, 100.

49. *El Cosmopolita*, October 21, 1840, 4.

50. Bustamante, *Diario histórico*, October 21, 1840.

51. Bustamante, *Diario histórico*, October 21, 1840. Rumors of French monarchical conspiracy had also circulated during a brief invasion by French troops that occupied Veracruz in December 1838. Costeloe, *Central Republic in Mexico*, 145.

52. *El Cosmopolita*, October 21, 1840, 4.

53. *El Mosquito Mexicano*, October 30, 1840, 3. Also referenced in Charles A. Hale, *Mexican Liberalism in the Age of Mora, 1821–1853* (New Haven, CT: Yale University Press, 1968), 27.

54. *El Mosquito Mexicano*, October 30, 1840, 3. Comparatively, a subscription to the biweekly *Mosquito Mexicano* cost one peso for an entire month.

55. Berrospe had served in the active militia, while Rivera's branch is not specified in the documents. He may have served in the active militia with Berrospe, who referred to him as his "compadre."

56. "Sumaria instruida," f. 4.

57. "Sumaria instruida," f. 6.

58. "Sumaria instruida," f. 6.

59. "Sumaria instruida," f. 10.

60. "Sumaria instruida," f. 10.

61. "Sumaria instruida," f. 11.

62. Rivera lost one of his presses in 1838 in a lawsuit after failing to pay rent. "D. Manuel de la Borda por la Sra. su madre política Da. Ma. Ignacia Palacios de Horcasitas contra el Capitán D. Martín Rivera sobre desocupación de casa," October 1838, AGN, TSJDF, caja 146, exp. s/n.

63. "Sumaria instruida," f. 79.

64. "Sumaria instruida," fs. 79–80.

65. "Sumaria instruida," f. 80.

66. "Sumaria instruida," f. 80.

67. "Sumaria instruida," f. 82.

68. Piccato, *Tyranny of Opinion*, 11.

69. The scandal generated condemnation from General Antonio López de Santa Anna (*El Diario del Gobierno*, October 23, 1840), President Bustamante (*El Mosquito Mexicano*, October 27, 1840, and *El Cosmopolita*, October 28, 1840), General Gabriel Valencia (*El Cosmopolita*, October 28, 1840), General José María Tornel, and others. *El Correo de Dos Mundos* (October 24, 1840) suggested Gutiérrez Estrada was a well-intentioned man led astray. *El Mosquito Mexicano* (October 30 and November 3, 1840) argued that government action might be overzealous.

70. *El Cosmopolita*, October 21, 24, 28, and November 4, 14, 18, 1840.

71. *El Cosmopolita*, October 24, 1840, 4.

72. *Diario del Gobierno*, October 26, 1840, 4.

73. Cumplido moved to Mexico City from Jalisco, where his father was a professor of medicine. Cumplido's family relationship to Juan Nepomuceno Cumplido, who served briefly as vice-governor and governor of Jalisco, perhaps facilitated the printer's career in Mexico City. Ramiro Villaseñor y Villaseñor, *Ignacio Cumplido, impresor tapatío* (Guadalajara, Mexico: Gobierno de Jalisco, Secretaría General, Unidad Editorial, 1987), 13.

74. Cumplido's commissioned works in the 1830s included pamphlets by the *santanistas* José María Tornel and Ignacio Sierra y Rosso, conservative president Anastasio Bustamante, and the Conde de la Cortina. For a detailed reconstruction of Cumplido's editorial activities, see María Esther Pérez Salas, "Ignacio Cumplido: un empresario a cabalidad," in *Empresa y cultura en tinta y papel: 1800–1860*, ed. Laura Suárez de la Torre and Miguel Ángel Castro (Mexico City: Instituto de Investigaciones Dr. José María Luis Mora / Universidad Nacional Autónoma de México, 2001); María Esther Pérez Salas Cantú, "Los secretos de una empresa exitosa: La imprenta de Ignacio Cumplido," in *Constructores de un cambio cultural: Impresores-editores y libreros en la ciudad de México, 1830–1855*, ed. Laura Suárez de la Torre (Mexico City: Instituto de Investigaciones Dr. José María Luis Mora, 2003).

75. Ignacio Cumplido, *Apelación al público* (Mexico City: Imprenta de Cumplido, 1840).

76. Cumplido, *Manifestación al público.*

77. "Defensa del impresor ciudadano Ignacio Cumplido, con motivo de su prision, verificada el 21 de octubre de 1840," *El Cosmopolita*, November 4, 1840.

78. "Defensa del impresor ciudadano Ignacio Cumplido, con motivo de su prision, verificada el 21 de octubre de 1840," *El Mosquito Mexicano*, November 6, 10, 13, 17, 20, 1840.

79. *Recopilación de leyes, decretos, reglamentos, circulares y providencias de los supremos poderes y otras autoridades de la república mexicana: Formada de orden del supremo gobierno por el Lic. Basilio José Arrillaga; Comprende este tomo todo el año de 1837* (Mexico City: Imprenta de J. M. Fernández de Lara, 1839), 320.

80. *Recopilación de leyes*, 321. On the vagrancy court that targeted underemployed artisans in Mexico City between 1828 and 1850, see Sonia Pérez Toledo, *Los hijos del trabajo: Los artesanos de la ciudad de México, 1780–1853* (Mexico City: El Colegio de México / Universidad Autónoma Metropolitana-Iztapalapa, 1996), 248–57.

81. Cumplido, *Apelación al público.*

82. Cumplido, *Apelación al público.*

83. Cumplido, *Manifestación al público*, 4–5.

84. Cumplido, *Manifestación al público*, 6.

85. Cumplido, *Manifestación al público*, 6.

86. Cumplido, *Manifestación al público*, 7 (emphasis in original).

87. Cumplido, *Manifestación al público*, 7.

88. Cumplido, *Manifestación al público*, 16–18.

89. "Sobre las dudas" June 1836, AGN, Justicia, vol. 132, exp. 22.

90. "Defensa del Impresor," *El Mosquito Mexicano*, November 6, 1840, 2–3.

91. "Defensa del Impresor," 3.

92. "Defensa del Impresor," 3.

93. *El Cosmopolita*, November 25, 1840, 4.

94. *El Cosmopolita*, November 25, 1840, 4; and Bustamante, *Diario histórico*, November 25, 1840.

95. Ignacio Cumplido, *Invitación que hace el impresor C. Ignacio Cumplido al juez de letras de lo criminal licenciado D. J. Gabriel Gómez de la Peña, a fin de que esponga las disposiciones legales á que se arregló para proceder á su prision y detenerlo treinta y tres días en la cárcel de la Acordada, como impresor del folleto que escribió D. J. M. Gutierrez Estrada* (Mexico City: Impreso por el autor, 1840), 7.

96. Cumplido, *Invitación que hace el impresor C. Ignacio Cumplido*, 13–14.

97. "Contra impreso de Eduardo Novoa en el Mosquito Mexicano," 7 November 1840, AGN, TSJDF, caja 151, exp. s/n.

98. *El Cosmopolita*, December 2, 1840, 4.

99. *El Mosquito Mexicano*, December 4, 1840, 4.

100. Francisco Berrospe, "Al público," *El Mosquito Mexicano*, January 1, 5, 8, 12, 15, 19, 22, 26, 29, and February 2, 5, 9, 12, 23, 26, 1841.

101. Berrospe, "Al público," January 5, 1841, 3.

102. Berrospe, "Al público," February 5, 1841, 1–2.

103. Berrospe, "Al público," February 26, 1841, 2.

104. "Sumaria instruida," fs. 116–18.

105. Gutiérrez Estrada may have stopped in Cuba on his voyage to Europe, as a second edition of his pamphlet was issued there the same year, featuring an imperfect copy of the original Mexican lithograph. José María Gutiérrez Estrada, *Carta dirigida al Escmo. Sr. Presidente de la República, sobre la necesidad de buscar en una convención el posible remedio de los males que aquejan á la República: Y opiniones del autor acerca del mismo asunto* (Havana: Imprenta de Francisco García, 1840).

106. Costeloe, *Central Republic in Mexico*, 216.

107. Costeloe, *Central Republic in Mexico*, 216; "Libertad de Imprenta: Sobre el Plan de dictadura," April–May 1842, AGN, Gobernación, leg. 176, exp. 2, no. 4; and "García Torres, Dn. Vicente, Impresor," June 1843, AGN, Archivo de Guerra, vol. 1218.

108. Examples of executive decrees specifically discussing responsibility include "Sobre responsabilidad personal de los dueños de lo que se publique," 1 December 1844, AGN, Gobernación, leg. 176, exp. 4, no. 31; and "Sobre responsabilidad de los autores, editores e impresores, de los escritos que protejan las miras de algún invasor, o que auxilien algún cambio en el orden establecido," 18 April 1846, AGN, Gobernación, leg. 176, exp. 6, no. 55.

109. Pérez Salas Cantú, "Los secretos de una empresa exitosa," 165.

110. In 1842, Santa Anna issued a decree that specifically targeted Cumplido and *El Siglo Diez y Nueve* by denying the right of congressional immunity to printers. Piccato, *Tyranny of Opinion*, 38.

111. On liberals' slow response to the conservative monarchist assault, see Hale, *Mexican Liberalism in the Age of Mora*, 32.

112. For a full account of the monarchist conspiracy, which sought to gain power after a coup by the conservative general Mariano Paredes, see Miguel Soto, *La conspiración monárquica en México, 1845–1846* (Mexico City: Editorial Offset, 1988).

113. On the monarchist platform of *El Tiempo* and the backlash that followed, see Soto, *La conspiración monárquica en México*; and Costeloe, *Central Republic in Mexico*. On promonarchist debates that reemerged between 1848 and 1850, see Palti, *La política del disenso*. *El Tiempo* was printed by the conservative printer José Mariano Lara. Laura Suárez de la Torre, "José Mariano Lara: Intereses empresariales—inquietudes intelectuales—compromisos políticos," in *Constructores de un cambio cultural: Impresores-editores y libreros en la ciudad de México, 1830–1855*, ed. Laura Suárez de la Torre (Mexico City: Instituto de Investigaciones Dr. José María Luis Mora, 2003).

114. José María Gutiérrez Estrada, *México en 1840 y 1847* (Mexico City: Imprenta de Vicente G. Torres, en el ex-convento del Espíritu Santo, 1848), 11.

CHAPTER FOUR. SELLING SCANDAL: *THE MYSTERIES OF THE INQUISITION*

1. V. de Féréal, *Misterios de la Inquisición y otras sociedades secretas de España* (Mexico City: Imprenta de V. García Torres, á cargo de L. Vidaurri, 1850).

2. Lithographer Charles Risso copied the French engravings for the New Orleans edition. *Misterios de la Inquisición y otras sociedades secretas de España* (New Orleans: Imprenta de J. L. Sollée, 1846). His tracing shows in the mirror image of the original illustrations. *Mystères de l'inquisition et autres sociètès secretes d'Espagne* (Paris: Boizard, 1845).

3. Elizabeth A. Fenton, *Religious Liberties: Anti-Catholicism and Liberal Democracy in Nineteenth-Century U.S. Literature and Culture* (New York: Oxford University Press, 2011), 4.

4. Daniel Muñoz, "The Abolition of the Inquisition and the Creation of a Historical Myth," *Hispanic Research Journal* 11, no. 1 (2010).

5. Pamela Voekel, *Alone Before God: The Religious Origins of Modernity in Mexico* (Durham, NC: Duke University Press, 2002).

6. Actas de Cabildo originales de sesiones secretas, 11 September 1849, AHCM, vol. 302A, discussed in Arturo Soberón, "Lucas Alamán y la presidencia del ayuntamiento de la ciudad de México en 1849," *Historias: Revista de la Dirección de Estudios Históricos del Instituto Nacional de Antropología e Historia*, no. 50 (2001): 42–43.

7. The simultaneous outbreak of indigenous rebellions in the Yucatán and Huasteca regions further challenged the state. Charles A. Hale, *Mexican Liberalism in the Age of Mora, 1821–1853* (New Haven, CT: Yale University Press, 1968), 12.

8. For an overview of the radical, moderate, and conservative perspectives see Will Fowler, *Mexico in the Age of Proposals, 1821–1853* (Westport, CT: Greenwood Press, 1998).

9. Pablo Mijangos y González, *Entre Dios y la república: La separación Iglesia-Estado en México, siglo XIX* (Valencia: CIDE / Tirant Lo Blanch, 2018), 99.

10. Brian F. Connaughton, *Clerical Ideology in a Revolutionary Age: The Guadalajara Church and the Idea of the Mexican Nation, 1788–1853*, trans. Mark Alan Healey (Calgary, AB: University of Calgary Press, 2002).

11. Michael P. Costeloe, *Church and State in Independent Mexico: A Study of the Patronage Debate, 1821–1857* (London: Royal Historical Society, 1978).

12. Michael P. Costeloe, *Church Wealth in Mexico: A Study of the "Juzgado de Capellanías" in the Archbishopric of Mexico 1800–1856* (London: Cambridge University Press, 1967).

13. *Colección de los decretos y ordenes de las Cortes de España, que se reputan vigentes en la república de los Estados-Unidos Mexicanos* (Mexico City: Imprenta de Galván á cargo de Mariano Arévalo, 1829), 153.

14. On the final phase of Mexico's Inquisition, see Gabriel Torres Puga, *Los últimos años de la Inquisición en la Nueva España* (Mexico City: Miguel Ángel Porrúa / CONACULTA-INAH, 2004).

15. In one exceptional 1829 case, the state intervened and stopped the activities of the London Bible Society in Mexico. Mijangos y González, *Entre Dios y la república*, 111–18.

16. "Acta de la Junta de Censura religiosa, conllevada en 20 de Septiembre de 1831," AGN, Bienes Nacionales, vol. 732, exp. 11.

17. Untitled document, 23 March 1831, AGN, Bienes Nacionales, caja 1139, exp. 11.

18. *Disposiciones legales y otros documentos relativos a la prohibición de impresos por la autoridad eclesiástica, mandados publicar de orden del Supremo Gobierno* (Mexico City: Imprenta de Ignacio Cumplido, 1850), 13.

19. Letter from Commission in "Proyecto de la comisión respectiva sobre libertad de imprenta," 27 May 1845, AGN, Gobernación, leg. 176, exp. 5, no. 41-Bis.

20. Letter from Commission, 27 May 1845.

21. "Discusión sobre reglamento de Libertad de Imprenta," minutes of 4 February 1845, AGN, Gobernación, leg. 176, exp. 5, no. 42-Bis.

22. "Discusión sobre reglamento de Libertad de Imprenta," minutes of 6 February 1845.

23. *Colección de leyes y decretos: Publicados desde 10 de Enero de 1844.* (Mexico City: Imprenta en Palacio, 1851), 487.

24. Carlos María de Bustamante, *Diario histórico de México, 1822–1848*, ed. Josefina Zoraida Vázquez and Héctor Cuauhtémoc Hernández Silva (Mexico City: El Colegio de México / Centro de Investigaciones y Estudios Superiores en Antropología Social, 2001), June 22, 1847.

25. "Reglamento de la libertad de imprenta," 14 November 1846, art. 65, *Colección de leyes y decretos*, 499.

26. "Décimo calendario de Cumplido para 1845," *El Siglo Diez y Nueve*, September 25, 1844; Reconocimiento (Juan O'Sullivan, Eduardo Nolan, Juan Baggally), 25 May 1852, AHN, Fermín Villa, Notary #719, f. 43; Compraventa (Boix Besserer y Compañía, O'Sullivan y Nolan), 29 July 1852, AHN, Miguel Diez de Bonilla, Notary #215, f. 9; Compraventa (Vicente Serralde, Serefino Serralde, Mariano Lazo, Luis Vidal), 13 October 1854, AHN, José de Jesús Piña, Notary #534; Compraventa (Santiago Pérez, Eduardo Trejo), 11 February 1856, AHN, Agustín Pérez de Lara, Notary #1001 (Hacienda), f. 50; and Edward Nolan to Hoe & Co, 5 March 1855, Columbia University Rare Book & Manuscript Library (RBML), Richard M. Hoe & Company Papers, box 3.

27. Dorothy Tanck Estrada, *La educación ilustrada, 1786–1836: Educación primaria en la ciudad de México*, 2nd ed. (Mexico City: El Colegio de México, 1984), 202.

28. Guillermo Prieto, *Memoria de mis tiempos 1828 a 1853* (Puebla: Editorial José M. Cajica Jr., 1970), 353.

29. Prieto, *Memoria de mis tiempos*, 355.

30. Cumplido to León Ortigosa, 12 August 1848, in Sylvia Cárdenas Iglesias and Delia de Peña Guajardo, eds., *Correspondencia de Ignacio Cumplido a León Ortigosa en la Biblioteca del Instituto Tecnológico y de Estudios Superiores de Monterrey* (Monterrey: Instituto Tecnológico y de Estudios Superiores de Monterrey, 1969).

31. Othón Nava Martínez, "La empresa editorial de Vicente García Torres, 1838–1853," in *Constructores de un cambio cultural: Impresores-editores y libreros en la ciudad de México, 1830–1855*, ed. Laura Suárez de la Torre (Mexico City: Instituto de Investigaciones Dr. José María Luis Mora, 2003), 256–57.

32. Fowler, *Mexico in the Age of Proposals*, 170.

33. "García Torres, Dn. Vicente, Impresor," June 1843, AGN, Archivo de Guerra, vol. 1218.

34. "Queja que hace D. Vicente García Torres contra el Sr. Gral. en Gefe del Ejército de Oriente por sus procedimientos," 26 July 1847, Archivo Histórico de la Suprema Corte de Justicia de la Nación (AHSCJN), Queja, Militar, J-1847-08-09-SCJ-2S-Q-Mx-3272.

35. Peter Guardino, *The Dead March: A History of the Mexican-American War* (Cambridge, MA: Harvard University Press, 2017), 249.

36. "Vicente García Torres, Teniente Coronel del Regimento de la Independencia a sus conciudadanos compañeros de armas," 1847, Sutro Library, SMBC6, Proclamaciones 1824–1888, no. 76.

37. Bustamante, *Diario histórico*, August 11, 1847.

38. Guillermo Prieto to Vicente García Torres, 23 September 1847, Biblioteca Nacional de México, Fondo Reservado, Archivos y Manuscritos, MS 10276, Cartas privadas de Guillermo Prieto a Don Vicente García Torres entre 1847 y 1861.

39. Guardino, *Dead March*, 364–68.

40. Guardino, *Dead March*, 280–85.

41. José Joaquín Castañares to Mariano Riva Palacio, 16 October 1847, BLAC, Mariano Riva Palacio Manuscript Collection (MRP), #2438.

42. Kenya Bello, "The American Star: El destino manifiesto y la difusión de una comunidad imaginaria," *Estudios de Historia Moderna y Contemporánea de México*, no. 31 (2006).

43. Pablo Piccato, *The Tyranny of Opinion: Honor in the Construction of the Mexican Public Sphere* (Durham, NC: Duke University Press, 2010), 38–39.

44. Granja had moved to New York after being expelled from Mexico along with others of Spanish origin in 1827. In the 1830s, he sold printing equipment from R. Hoe & Company throughout Latin America. Letterpress Book, 1836–1858, Columbia University RBML, Richard M. Hoe and Company Records, box 36, fol. 118. He later returned to Mexico, where he died. Juan de la Granja, *Epistolario: Con un estudio biográfico preliminar por Luis Castillo Ledón y notas de Nereo Rodríguez Barragán* (Mexico City: Talleres Gráficos del Museo Nacional de Arqueología y Etnografía, 1937), 387.

45. For thorough analysis of the Rafael-Cumplido polemic, see Javier Rodríguez Piña, "Rafael de Rafael y Vilá: El conservadurismo como empresa," in *Constructores de un cambio cultural: Impresores-editores y libreros en la ciudad de México, 1830–1855*, ed. Laura Suárez de la Torre (Mexico City: Instituto de Investigaciones Dr. José María Luis Mora, 2003); and Javier Rodríguez Piña, "La prensa y las ideas conservadores a mediados del siglo XIX," in *Tipos y caracteres: la prensa mexicana, 1822–1855*, ed. Miguel Ángel Castro (Mexico City: Universidad Nacional Autónoma de México, 2001).

46. R. Rafael, "Don Ignacio Cumplido y sus dependientes," *El Monitor Republicano*, December 1, 1847.

47. Compraventa Negocio, 8 March 1848, AHN, Daniel Méndez, Notary #433; and Rodríguez Piña, "Rafael de Rafael y Vilá," 161.

48. Fowler, *Mexico in the Age of Proposals*, 46.

49. Elías José Palti, *La política del disenso: La "polémica en torno al monarquismo" (México, 1848–1850) . . . y las aporías del liberalismo* (Mexico City: Fondo de Cultura Económica, 1998).

50. Soberón, "Lucas Alamán y la presidencia," 37.

51. "Denuncio del impreso titulado 'Muera D. Lucas Alamán,'" 5 December 1849, AGN, TSJDF, caja 258, exp. 20.

52. "Incidente de la causa que se instruye en el Juzgado 29 de lo Civil por el Lic. Pérez de Lebrija contra D. Vicente García Torres como responsable . . . ," November 1849, AGN, TSJDF, caja 262, exp. s/n.

53. "Expediente instruido a consecuencia de la Consulta hecha por la 3a Sala de esta Suprema Corte con motivo de las dudas que han ocurrido relativas a la ley [relativa] de imprenta," 14 January 1850, AHSCJN, Consulta, Diversas, J-1850-01-17-SCJ-TP-Con-Mx-3668.

54. May 1 prospectus reprinted as "Misterios de la Inquisición," *El Siglo Diez y Nueve*, June 19, 1850.

55. May 1 prospectus, 2.

56. May 1 prospectus.

57. Muñoz, "Abolition of the Inquisition," 72–73.

58. Marie Léger-St-Jean, "Price One Penny: A Database of Cheap Literature, 1837–1860," last updated September 9, 2020, http://priceonepenny.info.

59. For example, see Vicente García Torres to Sres. Redactores, *El Monitor Republicano*, March 12, 1846, 4.

60. "Misterios de la Inquisición," *El Siglo Diez y Nueve*, May 28, 1850. On press debates over the *Mysteries of Paris*, see Javier Rodríguez Piña, "Los conservadores-católicos mexicanos ante *Los Misterios de París de Eugenio Sue*," in *Tras las huellas de Eugenio Sue: Lectura, circulación y apropiación de Los misterios de París, Siglo XIX*, ed. Laura Suárez de la Torre (Mexico City: Instituto de Investigaciones Dr. José María Luis Mora, 2015).

61. "Misterios de la Inquisición," *El Monitor Republicano*, June 12, 1850.

62. "Misterios de la Inquisición," *El Siglo Diez y Nueve*, June 14, 1850.

63. See, for example, Ignacio Cumplido, "Al público mexicano," in *Cuarto calendario portátil de I. Cumplido, para el año de 1839: Arreglado al meridiano de México* (Mexico City: Impreso por el Propietario, en la oficina de la calle de los Rebeldes Num. 2, 1839).

64. Ryan Cordell, "Reprinting, Circulation, and the Network Author in Antebellum Newspapers," *American Literary History* 27, no. 3 (Fall 2015): 418.

65. Cordell, "Reprinting, Circulation, and the Network Author," 418.

66. Meredith L. McGill, *American Literature and the Culture of Reprinting, 1834–1853* (Philadelphia: University of Pennsylvania Press, 2003).

67. "Desenfreno de la prensa—Los Misterios de la Inquisición," *El Universal*, June 15, 1850.

68. "Desenfreno de la prensa."

69. "Los Misterios de la Inquisición," *El Monitor Republicano*, June 17, 1850; "Los Misterios de la Inquisición," *El Siglo Diez y Nueve*, June 19, 1850; and "El Siglo XIX y los 'Misterios de la Inquisición,'" *El Universal*, June 21, 1850.

70. "El Siglo XIX y los 'Misterios de la Inquisición.'"

71. Féréal, *Misterios de la Inquisicion* (Mexico City), 46.

72. "Los Misterios de la Inquisición," *El Siglo Diez y Nueve*, June 29, 1850.

73. "Los Misterios de la Inquisición y el Universal," *El Siglo Diez y Nueve*, July 13, 1850. Other attacks included "Despique de los Loretos," *El Siglo Diez y Nueve*, July 3, 1850; and "Mala fé y charlatanería del Universal," *El Siglo Diez y Nueve*, July 10, 1850.

74. "Misterios de la Inquisición," *El Monitor Republicano*, July 18, 1850.

75. Marta Eugenia García Ugarte, *Poder político y religioso: México siglo XIX* (Mexico City: Universidad Nacional Autónoma de México, Instituto de Investigaciones Sociales / M.A. Porrúa, 2010), 1:349.

76. José María Barrientos decree, in "El E. S. Ministro de Justicia inserta su oficio del S. Vicario Capitular sobre que se recoja todos los ejemplares de la obra titulada 'Misterios de la Inquisición,'" 5 September 1850, AGN, Gobernación, s/s, caja 378, exp. 1.

77. José María Diez de Sollano, *Dictamen que el doctor Don José María Diez de Sollano, cura interino del Sagrario Metropolitano, y Rector del colegio de S. Gregorio, emitió sobre la obra intitulada Misterios de la Inquisición y que hizo suyo la Junta diocesana de censura, y ha mandado publicar el Sr. Vicario Capitular de este arzobispado* (Mexico City: Tipografía de R. Rafael, 1850).

78. Diez de Sollano, *Dictamen que el doctor Don José María Diez de Sollano*, 4.

79. See, for example, "Asuntos concluidos en el provisorato durante el mes de julio de 1852," and "Asuntos concluidos en el provisorato en el mes de mayo de 1852," Archivo Histórico del Arzobispado de México (AHAM), Base Siglo XIX, caja 85, exps. 20–21.

80. Diez de Sollano, *Dictamen que el doctor Don José María Diez de Sollano*, 3.

81. Diez de Sollano, *Dictamen que el doctor Don José María Diez de Sollano*, 58, 46.

82. Diez de Sollano, *Dictamen que el doctor Don José María Diez de Sollano*, 43.

83. *Disposiciones legales*, 3–4.

84. *Disposiciones legales*, 9.

85. *Disposiciones legales*, 9.

86. *Disposiciones legales*, 10.

87. *Disposiciones legales*, 11.

88. *Disposiciones legales*, 10.

89. *Disposiciones legales*, 11.

90. *Disposiciones legales*, 11.

91. *Disposiciones legales*, 11.

92. *Disposiciones legales*, 12.

93. *Disposiciones legales*, 8.

94. *Disposiciones legales*, 13.

95. *Disposiciones legales*, 14.

96. *Disposiciones legales*, 15.

97. *Disposiciones legales*, 15.

98. *Disposiciones legales*, 16.

99. *Disposiciones legales*, 16.

100. *Disposiciones legales*, 18.

101. "Juicio crítico de los Misterios de la Inquisición," *El Monitor Republicano*, September 11, 1850.

102. *Defensa del editor de la obra titulada los Misterios de la Inquisición, contestando el dictamen del Sr. Consultor de la Junta Diocesana de Censura, en virtud del cual se declaró prohibido, y se fulminó por el señor vicario capitular una excomunicación mayor* (Mexico City: Imprenta de V. G. Torres, 1850), 4–5.

103. *Defensa del editor de la obra titulada los Misterios de la Inquisición*, 14.

104. *Defensa del editor de la obra titulada los Misterios de la Inquisición*, 49.

105. *Defensa del editor de la obra titulada los Misterios de la Inquisición*, 49.

106. *Defensa del editor de la obra titulada los Misterios de la Inquisición*, 50 (emphasis in original).

107. *Disposiciones legales*, 57.

108. *Disposiciones legales*, 57.

109. "Sobre que la Junta de Censura revise el periódico titulado *Monitor Republicano* en uno de sus párrafos," August 1851, AGN, Bienes Nacionales, caja 732, exp. 19.

110. "Asuntos concluidos en el provisorato en el mes de mayo de 1852 a saber: Sobre los numeros 2514 y 2515 del *Monitor*, remitidos a la Junta de Censura," April 1852, AHAM, Base Siglo XIX, caja 85, exp. 21.

111. "Misterios de la Inquisición," *El Monitor Republicano*, November 23, 1850.

112. "Misterios de la Inquisición," November 23, 1850.

113. Manuel Dublán and José María Lozano, *Legislación mexicana ó: Colección completa de las disposiciones legislativas expedidas desde la independencia de la República* (Mexico City: Imprenta del Comercio de E. Dublán y Comp., 1876), 1:337.

114. *Colección de leyes y decretos*, 490.

115. Mijangos y González, *Entre Dios y la república*.

116. The deposit system drew from 1852 French press laws. Laurence Coudart, "La regulación de la libertad de prensa (1863–1867)," *Historia Mexicana* 65, no. 2 (2015): 650.

CHAPTER FIVE. THE BUSINESS OF NATION BUILDING

1. The decree's author was acting interim governor of Mexico City but had close ties to the national government (having recently served in the Ministry of Hacienda). The municipal government probably received some special access to the national presses at times. Bando and Circular, José Ignacio Esteva, 24 December 1827, AGN, Gobernación, leg. 60, exp. 17.

2. "Cuenta de los gastos erogados en la Imprenta nacional del Supremo Gobierno de los Estados unidos mexicanos en el año de 1824," 28 February 1825, in "Cuenta general documentada del año de 1824," AGN, Gobernación, leg. 42, exp. 11, fs. 2–5.

3. Ramón Gutiérrez del Mazo to Joaquín de Miramón, 21 April 1823, in "Números de Gacetas desde el 21 al 30 de Abril de 1823," AGN, Gobernación, leg. 81, exp. 4.

4. "Imprenta Nacional del S.G. de M, Cuenta general de diferentes gastos," 8 January 1824, AGN, Gobernación, s/s, caja 59/1, exp. 28, f. 2v.

5. Joaquín de Miramón to Ministro de Relaciones, 25 April 1823, in "Números de Gacetas desde el 21 al 30 de Abril de 1823," AGN, Gobernación, leg. 81, exp. 4, fs. 4–6.

6. "Cuenta de los gastos erogados en la Imprenta nacional del Supremo Gobierno de los Estados unidos mexicanos en el año de 1824," 28 February 1825, in "Cuenta general documentada del año de 1824," AGN, Gobernación, leg. 42, exp. 11, fs. 2-5.

7. "Cuenta de los gastos erogados en la Imprenta nacional del Supremo Gobierno de los Estados unidos mexicanos en el año de 1824"; and "Cuenta de diferentes gastos extraordinarios," 24 February 1824, in "Cuentas," AGN, Imprenta del Gobierno, vol. 1.

8. In 1824, job work covered over one-quarter of the imprenta's budget shortfall. "Cuenta de los gastos erogados en la Imprenta nacional del Supremo Gobierno de los Estados unidos mexicanos en el año de 1824," 28 February 1825, in "Cuenta general documentada del año de 1824," AGN, Gobernación, leg. 42, exp. 11, fs. 2–5. For examples of such printing, see sonnet in "Cuenta documentada de los impresos que se han hecho a particulares en el mes de Octubre de 1823," AGN, Gobernación, s/s, caja 55, exp. 2, f. 14; and miscellaneous ephemera, 1826–27, AGN, Gobernación, leg. 60, exp. 9 and Gobernación, s/s, caja 59-7, exp. 23, f. 157.

9. Cédulas de confesión, 1828(?), AGN, Gobernación, leg. 71, exp. 1.

10. Claudia Ferreira Ascencio, "Los padrones de confesión y comunión del Sagrario de México: Una aproximación a la praxis sacramental en el orden canónico indiano (1676–1825)," in *Normatividades e instituciones eclesiasticas en la Nueva Espana, siglos XVI–XIX*, ed. Benedetta Albani, Otto Danwerth, and Thomas Duve (Frankfurt: Max Planck Institute for European Legal History, 2018), 180.

11. "Cuentas," January–December 1824, AGN, Imprenta del Gobierno, vols. 1–2.

12. The constitution's printing is documented in "Cuentas," vol. 2.

13. "Cuenta de lo trabajado en el departamento de composición del S.P.E. del Domingo 5 al sabado 11 de Dic. de 1824," in "Cuentas," AGN, Imprenta del Gobierno, vol. 2.

14. Contrato (Joaquín Miramón, José Jimeno, Supremo Gobierno de la Nación), 19 July 1828, AHN, Francisco Calapiz, Notary #155.

15. "Sobre que las Cámaras del Congreso acuerden lo conducente para que las sesiones no se publiquen por particular alguno, antes que se haga por el Periódico Oficial," 4 July 1844, AGN, Gobernación, leg. 176, exp. 4, no. 26.

16. See, for example, multiple records on subscriptions and "fomento de periódicos" from 1833 in AGN, Gobernación, leg. 140, exp. 2 and from 1851–1852 in leg. 248, exps. 1 and 2.

17. Isidro Gondra to José María Ortíz Monasterio, 23 November 1840, AGN, Gobernación, leg. 139, exp. 1.

18. José Jimeno (also written Ximeno), formerly the overseer for Alejandro Valdés (discussed in chapter 2), oversaw the Imprenta del Aguila.

19. Certain specific printing jobs, like lottery tickets, were auctioned more frequently to a wider set of contractors. See, for example, Contrato (José Mariano Fernández de Lara), 13 May 1836, AHN, Miguel Diez de Bonilla, Notary #215, f. 28.

20. A new five-year contract was signed in 1839, extended several times, and formally renewed in 1848. "Se acompañan al Ministro de Hacienda 7 cuadernos sobre contrato para las impresiones del Supremo Gobierno," 1848, AGN, Gobernación, leg. 47, exp. 33.

21. "Sobre que los trabajos que deben [illeg] para la impresión del registro oficial se remitan con la oportunidad debida," April 1830, AGN, Gobernación, leg. 140, exp. 5; and "Orden al Administrador del Registro Oficial diciéndole que el número de los días del Correo lo remita precisamente en él," March 1832, AGN, Gobernación, leg. 140, exp. 3.

22. "El contratista de las impresiones del Gobierno remitiendo las cuentas de las que se han causado en los meses de enero a julio inclusive de este año," September 1829, AGN, Gobernación, leg. 82, exp. 1.

23. Ignacio Díaz de Triujeque to Ministro de Relaciones, 19 September 1851, in "Periódico Oficial: Orden para que cese su publicación en la imprenta de la calle de Medinas," AGN, Gobernación, leg. 248, exp. 1, fs. 202–7.

24. Compraventa (Mariano Esteva, Vicente Cerralde, Mariano Arévalo, Víctor Cerralde, Mariano Bustos), 13 April 1853, AHN, Ramon de la Cueva, Notary #169.

25. Compraventa (Boix, Besserer & Compañia, O'Sullivan and Nolan), 29 July 1852, AHN, Miguel Diez de Bonilla, Notary #215, f. 9v.

26. "Periódico Oficial: Orden para que se dén a D. Vicente García Torres 76 pesos diarios," September 1851, AGN, Gobernación, leg. 248, exp. 1, fs. 208–21.

27. *Reglamento para las impresiones del gobierno* (Mexico City: Tipografía de Vicente García Torres, 1852), art. 37.

28. See, for example, numerous discussions between Ignacio Cumplido and government administrators, 1853, AGN, Gobernación, leg. 247, exp. 3.

29. Ignacio Cumplido to Mariano Riva Palacio, 23 June 1845, BLAC, MRP, #1827; and Ignacio Cumplido to Mariano Riva Palacio, 1 February 1850, BLAC, MRP, #3808.

30. Mariano Riva Palacio to Ignacio Cumplido, 6 June 1850, BLAC, MRP #4257; and Ignacio Cumplido to Mariano Riva Palacio, 12 July 1850, BLAC, MRP, #4446.

31. Víctor Manuel Macías-González, "Masculine Friendships, Sentiment, and Homoerotics in Nineteenth-Century Mexico: The Correspondence of José María Calderón y Tapia, 1820s–1850s," *Journal of the History of Sexuality* 16, no. 3 (2007): 419.

32. Vicente García Torres, 1853, in "Periódico Oficial: Contrata celebrada con D. Vicente García Torres para la impresión de dicho periódico," AGN, Gobernación, leg. 248, exp. 1, fs. 115–18.

33. García Torres, 1853, in "Periódico Oficial."

34. Lucas Alamán to Ministry of Hacienda, 16 May 1853 in "Periódico Oficial," f. 119.

35. "Impresiones," 1853, AGN, Gobernación, leg. 248, exp. 1, f. 987.

36. *El archivo mexicano: Colección de leyes, decretos, circulares y otros documentos* (Mexico City: Imprenta de Vicente G. Torres, 1856), 1:203.

37. Javier Rodríguez Piña, "Rafael de Rafael y Vilá: El conservadurismo como empresa," in *Constructores de un cambio cultural: Impresores-editores y libreros en la ciudad de México, 1830–1855,* ed. Laura Suárez de la Torre (Mexico City: Instituto de Investigaciones Dr. José María Luis Mora, 2003)," 371; Compraventa (Francisco Javier Miranda, Rafael Rafael, José María Andrade, Felipe Escalante), 30 June 1854, AHN, Francisco Villalon, Notary #722, f. 185; and Compraventa Negocio, 8 March 1848, AHN, Daniel Mendez, Notary #433.

38. In Cuba, Rafael published *La Voz de Cuba,* and his antifreemasonry writings were later compiled as Rafael de Rafael and Antonio Juan de Vildósola, *La masonería pintada por sí misma: Artículos publicados en el periódico "La Voz de Cuba," de la Habana* (Madrid: Impr. de A. P. Dubrull, 1883).

39. "Impresiones: D. Vicente García Torres solicitando se supenda la convocatoria," 14 May 1857, AGN, Gobernación, leg. 1249, exp. 3.

40. "Impresiones."

41. AHCM, Ayuntamiento, Biblioteca: Publicaciones de Boletín y Actas de Cabildo, vol. 431, exp. 27.

42. "El Ministerio de Gobernación, comunica la contrata hecho con la viuda y albacea de Boix para las impresiones del Supremo Gobierno," 1858, AGN, Justicia, vol. 624, exp. 39, fs. 275–77, and exp. 93, fs. 437–43.

43. Liberals paid Rafael de Zayas, Domingo Cabrera, and Manuel Díaz Mirón in 1860. Miscellaneous documents, 1860, AGN, Gobernación, leg. 1046, exp 1.

44. Annita Melville Ker, *Mexican Government Publications: A Guide to the More Important Publications of the National Government of Mexico, 1821–1936* (Washington, DC: US Government Printing Office, 1940), 21.

45. AHCM, Ayuntamiento, Biblioteca, vol. 431, exp. 32.

46. Worldcat searches for 1858–1860 returned just a single volume.

47. Quoted in Robert H. Duncan, "Maximilian and the Construction of the Liberal State, 1863-1866," in *The Divine Charter: Constitutionalism and Liberalism in Nineteenth-Century Mexico,* ed. Jaime E. Rodríguez O. (Lanham, MD: Rowman & Littlefield, 2005), 152.

48. Memorandum to Sub-Secretario del Despacho de Hacienda, 15 July 1863, AGN, Gobernación, leg. 1127, exp. 1; and "Impresiones: Puebla. D. Vicente García Torres pidiendo el pago de una cantidad por un contrato de impresiones que celebró con el Gobierno de Puebla," 4 April 1865, AGN, Gobernación, leg. 1046, exp. 4.

49. "Contestando el Sr. Subsecrio. de Hacienda sobre la pregunta que se le hizo, de si pulsaba algún inconveniente en la solicitud del Sr. Lic. D. Basilio Arrillaga," April–October 1864, AGN, Gobernación, leg. 1127, exp. 2.

50. "El Señor Don Francisco Díaz de León, Tipógrafo," *El Socialista,* September 19, 1881.

51. See petitions in AGN, Gobernación, leg. 1127, exps. 1, 2, 4, and leg. 1046, exp. 3.

52. Request from Manuel Ramírez, 5 December 1864, AGN, Gobernación, leg. 1237, exp. 4.

53. On continuities between Maximilian's regime and previous Mexican governments, see Erika Pani, *Para mexicanizar el Segundo Imperio: El imaginario político de los imperialistas* (Mexico City: El Colegio de México / Instituto de Investigaciones Dr. José María Luis Mora, 2001).

54. Laurence Coudart, "La regulación de la libertad de prensa (1863–1867)," *Historia Mexicana* 65, no. 2 (2015): 647–48.

55. Press clippings, 1866, AGN, Gobernación, leg. 1862, exp. 1.

56. Order from Ministro de Gobernación to Prefecto Político de México, 25 April 1865, AGN, Gobernación, leg. 1046, exp. 3.

57. "El Prefecto de León, sobre que el Prefecto Superior de Guanajuato mandó suspender el periódico *La Paz,* que allí se publicaba," 9 March 1864, AGN, Gobernación, leg. 1046, exp. 2.

58. Robert H. Duncan, "Political Legitimation and Maximilian's Second Empire in Mexico, 1864–1867," *Mexican Studies* 12, no. 1 (1996): 34.

59. Circular no. 23, 20 June 1865, AGN, Gobernación, leg. 1046, exp. 3.

60. Prefectura de Guanajuato to Subsecretario de Gobernación, 26 March 1864, AGN, Gobernación, leg. 1127, exp. 2.

61. Prefectura de Jalisco and Ministerio de Gobernación, 12 June 1865, Archivo Histórico de Jalisco (AHJ), Gobernación, Prensa e Imprenta del Gobierno, clasificación G-3-862, caja 2, no. 6286.

62. Duncan, "Political Legitimation," 37.

63. Decree, 2 October 1865, in "De Miguel Zornoza sobre el pago de varios impresiones de esta Secretaria," AGN, Gobernación, leg. 1046, exp. 5.

64. Decree, 2 October 1865. I hazard this claim based on observations of extant government printing records consulted in the AGN.

65. Esteva to Prefectos, 3 October 1865, in "De Miguel Zornoza sobre el pago de varios impresiones de esta Secretaria," AGN, Gobernación, leg. 1046, exp. 5.

66. "Maximiliano, Emperador de México," 2 October 1865, copy in The Bancroft Library, University of California, Berkeley.

67. Mark Morris, "Language in Service of the State: The Nahuatl Conterinsurgency Broadsides of 1810," *Hispanic American Historical Review* 87, no. 3 (2007).

68. Magdalena Chocano Mena, "Colonial Printing and Metropolitan Books: Printed Texts and the Shaping of Scholarly Culture in New Spain, 1539–1700," *Colonial Latin American Historical Review* 6, no. 1 (1997): 72. On the typography of indigenous language printing, see Garone Gravier, *Historia de la tipografía colonial para lenguas indígenas* (Mexico City: CIESAS / Universidad Veracruzana, 2014).

69. Erika Pani, "¿'Verdaderas figuras de Cooper' o 'Pobres inditos infelices'? La política indigenista de Maximiliano," *Historia Mexicana* 47, no. 3 (1998): 594.

70. Brian R. Hamnett, *Juárez* (London: Longman, 1994), 183.

71. Inventory, 1870, in "Impresiones: Sobre compra de tipos para el Diario Oficial," AGN, Gobernación, leg. 1305, caja 2, exp. 2, f. 38.

72. The director, José María Sandoval, apparently loaned one of Escalante's printing presses to another printer, who resisted later requests to give it back. "Sobre que se le recoja al C. Gregorio Pérez Jardón la prensa mecánica que tiene en calidad de préstamo," August 1870, AGN, Gobernación, leg. 1350, caja 2, exp. 2, fs. 1–13.

73. Bancroft's purchase became a core of the University of California at Berkeley's library in the early twentieth century. Miguel Ángel Castro, "Un par de lecturas posibles del Catálogo de la Biblioteca de José María Andrade," in *Empresa y cultura en tinta y papel: 1800–1860*, ed. Laura Suárez de la Torre and Miguel Ángel Castro (Mexico City: Instituto de Investigaciones Dr. José María Luis Mora / Universidad Nacional Autónoma de México, 2001), 288–89.

74. Discussed in Conrado Hernández López, "Querétaro en 1867 y la división en la historia (sobre una carta enviada por Silverio Ramírez a Tomás Mejía el 10 de abril de 1867)," *Historia Mexicana* 57, no. 4 (2008): 1203.

75. Quarter-leather binding cut down on the cost of materials and was frequently used for ledgers or economical volumes.

76. Juan Pablo Ortiz Dávila, "Visiones desde la prensa: Las relaciones entre los conservadores y los confederados durante el Segundo Imperio, 1863–1866," *Estudios de Historia Moderna y Contemporánea de México* 52 (2016): 31.

77. Maury's text supported Maximilian's own decision to sideline his ultramontane supporters in favor of establishing a national church subordinated to the state.

78. "Reglamento para la Imprenta del Supremo Gobierno," in Manuel Dublán and José María Lozano, *Legislación mexicana ó: Colección completa de las disposiciones legislativas expedidas desde la independencia de la República* (Mexico City: Imprenta del Comercio de E. Dublán y Comp., 1882), 12:515.

79. See, for example, "Imprenta del Gobierno: Cuenta de Impresiones," November 1875, AGN, Gobernación, leg. 1322, exp. 1.

80. The archivist asked officials to cut their remittances down to one hundred copies, and the government obliged. Jefe del Archivo General to Oficial Mayor de Gobernación, 4 June 1877, AGN, Gobernación, leg. 1264, exp. 2, no. 71, f. 1.

81. See, in particular, Raymond B. Craib, *Cartographic Mexico: A History of State Fixations and Fugitive Landscapes* (Durham, NC: Duke University Press, 2004); and Magali M. Carrera, *Traveling from New Spain to Mexico: Mapping Practices of Nineteenth-Century Mexico* (Durham, NC: Duke University Press, 2011).

82. "Inventario de las obras que existen en el Archivo de la Imprenta del Supremo Gobierno," May 1877, AGN, Gobernación, leg. 1264, exp. 3, fs. 25–31.

83. Oz Frankel, *States of Inquiry: Social Investigations and Print Culture in Nineteenth-Century Britain and the United States* (Baltimore, MD: Johns Hopkins University Press, 2006), 2.

84. Order to close government printing office, 22 November 1862, AHJ, Gobernación, Prensa e Imprenta del Gobierno, clasificación G-3-862, caja 2, no. 6267.

85. Dublán and Lozano, *Legislación mexicana*, 12:515.

86. "Guillermo Prieto pide la impresión de su obra 'Romancero Nacional' de la Imprenta de la Secretaría de Fomento," 2 June 1885, AGN, Instrucción Pública y Bellas Artes, vol. 226, exp. 52.

87. This can be seen in the monthly accounting reports provided by the national printing shop directors. See, for example, "Impresiones: Cortes de Caja," 1870, AGN, Gobernación, leg. 1305, caja 2, exps. 1–2; and "Imprenta: Cuenta comprobada de las impresiones oficiales," 1875, leg. 1322, exp. 1.

88. Craib, *Cartographic Mexico*, 8.

89. This accounts for the 44 typesetters I identified on payroll from 1870, 1872, and 1875, plus scattered associated printers. The 1879 census counted 264 adult male printers. Susie S. Porter, *Working Women in Mexico City: Public Discourses and Material Conditions, 1879–1931* (Tucson: University of Arizona Press, 2003), 12.

CHAPTER SIX. WORKERS OF THOUGHT

1. Guillermo Prieto, *Lecciones elementales de economía política, dadas en la escuela de jurisprudencia de México en el curso de 1871* (Mexico City: Imprenta del Gobierno, en Palacio, a cargo de José María Sandoval, 1871), 1.

2. Prieto, *Lecciones elementales*, 27, 29.

3. Prieto, *Lecciones elementales*, 39.

4. Prieto, *Lecciones elementales*, 29.

5. "El cajista," *El Socialista*, June 13, 1875.

6. Martha Celis de la Cruz, "La propiedad literaria: El caso Carlos Nebel contra Vicente García Torres (1840)," in *Empresa y cultura en tinta y papel: 1800–1860*, ed. Laura Suárez de la Torre and Miguel Ángel Castro (Mexico City: Instituto de Investigaciones Dr. José María Luis Mora / Universidad Nacional Autónoma de México, 2001).

7. Francisco Zarco, *Escritos sobre la libertad de imprenta* (Mexico City: Consejo Nacional para la Cultura y las Artes, Dirección General de Publicaciones, 2013), 225.

8. Ignacio Cumplido to Secretario del Ayuntamiento, 12 November 1869, AHCM, Ayuntamiento, Justicia, Jurados de Imprenta, exp. 65.

9. Pablo Piccato, *The Tyranny of Opinion: Honor in the Construction of the Mexican Public Sphere* (Durham, NC: Duke University Press, 2010). On liberals' exceptions to the new rules of press freedom, see Fausta Gantús, "Amagada, perseguida y ¿sometida? Discurso satírico-visual y normativa legal sobre la libertad de imprenta. Ciudad de México, 1868–1883," *Historia Mexicana* 69, no. 1 (2019): 265.

10. Carlos Illades, *Hacia la república del trabajo: La organización artesanal en la Ciudad de México, 1853–1876* (Mexico City: El Colegio de México, 1996).

11. Carlos Illades, *Las otras ideas: Estudio sobre el primer socialismo en México, 1850–1935* (Mexico City: Ediciones Era / Universidad Autónoma Metropolitana Cuajimalpa, 2008).

12. Jacques Rancière, "The Myth of the Artisan: Critical Reflections on a Category of Social History," *International Labor and Working-Class History*, no. 24 (1983): 11 (emphasis in original).

13. "El cajista," *El Socialista*, June 13, 1875.

14. "El cajista."

15. Pierre Bourdieu, *Distinction: A Social Critique of the Judgement of Taste* (London: Routledge, 2012), 328.

16. Ireneo Paz, *Datos tocantes al periodismo en México,* ca. 1884–1885, Bancroft Library, MSS M-M371, f. 4.

17. Vicente Riva Palacio and Manuel Payno, *El libro rojo, 1820–1867* (Mexico City: Díaz de León y White, 1870).

18. Vieyra Sánchez, *"La Voz de México" (1870–1875), la prensa católica y la reorganización conservadora* (Mexico City: Universidad Nacional Autónoma de México, Instituto de Investigaciones Bibliográficas / Instituto Nacional de Antropología e Historia, 2008), 61.

19. Rafael Barajas, *El país de El Ahuizote: La caricatura mexicana de oposición durante el gobierno de Sebastián Lerdo de Tejada, 1872–1876* (Mexico City: Fondo de Cultura Económica, 2005).

20. My reconstruction of the government printing shop comes from an inventory prepared by its director, José María Sandoval. "Inventario general de los útiles, muebles, enseres y demás objetos que existen en esta oficina" 31 December 1870, in "Impresiones: Sobre compra de tipos para el Diario Oficial," AGN, Gobernación, leg. 1305, caja 2, exp. 2.

21. Juan Josef Sigüenza y Vera, *Mecanismo del arte de la imprenta para facilidad de los operarios que le exerzan* (Madrid: Imprenta de la Compañia, 1811), 29.

22. Emilio Rabasa, *La gran ciencia: El cuarto poder* (Tuxtla Gutiérrez, Chiapas: Consejo Estatal para la Cultura y las Artes de Chiapas, 2000), 210.

23. The protagonist in Elena Poniatowska's testimonial novel *Here's to You, Jesusa!* is based on her interviews with a woman who worked as a cleaner in a Mexico City printing shop in the twentieth century, where she washed type and took home the workers' aprons to soak in solvent. I am grateful to the anonymous reviewer who recommended this work. Elena Poniatowska, *Here's to You, Jesusa!,* trans. Deanna Heikkinen (New York: Farrar, Straus and Giroux, 2001), ix.

24. "Reglamento para la Imprenta del Supremo Gobierno," 14 November 1873, in Manuel Dublán and José María Lozano, *Legislación mexicana ó: Colección completa de las disposiciones legislativas expedidas desde la independencia de la República* (Mexico City: Imprenta del Comercio de E. Dublán y Comp., 1882), 12:516.

25. This practice runs contrary to the findings in D. F. McKenzie's landmark 1969 bibliographical study that revealed simultaneous composition practices in eighteenth-century England. D. F. McKenzie, *Making Meaning: "Printers of the Mind" and Other Essays* (Amherst: University of Massachusetts Press, 2002).

26. "Interlíneas," *La Imprenta,* May 25, 1884, 6.

27. Incomplete records made it impossible to envision a complete overview of compositors' wages in the government printing shop at any given time, since administrators tabulated composition work for the *Diario Oficial* separately from other jobs.

28. Composition records of the *Diario Oficial,* 18 December 1875, in "Imprenta de Gobierno. Cuenta de Impresiones," AGN, Gobernación, leg. 1322, caja 1, exp. 1, f. 35.

29. "Corte de caja de Agosto de 1872," in "Impresiones Oficiales: El Director de la Imprenta del Gobierno remite sus cortes de caja," 1872, AGN, Gobernación, leg. 1208, exp. 3, f. 67.

30. "Impresiones: Fallecimiento del formador José María Sierra y nombramiento de Tomás Vazquez," September 1875, AGN, Gobernación, leg. 1322, exp. 2.

31. Composition records of the *Diario Oficial*, December 1875, in "Imprenta de Gobierno: Cuenta de Impresiones," AGN, Gobernación, leg. 1322, caja 1, exp. 1, fs. 34–37.

32. See "Imprenta de Gobierno: Cuenta de Impresiones," 1870, AGN, Gobernación, leg. 1305, caja 2, exps. 1–3; 1872, leg. 1280, exp. 3; 1875, leg. 1322, exps. 1–5.

33. Dublán and Lozano, *Legislación mexicana*, 12:516–17.

34. "Impresiones del Gobierno: El C. Ramón Arce pide aumento de sueldo," January 1870, AGN, Gobernación, leg. 1305, caja 2, exp. 1.

35. I am grateful to Manuel Suárez Rivera for notifying me about "Asociación Artística La Fraternidad Tipográfica, Circular," 29 March 1853, Sutro Library, SMMS, HG1 Folder 9.

36. On the Sociedad de Socorros Mutuos de Impresores, see José Woldenberg K., "Asociaciones artesanas del siglo XIX (Sociedad Socorros Mutuos de Impresores, 1874–1875)," *Revista Mexicana de Ciencias Políticas y Sociales* 21, no. 83 (1976)." The rules of the Sociedad Mexicana de Tipografía can be consulted in Carlos Illades, *Estudios sobre el artesanado urbano del siglo XIX*, 2nd. ed. (México: Universidad Autónoma Metropolitana; M. A. Porrúa, 2001), 198.

37. *La Firmeza*, April 15, 1874.

38. Illades, *Hacia la república del trabajo*, 31.

39. Federico Gamboa, *Impresiones y recuerdos* (Buenos Aires: A. Moen, 1893), 66.

40. For select examples see Letter to the Editor, *El Mosquito Mexicano*, May 25, 1838, 4; "Pronunciamiento," *El Universal*, August 1, 1850; "Corrección," *El Siglo Diez y Nueve*, August 3, 1861; and "Erratas," *El Monitor Republicano*, December 26, 1867.

41. María Esther Pérez Salas, *Costumbrismo y litografía en México: Un nuevo modo de ver* (Mexico City: Universidad Nacional Autónoma de México, Instituto de Investigaciones Estéticas, 2005).

42. Edward Wright-Rios, *Searching for Madre Matiana: Prophecy and Popular Culture in Modern Mexico* (Albuquerque: University of New Mexico Press, 2014), 99–100.

43. John Lear, *Workers, Neighbors, and Citizens: The Revolution in Mexico City* (Lincoln: University of Nebraska Press, 2001), 64.

44. "Discurso pronunciado por el C Lic. Ignacio M. Altamirano en la celebración del 20 aniversario de la Sociedad de Socorros Mutuos de Impresores," *La Firmeza*, February 13, 20, 1875; and "El Sr. José Martí," *La Firmeza*, February 20, 1875.

45. Lorenzo Agoitia, "Las clases obreras," *La Firmeza*, January 30, 1875.

46. Juan N. Serrano, "Nuestra sociedad," *La Firmeza*, January 30, 1875.

47. Serrano, "Nuestra sociedad."

48. Jesús Laguna, "El cajista," *El Desheredado*, February 14, 1875.

49. Luis Alva, "Los obreros de la luz," *La Imprenta*, June 1, 1884.

50. "Bajo qué bases deben asociarse los tipógrafos," *La Imprenta*, June 22, 1884.

51. "La enseñanza industrial," *La Imprenta*, May 25, 1884.

52. "La imprenta," *La Imprenta*, June 22, 1884. Another article, "El Cajista," charted a similar tale of decline in *El Desheredado*, February 14, 1875. For a progressive narrative, "Los obreros de la luz," *La Imprenta*, June 1, 1884.

53. "Imprenta del Gobierno: Se nombran; Al C. José Ponce de León Director de la Imprenta del Gobierno . . .," December 1876, AGN, Gobernación, leg. 1264, exp. 3.

54. Luis I. Mata, *Filomeno Mata* (Mexico City: Secretaría de Educación Pública, 1945), 14–15. On Paz's political publishing activities, see Antonia Pi-Suñer Llorens, "Entre la historia y la novela. Ireneo Paz," in *La república de las letras: Asomos a la cultura escrita del México decimonónico*, ed. Belem Clark de Lara and Elisa Speckman (Mexico City: Universidad Nacional Autónoma de México, 2005).

55. "Informe rendido por el C. Filomeno Mata acerca del estado que guarda la Imprenta del Gobierno," 12 January 1877, AGN, Gobernación, leg. 1264, exp. 3.

56. "Informe rendido por el C. Filomeno Mata."

57. "Informe rendido por el C. Filomeno Mata."

58. Sandoval's 1870 inventory reported that the government printing shop owned type from the Bruce Foundry. For an example of Bruce's jocular specimens, see *An Abridged Specimen of Printing Types, Made at Bruce's New York Type-Foundry* (New York: George Bruce's Son & Co., 1869).

59. For references to all of these specimens, see Marina Garone Gravier, "Muestras tipográficas mexicanas: Comentarios en torno a nuevos hallazgos (siglos XVIII–XX)," in *Las muestras tipográficas y el estudio de la cultura impresa*, ed. Marina Garone Gravier and María Esther Pérez Salas Cantú (Mexico City: Universidad Nacional Autónoma de México, 2012). The typography of Manuel Antonio Valdés's more recently rediscovered specimen is analyzed in Marina Garone Gravier, "La muestra de letras de Manuel Antonio Valdés (México, 1814): Noticias sobre una fuente para la historia de la cultura impresa novohispana," *Historia Mexicana* 70, no. 1 (2020).

60. On Cumplido's liberal performance, see María Esther Pérez Salas Cantú, "Tipografía e ideología en el Libro de Muestras de Ignacio Cumplido," in *Las muestras tipográficas y el estudio de la cultura impresa*, ed. Marina Garone Gravier and María Esther Pérez Salas Cantú (Mexico City: Universidad Nacional Autónoma de México, 2012). For an analysis of US type specimens as printing shop literature, see Alastair Johnston, *Alphabets to Order: The Literature of Nineteenth-Century Typefounders' Specimens* (New Castle, DE: Oak Knoll Press, 2000).

61. Ángel Rama, *The Lettered City*, trans. John Chasteen (Durham, NC: Duke University Press, 1996), 22.

62. To analyze this document, I quantified the 88 percent of its 288 references that could be assigned some kind of geographic attribute and also experimented with categorical denominations (political figures, artists, writers, etc.). This exercise informed the qualitative analysis presented here.

63. Magali M. Carrera, *Traveling from New Spain to Mexico: Mapping Practices of Nineteenth-Century Mexico* (Durham, NC: Duke University Press, 2011), 169–71.

64. Charles A. Hale, *The Transformation of Liberalism in Late Nineteenth-Century Mexico* (Princeton, NJ: Princeton University Press, 1989), 41. Castelar's

column appeared alongside various reprinted speeches by Spanish republican presidents including Pi y Magall and Salmerón, both of whom appear in the *muestras*. Castelar and his cohort became models of conservative liberalism for Mexican politicians and were influential in the adoption of "scientific politics" under the Porfirian regime.

65. Erika Pani, *Para mexicanizar el Segundo Imperio: El imaginario político de los imperialistas* (Mexico City: El Colegio de México / Instituto de Investigaciones Dr. José María Luis Mora, 2001), 67.

66. Mario Trujillo Bolio, "El entramado de la cultura obrera entre los trabajadores urbanos (1864–1880)," in *Cultura y trabajo en México: Estereotipos, prácticas y representaciones*, ed. Rocío Guadarrama (Mexico City: Universidad Autónoma Metropolitana, 1998), 57.

67. Susie S. Porter, *Working Women in Mexico City: Public Discourses and Material Conditions, 1879–1931* (Tucson: University of Arizona Press, 2003), 13.

68. This supports the observations of scholars of nineteenth-century masculinity who emphasize the importance of homosocial ties and friendship in the narration of national dramas and the navigation of interpersonal relationships and power. Robert McKee Irwin, *Mexican Masculinities* (Minneapolis: University of Minnesota Press, 2003); and Victor Manuel Macías-González, "Masculine Friendships, Sentiment, and Homoerotics in Nineteenth-Century Mexico: The Correspondence of José María Calderón y Tapia, 1820s–1850s," *Journal of the History of Sexuality* 16, no. 3 (2007): 420.

69. Rebecca Earle, *The Return of the Native: Indians and Myth-Making in Spanish America, 1810–1930* (Durham, NC: Duke University Press, 2007), 107.

70. James E. Sanders, *The Vanguard of the Atlantic World: Creating Modernity, Nation, and Democracy in Nineteenth-Century Latin America* (Durham, NC: Duke University Press, 2014), 5.

71. Jesse Hoffnung-Garskof, "To Abolish the Law of Castes: Merit, Manhood and the Problem of Colour in the Puerto Rican Liberal Movement, 1873–92," *Social History* 36, no. 3 (2011): 314.

72. William H. Sewell, *Work and Revolution: The Language of Labor from the Old Regime to 1848* (New York: Cambridge University Press, 1980), 14.

73. Emilio Rabasa skewered this character when he described "that privilege that men of talent have, of talking about everything, assured of doing it well, and thus not understanding the issue in question" in his novel *El cuarto poder*. Rabasa, *La gran ciencia: El cuarto poder*, 239.

74. Carrera, *Traveling from New Spain to Mexico*, 171.

75. "Imprenta: Nombramiento al C. Sabás Munguia, de Administrador de la Imprenta del Gobierno," 23 May 1877, AGN, Gobernación, leg. 1264, exp. 2.

76. Rafael Martínez, "Ecce Homo," *El Socialista*, August 11, 1878.

77. Press accounts of lowered wages conflict with the available data from the government printing shop; perhaps press operator wages went down while type compositors' pay rates remained constant. Illades, *Hacia la república del trabajo*, 172; and J. G. M., "Las artes y los oficios," *El Hijo del Trabajo*, November 11, 1883.

78. Wages compiled from available records for the years 1875, 1880, 1883, 1884, 1888, 1895, and 1900 from AGN, Gobernación: "Imprenta de Gobierno: Cuenta de Impresiones," January–December 1875, leg. 1322, caja 2, exps. 1–5; "Imprenta. Cortes de caja," January–December 1880, leg. 945, exps. 1–2; "Imprenta: Cuentas comprobadas," January 1883, leg. 945, exp. 3; "Imprenta del Gobierno: Cuentas comprobadas," June–August 1884, s/s, caja 639, exp. 10-3; "Diario Oficial e Imprenta del Gobierno: Cuentas comprobadas," November–December 1888, s/s, caja 654, exp. 3-1; "Imprenta del Gobierno: Sus cuentas comprobadas," January–December 1895, s/s, caja 782, exp. 2; and "Imprenta del Gobierno: Sus cuentas comprobadas," March–November 1900, s/s, caja 747, exps. 1–3.

79. "Reglamento para el régimen interior de la Imprenta del Gobierno," January 1880, AGN, Gobernación, leg. 945, exp. 1, art. 5.

80. *Informe presentado al Señor Secretario de Fomento por el director de la imprenta de la misma secretaría, en cumplimiento del artículo 18 del reglamento que rige en dicha oficina* (Mexico City: Oficina Tipográfica de la Secretaría de Fomento, 1889), 9.

81. Luis Rubin, *Cuentos de mi tía, por Luis G. Rubin.* Ed. publicada con el patrocinio del Señor Secretaría de Fomento, General D. Carlos Pacheco (Mexico City: Oficina Tip. de la Secretaría de Fomento, 1890); and Luis Rubin, *Mi libro* (Mexico City: Oficina Tip. de la Secretaría de Fomento, 1897).

82. Gamin [Aurelio Garay], "La Hidra (memorias de un suicida)," *El Socialista*, September 5, 1883.

83. Aurelio Garay, "La Hidra," *El Socialista*, April 2, 1884, folletín no. 37.

84. Gamboa, *Impresiones y recuerdos*, 63.

85. Gamboa, *Impresiones y recuerdos*, 65.

86. Hale, *Transformation of Liberalism*.

CHAPTER SEVEN. CRIMINALIZING THE PRINTING PRESS

1. "Sobre cesión de una prensa tipográfica de pie 'Gordon' y unos tipos pertenecientes a la imprenta de 'El Hijo del Ahuizote,'" 14 August 1906, AGN, Secretaría de Justicia, caja 559, exp. 1284; and "Sobre cesión de una prensa de mano sistema 'Campbell,' dos peinazos y 16 cajones con letra pertenecientes a la imprenta del periódico 'Vesper,'" 14 August 1906, AGN, Secretaría de Justicia, caja 559, exp. 1285.

2. "Las imprentas del gobierno en México," *El Arte Tipográfico*, July 1910, 3–16.

3. Timo H. Schaefer, *Liberalism as Utopia: The Rise and Fall of Legal Rule in Post-Colonial Mexico, 1820–1900* (New York: Cambridge University Press, 2017), 203.

4. Charles A. Hale, *The Transformation of Liberalism in Late Nineteenth-Century Mexico* (Princeton, NJ: Princeton University Press, 1989), 3.

5. Robert Buffington, *Criminal and Citizen in Modern Mexico* (Lincoln: University of Nebraska Press, 2000), 40; Pablo Piccato, *City of Suspects: Crime in Mexico City, 1900–1931* (Durham, NC: Duke University Press, 2001), 51; and Elisa Speckman Guerra, "Infancia es destino: Menores delincuentes en la ciudad de México

(1884–1910)," in *De normas y transgresiones: Enfermedad y crimen en América Latina, 1850–1950*, ed. Claudia Agostoni and Elisa Speckman Guerra (Mexico City: Universidad Nacional Autónoma de México, Instituto de Investigaciones Históricas, 2005), 238.

6. Ann S. Blum, "Conspicuous Benevolence: Liberalism, Public Welfare, and Private Charity in Porfirian Mexico City, 1877–1910," *The Americas* 58, no. 1 (2001): 38.

7. On Porfirian and revolutionary vocational training programs, see Mary Kay Vaughan, *The State, Education, and Social Class in Mexico, 1880–1928* (DeKalb: Northern Illinois University Press, 1982); and Patience A. Schell, *Church and State Education in Revolutionary Mexico City* (Tucson: University of Arizona Press, 2003).

8. Lisa Gitelman, *Paper Knowledge: Toward a Media History of Documents* (Durham, NC: Duke University Press, 2014), 25.

9. Robert Buffington, *A Sentimental Education for the Working Man: The Mexico City Penny Press, 1900–1910* (Durham, NC: Duke University Press, 2015), 24.

10. Manuel Ceballos Ramírez, "Las lecturas católicas: Cincuenta años de literatura paralela, 1867–1917," in *Historia de la lectura en México*, ed. Seminario de Historia de la Educación de México (Mexico City: Colegio de Mexico, 1997), 155.

11. Florence Toussaint Alcaraz, *Escenario de la prensa en el Porfiriato* (Mexico City: Fundación Manuel Buendía / Universidad de Colima, 1989), 21; Juan Garibay Mendoza, ed., *El Mundo Ilustrado de Rafael Reyes Spíndola* (Mexico City: Grupo Carso, 2003); and Clara Guadalupe García, *El Imparcial: Primer periódico moderno de México* (Mexico City: Centro de Estudios Históricos del Porfiriato, A. C., 2003).

12. Ariel Rodríguez Kuri, "El discurso del miedo: El Imparcial y Francisco I. Madero," *Historia Mexicana* 40, no. 4 (1991): 701.

13. One observer credited Vicente García Torres with introducing steam power to his mechanical presses in 1873. *Manual de tipografía escrito expresamente para las alumnas impresoras del conservatorio de música y declamación* (Mexico City: Imprenta del Conservatorio, 1875), 28.

14. Edward Beatty, *Technology and the Search for Progress in Modern Mexico* (Oakland: University of California Press, 2015), 4.

15. Manuel Fernández Leal, *Memoria presentada al Congreso de la Unión por el Secretario de Estado y del Despacho de Fomento, Colonización e Industria de la República Mexicana Ingeniero Manuel Fernández de Leal: Corresponde a los años transcurridos de 1892 a 1896* (Mexico City: Oficina Tip. de la Secretaría de Fomento, 1897), 120.

16. *Legislación mejicana, o sea colección completa de las leyes, decretos y circulares que se han expedido desde la consumación de la independencia* (Mejico: Imprenta de Juan R. Navarro, 1855), 647.

17. "R. Hoe y Compañia," *El Siglo Diez y Nueve*, February 11, 1874.

18. Ignacio Cumplido visited New York as a young man and secured the advertising business of major firms like R. Hoe & Company and George Bruce & Sons. See advertisement in *El Siglo Diez y Nueve*, April 16, 1874. On Porfirian-era retailers, see Beatty, *Technology and the Search for Progress*, 79, 87.

19. See, for example, *La Tipografía Mexicana: Circular de Ellis Read,* July 1878; *Gran depósito de útiles para imprenta* (Mexico City: G. Lohse y Comp., Sucs., 1885); and "Antigua ferretería y mercería de la Palma de G. Lohse y Cia.," *El Correo Español,* December 29, 1895.

20. Beatty, *Technology and the Search for Progress,* 206; and Ana María Otero-Cleves, "Foreign Machetes and Cheap Cotton Cloth: Popular Consumers and Imported Commodities in Nineteenth-Century Colombia," *Hispanic American Historical Review* 97, no. 3 (2017): 448.

21. Pedro Loza, *Carta pastoral del Ilmo. y Rvmo. Sr. Doctor D. Pedro Loza, Arzobispo de Guadalajara, sobre los malos periódicos* (Guadalajara, Mexico: Ant. Tip. de N. Parga, 1897), 6–7.

22. Ceballos Ramírez, "Las lecturas católicas," 154.

23. Ceballos Ramírez, "Las lecturas católicas," 155, 168–69.

24. Edward Wright-Rios, *Searching for Madre Matiana: Prophecy and Popular Culture in Modern Mexico* (Albuquerque: University of New Mexico Press, 2014), 71.

25. Wright-Rios, *Searching for Madre Matiana,* 132.

26. Blum, "Conspicuous Benevolence," 15.

27. The 1891 encyclical *Rerum Novarum* fueled official calls for renewed engagement in print. Erika Pani, "'Para difundir las doctrinas ortodoxas y vindicarlas de los errores dominantes': Los periódicos católicos y conservadores en el siglo XIX," in *La república de las letras: Asomos a la cultura escrita del México decimonónico; Publicaciones periódicos y otros impresos,* ed. Belem Clark de Lara and Elisa Speckman (Mexico City: Universidad Nacional Autónoma de México, 2005), 129.

28. Loza, *Carta pastoral,* 11.

29. Susie S. Porter, *Working Women in Mexico City: Public Discourses and Material Conditions, 1879–1931* (Tucson: University of Arizona Press, 2003), 11; and Dirección General de Estadística, *Estadística general de la república mexicana, á cargo del Dr. Antonio Peñafiel* (Mexico City: Oficina Tipográfica de la Secretaría de Fomento, 1892), 6:902. Statistics that counted the number of printing shops may be even more unreliable. While Sonia Pérez Toledo counts forty-five shops in 1842 and fifty-eight in 1865, Carlos Illades identifies twenty-one in 1865, and Susie Porter counts thirty-three in 1879. The increase in printers likely reflects a combination of proliferating smaller workshops and the growth of large firms who employed more workers. Sonia Pérez Toledo, *Trabajadores, espacio urbano y sociabilidad en la ciudad de México, 1790–1867* (Mexico City: Universidad Autónoma Metropolitana, Unidad Iztapalapa / Miguel Ángel Porrúa, 2011), 81; Carlos Illades, *Hacia la república del trabajo: La organización artesanal en la ciudad de México, 1853–1876* (Mexico City: El Colegio de México, 1996), 31; and Porter, *Working Women in Mexico City.*

30. Steven B. Bunker, *Creating Mexican Consumer Culture in the Age of Porfirio Díaz* (Albuquerque: University of New Mexico Press, 2012), 26.

31. John Lear, *Workers, Neighbors, and Citizens: The Revolution in Mexico City* (Lincoln: University of Nebraska Press, 2001), ch. 3.

32. "Una visita a la imprenta de la Secretaría de Fomento," *El Socialista*, August 22, 1886; and "La paniconografía Gillot y el foto-grabado mexicano," *El Socialista*, October 21, 1877.

33. "Máquinas para componer y distribuir," *El Socialista*, July 12, 1885.

34. "Prodigios de la linotipía: La máquina educará al obrero," *El Imparcial*, September 22, 1899.

35. For a primer on linotype, see David Loeb Weiss and Carl Schlesinger, *Farewell: ETAOIN SHRDLU* (New York Times, 1975), https://vimeo.com/127605643.

36. "Un establecimiento tipográfico modelo," *El Arte Tipográfico*, October 1909, 136.

37. "Un establecimiento tipográfico modelo," 136–38.

38. "Una industria que progresa," *El Imparcial*, September 1, 1897.

39. Stephen P. Rice, *Minding the Machine: Languages of Class in Early Industrial America* (Berkeley: University of California Press, 2004), 117–18.

40. J. López Tilghman, "El problema del costo y los presupuestos de imprenta," *El Arte Tipográfico*, April 1908, 57.

41. Phyllis Lynn Smith, "Contentious Voices amid the Order: The Porfirian Press in Mexico City, 1876–1911" (PhD diss., University of Arizona, 1996), 99.

42. "El progreso de la prensa mexicana," *El Imparcial*, July 24, 1897.

43. "El progreso de la prensa mexicana."

44. "La circulación de *El Imparcial*," *El Imparcial*, March 16, 1897.

45. "Letra nueva y costumbres viejas," *El Hijo del Ahuizote*, May 20, 1894.

46. "Prensas mecánicas de venta," *El Diario del Hogar*, January 17, 1908.

47. "El éxito de nuestro semanario: Un resultado de la libertad de pensar," *El Ahuizote*, September 30, 1911.

48. Fausta Gantús, *Caricatura y poder político: Crítica, censura y represión en la ciudad de México, 1876–1888* (Mexico City: El Colegio de México / Instituto de Investigaciones Dr. José María Luis Mora, 2009), 125.

49. Hale, *Transformation of Liberalism*, 130.

50. On García Torres as an icon of late nineteenth-century journalism, see Pablo Piccato, *The Tyranny of Opinion: Honor in the Construction of the Mexican Public Sphere* (Durham, NC: Duke University Press, 2010), 67–68.

51. Piccato, *Tyranny of Opinion*, 161.

52. Piccato, *Tyranny of Opinion*, 159.

53. Elisa Speckman Guerra, *Crimen y castigo: Legislación penal, interpretaciones de la criminalidad y administración de justicia (Ciudad de México, 1872–1910)* (Mexico City: El Colegio de México / Universidad Nacional Autónoma de México, 2002), 14.

54. "Da. Brigida Piña solicitando se le vuelva su imprenta," 11 July 1854, AGN, Gobernación, leg. 1251, exp. 1; "Sobre que el Gobernador del Distrito devuelva la imprenta de D. Vicente García Torres, Da. Mariana Deriar, sin que sea molestada," 8 July 1854, AGN, Gobernación, leg. 1251, exp. 1; and Juan Baz to President of

Ayuntamiento re: Brigida Piña, 10 January 1856, AHCM, Ayuntamiento, Justicia, Jurados de Imprenta, vol. 2740, exp. 37.

55. "Sobre que se le recoja al C. Gregorio Pérez Jardón la prensa mecánica que tiene en calidad de préstamo," August 1870, AGN, Gobernación, leg. 1350, caja 2, exp. 2, fs. 1–13.

56. "El ciudadano Rafael Núñez hace presente que por haber pertenecido a los de la Acordada se proyectó por el señor Alamán y por Martín Rivera exterminar su imprenta," 16 November 1833, AGN, Justicia, vol. 151, exp. 27.

57. Examples of printing shop sackings include Martín Rivera's Imprenta del Sol in the 1820s, Rafael de Rafael's printing shop in 1855, the offices of *El Pájaro Verde* in 1861, and the Imprenta Políglota in 1880.

58. *Proyecto de Código penal para el Distrito Federal y territorio de la Baja California sobre delitos del fuero comun y para toda la república sobre delitos contra la federación* (Mexico City: Imprenta del Gobierno, 1871), 108.

59. *Código de procedimientos penales para el Distrito y territorios federales, expedido por el ejecutivo en virtud de la autorización que se le concedió por el Congreso de la Unión en 3 de junio de 1891* (Mexico City: Imp. y Lit. de F. Díaz de León Sucesores, Sociedad Anónima, 1894), 23.

60. "Toca al juicio de amparo promovido por Daniel Cabrera," 27 March 1900, AHSCJN, Amparo, exp. 730. Anti-Spanish sentiment had appeared frequently in *El Hijo del Ahuizote*, unfolding as part of a broader hemispheric conversation about national sovereignty spurred by the US intervention in Cuba and Puerto Rico, and which the newspaper's editors leveraged to indirectly criticize Porfirian courting of foreign investment. Tomás Pérez Vejo, "La conspiración gachupina en 'El Hijo del Ahuizote,'" *Historia Mexicana* 54, no. 4 (2005).

61. Daniel Cosío Villegas, *La república restaurada: Vida política*, vol. 1, *Historia moderna de México* (Mexico City: Editorial Hermes, 1955), 530.

62. Gantús, *Caricatura y poder político*, 143.

63. Porfirio Díaz to Filomeno Mata, 23 May 1888, Universidad Iberoamericana, Colección Porfirio Díaz, doc. 4779.

64. Porfirio Díaz to the Associated Press, 28 February 1892, Universidad Iberoamericana, Colección Porfirio Díaz, doc. 4401–3.

65. "Toca al juicio de amparo promovido por Daniel Cabrera," 27 March 1900, AHSCJN, Amparo, exp. 730.

66. "Sobre cesión de una prensa tipográfica de pie 'Gordon' y unos tipos pertenecientes a la imprenta de 'El Hijo del Ahuizote,'" 14 August 14 1906, AGN, Secretaría de Justicia, caja 559, exp. 1284.

67. "Toca al juicio de amparo promovido por Santiago de la Hoz," 23 May 1903, AHSCJN, Amparo, exp. 1678.

68. "Subvención. A Filomeno Mata se le dan $150 mensuales por publicación del periódico del Gran Círculo de Obreros," 4 June 1879, AGN, Instrucción Pública y Bellas Artes, caja 232, exp. 37.

69. Daniel Cosío Villegas, *El Porfiriato: Vida política interior, primera parte*, vol. 8, *Historia moderna de México* (Mexico City: Editorial Hermes, 1955), 109; and

Florence Toussaint Alcaraz, "Diario del Hogar: De lo doméstico a lo político," *Revista Mexicana de Ciencias Políticas y Sociales* 28, no. 109 (1982).

70. Ana María Serna, *Un análisis de los casos relativos a la libertad de imprenta: Los juicios de amparo de Filomeno Mata Rodríguez en 1901 y 1910* (Mexico City: Suprema Corte de Justicia de la Nación, 2013), 5.

71. Claudio Lomnitz-Adler, *The Return of Comrade Ricardo Flores Magón* (Brooklyn, NY: Zone Books, 2014), 58–59.

72. Lomnitz-Adler, *Return of Comrade Ricardo Flores Magón*, ch. 6.

73. Serna, *Un análisis de los casos*, 17. "Toca al juicio de amparo promovido por Jesús Flores Magón y Socios," 31 May 1901, AHSCJN, Amparo, exp. 1417; and "Toca al juicio de Amparo promovido por Filomeno Mata," 17 June 1901, AHSCJN, Amparo, exp. 1528.

74. "Toca al juicio de amparo promovido por Filomeno Mata," 11 November 1907, AHSCJN, Amparo, exp. 3462.

75. "Nuestro periódico ante los tribunales," *El Diario del Hogar*, November 3, 1907.

76. The printer of *La Iberia* produced *El Diario del Hogar* for approximately one month. "El asunto del *Diario del Hogar*," *El Tiempo*, November 27, 1907.

77. "Dos periódicos extranjeros y varios nacionales," *El Diario del Hogar*, November 6, 1907.

78. "La prision de nuestro director," *El Diario del Hogar*, November 8, 1907.

79. "Toca al juicio de amparo promovido por Filomeno Mata," 7 November 1907, AHSCJN, Amparo, exp. 3411.

80. Filomeno Mata, "La persecución a nuestro periódico," *El Diario del Hogar*, December 4, 1907.

81. "El asunto del *Diario del Hogar*."

82. "La prensa y la prisión de nuestro director," *El Diario del Hogar*, November 17, 1907.

83. "Por los estados," *El Diario del Hogar*, November 17, 1907.

84. "La prensa y la persecución a nuestro periódico," *El Diario del Hogar*, November 20, 1907.

85. "La prensa y la prisión de nuestro director," *El Diario del Hogar*, November 17, 1907.

86. Luciano Mascorro, "La prisión de D. Filomeno Mata," *El Diario del Hogar*, November 23, 1907.

87. "Toca al juicio de amparo promovido por Filomeno Mata," 7 November 1907, AHSCJN, Amparo exp. 3411.

88. *El Tiempo* cast doubt on the judge's intentions, reprinted in "Seguimos sufriendo el despojo de nuestros talleres," *El Diario del Hogar*, November 24, 1907.

89. "La ocupación de la imprenta del 'Diario del Hogar,'" reprinted in *El Diario del Hogar*, November 27, 1907 (capitals in original).

90. "La prensa y la persecución a nuestro periódico," *El Diario del Hogar*, December 4, 1907.

91. "La prensa y la persecución a nuestro periódico," *El Diario del Hogar*, December 5, 1907.

92. "La persecución a nuestro periódico," *El Diario del Hogar*, December 17, 1907.

93. "Persecuciones al 'Diario del Hogar,'" *El Diario del Hogar*, November 27, 1907.

94. "Persecuciones al 'Diario del Hogar.'"

95. "Toca al juicio de amparo promovido por Filomeno Mata," 7 November 1907, AHSCJN, Amparo, exp. 3411.

96. Serna, *Un análisis de los casos*, 19–21.

97. John Mraz, *Photographing the Mexican Revolution: Commitments, Testimonies, Icons* (Austin: University of Texas Press, 2012); and Marion Gautreau, *De la crónica al icono: La fotografía de la revolución mexicana en la prensa ilustrada capitalina (1910–1940)* (Mexico City: Secretaría de Cultura, Instituto Nacional de Antropología e Historia, 2016), 28.

98. R. Osorno to Emiliano Zapata, 2 November 1915, AGN, Fondo Emiliano Zapata (FEZ), caja 16, exp. 3, f. 3; and Prudencio Casals to Emiliano Zapata, 3 December 1915, AGN, FEZ, caja 10, exp. 10, fs. 21–22.

99. Telegram from M. Palafox, 25 November 1914, AGN, FEZ, caja 15, exp. 3, f. 25; and Manuel Palafox to Francisco Ayala Martínez, 2 February 1915, AGN, FEZ, caja 4, exp. 3, f. 105.

100. M. Palafox to Jenaro Amezcua, 26 November 1915, AGN, FEZ, caja 16, exp. 4, f. 41; and Ariel Arnal, *Atila de tinta y plata: Fotografía del zapatismo en la prensa de la Ciudad de México entre 1910 y 1915* (Mexico City: Instituto Nacional de Antropología e Historia, 2010).

101. "Adiós! . . . a nuestra vieja prensa," *El Diario del Hogar*, May 31, 1911.

102. "Telegrama de Filomeno Mata a Francisco I. Madero felicitándolo a nombre del *Diario del Hogar*," 17 May 1911, Biblioteca Nacional de México, Fondo Reservado, Archivos y Manuscritos, Ms.M/T. 1031 c. 10; and "Telegrama de Francisco I. Madero a Filomeno Mata agradeciendo sus felicitaciones," 18 May 1911, Biblioteca Nacional de México, Fondo Reservado, Archivos y Manuscritos, Ms.M/T. 1059 c. 10.

103. Alfredo Ayala Mendoza, "Honra a su memoria"; Juan Sarabia, "Queda siempre un nombre que pronunciar con respeto"; and Lic. Blas Urrea (Luis Cabrera Lobato), "Sincero homenaje a Filomeno Mata, con motive de su sentida muerte," *El Diario del Hogar*, July 3, 1911.

104. *El Diario del Hogar*, July 3, 1911.

105. "Constitución política de los Estados Unidos Mexicanos," *Diario Oficial*, February 5, 1917.

106. "Ley sobre delitos de imprenta," *Diario Oficial*, April 12, 1917.

CONCLUSION

1. "Incidente de la causa que se instruye en el Juzgado 20 de lo Civil por el Lic. P. de Lebrija contra D. Vicente G. Torres como responsable de un art.o publicado en el Monitor," 1849, AGN, TSJDF, caja 262, exp. s/n.

2. Will Fowler, *Malcontents, Rebels, and Pronunciados: The Politics of Insurrection in Nineteenth-Century Mexico* (Lincoln: University of Nebraska Press, 2012), xxiv.

3. For example, see "Apertura del Congreso," *El Hijo del Ahuizote*, April 4, 1886; "¿D. Sebastián se vindicará?," *El Hijo del Ahuizote*, March 13, 1887; "Cuestión de Pantalones," *El Hijo del Ahuizote*, July 3, 1887; and "Esquelas de Invitación," *El Hijo del Ahuizote*, September 16, 1894.

4. On media scandals as socially constructed, see Vanessa Freije, *Citizens of Scandal: Journalism, Secrecy, and the Politics of Reckoning in Mexico* (Durham, NC: Duke University Press, 2020), 15.

5. "Esposición que dirigen a la augusta representación nacional los impresores que la suscriben, para que se permita la libre introducción de papel sin cola a la república," *El Siglo Diez y Nueve*, March 19, 1844.

6. Printer poem, [1820?], Sutro Library, Mexican Pamphlet Collection, vol. 292.

7. "El cajista," *El Socialista*, June 13, 1875.

8. Anne Rubenstein, *Bad Language, Naked Ladies, and Other Threats to the Nation: A Political History of Comic Books in Mexico* (Durham, NC: Duke University Press, 1998), 142–43.

9. Paul Gillingham, Michael Lettieri, and Benjamin T. Smith, eds., *Journalism, Satire, and Censorship in Mexico* (Albuquerque: University of New Mexico Press, 2018), 11.

10. Pablo Piccato, *History of Infamy: Crime, Truth, and Justice in Mexico* (Oakland: University of California Press, 2017), 64.

11. Benjamin T. Smith, *The Mexican Press and Civil Society, 1940–1976: Stories from the Newsroom, Stories from the Street* (Chapel Hill: University of North Carolina Press, 2018), 22.

12. *Dictamen de las Comisiones Unidas Primera de Hacienda e Industria de la Camara del Senado, sobre que no se disminuyan los derechos al papel sin cola para impresiones, presentado en la sesion de 16 de abril del corriente año* (Mexico City: Impreso en papel mexicano en la calle de la Palma Num. 4, 1845).

13. Freije, *Citizens of Scandal*, 8.

14. Meeting notes, 28 March 1909, AGN, Actas de Union Linotipográfica, Archivos Incorporados, Documentos Textuales, caja 1.

15. "Los tipógrafos más antiguos de México," *Revista de Revistas*, April 26, 1925, 15.

16. Dr. Atl, *Las artes populares en México*, 2 vols. (México: Librería "Cvltvra," 1921); and José Guadalupe Posada et al., *Monografía: Las obras de José Guadalupe Posada, grabador mexicano* (México: Mexican Folkways, 1930).

17. John Lear, *Picturing the Proletariat: Artists and Labor in Revolutionary Mexico, 1908–1940* (Austin: University of Texas Press, 2017), 57.

18. Salvador Albiñana, ed. *México ilustrado: Libros, revistas y carteles, 1920–1950* (Mexico City: Editorial RM, 2010).

19. See, for example, José Toribio Medina, *La imprenta en México (1539–1821)*, 8 vols. (Santiago, Chile: Impreso en casa del autor, 1912); and Enrique Fernández Ledesma, *Historia crítica de la tipografía en la ciudad de México* (Mexico City: Ediciones del Palacio de Bellas Artes, 1934).

20. Fernández Ledesma, *Historia crítica*.

21. Medina, *La imprenta en México*, 1:xiv.

22. *Calavera de la prensa* (Mexico City: Tip. de la Test. de Antonio Vanegas Arroyo, 1919).

23. Claudio Lomnitz-Adler, *Death and the Idea of Mexico* (Brooklyn, NY: Zone Books, 2005), 347.

BIBLIOGRAPHY

ARCHIVES

Mexico City

Archivo General de la Nación (AGN)

> Archivos Incorporados: Actas de Union Linotipográfica
> Fondo Archivo de Guerra
> Fondo Bienes Nacionales
> Fondo Emiliano Zapata (FEZ)
> Fondo General de Parte
> Fondo Gobernación
> Fondo Hacienda
> Fondo Imprenta del Gobierno
> Fondo Impresos Oficiales
> Fondo Indiferente de Guerra
> Fondo Inquisición
> Fondo Instrucción Pública y Bellas Artes
> Fondo Justicia
> Fondo Operaciones de Guerra
> Fondo Secretaría de Justicia
> Fondo Tribunal Superior de Justicia del Distrito Federal (TSJDF)

Archivo Histórico de la Ciudad de México (AHCM)

> Fondo Actas de Cabildo, Actas de Cabildo originales de sesiones secretas
> Fondo Ayuntamiento

Biblioteca: Publicaciones de Boletín y Actas de Cabildo

Justicia: Jurados de Imprenta

Archivo Histórico de la Suprema Corte de Justicia de la Nación (AHSCJN)

Archivo Histórico de Notarías (AHN)

Archivo Histórico del Arzobispado de México, Base Siglo XIX (AHAM)

Biblioteca Nacional de México, Fondo Reservado, Archivos y Manuscritos

Universidad Iberoamericana, Colección Porfirio Díaz

Guadalajara, Mexico

Archivo de la Real Audiencia de la Nueva Galicia, Ramo Criminal (ARANG)

Archivo Histórico de Jalisco, Fondo Gobernación, Prensa e Imprenta del Gobierno (AHJ)

Seville, Spain

Archivo General de Indias, Gobierno, Audiencia de México (AGI)

Berkeley, California

Bancroft Library, University of California, Berkeley

San Francisco, California

California State Library, Sutro Branch (Sutro Library)

New York City

Columbia University Rare Book and Manuscript Library (RBML)

Austin, Texas

Nettie Lee Benson Latin American Collection, University of Texas at Austin (BLAC)

Juan E. Hernández y Dávalos Manuscript Collection (HD)

Mariano Riva Palacio Collection (MRP)

Chicago, Illinois

The Newberry Library

PERIODICALS

Mexico City

El Ahuizote
The American Star
El Conductor Eléctrico
El Correo de Dos Mundos
El Correo Español
El Cosmopolita
El Desheredado
El Diario de México
El Diario del Gobierno
El Diario del Hogar
El Diario Oficial
La Firmeza
La Gaceta del Gobierno de México
Gaceta Extraordinaria del Gobierno de México
La Gazeta de Literatura de México
La Gazeta de México
El Hijo del Ahuizote
El Imparcial
La Imprenta
El Monitor Republicano
El Mosquito Mexicano
Revista de Revistas
El Siglo Diez y Nueve
El Socialista
Suplemento a la Gazeta de México
El Tiempo
La Tipografía Mexicana: Circular de Elis Reed
El Universal

New York

El Arte Tipográfico

An Abridged Specimen of Printing Types, Made at Bruce's New York Type-Foundry. New York: George Bruce's Son & Co., 1869.

Alamán, Lucas. *Historia de Méjico desde los primeros momentos que prepararon su independencia en el año de 1808 hasta la época presente.* Vol. 4. Mexico City: Imprenta de J. M. Lara, calle de la Palma Num. 4, 1851.

El archivo mexicano: Colección de leyes, decretos, circulares y otros documentos. Vol. 1. Mexico City: Imprenta de Vicente G. Torres, 1856.

Barazábal, Mariano. *Mordaza al liberal que se dice.* Mexico City: Alejandro Valdés, en su oficina, calle de Sto. Domingo, 1820.

Bustamante, Carlos María de. *Cuadro histórico de la revolución mexicana, comenzada en 15 de septiembre de 1810 por el ciudadano Miguel Hidalgo y Costilla.* Vol. 1. Mexico City: Impr. de J. M. Lara, 1843.

———. *Diario histórico de México, 1822–1848.* Edited by Josefina Zoraida Vázquez and Héctor Cuauhtémoc Hernández Silva. Mexico City: El Colegio de México / Centro de Investigaciones y Estudios Superiores en Antropología Social, 2001. CD-ROM.

Calavera de la prensa. Mexico City: Tip. De la Test. de Antonio Vanegas Arroyo, 1919.

Calderón de la Barca, Frances. *Life in Mexico.* Berkeley: University of California Press, 1982. First published 1843.

Campomanes, Pedro Rodríguez de. *Discurso sobre la educación popular de los artesanos y su fomento.* Madrid: Impr. de D. A. de Sancha, 1775.

Cárdenas Iglesias, Sylvia, and Delia de Peña Guajardo, eds. *Correspondencia de Ignacio Cumplido a León Ortigosa en la Biblioteca del Instituto Tecnológico y de Estudios Superiores de Monterrey.* Monterrey: Instituto Tecnológico y de Estudios Superiores de Monterrey, 1969.

Código de procedimientos penales para el Distrito y territorios federales, expedido por el ejecutivo en virtud de la autorización que se le concedió por el Congreso de la Unión en 3 de junio de 1891. Mexico City: Imp. y Lit. de F. Díaz de León Sucesores, Sociedad Anónima, 1894.

Colección de leyes y decretos: Publicados desde 10 de Enero de 1844. Mexico City: Imprenta en Palacio, 1851.

Colección de los decretos y ordenes de las Cortes de España, que se reputan vigentes en la república de los Estados-Unidos Mexicanos. Mexico City: Imprenta de Galván á cargo de Mariano Arévalo, 1829.

Cumplido, Ignacio. "Al público mexicano." In *Cuarto calendario portátil de I. Cumplido, para el año de 1839: Arreglado al meridiano de México.* Mexico City: Impreso por el Propietario, en la oficina de la calle de los Rebeldes Num. 2, 1839.

———. *Apelación al público.* Mexico City: Imprenta de Cumplido, 1840.

———. *Impresiones de viaje.* Mexico City: Tip. de I. Cumplido, 1884.

———. *Invitación que hace el impresor C. Ignacio Cumplido al juez de letras de lo criminal licenciado D. J. Gabriel Gómez de la Peña, a fin de que esponga las* disposiciones legales á que se arregló para proceder á su prision y detenerlo treinta y tres días en la cárcel de la Acordada, como impresor del folleto que escribió D. J. M. Gutierrez Estrada. Mexico City: Impreso por el autor, 1840.

———. *Manifestación al público del impresor ciudadano Ignacio Cumplido, con motivo de su prisión, verificada el 21 de octubre de 1840.* Mexico City: Imprenta de Cumplido, 1840.

Dávila, Rafael. *La verdad amarga, pero es preciso decirla.* Mexico City: Imprenta de J. M. de Benavente y Socios, 1820.

Defensa del editor de la obra titulada los Misterios de la Inquisición, contestando el dictamen del Sr. Consultor de la Junta Diocesana de Censura, en virtud del cual se declaró prohibido, y se fulminó por el señor vicario capitular una excomunicación mayor. Mexico City: Imprenta de V. G. Torres, 1850.

Diálogo entre D. Ruperto y el Impresor: Traslado al Observador del Observador J. y suplemento al Noticioso General num 751. Mexico City: Impreso en la oficina de D. J. M. Benavente y Socios, 1820.

Dictamen de las Comisiones Unidas Primera de Hacienda e Industria de la Camara del Senado, sobre que no se disminuyan los derechos al papel sin cola para impresiones, presentado en la sesion de 16 de abril del corriente año. Mexico City: Impreso en papel mexicano en la calle de la Palma n. 4, 1845.

Diez de Sollano, José María. *Dictamen que el doctor Don José María Diez de Sollano, cura interino del Sagrario Metropolitano, y Rector del colegio de S. Gregorio, emitió sobre la obra intitulada Misterios de la Inquisición y que hizo suyo la Junta diocesana de censura, y ha mandado publicar el Sr. Vicario Capitular de este arzobispado.* Mexico City: Tipografía de R. Rafael, 1850.

Dirección General de Estadística. *Estadística general de la república mexicana, á cargo del Dr. Antonio Peñafiel.* Vol. 6. Mexico City: Oficina Tipográfica de la Secretaría de Fomento, 1892.

Disposiciones legales y otros documentos relativos a la prohibición de impresos por la autoridad eclesiástica, mandados publicar de orden del Supremo Gobierno. Mexico City: Imprenta de Ignacio Cumplido, 1850.

Dr. Atl. *Las artes populares en México.* 2 vols. México: Librería "Cvltvra," 1921.

Dublán, Manuel, and José María Lozano. *Legislación mexicana ó: Colección completa de las disposiciones legislativas expedidas desde la independencia de la República.* Vol. 1. Mexico City: Imprenta del Comercio de E. Dublán y Comp., 1876.

———. *Legislación mexicana ó: Colección completa de las disposiciones legislativas expedidas desde la independencia de la República.* Vol. 3. Mexico City: Imprenta del Comercio, a cargo de Dublán y Lozano, Hijos, 1876.

———. *Legislación mexicana ó: Colección completa de las disposiciones legislativas expedidas desde la independencia de la República.* Vol. 12. Mexico City: Imprenta del Comercio de E. Dublán y Comp., 1882.

Eguiara y Eguren, Juan José de. *Prólogos a la Biblioteca mexicana.* 2nd ed. Translated [from Latin] by Agustín Millares Carlo. Mexico City: Fondo de Cultura Económica, 1944.

Féréal, V. de. *Misterios de la Inquisición y otras sociedades secretas de España*. New Orleans: Imprenta de J. L. Sollée, 1846.

———. *Misterios de la Inquisición y otras sociedades secretas de España*. Mexico City: Imprenta de V. García Torres, á cargo de L. Vidaurri, 1850.

———. *Mystères de l'inquisition et autres sociètès secretes d'Espagne*. Paris: Boizard, 1845.

Fernández de Lizardi, José Joaquín. *Maldita sea la libertad de imprenta*. Mexico City: Oficina de Betancourt, 1820.

———. *The Mangy Parrot: The Life and Times of Periquillo Sarniento; Written by Himself for His Children*. Translated by David L. Frye. Indianapolis, IN: Hackett Publishing, 2004.

———. *Obras: IV: Periódicos*. Mexico City: Universidad Nacional Autónoma de México, 1970.

———. *Obras, X: Folletos (1811–1820)*. Mexico City: Universidad Nacional Autónoma de México, 1981.

———. *Sociedad Pública de Lectura: Por el Pensador Mexicano*. Mexico City: En la oficina de D. Juan Bautista de Arizpe, 1820.

Fernández de San Salvador, Agustín Pomposo. *Convite a los verdaderos amantes de la religion católica y de la patria*. Mexico City: En la oficina de Ontiveros, 1812.

Fernández Leal, Manuel. *Memoria presentada al Congreso de la Unión por el Secretario de Estado y del Despacho de Fomento, Colonización e Industria de la República Mexicana Ingeniero Manuel Fernández de Leal: Corresponde a los años transcurridos de 1892 a 1896*. Mexico City: Oficina Tip. de la Secretaría de Fomento, 1897.

Fernández Ledesma, Enrique. *Historia crítica de la tipografía en la ciudad de México*. Mexico City: Ediciones del Palacio de Bellas Artes, 1934.

F. M. [Merino, Félix]. *El liberal a los bajos escritores*. Puebla, Mexico: Oficina del Gobierno, 1820.

Galán, Manuel. *Prisión en la ciudadela del teniente Galan*. Mexico City: Imprenta de D. J. M. de Benavente y Socios, 1820.

Gamboa, Federico. *Impresiones y recuerdos*. Buenos Aires: A. Moen, 1893.

García Icazbalceta, Joaquín. "Tipografía Mexicana." In *Diccionario universal de historia y de geografía*, edited by Lucas Alamán, 961–77. Vol. 5. Mexico City: Imp. de F. Escalente y Ca.; Librería de Andrade, 1854.

Gran depósito de útiles para imprenta. Mexico City: G. Lohse y Comp., Sucs., 1885.

Granja, Juan de la. *Epistolario: Con un estudio biográfico preliminar por Luis Castillo Ledón y notas de Nereo Rodríguez Barragán*. Mexico City: Talleres Gráficos del Museo Nacional de Arqueología y Etnografía, 1937.

Gutiérrez Estrada, José María. *Carta dirigida al Escmo. Sr. Presidente de la República, sobre la necesidad de buscar en una convención el posible remedio de los males que aquejan á la República: Y opiniones del autor acerca del mismo asunto*. Mexico City: Impresa por I. Cumplido, 1840.

———. *Carta dirigida al Escmo. Sr. Presidente de la República, sobre la necesidad de buscar en una convención el posible remedio de los males que aquejan á la República:*

Y opiniones del autor acerca del mismo asunto. Havana: Imprenta de Francisco García, 1840.

———. *México en 1840 y 1847.* Mexico City: Imprenta de Vicente G. Torres, en el ex-convento del Espíritu Santo, 1848.

Hernández y Dávalos, J. E. *Colección de documentos para la historia de la guerra de independencia de Mexico de 1808 a 1821.* Vol. 1. Mexico City: J. M. Sandoval, impresor, 1877.

Informe presentado al Señor Secretario de Fomento por el director de la imprenta de la misma secretaría, en cumplimiento del artículo 18 del reglamento que rige en dicha oficina. Mexico City: Oficina Tipográfica de la Secretaría de Fomento, 1889.

J. N. *Predicar en desierto sermon perdido.* Mexico City: Impreso en la Oficina de D. J. M. Benavente y Socios, 1820.

Legislación mejicana, o sea colección completa de las leyes, decretos y circulares que se han expedido desde la consumación de la independencia. Mexico City: Imprenta de Juan R. Navarro, 1855.

El Licenciado Cachaza. *Cortadillos de imprenta (*) de coco y almendra.* Mexico City: En la imprenta de D. Juan Bautista de Arizpe, 1820.

López Cancelada, Juan. *Decreto de Napoleón, emperador de los franceses sobre los judíos residentes en Francia, y deliberaciones que tomaron estos en su cumplimiento, con un resúmen de otros sucesos interesantes.* Mexico City: En la oficina de Don Mariano de Zúñiga y Ontiveros, calle del Espíritu Santo, 1807.

———. *Sucesos de Nueva España hasta la coronación de Iturbide.* Mexico City: Instituto Mora, 2008. First published 1828–1829.

———. *La verdad sabida y buena fé guardada: Orígen de la espantosa revolución de Nueva España comenzada en 15 de setiembre de 1810.* Cádiz: Imprenta de D. Manuel Santiago de Quintana, 1811.

Loza, Pedro. *Carta pastoral del Ilmo. y Rvmo. Sr. Doctor D. Pedro Loza, Arzobispo de Guadalajara, sobre los malos periódicos.* Guadalajara, Mexico: Ant. Tip. de N. Parga, 1897.

Manual de tipografía escrito expresamente para las alumnas impresoras del conservatorio de música y declamación. Mexico City: Imprenta del Conservatorio, 1875.

Medina, José Toribio. *La imprenta en México (1539–1821).* 8 vols. Santiago, Chile: Impreso en casa del autor, 1912.

Merino, Félix. *El liberal al público.* Puebla, Mexico: Imprenta Liberal, 1820.

Mier Noriega y Guerra, José Servando Teresa de. *Historia de la revolución de Nueva España antiguamente Anáhuac, ó Verdadero origen y causas de ella, con la relación de sus progresos hasta el presente año de 1813.* 2 vols. London: Impr. de G. Glindon, 1813.

El Observador J. V. *La Inquisición se quitó pero sus usos quedaron.* Mexico City: Imprenta de Ontiveros, 1820.

La Observadora. *La libertad de imprenta todo lo cuenta.* Mexico City: Oficina de Betancourt, 1822.

El papel moneda se quita. Mexico City: En la Imprenta Imperial de Sr. D. Alexandro Valdés, 1823.

Poniatowska, Elena. *Here's to You, Jesusa!* Translated by Deanna Heikkinen. New York: Farrar, Straus and Giroux, 2001.

Posada, José Guadalupe, Diego Rivera, Frances Toor, Pablo O'Higgins, and Blas Vanegas Arroyo. *Monografía: Las obras de José Guadalupe Posada, grabador mexicano.* Mexico City: Mexican Folkways, 1930.

Prieto, Guillermo. *Lecciones elementales de economía política, dadas en la escuela de jurisprudencia de México en el curso de 1871.* Mexico City: Imprenta del Gobierno, en Palacio, a cargo de José María Sandoval, 1871.

———. *Memoria de mis tiempos 1828 a 1853.* Puebla: Editorial José M. Cajica Jr., 1970. First published 1906.

Proyecto de código penal para el Distrito Federal y territorio de la Baja California sobre delitos del fuero comun y para toda la república sobre delitos contra la federación. Mexico City: Imprenta del Gobierno, 1871.

Rabasa, Emilio. *La gran ciencia* [and] *El cuarto poder.* Tuxtla Gutiérrez, Chiapas: Consejo Estatal para la Cultura y las Artes de Chiapas, 2000. First published 1887–1888.

Rafael, Rafael de, and Antonio Juan de Vildósola. *La masonería pintada por sí misma: Artículos publicados en el periódico "La Voz de Cuba," de la Habana.* Madrid: Impr. de A. P. Dubrull, 1883.

Recopilación de leyes, decretos, reglamentos, circulares y providencias de los supremos poderes y otras autoridades de la república mexicana: Formada de orden del supremo gobierno por el Lic. Basilio José Arrillaga; Comprende este tomo todo el año de 1837. Mexico City: Imprenta de J. M. Fernández de Lara, 1839.

Reglamento para las impresiones del gobierno. Mexico City: Tipografía de Vicente García Torres, 1852.

Riva Palacio, Vicente, and Manuel Payno. *El libro rojo, 1820–1867.* Mexico City: Díaz de León y White, 1870.

Rubin, Luis. *Cuentos de mi tía, por Luis G. Rubin.* Ed. publicada con el patrocinio del Señor Secretaría de Fomento, General D. Carlos Pacheco. Mexico City: Oficina Tip. de la Secretaría de Fomento, 1890.

———. *Mi libro.* Mexico City: Oficina Tip. de la Secretaría de Fomento, 1897.

Sigüenza y Vera, Juan Josef. *Mecanismo del arte de la imprenta para facilidad de los operarios que le exerzan.* Madrid: Imprenta de la Compañia, 1811.

Sobre el abuso de la libertad de imprenta. Mexico City: En la oficina de D. Alejandro Valdés, 1820.

Solicitud de un ciudadano por la libertad de Dávila. Mexico City: Imprenta de Ontiveros, 1820.

Torres Palacios, José Gregorio de. *Al que le venga el saco que se lo ponga: Por varios rumbos y distintos modos que se cumpla la ley queremos todos.* Mexico City: Oficina de D. J. M. Benavente y Socios, 1820.

Valdés, Alejandro. *La prensa libre.* Mexico City: En su oficina, 1820.

Weiss, David Loeb, and Carl Schlesinger. *Farewell: ETAOIN SHRDLU.* New York Times Company, 1975. https://vimeo.com/127605643. Video, 29 min.

Zarco, Francisco. *Escritos sobre la libertad de imprenta.* Mexico City: Consejo Nacional para la Cultura y las Artes, Dirección General de Publicaciones, 2013.

Acree Jr., William G. *Everyday Reading: Print Culture and Collective Identity in the Río de la Plata, 1780–1910*. Nashville, TN: Vanderbilt University Press, 2011.

Adelman, Joseph M. *Revolutionary Networks: The Business and Politics of Printing the News, 1763–1789*. Baltimore, MD: Johns Hopkins University Press, 2019.

Albiñana, Salvador, ed. *México ilustrado: Libros, revistas y carteles, 1920–1950*. Mexico City: Editorial RM, 2010.

Anderson, Benedict. *Imagined Communities*. Rev. ed. London: Verso, 1991.

Anna, Timothy E. *The Fall of the Royal Government in Mexico City*. Lincoln: University of Nebraska Press, 1978.

Arnal, Ariel. *Atila de tinta y plata: Fotografía del zapatismo en la prensa de la ciudad de México entre 1910 y 1915*. Mexico City: Instituto Nacional de Antropología e Historia, 2010.

Bailyn, Bernard. *The Ideological Origins of the American Revolution*. Cambridge, MA: Belknap Press of Harvard University Press, 1967.

Barajas, Rafael. *El país de El Ahuizote: La caricatura mexicana de oposición durante el gobierno de Sebastián Lerdo de Tejada, 1872–1876*. Mexico City: Fondo de Cultura Económica, 2005.

Bátiz Vázquez, José Antonio, and José Enrique Covarrubias. *La moneda en México, 1750–1920*. Mexico City: Instituto Mora / El Colegio de Michoacán / El Colegio de México / Instituto de Investigaciones Históricas, UNAM, 1998.

Beatty, Edward. *Technology and the Search for Progress in Modern Mexico*. Oakland: University of California Press, 2015.

Bello, Kenya. "The American Star: El destino manifiesto y la difusión de una comunidad imaginaria." *Estudios de Historia Moderna y Contemporánea de México*, no. 31 (2006): 31–56.

Bleichmar, Daniela. *Visible Empire: Botanical Expeditions and Visual Culture in the Hispanic Enlightenment*. Chicago: University of Chicago Press, 2012.

Blum, Ann S. "Conspicuous Benevolence: Liberalism, Public Welfare, and Private Charity in Porfirian Mexico City, 1877–1910." *The Americas* 58, no. 1 (2001): 7–38.

Bourdieu, Pierre. *Distinction: A Social Critique of the Judgement of Taste*. London: Routledge, 2012. First published 1984.

Braga-Pinto, César. "Journalists, Capoeiras, and the Duel in Nineteenth-Century Rio de Janeiro." *Hispanic American Historical Review* 94, no. 4 (2014): 581–614.

Breña, Roberto. "The Cádiz Liberal Revolution and Spanish American Independence." In *New Countries: Capitalism, Revolutions, and Nations in the Americas, 1750–1870*, edited by John Tutino, 71–104. Durham, NC: Duke University Press, 2016.

Briggs, Ronald. *The Moral Electricity of Print: Transatlantic Education and the Lima Women's Circuit, 1876–1910*. Nashville, TN: Vanderbilt University Press, 2017.

Buffington, Robert. *Criminal and Citizen in Modern Mexico*. Lincoln: University of Nebraska Press, 2000.

————. *A Sentimental Education for the Working Man: The Mexico City Penny Press, 1900–1910*. Durham, NC: Duke University Press, 2015.

Bunker, Steven B. *Creating Mexican Consumer Culture in the Age of Porfirio Díaz*. Albuquerque: University of New Mexico Press, 2012.

Caplan, Karen Deborah. *Indigenous Citizens: Local Liberalism in Early National Oaxaca and Yucatán*. Stanford, CA: Stanford University Press, 2010.

Carrera, Magali M. *Traveling from New Spain to Mexico: Mapping Practices of Nineteenth-Century Mexico*. Durham, NC: Duke University Press, 2011.

Casper, Scott, Jeffrey D. Groves, Stephen W. Nissenbaum, and Michael Winship, eds. *The Industrial Book, 1840–1880*. Vol. 3 of *A History of the Book in America*. Chapel Hill: University of North Carolina Press, 2007.

Castañeda, Carmen. "Periodismo en la ciudad de México: Siglo XVIII." In *Historia de la literatura mexicana: Desde sus orígenes hasta nuestros días*, edited by Nancy Vogeley and Manuel Ramos Medina, 128–49. Mexico City: Siglo XXI / Universidad Nacional Autónoma de México, Facultad de Filosofía y Letras, 2011.

Castro, Miguel Ángel, ed. *Tipos y caracteres: La prensa mexicana, 1822–1855*. Mexico City: Universidad Nacional Autónoma de México, 2001.

————. "Un par de lecturas posibles del Catálogo de la Biblioteca de José María Andrade." In *Empresa y cultura en tinta y papel: 1800–1860*, edited by Laura Suárez de la Torre and Miguel Ángel Castro, 285–93. Mexico City: Instituto de Investigaciones Dr. José María Luis Mora / Universidad Nacional Autónoma de México, 2001.

Castro Klarén, Sara, and John Chasteen, eds. *Beyond Imagined Communities: Reading and Writing the Nation in Nineteenth-Century Latin America*. Baltimore, MD: Johns Hopkins University Press, 2003.

Ceballos Ramírez, Manuel. "Las lecturas católicas: Cincuenta años de literatura paralela, 1867–1917." In *Historia de la lectura en México*, edited by Seminario de Historia de la Educación de México, 153–204. Mexico City: Colegio de Mexico, 1997.

Celis de la Cruz, Martha. "La propiedad literaria: El caso Carlos Nebel contra Vicente García Torres (1840)." In *Empresa y cultura en tinta y papel: 1800–1860*, edited by Laura Suárez de la Torre and Miguel Ángel Castro, 489–504. Mexico City: Instituto de Investigaciones Dr. José María Luis Mora / Universidad Nacional Autónoma de México, 2001.

Chambers, Sarah C. *From Subjects to Citizens: Honor, Gender, and Politics in Arequipa, Peru, 1780–1854*. University Park: Pennsylvania State University Press, 1999.

Chartier, Roger. "Laborers and Voyagers: From the Text to the Reader." *Diacritics* 22, no. 2 (1992): 49–61.

Chávez Lomelí, Elba. *Lo público y lo privado en los impresos decimonónicos: Libertad de imprenta, 1810–1882*. Mexico City: Universidad Nacional Autónoma de México / Facultad de Estudios Superiores Aragón / M. A. Porrúa, 2009.

Chocano Mena, Magdalena. "Colonial Printing and Metropolitan Books: Printed Texts and the Shaping of Scholarly Culture in New Spain, 1539–1700." *Colonial Latin American Historical Review* 6, no. 1 (1997): 69–90.

———. *La fortaleza docta: Elite letrada y dominación social en México colonial (siglos XVI–XVII)*. Barcelona: Ediciones Bellaterra, 2000.

Connaughton, Brian F. *Clerical Ideology in a Revolutionary Age: The Guadalajara Church and the Idea of the Mexican Nation, 1788–1853*. Translated by Mark Alan Healey. Calgary, AB: University of Calgary Press, 2002.

Corbeto, Albert. "Tipografía y patrocinio real: La intervención del gobierno en la importación de tipos de imprenta en España." In *Imprenta Real: Fuentes de la tipografía española*, edited by José María Ribagorda, 29–46. Madrid: Ministerio de Asuntos Exteriores y de Cooperación / AECID, 2009.

Cordell, Ryan. "Reprinting, Circulation, and the Network Author in Antebellum Newspapers." *American Literary History* 27, no. 3 (Fall 2015): 417–45.

Coronado, Raúl. *A World Not to Come: A History of Latino Writing and Print Culture*. Cambridge, MA: Harvard University Press, 2013.

Cosío Villegas, Daniel. *El Porfiriato: Vida política interior, primera parte*. Vol. 8 of *Historia moderna de México*. Mexico City: Editorial Hermes, 1955.

———. *La república restaurada: Vida política*. Vol. 1 of *Historia moderna de México*. Mexico City: Editorial Hermes, 1955.

Costa, Emília Viotti da. *The Brazilian Empire: Myths and Histories*. Chicago: University of Chicago Press, 1985.

Costeloe, Michael P. *The Central Republic in Mexico, 1835–1846: Hombres de Bien in the Age of Santa Anna*. New York: Cambridge University Press, 1993.

———. *Church and State in Independent Mexico: A Study of the Patronage Debate, 1821–1857*. London: Royal Historical Society, 1978.

———. *Church Wealth in Mexico: A Study of the "Juzgado de Capellanías" in the Archbishopric of Mexico 1800–1856*. London: Cambridge University Press, 1967.

Coudart, Laurence. "El 'Diario de México' y la era de la 'Actualidad.'" In *Bicentenario del Diario de México: Los albores de la cultura letrada en el México independiente, 1805–2005*, edited by Esther Martínez Luna, 197–225. Mexico City: Universidad Nacional Autónoma de México, 2009.

———. "En torno al correo de lectores de *El Sol* (1823–1832): Espacio periodístico y 'opinión pública.'" In *Transición y cultura política: de la colonia al México independiente*, edited by Cristina Gómez Álvarez and Miguel Soto, 67–110. Mexico City: Facultad de Filosofía y Letras, Universidad Nacional Autónoma de México, 2004.

———. "La regulación de la libertad de prensa (1863–1867)." *Historia Mexicana* 65, no. 2 (2015): 629–87.

Craib, Raymond B. *Cartographic Mexico: A History of State Fixations and Fugitive Landscapes*. Durham, NC: Duke University Press, 2004.

Darnton, Robert. *The Forbidden Best-Sellers of Pre-revolutionary France*. New York: W. W. Norton, 1995.

Deans-Smith, Susan. *Bureaucrats, Planters, and Workers: The Making of the Tobacco Monopoly in Bourbon Mexico*. Austin: University of Texas Press, 1992.

———. "'A Natural and Voluntary Dependence': The Royal Academy of San Carlos and the Cultural Politics of Art Education in Mexico City, 1786–1797." *Bulletin of Latin American Research* 29, no. 3 (2010): 278–95.

Delgado Carranco, Susana María. *Libertad de imprenta, política y educación: Su planteamiento y discusión en el Diario de México, 1810–1817.* Mexico City: Instituto de Investigaciones Dr. José María Luis Mora, 2006.

Donahue-Wallace, Kelly. *Art and Architecture of Viceregal Latin America, 1521–1821.* Albuquerque: University of New Mexico Press, 2008.

———. *Jerónimo Antonio Gil and the Idea of the Spanish Enlightenment.* Albuquerque: University of New Mexico Press, 2017.

———. "Prints and Printmakers in Viceregal Mexico City, 1600–1800." PhD diss., University of New Mexico, 2000.

———. "Publishing Prints in Eighteenth-Century Mexico City." *Print Quarterly* 23, no. 2 (2006): 134–54.

Ducey, Michael T. "Liberal Theory and Peasant Practice: Land and Power in Northern Veracruz, Mexico, 1826–1900." In *Liberals, the Church, and Indian Peasants: Corporate Lands and the Challenge of Reform in Nineteenth-Century Spanish America,* edited by Robert H. Jackson, 65–93. Albuquerque: University of New Mexico Press, 1997.

Duncan, Robert H. "Maximilian and the Construction of the Liberal State, 1863–1866." In *The Divine Charter: Constitutionalism and Liberalism in Nineteenth-Century Mexico,* edited by Jaime E. Rodríguez O., 134–66. Lanham, MD: Rowman & Littlefield, 2005.

———. "Political Legitimation and Maximilian's Second Empire in Mexico, 1864–1867." *Mexican Studies* 12, no. 1 (Winter 1996): 27–66.

Earle, Rebecca. "Information and Disinformation in Late Colonial New Granada." *The Americas* 54, no. 2 (1997): 167–84.

———. *The Return of the Native: Indians and Myth-Making in Spanish America, 1810–1930.* Durham, NC: Duke University Press, 2007.

———. "The Role of Print in the Spanish Wars of Independence." In *The Political Power of the Word: Press and Oratory in Nineteenth-Century Latin America,* edited by Iván Jaksic, 9–33. London: Institute of Latin American Studies, University of London, 2002.

Eisenstein, Elizabeth L. *Divine Art, Infernal Machine: The Reception of Printing in the West from First Impressions to the Sense of an Ending.* Philadelphia: University of Pennsylvania Press, 2011.

Fenton, Elizabeth A. *Religious Liberties: Anti-Catholicism and Liberal Democracy in Nineteenth-Century U.S. Literature and Culture.* New York: Oxford University Press, 2011.

Fernández Sebastián, Javier. "From the 'Voice of the People' to the Freedom of the Press: The Birth of Public Opinion." In *The Spanish Enlightenment Revisited,* edited by Jesús Astigarraga, 213–34. Oxford: Voltaire Foundation, 2015.

Ferreira Ascencio, Claudia. "Los padrones de confesión y comunión del Sagrario de México: Una aproximación a la praxis sacramental en el orden canónico indiano (1676–1825)." In *Normatividades e instituciones eclesiasticas en la Nueva Espana, siglos XVI–XIX,* edited by Benedetta Albani, Otto Danwerth, and Thomas Duve, 169–93. Frankfurt am Main: Max Planck Institute for European Legal History, 2018.

Fowler, Will. *Malcontents, Rebels, and Pronunciados: The Politics of Insurrection in Nineteenth-Century Mexico*. Lincoln: University of Nebraska Press, 2012.

———. *Mexico in the Age of Proposals, 1821–1853*. Westport, CT: Greenwood Press, 1998.

Franco, Jean. "En espera de una burgesía: La formación de la inteligencia mexicana en la época de la Independencia." In *Actas del VIII Congreso de la Asociación Internacional de Hispanistas*, edited by David Kosoff et al., 21–36. Madrid: Istmo, 1986.

Frankel, Oz. *States of Inquiry: Social Investigations and Print Culture in Nineteenth-Century Britain and the United States*. Baltimore, MD: Johns Hopkins University Press, 2006.

Freije, Vanessa. *Citizens of Scandal: Journalism, Secrecy, and the Politics of Reckoning in Mexico*. Durham, NC: Duke University Press, 2020.

French, William E. "The Conjunction of the Lettered City and the Lettered Countryside in 19th-Century Mexico." In *Oxford Research Encyclopedia of Latin American History* (May 9, 2016). https://oxfordre.com/latinamericanhistory/view/10.1093/acrefore/9780199366439.001.0001/acrefore-9780199366439-e-10.

Frye, David L. "Translator's Note." In *The Mangy Parrot: The Life and Times of Periquillo Sarniento; Written by Himself for His Children*, by José Joaquín Fernández de Lizardi, xxxi–xl. Translated by David L. Frye. Indianapolis, IN: Hackett Publishing, 2004.

Gantús, Fausta. "Amagada, perseguida y ¿sometida? Discurso satírico-visual y normativa legal sobre la libertad de imprenta; Ciudad de México, 1868–1883." *Historia Mexicana* 69, no. 1 (2019): 257–310.

———. *Caricatura y poder político: Crítica, censura y represión en la ciudad de México, 1876–1888*. Mexico City: El Colegio de México / Instituto de Investigaciones Dr. José María Luis Mora, 2009.

———. "La libertad de imprenta en el siglo XIX: Vaivenes de su regulación. Presentación." *Historia Mexicana* 69, no. 1 (2019): 93–114.

García, Clara Guadalupe. *El Imparcial: Primer periódico moderno de México*. Mexico City: Centro de Estudios Históricos del Porfiriato, A. C., 2003.

García Ugarte, Marta Eugenia. *Poder político y religioso: México siglo XIX*. 2 vols. Mexico City: Universidad Nacional Autónoma de México, Instituto de Investigaciones Sociales / M. A. Porrúa, 2010.

García-Bryce, Iñigo L. *Crafting the Republic: Lima's Artisans and Nation Building in Peru, 1821–1879*. Albuquerque: University of New Mexico Press, 2004.

Garibay Mendoza, Juan, ed. *El Mundo Ilustrado de Rafael Reyes Spíndola*. Mexico City: Grupo Carso, 2003.

Garone Gravier, Marina. *El Arte de ymprenta de don Alejandro Valdés (1819): Estudio y paleografía de un tratado de tipografía inédito*. Toluca de Lerdo, Mexico: Fondo Editorial Estado de México, 2015.

———. "El comercio tipográfico matritense en México durante el siglo XVIII." *Secuencia* 88 (enero–abril 2014): 9–36.

———. *Historia de la imprenta y la tipografía colonial en Puebla de los Ángeles, 1642–1821*. Mexico City: Instituto de Investigaciones Bibliográficas, Universidad Nacional Autónoma de México, 2014.

———. *Historia de la tipografía colonial para lenguas indígenas*. Mexico City: CIESAS / Universidad Veracruzana, 2014.

———. "La influencia de la Imprenta Real en América: El caso de México." In *Imprenta Real: Fuentes de la tipografía española*, edited by José María Ribagorda, 87–100. Madrid: Ministerio de Asuntos Exteriores y de Cooperación / AECID, 2009.

———. "La muestra de letras de Manuel Antonio Valdés (México, 1814): Noticias sobre una fuente para la historia de la cultura impresa novohispana." *Historia Mexicana* 70, no. 1 (julio–septiembre 2020): 423–70.

———. *La tipografía en México: Ensayos históricos (siglos XVI al XIX)*. Mexico City: Universidad Nacional Autónoma de México, 2012.

———. "Muestras tipográficas mexicanas: Comentarios en torno a nuevos hallazgos (siglos XVIII–XX)." In *Las muestras tipográficas y el estudio de la cultura impresa*, edited by Marina Garone Gravier and María Esther Pérez Salas Cantú, 233–66. Mexico City: Universidad Nacional Autónoma de México, 2012.

Gaskell, Philip. *A New Introduction to Bibliography*. New Castle, DE: Oak Knoll Press / St. Paul's Bibliographies, 2012. First printed 1995.

Gautreau, Marion. *De la crónica al icono: La fotografía de la revolución mexicana en la prensa ilustrada capitalina (1910–1940)*. Mexico City: Secretaría de Cultura, Instituto Nacional de Antropología e Historia, 2016.

Gayol, Víctor. "Escritores cortesanos y rebelión: La breve respuesta de los letrados a los sucesos de 1810 en México." In *Las guerras de independencia en la América española*, edited by Marta Terán and José Antonio Serrano Ortega, 149–64. Mexico City: Colegio de Michoacán / Universidad Michoacana de San Nicolás de Hidalgo / Instituto Nacional de Antropología e Historia, 2002.

Geggus, David P. "Print Culture and the Haitian Revolution: The Written and the Spoken Word." *Proceedings of the American Antiquarian Society* 116, no. 2 (2006): 299–316.

Genette, Gérard. *Paratexts: Thresholds of Interpretation*. New York: Cambridge University Press, 1997.

Gillingham, Paul, Michael Lettieri, and Benjamin T. Smith, eds. *Journalism, Satire, and Censorship in Mexico*. Albuquerque: University of New Mexico Press, 2018.

Gitelman, Lisa. *Paper Knowledge: Toward a Media History of Documents*. Durham, NC: Duke University Press, 2014.

Godoi, Rodrigo Camargo de. *Francisco de Paula Brito: A Black Publisher in Imperial Brazil*. Translated by H. Sabrina Gledhill. Nashville, TN: Vanderbilt University Press, 2020.

Goldgel, Víctor. *Cuando lo nuevo conquistó América: Prensa, moda y literatura en el siglo XIX*. Buenos Aires: Siglo Veintiuno Editores, 2013.

Goldgel-Carballo, Víctor. "'High-Speed Enlightenment': Latin American Literature and the New Medium of Periodicals." *Media History* 18, no. 2 (2012): 1–13.

Gómez Álvarez, Cristina, and Guillermo Tovar de Teresa. *Censura y revolución: Libros prohibidos por la Inquisición de México (1790–1819)*. Madrid: Trama Editorial / Consejo de la Crónica de la Ciudad de México, 2009.

González Casanova, Pablo. *La literatura perseguida en la crisis de la Colonia*. Mexico City: Colegio de México, 1958.

Grañén Porrúa, María Isabel. "El ambito socio-laboral de las imprentas novohispanas: Siglo XVI." *Anuario de Estudios Americanos* 48 (1991): 49–94.

Guardino, Peter. *The Dead March: A History of the Mexican-American War*. Cambridge, MA: Harvard University Press, 2017.

———. *The Time of Liberty: Popular Political Culture in Oaxaca, 1750–1850*. Durham, NC: Duke University Press, 2005.

———. "The War of Independence in Guerrero, New Spain, 1808–1821." In *The Wars of Independence in Spanish America*, edited by Christon I. Archer, 93–140. Wilmington, DE: Scholarly Resources, 2000.

Guerra, François-Xavier. *Modernidad e independencias: Ensayos sobre las revoluciones hispánicas*. 2nd ed. Mexico City: Editorial MAPFRE / Fondo de Cultura Económica, 1993.

———. "'Voces del pueblo': Redes de comunicación y orígenes de la opinión en el mundo hispánico (1808–1814)." *Revista de Indias* 62, no. 225 (2002): 357–84.

Guibovich Pérez, Pedro. *Censura, libros e inquisición en el Perú colonial, 1570–1754*. Seville: Consejo Superior de Investigaciones Científicas / Universidad de Sevilla / Diputación de Sevilla, 2003.

———. *Imprimir en Lima durante la colonia: Historia y documentos, 1584–1750*. Madrid: Iberoamericana / Vervuert, 2019.

Habermas, Jürgen. *The Structural Transformation of the Public Sphere: An Inquiry into a Category of Bourgeois Society*. Cambridge, MA: MIT Press, 1995. First published 1962.

Hale, Charles A. *Mexican Liberalism in the Age of Mora, 1821–1853*. New Haven, CT: Yale University Press, 1968.

———. *The Transformation of Liberalism in Late Nineteenth-Century Mexico*. Princeton, NJ: Princeton University Press, 1989.

Hamill, Hugh M. *The Hidalgo Revolt: Prelude to Mexican Independence*. Gainesville: University of Florida Press, 1966.

———. "Royalist Propaganda and 'La Porción Humilde del Pueblo' during Mexican Independence." *The Americas* 36, no. 4 (1980): 423–44.

Hamnett, Brian R. *Juárez*. London: Longman, 1994.

Haynes, Christine. *Lost Illusions: The Politics of Publishing in Nineteenth-Century France*. Cambridge, MA: Harvard University Press, 2010.

Henkin, David M. *City Reading: Written Words and Public Spaces in Antebellum New York*. New York: Columbia University Press, 1998.

Herzog, Tamar. *Defining Nations: Immigrants and Citizens in Early Modern Spain and Spanish America*. New Haven, CT: Yale University Press, 2003.

Hoffnung-Garskof, Jesse. *Racial Migrations: New York City and the Revolutionary Politics of the Spanish Caribbean*. Princeton, NJ: Princeton University Press, 2019.

———. "To Abolish the Law of Castes: Merit, Manhood and the Problem of Colour in the Puerto Rican Liberal Movement, 1873–92." *Social History* 36, no. 3 (2011): 312–42.

Illades, Carlos. *Estudios sobre el artesanado urbano del siglo XIX.* 2nd. ed. Mexico City: Universidad Autónoma Metropolitana / M. A. Porrúa, 2001.

———. *Hacia la república del trabajo: La organización artesanal en la ciudad de México, 1853–1876.* Mexico City: El Colegio de México, 1996.

———. *Las otras ideas: Estudio sobre el primer socialismo en México, 1850–1935.* Mexico City: Ediciones Era / Universidad Autónoma Metropolitana Cuajimalpa, 2008.

Irwin, Robert McKee. *Mexican Masculinities.* Minneapolis: University of Minnesota Press, 2003.

Johns, Adrian. *The Nature of the Book: Print and Knowledge in the Making.* Chicago: University of Chicago Press, 1998.

Johnston, Alastair. *Alphabets to Order: The Literature of Nineteenth-Century Type-founders' Specimens.* New Castle, DE: Oak Knoll Press, 2000.

Juárez Nieto, Carlos. "El intendente Manuel Merino y la insurgencia en Valladolid de Michoacán, 1810–1821." In *Las guerras de independencia en la América española,* edited by Marta Terán and José Antonio Serrano Ortega, 193–203. Mexico City: Colegio de Michoacán / Universidad Michoacana de San Nicolás de Hidalgo / Instituto Nacional de Antropología e Historia, 2002.

Ker, Annita Melville. *Mexican Government Publications: A Guide to the More Important Publications of the National Government of Mexico, 1821–1936.* Washington, DC: US Government Printing Office, 1940.

Konove, Andrew. *Black Market Capital: Urban Politics and the Shadow Economy in Mexico City.* Oakland: University of California Press, 2018.

Kuri, Ariel Rodríguez. "El discurso del miedo: El Imparcial y Francisco I. Madero." *Historia Mexicana* 40, no. 4 (1991): 697–740.

Landavazo, Marco Antonio. "Guerra, discurso y terror en la independencia de México." In *Creación de estados de opinión en el proceso de independencia mexicano (1808–1823),* edited by Laura Suárez de la Torre, 99–124. Mexico City: Instituto de Investigaciones Dr. José María Luis Mora, 2010.

Larkin, Brian R. *The Very Nature of God: Baroque Catholicism and Religious Reform in Bourbon Mexico City.* Albuquerque: University of New Mexico Press, 2010.

Lazo, Rodrigo. *Letters from Filadelfia: Early Latino Literature and the Trans-American Elite.* Charlottesville: University of Virginia Press, 2020.

Lear, John. *Picturing the Proletariat: Artists and Labor in Revolutionary Mexico, 1908–1940.* Austin: University of Texas Press, 2017.

———. *Workers, Neighbors, and Citizens: The Revolution in Mexico City.* Lincoln: University of Nebraska Press, 2001.

Léger-St-Jean, Marie. "Price One Penny: A Database of Cheap Literature, 1837–1860." Last updated September 9, 2020. http://priceonepenny.info/.

Lomnitz-Adler, Claudio. *Death and the Idea of Mexico.* Brooklyn, NY: Zone Books, 2005.

———. "Nationalism as a Practical System: Benedict Anderson's Theory of Nationalism from the Vantage Point of Spanish America." In *The Other Mirror: Grand Theory through the Lens of Latin America*, edited by Miguel Angel Centeno and Fernando López-Alves, 329–60. Princeton, NJ: Princeton University Press, 2001.

———. *The Return of Comrade Ricardo Flores Magón*. Brooklyn, NY: Zone Books, 2014.

López, Conrado Hernández. "Querétaro en 1867 y la división en la historia (sobre una carta enviada por Silverio Ramírez a Tomás Mejía el 10 de abril de 1867)." *Historia Mexicana* 57, no. 4 (2008): 1201–14.

Loughran, Trish. *The Republic in Print: Print Culture in the Age of U.S. Nation Building, 1770–1870*. New York: Columbia University Press, 2007.

Macías, Anna. "Cómo fue publicada la Constitución de Apatzingán." *Historia Mexicana* 19, no. 1 (1969): 10–22.

Macías-González, Víctor Manuel. "Masculine Friendships, Sentiment, and Homoerotics in Nineteenth-Century Mexico: The Correspondence of José María Calderón y Tapia, 1820s–1850s." *Journal of the History of Sexuality* 16, no. 3 (2007): 416–35.

Mallon, Florencia E. *Peasant and Nation: The Making of Postcolonial Mexico and Peru*. Berkeley: University of California Press, 1995.

Maruca, Lisa. *The Work of Print: Authorship and the English Text Trades, 1660–1760*. Seattle: University of Washington Press, 2007.

Mata, Luis I. *Filomeno Mata*. Mexico City: Secretaría de Educación Pública, 1945.

McGill, Meredith L. *American Literature and the Culture of Reprinting, 1834–1853*. Philadelphia: University of Pennsylvania Press, 2003.

McKenzie, D. F. *Making Meaning: "Printers of the Mind" and Other Essays*. Amherst: University of Massachusetts Press, 2002.

Mijangos y González, Pablo. *Entre Dios y la república: La separación Iglesia-Estado en México, siglo XIX*. Valencia: CIDE / Tirant Lo Blanch, 2018.

———. *The Lawyer of the Church: Bishop Clemente de Jesús Munguía and the Clerical Response to the Mexican Liberal Reforma*. Lincoln: University of Nebraska Press, 2015.

Montiel Ontiveros, Ana Cecilia. *En la esquina de Tacuba y Santo Domingo: La imprenta de María Fernández de Jáuregui, testigo y protagonista de la cultura impresa 1801–1817*. Mexico City: Coalición de Libreros / Sísifo Ediciones, 2015.

Moreno Gamboa, Olivia. "La imprenta y los autores novohispanos: La transformación de una cultura impresa colonial bajo el régimen borbónico (1701–1821)." PhD diss., Universidad Nacional Autónoma de México, 2013.

Moriuchi, Mey-Yen. *Mexican Costumbrismo: Race, Society, and Identity in Nineteenth-Century Art*. University Park: Pennsylvania State University Press, 2018.

Morris, Mark. "Language in Service of the State: The Nahuatl Conterinsurgency Broadsides of 1810." *Hispanic American Historical Review* 87, no. 3 (2007): 433–70.

Mraz, John. *Photographing the Mexican Revolution: Commitments, Testimonies, Icons*. Austin: University of Texas Press, 2012.

Muñoz, Daniel. "The Abolition of the Inquisition and the Creation of a Historical Myth." *Hispanic Research Journal* 11, no. 1 (February 2010): 71–81.

Nava Martínez, Othón. "La empresa editorial de Vicente García Torres, 1838–1853." In *Constructores de un cambio cultural: Impresores-editores y libreros en la ciudad de México, 1830–1855*, edited by Laura Suárez de la Torre, 253–304. Mexico City: Instituto de Investigaciones Dr. José María Luis Mora, 2003.

Neal, Clarice. "Freedom of the Press in New Spain, 1810–1820." In *Mexico and the Spanish Cortes, 1810–1822: Eight Essays*, edited by Nettie Lee Benson, 87–112. Austin: University of Texas Press, Institute of Latin American Studies, 1966.

Nesvig, Martin Austin. "'Heretical Plagues' and Censorship Cordons: Colonial Mexico and the Transatlantic Book Trade." *Church History* 75, no. 1 (2006): 1–37.

Newman, Richard S. "Liberation Technology: Black Printed Protest in the Age of Franklin." *Early American Studies: An Interdisciplinary Journal* 8, no. 1 (Winter 2010): 173–98.

Ogborn, Miles. *Indian Ink: Script and Print in the Making of the English East India Company*. Chicago: University of Chicago Press, 2007.

O'Gorman, Edmundo. *La supervivencia política novo-hispana: Reflexiones sobre el monarquismo mexicano*. 2nd ed. Mexico City: Fundación Cultural de Condumex, Centro de Estudios de Historia de México, 1969.

Ortiz Dávila, Juan Pablo. "Visiones desde la prensa: Las relaciones entre los conservadores y los confederados durante el Segundo Imperio, 1863–1866." *Estudios de Historia Moderna y Contemporánea de México* 52 (2016): 18–38.

Otero-Cleves, Ana María. "Foreign Machetes and Cheap Cotton Cloth: Popular Consumers and Imported Commodities in Nineteenth-Century Colombia." *Hispanic American Historical Review* 97, no. 3 (2017): 423–56.

Ozuna Castañeda, Mariana, and María Esther Guzmán Gutiérrez. "Para que todos lean: La Sociedad Pública de Lectura de El Pensador Mexicano." In *Empresa y cultura en tinta y papel: 1800–1860*, edited by Laura Suárez de la Torre and Miguel Ángel Castro, 273–84. Mexico City: Instituto de Investigaciones Dr. José María Luis Mora / Universidad Nacional Autónoma de México, 2001.

Palacios, Albert A. "Preventing 'Heresy': Censorship and Privilege in Mexican Publishing, 1590–1612." *Book History* 17 (2014): 117–64.

Palti, Elías José. *La invención de una legitimidad: Razón y retórica en el pensamiento mexicano del siglo XIX (un estudio sobre las formas del discurso político)*. Mexico City: Fondo de Cultura Económica, 2005.

———. *La política del disenso: La "polémica en torno al monarquismo" (México, 1848–1850) . . . y las aporías del liberalismo*. Mexico City: Fondo de Cultura Económica, 1998.

Pani, Erika. "Monarchism and Liberalism in Mexico's Nineteenth Century." Working paper presented at the "Liberalism, Monarchy and Empire: Ambiguous Relationships" conference, School of Advanced Study, University of London, 2012.

———. "'Para difundir las doctrinas ortodoxas y vindicarlas de los errores dominantes': Los periódicos católicos y conservadores en el siglo XIX." In *La república de las letras: Asomos a la cultura escrita del México decimonónico; Publicaciones periódicos y otros impresos*, edited by Belem Clark de Lara and Elisa Speckman, 119–30. Mexico City: Universidad Nacional Autónoma de México, 2005.

———. *Para mexicanizar el Segundo Imperio: El imaginario político de los imperialistas*. Mexico City: El Colegio de México / Instituto de Investigaciones Dr. José María Luis Mora, 2001.

———. "'¿Verdaderas figuras de Cooper' o 'Pobres inditos infelices'? La política indigenista de Maximiliano." *Historia Mexicana* 47, no. 3 (1998): 571–604.

Paquette, Gabriel B. *Enlightenment, Governance, and Reform in Spain and Its Empire 1759–1808*. Basingstoke, UK: Palgrave Macmillan, 2008.

Pérez Salas, María Esther. *Costumbrismo y litografía en México: Un nuevo modo de ver*. Mexico City: Universidad Nacional Autónoma de México, Instituto de Investigaciones Estéticas, 2005.

———. "Ignacio Cumplido: Un empresario a cabalidad." In *Empresa y cultura en tinta y papel: 1800–1860*, edited by Laura Suárez de la Torre and Miguel Ángel Castro, 145–56. Mexico City: Instituto de Investigaciones Dr. José María Luis Mora / Universidad Nacional Autónoma de México, 2001.

Pérez Salas Cantú, María Esther. "Los secretos de una empresa exitosa: La imprenta de Ignacio Cumplido." In *Constructores de un cambio cultural: Impresores-editores y libreros en la ciudad de México, 1830–1855*, edited by Laura Suárez de la Torre, 101–82. Mexico City: Instituto de Investigaciones Dr. José María Luis Mora, 2003.

———. "Tipografía e ideología en el Libro de Muestras de Ignacio Cumplido." In *Las muestras tipográficas y el estudio de la cultura impresa*, edited by Marina Garone Gravier and María Esther Pérez Salas Cantú, 83–112. Mexico City: Universidad Nacional Autónoma de México, 2012.

Pérez Toledo, Sonia. *Los hijos del trabajo: Los artesanos de la ciudad de México, 1780–1853*. Mexico City: El Colegio de México / Universidad Autónoma Metropolitana-Iztapalapa, 1996.

———. *Trabajadores, espacio urbano y sociabilidad en la ciudad de México, 1790–1867*. Mexico City: Universidad Autónoma Metropolitana-Iztapalapa / Miguel Ángel Porrúa, 2011.

Pérez Vejo, Tomás. "La conspiración gachupina en 'El Hijo del Ahuizote.'" *Historia Mexicana* 54, no. 4 (2005): 1105–53.

Pérez Vejo, Tomás, and Marta Yolanda Quezada. *De novohispanos a mexicanos: Retratos e identidad colectiva en una sociedad en transición*. Mexico City: Instituto Nacional de Antropología e Historia, 2009.

Peterson, Derek R., Emma Hunter, and Stephanie Newell, eds. *African Print Cultures: Newspapers and Their Publics in the Twentieth Century*. Ann Arbor: University of Michigan Press, 2016.

Piccato, Pablo. *City of Suspects: Crime in Mexico City, 1900–1931*. Durham, NC: Duke University Press, 2001.

———. *History of Infamy: Crime, Truth, and Justice in Mexico*. Oakland: University of California Press, 2017.

———. "Jurados de imprenta en México: El honor en la construcción de la esfera pública, 1821–1882." In *Construcciones impresas: Panfletos, diarios y revistas en la formación de los estados nacionales en América Latina, 1820–1920*, edited by Paula Alonso and José Antonio Aguilar Rivera, 139–66. Mexico City: Fondo de Cultura Económica, 2004.

———. *The Tyranny of Opinion: Honor in the Construction of the Mexican Public Sphere*. Durham, NC: Duke University Press, 2010.

Pi-Suñer Llorens, Antonia. "Entre la historia y la novela: Ireneo Paz." In *La república de las letras: Asomos a la cultura escrita del México decimonónico*, edited by Belem Clark de Lara and Elisa Speckman, 379–92. Mexico City: Universidad Nacional Autónoma de México, 2005.

Popkin, Jeremy D. "A Colonial Media Revolution: The Press in Saint-Domingue, 1789–1793." *The Americas* 75, no. 1 (2018): 3–25.

———. *Revolutionary News: The Press in France, 1789–1799*. Durham, NC: Duke University Press, 1990.

Porter, Susie S. *Working Women in Mexico City: Public Discourses and Material Conditions, 1879–1931*. Tucson: University of Arizona Press, 2003.

Premo, Bianca. *The Enlightenment on Trial: Ordinary Litigants and Colonialism in the Spanish Empire*. New York: Oxford University Press, 2017.

———. "Legal Writing, Civil Litigation, and Agents in the 18th-Century Spanish Imperial World." In *Oxford Research Encyclopedia of Latin American History* (February 27, 2017). https://oxfordre.com/latinamericanhistory/view/10.1093/acrefore/9780199366439.001.0001/acrefore-9780199366439-e-247.

Price, Leah. *How to Do Things with Books in Victorian Britain*. Princeton, NJ: Princeton University Press, 2012.

Rama, Ángel. *The Lettered City*. Translated by John Chasteen. Durham, NC: Duke University Press, 1996.

Rancière, Jacques. "The Myth of the Artisan: Critical Reflections on a Category of Social History." *International Labor and Working-Class History*, no. 24 (1983): 1–16.

———. *Proletarian Nights: The Workers' Dream in Nineteenth-Century France*. London: Verso Books, 2012.

Rappaport, Joanne, and Tom Cummins. *Beyond the Lettered City: Indigenous Literacies in the Andes*. Durham, NC: Duke University Press, 2012.

Reyes Heroles, Jesús. *Los orígenes*. Vol. 1 of *El liberalismo mexicano*. Mexico City: Universidad Nacional de México, Facultad de Derecho, 1957.

Rice, Stephen P. *Minding the Machine: Languages of Class in Early Industrial America*. Berkeley: University of California Press, 2004.

Ricketts, Mónica. *Who Should Rule? Men of Arms, the Republic of Letters, and the Fall of the Spanish Empire*. New York: Oxford University Press, 2017.

Ríos Zúñiga, Rosalina. *Formar ciudadanos: Sociedad civil y movilización popular en Zacatecas, 1821–1853*. Mexico City: ESU Plaza y Valdés, 2005.

Rodríguez Piña, Javier. "Los conservadores-católicos mexicanos ante *Los Misterios de París de Eugenio Sue*." In *Tras las huellas de Eugenio Sue: Lectura, circulación y apropiación de Los Misterios de París, Siglo XIX*, edited by Laura Suárez de la Torre, 202–20. Mexico City: Instituto de Investigaciones Dr. José María Luis Mora, 2015.

———. "La prensa y las ideas conservadores a mediados del siglo XIX." In *Tipos y caracteres: La prensa mexicana, 1822–1855*, edited by Miguel Ángel Castro, 253–64. Mexico City: Universidad Nacional Autónoma de México, 2001.

———. "Rafael de Rafael y Vilá: El conservadurismo como empresa." In *Constructores de un cambio cultural: Impresores-editores y libreros en la ciudad de México, 1830–1855*, edited by Laura Suárez de la Torre, 305–80. Mexico City: Instituto de Investigaciones Dr. José María Luis Mora, 2003.

Rojas, Rafael. "Una maldición silenciada: El panfleto político en el México independiente." *Historia Mexicana* 47, no. 1 (1997): 35–67.

Rojas Rendón, María José Patricia. "Los impresos poblanos efímeros: Una mirada a 'Tertulia de pulquería,' de José A. Arrieta, 1851." *Inmediaciones de la Comunicación* 12, no. 2 (2017): 49–71.

Rubenstein, Anne. *Bad Language, Naked Ladies, and Other Threats to the Nation: A Political History of Comic Books in Mexico*. Durham, NC: Duke University Press, 1998.

Sabato, Hilda. *Republics of the New World: The Revolutionary Political Experiment in Nineteenth-Century Latin America*. Princeton, NJ: Princeton University Press, 2018.

Sánchez, Vieyra. *"La Voz de México" (1870–1875), la prensa católica y la reorganización conservadora*. Mexico City: Universidad Nacional Autónoma de México, Instituto de Investigaciones Bibliográficas / Instituto Nacional de Antropología e Historia, 2008.

Sánchez Archundia, Alejandra. "Legislación de imprenta y voceo de papeles en las calles de la ciudad de México, 1821–1834." In *Miradas y acercamientos a la prensa decimonónica*, edited by Adriana Pineda Soto and Fausta Gantús, 133–60. Mexico City: Universidad Michoacana de San Nicolás de Hidalgo / Red de Historiadores de la Prensa y el Periodismo en Iberoamérica, 2013.

Sanders, Frank J. "Jose María Gutiérrez Estrada: Monarchist Pamphleteer." *The Americas* 27, no. 1 (1970): 56–74.

Sanders, James E. *The Vanguard of the Atlantic World: Creating Modernity, Nation, and Democracy in Nineteenth-Century Latin America*. Durham, NC: Duke University Press, 2014.

Sartorius, David. *Ever Faithful: Race, Loyalty, and the Ends of Empire in Spanish Cuba*. Durham, NC: Duke University Press, 2013.

Schaefer, Timo H. *Liberalism as Utopia: The Rise and Fall of Legal Rule in Post-Colonial Mexico, 1820–1900*. New York: Cambridge University Press, 2017.

Schell, Patience A. *Church and State Education in Revolutionary Mexico City*. Tucson: University of Arizona Press, 2003.

Schwartz, Kathryn A. "The Political Economy of Private Printing in Cairo as Told from a Commissioning Deal Turned Sour, 1871." *International Journal of Middle East Studies* 49, no. 1 (2017): 25–45.

Sellers-García, Sylvia. *Distance and Documents at the Spanish Empire's Periphery*. Stanford, CA: Stanford University Press, 2014.

Sennett, Richard. *The Craftsman*. New Haven, CT: Yale University Press, 2008.

Serna, Ana María. *Un análisis de los casos relativos a la libertad de imprenta: Los juicios de amparo de Filomeno Mata Rodríguez en 1901 y 1910.* Mexico City: Suprema Corte de Justicia de la Nación, 2013.

Sewell, William H. *Work and Revolution in France: The Language of Labor from the Old Regime to 1848.* New York: Cambridge University Press, 1980.

Smith, Benjamin T. *The Mexican Press and Civil Society, 1940–1976: Stories from the Newsroom, Stories from the Street.* Chapel Hill: University of North Carolina Press, 2018.

———. *The Roots of Conservatism in Mexico: Catholicism, Society, and Politics in the Mixteca Baja, 1750–1962.* Albuquerque: University of New Mexico Press, 2012.

Smith, Phyllis Lynn. "Contentious Voices amid the Order: The Porfirian Press in Mexico City, 1876–1911." PhD diss., University of Arizona, 1996.

Soberón, Arturo. "Lucas Alamán y la presidencia del ayuntamiento de la ciudad de México en 1849." *Historias: Revista de la Dirección de Estudios Históricos del Instituto Nacional de Antropología e Historia,* no. 50 (2001): 33–49.

Sordo Cedeño, Reynaldo. "La libertad de prensa en la construcción del estado laico: 1810–1857." In *El Estado laico y los derechos humanos en México: 1810–2010,* edited by Margarita Moreno Bonett and Rosa María Álvarez de Lara, 133–47. Mexico City: Universidad Nacional Autónoma de México, 2012.

Soriano, Cristina. *Tides of Revolution: Information, Insurgencies, and the Crisis of Colonial Rule in Venezuela.* Albuquerque: University of New Mexico Press, 2018.

———. "'A True Vassal of the King': Pardo Literacy and Political Identity in Venezuela during the Age of Revolutions." *Atlantic Studies* 14, no. 3 (2017): 275–95.

Soto, Miguel. *La conspiración monárquica en México, 1845–1846.* Mexico City: Editorial Offset, 1988.

Speckman Guerra, Elisa. *Crimen y castigo: Legislación penal, interpretaciones de la criminalidad y administración de justicia (Ciudad de México, 1872–1910).* Mexico City: El Colegio de México / Universidad Nacional Autónoma de México, 2002.

———. "Infancia es destino: Menores delincuentes en la ciudad de México (1884–1910)." In *De normas y transgresiones: Enfermedad y crimen en América Latina, 1850-1950,* edited by Claudia Agostoni and Elisa Speckman Guerra, 225–53. Mexico City: Universidad Nacional Autónoma de México, Instituto de Investigaciones Históricas, 2005.

Suárez de la Torre, Laura, ed. *Constructores de un cambio cultural: Impresores-editores y libreros en la ciudad de México, 1830–1855.* Mexico City: Instituto de Investigaciones Dr. José María Luis Mora, 2003.

———. "Editores para el cambio: Expresión de una nueva cultura política, 1808–1855." In *Transición y cultura política: De la colonia al México independiente,* edited by Cristina Gómez Álvarez and Miguel Soto, 43–66. Mexico City: Facultad de Filosofía y Letras, Universidad Nacional Autónoma de México, 2004.

———. "José Mariano Lara: Intereses empresariales—inquietudes intelectuales—compromisos políticos." In *Constructores de un cambio cultural: Impresores-editores y libreros en la ciudad de México, 1830–1855,* edited by Laura Suárez de la

Torre, 183–252. Mexico City: Instituto de Investigaciones Dr. José María Luis Mora, 2003.

Suárez de la Torre, Laura, and Miguel Ángel Castro, eds. *Empresa y cultura en tinta y papel: 1800–1860*. Mexico City: Instituto de Investigaciones Dr. José María Luis Mora / Universidad Nacional Autónoma de México, 2001.

Suárez Rivera, Manuel. *Dinastía de tinta y papel: Los Zúñiga Ontiveros en la cultura novohispana (1756–1825)*. Mexico City: Instituto de Investigaciones Bibliográficas, Universidad Nacional Autónoma de México, 2019.

———. "El periodismo en construcción: Estrategias comerciales de la *Gazeta de México*, 1784–1785." *Relaciones* 143 (verano 2015): 207–31.

———. "Se buscan lectores: El modelo de suscripción en los impresos novohispanos a finales del siglo XVIII." In *Libros y lectores en las sociedades hispanas: España y Nueva España (Siglos XVI–XVIII)*, edited by Francisco Javier Cervantes Bello, 367–406. Puebla, Mexico: Benemérita Universidad Autónoma de Puebla / Educación y Cultura, 2016.

Tanck Estrada, Dorothy. *La educación ilustrada, 1786–1836: Educación primaria en la ciudad de México*. 2nd ed. Mexico City: El Colegio de México, 1984.

Taylor, William B. *Theater of a Thousand Wonders: A History of Miraculous Images and Shrines in New Spain*. New York: Cambridge University Press, 2016.

Thomson, Guy P. C. "Popular Aspects of Liberalism in Mexico, 1848–1888." *Bulletin of Latin American Research* 10, no. 3 (1991): 265–92.

Torres Puga, Gabriel. "Inquisición y literatura clandestina en el siglo XVIII." In *Historia de la literatura mexicana: Desde sus orígenes hasta nuestros días*, edited by Nancy Vogeley and Manuel Ramos Medina, 150–72. Mexico City: Siglo XXI / Universidad Nacional Autónoma de México, Facultad de Filosofía y Letras, 2011.

———. *Opinión pública y censura en Nueva España: Indicios de un silencio imposible (1767–1794)*. Mexico City: El Colegio de México, 2010.

———. "La transformación de la *Gazeta de México*, 1805–1808." In *Guerra, política y cultura en las independencias hispanoamericanas*, edited by Marco Antonio Landavazo and Moisés Guzmán, 21–58. Morelia: Universidad Michoacana / El Colegio de Jalisco, 2013.

———. *Los últimos años de la Inquisición en la Nueva España*. Mexico City: Miguel Ángel Porrúa / CONACULTA-INAH, 2004.

Toussaint Alcaraz, Florence. "Diario del Hogar: De lo doméstico a lo político." *Revista Mexicana de Ciencias Políticas y Sociales* 28, no. 109 (1982): 103–16.

———. *Escenario de la prensa en el Porfiriato*. Mexico City: Fundación Manuel Buendía / Universidad de Colima, 1989.

Trujillo Bolio, Mario. "El entramado de la cultura obrera entre los trabajadores urbanos (1864–1880)." In *Cultura y trabajo en México: Estereotipos, prácticas y representaciones*, edited by Rocío Guadarrama, 55–84. Mexico City: Universidad Autónoma Metropolitana, 1998.

Valdez Garza, Dalia. *Libros y lectores en la Gazeta de literatura de México (1788–1795) de José Antonio Alzate*. Mexico City: Bonilla Artigas Editores / Instituto Tecnológico y de Estudios Superiores de Monterrey / Iberoamericana, 2014.

Van Young, Eric. "Agrarian Rebellion and Defense of Community: Meaning and Collective Violence in Late Colonial and Independence-Era Mexico." *Journal of Social History* 27, no. 2 (1993): 245–69.

———. "Islands in the Storm: Quiet Cities and Violent Countrysides in the Mexican Independence Era." *Past and Present* 118, no. 1 (1988): 130–55.

———. *The Other Rebellion: Popular Violence, Ideology, and the Mexican Struggle for Independence, 1810–1821.* Stanford, CA: Stanford University Press, 2001.

Vaughan, Mary Kay. "Primary Education and Literacy in Nineteenth-Century Mexico: Research Trends, 1968–1988." *Latin American Research Review* 25, no. 1 (1990): 31–66.

———. *The State, Education, and Social Class in Mexico, 1880–1928.* DeKalb: Northern Illinois University Press, 1982.

Velayos, Emmanuel. "Painting Words, Drawing Republics: Embodied Arts and New Beginnings in Simón Rodríguez." *Hispanic Review* 87, no. 2 (2019): 133–58.

Villa-Flores, Javier. "Reframing a 'Dark Passion': Bourbon Morality, Gambling, and the Royal Lottery in New Spain." In *Emotions and Daily Life in Colonial Mexico*, edited by Javier Villa-Flores and Sonya Lipsett-Rivera, 148–67. Albuquerque: University of New Mexico Press, 2014.

Villaseñor y Villaseñor, Ramiro. *Ignacio Cumplido, impresor tapatío.* Guadalajara, Mexico: Gobierno de Jalisco, Secretaría General, Unidad Editorial, 1987.

Voekel, Pamela. *Alone before God: The Religious Origins of Modernity in Mexico.* Durham, NC: Duke University Press, 2002.

Vogeley, Nancy J. *The Bookrunner: A History of Inter-American Relations—Print, Politics, and Commerce in the United States and Mexico, 1800–1830.* Philadelphia, PA: American Philosophical Society, 2011.

———. "Las vicisitudes editoriales de 'La Quijotita y su prima.'" *Legajos: Boletín del Archivo General de la Nación*, no. 18 (octubre–diciembre 2013): 135–93.

Ward, Kenneth C. "'Mexico, Where They Coin Money and Print Books': The Calderón Dynasty and the Mexican Book Trade, 1630–1730." PhD diss., University of Texas at Austin, 2013.

Warren, Richard A. *Vagrants and Citizens: Politics and the Masses in Mexico City from Colony to Republic.* Wilmington, DE: SR Books, 2001.

Wasserman, Mark. *Everyday Life and Politics in Nineteenth Century Mexico: Men, Women, and War.* Albuquerque: University of New Mexico Press, 2000.

Whittaker, Martha Ellen. "La cultura impresa en la ciudad de México, 1700–1800: Las imprentas, las librerías y las bibliotecas." In *Historia de la literatura mexicana: Desde sus orígenes hasta nuestros días*, edited by Nancy Vogeley and Manuel Ramos Medina, 37–52. Mexico City: Siglo XXI / Universidad Nacional Autónoma de México, Facultad de Filosofía y Letras, 2011.

———. "Jesuit Printing in Bourbon Mexico City: The Press of the Colegio de San Ildefonso, 1748–1767." PhD diss., University of California, Berkeley, 1998.

Wold, Ruth. *El Diario de México: Primer cotidiano de Nueva España.* Madrid: Editorial Gredos, 1970.

Woldenberg K., José. "Asociaciones artesanas del siglo XIX (Sociedad Socorros Mutuos de Impresores, 1874–1875)." *Revista Mexicana de Ciencias Políticas y Sociales* 21, no. 83 (enero–marzo 1976): 71–112.

Wright-Rios, Edward. *Searching for Madre Matiana: Prophecy and Popular Culture in Modern Mexico*. Albuquerque: University of New Mexico Press, 2014.

Zeltsman, Corinna. "Defining Responsibility: Printers, Politics, and the Law in Early Republican Mexico City." *Hispanic American Historical Review* 98, no. 2 (2018): 189–222.

Zúñiga Saldaña, Marcela. "Licencias para imprimir libros en la Nueva España, 1748–1770." In *Del autor al lector: Libros y libreros en la historia*, edited by Carmen Castañeda García, 163–78. Mexico City: Centro de Investigaciones y Estudios Superiores en Antropología Social, 2002.

INDEX

booksellers, 24, 133

bookstores, 67, 77, 93, 96, 268n70

Bourbon Reforms, 18, 20–21, 30–32

Bourdieu, Pierre, 173

broadsides, 79, 124, 243–45; controversial, 1–2, 53, 75, 102. *See also Liberal a los bajos escritores, El* (Merino)

Bruce & Co. type foundry, 190

Buen Tono, El, 212

Burke, Edmund, 137

Bustamante, Anastasio, 87, 93, 102, 107

Bustamante, Carlos María de: *El Diario de México*, 37; diary observations of, 86–87, 95, 96, 122; *El Juguete Rabioso*, 60–61; views on press abuses, 118

Cabrera, Daniel, 19, 205, 209, 218–19, 222–24

Cacho de Navarrete, Luisa, 152, 153

Café de Verolí, 108

cajistas. See compositors

Calavera de la Prensa, 243

Calderón de la Barca, Fanny, 82

Calderón printing family, 24

Calleja, Félix, 59

Calvin, John, 199

Campeche, 81

Campomanes, Pedro Rodríguez de, 22, *Discurso sobre la educación popular de los artesanos y su fomento*, 30–31

Cancelada, Juan López, 38, 39–41, 44–47

Carlos III (king of Spain), 31, 34

Carlota (empress of Mexico), 159

Carta dirigida al Ecsmo. Sr. Presidente de la república (Gutiérrez Estrada), 81–82; audience and circulation of, 93–95, 96; design of, 92–93; investigation into, 95–96, 97–101; press coverage of, 96, 101–2, 107; publisher's defense, 101–6

cartillas, 24, 65

Castelar, Emilio, 196

Catholic Church, 7, 8; attitudes towards printing, 210–12, 296n27; relationship with state, 1, 116–17, 119, 132–36, 138–41, 211. *See also* censorship: religious; printing: religious

cédulas de confesión y comunión, 149, 150

censorship, 80, 118; colonial-era, 23, 30, 61, 70–71, 80, 257n4; religious, 18, 112–13, 116–17, 129–31, 133–34, 139–40, 237; during the Second Empire, 158. *See also* Inquisition; *junta de censura; junta eclesiastica de censura*

centralists, 83–84; conflicts with federalists, 7, 81, 87; press laws of, 88, 90–91, 109, 117, 142

Chamber of Deputies, 95, 110

Chartier, Roger, 16

Chihuahua, 160

Chilpancingo, 50

china poblana, 12–13

científicos, 204, 208

circular (memo), 143

citizenship, 13, 19, 52, 83, 102, 255n35; the "printer citizen," 102–3, 106; and private property rights, 140–41

Colegio de San Ildefonso, 24

Colegio de San Pablo, 113

Columbus, Christopher, 197

compositors, 90, 148, 174, 188–90, 208; 1878 strike by, 201; and cleanliness, 176; descriptions of, as "vice-ridden," 181, 242; as destabilizing figures, 180–82; journalism and literature by, 15, 170–71, 184–86, 192–201, 202–3, 240; and liberalism, 15, 198; and linotype, 212–13, 242; and literacy, 212–13; literary representations of, 178, 179, 181–82, 203, 210, 245; work rhythms and wages of, 177–79. *See also muestras* of 1877

Conductor Eléctrico, El, 64, 66, 67

confederates, 165

Congress of Anáhuac, 50

conservatism, 115, 124, 169, 173. *See also* centralists

constitutions, 50–51, 55, 68, 75, 78, 111, 239; 1857 constitution, 146, 209, 219; article 7 (1857 constitution), 220–21; article 7 (1917 constitution), 231–33; Cádiz constitution (1812), 53, 61; centralist constitution (Siete Leyes, 1836), 83, 102; federalist constitution (1824), 149; federalist constitution (1847), 119, 131; revolutionary constitution (1917), 231–33, 241

contracts, 41, 65–66. *See also* government printing: outsourcing of

fomento de periódicos. See newspapers: state subsidies for
formador, 179
forms, 149
France, 81, 196
Frankel, Oz, 166
Franklin, Benjamin, 25, 194
freedom of religion, 114
freedom of the press, 4, 7, 12, 46; anxieties about, 61–62, 70, 118–19, 236; Cádiz Constitution and, 60–63; limits placed on, 8, 63, 77, 118–19, 120, 123; material and social dimensions of, 9–10, 79, 232, 235–36; partisan attitudes towards, 76, 91, 105–6, 118–19, 142, 236–37; and the power of printers, 53, 64–66, 68, 79, 235; and printers' freedom, 11, 19, 65–66, 120, 171, 226, 232, 238; and private property rights, 132, 140–41, 171, 238; reform of article 7 of the constitution and, 220; revolutionary constitution and, 231–32. See also junta de censura; press jury; press laws and regulations
French Revolution, 30, 36

Galán, Manuel, 71–72, 73–74
Galván Rivera, Mariano, 190, 194
Gálvez, Matías de, 34
Gamboa, Federico, 181, 185, 203, 219
Gantús, Fausta, 223
Garay, Aurelio, 202–3, 249; The Hydra: Memoir of a Suicide, 202
García Cubas, Antonio, 194; Curso elemental de geografía universal, 194
García Icazbalceta, Joaquín: 6
García Torres, Vicente, 7, 18, 111, 253n18; assault on the Catholic Church by, 130–32, 140–41, 240; confrontational persona of, 122–23; Defense of the Publisher of the Work Entitled "Mysteries of the Inquisition," 136–38; government contracts of, 153–54, 155–57, 167; and El Monitor Republicano, 113–14; and The Mysteries of the Inquisition, 112, 126–28, 130; radical activism of, 113, 116–17, 139, 158, 219, 238; wealth of, 173
Garibay, Pedro de, 38, 40
Garone, Marina, 29

Gazeta del Gobierno, La, 42, 44–45
Gazeta de Madrid, La, 36, 43
Gazeta de México, La, 18, 20–22, 34–37, 52; and 1808 crisis, 37, 38–39, 40–46; news from Madrid in, 36–37, 43
gender, 14, 29, 197; liberal definitions of work and, 169
Germillan, Victorine (pseud. V. de Féréal), 125
Gil, Jerónimo Antonio, 32–33
Girardin, Émile de, 196
Gobernación. See Ministry of the Interior
Godoy, Manuel, 38
Gómez de la Peña, José Gabriel, 95, 97, 99
Gómez Farías, Valentín, 116
González, Manuel, 220
government gazette, 86, 143, 156, 188; circulation among officials of, 152, 159; reliability of news in, 36, 38, 151–52. See also Diario Oficial, El; Gazeta del Gobierno, La; Gazeta de México, La
government printing: colonial-era, 40–41, 53–54, 139; correctional schools and, 205; of legal compilations, 157–58; municipal and regional, 156, 159–60, 167; outsourcing of, 85, 142, 145–46, 147, 149, 150–57, 158, 236, 285n19; and "print statism," 166; regulations for, 154, 165–66, 201–2; as a "state fixation," 168. See also decreto negro; "print clientelism"; state formation; Traidores pintados por sí mismos, Los
government printing shop: commandeering of, 152, 231; Imprenta del Gabinete Civil (1865–1867), 146–47, 158, 160, 163; Imprenta del Gobierno Federal (1867–1920), 147, 163–68, 169, 173, 174–80, 187–92, 199–202; Imprenta Nacional del Supremo Gobierno de México (1823–1828), 8, 85, 144–45, 147–50; of the Ministry of Public Works (Fomento, 1883–1920), 202
Gran Círculo de Obreros (Great Workers' Circle), 180
Granja, Juan de la, 123, 280n44
Gran Teatro Nacional, 196
Guadalajara, 55, 117, 160, 167, 226
Guadalupe, Virgin of, 56

Morelos, José María, 50–51

Mosquito Mexicano, El, 95, 96, 97, 99, 101, 102, 107

muestras of 1877: as compositors' treatise, 192–201; production context of, 187–90; as type specimen, 191–92

mules, 13, 176

Müller Brothers, 213, 214

mutual aid societies, 172, 180, 184, 202. *See also names of individual societies*

Mysteries of the Inquisition (Germillan), 18, 112–13, 116, 141, 153, 165, 173; audience for, 127, 133–34, 136; church censorship of, 129–31, 134, 140, 239; press polemic over, 127–29, 141; publicity for, 125–26, 129; publisher's defense of, 136–38, 140; state response to, 139–40

Napoleon III (emperor of France), 1, 146, 157, 163

Nariño, Antonio, 36

National Palace: bombardment of, 81; as site of government printing shop, 8, 85, 144, 158, 163–64, 166, 168

National Paper and Type Company, 214

nation building: liberal publishing projects and, 165, 173, 181; print and, 4–5, 6, 11, 169

Navarrete, Juan Gómez de, 152

Nezahualcoyotl, 197

newspapers, 123; binding of, 35, 134; Catholic, 173, 208, 210–11; Catholic Church's views on, 133, 211; commercial press, 208, 215–16, 241; development of, in Mexico, 21, 34–35; literature in, 10, 112, 125, 126, 127, 140; *nota roja*, 241; *papeleros* (vendors), 232; polemics of, 110–11, 113–16, 120, 124, 127–29; and printing technology, 120–21, 215; readership of, 121, 127, 128, 133–34; state subsidies for, 41–42, 86, 151, 208, 215, 223, 241; subscriptions, 11, 36–37, 38, 151, 159; as symbols of political awareness, 12, 239; for workers, 172, 182, 184–86, 201, 202, 208, 212. *See also under titles of specific newspapers*

New York, 85, 123

Noriega, Francisco José de, 42–45

novels, 113, 116, 125, 128, 182, 202–3. See also *Hydra: Memoir of a Suicide, The* (Garay)

Oaxaca, 51, 55

oficiales (journeymen), 25

Olaguíbel, Francisco M. de, 138

Otero, Mariano, 154

Padre Cobos, 188

País, El, 228

pamphlets, 72, 76, 84–85, 102, 139; controversial, 78; cost of, 96. See also *Carta dirigida al Ecsmo. Sr. Presidente de la república* (Gutiérrez Estrada)

papeles públicos (public papers), 10, 61, 76

papel sellado, 54–55

paper, 85, 125, 160, 176; imports, 6, 23, 241; making, 31; scarcity of, 24, 55; state subsidies of, 36, 241–42. See also *papel sellado*

pasquinades, 4, 29

patronage networks, 45, 85, 92, 154, 187–88; and complication of Habermasian ideal of the public sphere, 11; critiques of, 37–38, 44, 64, 79, 215; printers' cultivation of political, 6, 20–21, 24–25, 36, 41, 73, 102, 124; in printers' cultural imaginary, 26–29. *See also* newspapers: state subsidies for; *subvención*

Patronato, 116

Patti, Adelina, 196, 197

Paz, Ireneo, 173, 188

Pensador Mexicano, El, 61

Peralta, Ángela, 196, 197

Pérez Vejo, Tomás, 47

Periquillo sarniento, El (Lizardi), 64

Philadelphia, 47, 85

Philippines, 53

Piccato, Pablo, 123, 220

pie de imprenta. See imprint (*pie de imprenta*)

PIPSA (Productora e Importadora de Papel). *See* Producer and Importer of Paper (PIPSA)

Plan de Ayala, 231

political caricatures, 39, 40*fig.*, 219–20, 220*fig.*

political clubs, 230

politics: printing as arena of, 4, 9, 69, 84, 239; embodied dimensions of, 16; of running a printing business, 5–6, 11–12, 42–43, 53, 72–73, 79–80, 157, 221–22
Porfiriato, 206–7; and commercial press, 208, 215–16; and *doctrina psicológica* during, 219; expansion of printing during, 207–8, 226–27, 230; and opposition printers, 218–19, 223; patronage during, 219; press freedom during, 206, 223
Portal de Mercaderes, 71, 108
Posada, José Guadalupe, 242, 243
Posada y Garduño, Manuel, 117, 133
positivism, 198, 219; and scientific politics, 204, 207
press jury, 10, 88, 131, 132, 140, 171 142, 237
press laws and regulations, 8; criminal reforms of, 90–91, 207, 220–21, 222; Lafragua Law (1846), 118–19, 121, 124, 141; "Ley Lares" (1853), 142, 155; "Ley Zarco" (1861, 1868), 171, 220; Press Law (1813), 62, 132, 141, 267n51; Press Law (1820), 63, 117; Press Law (1917), 233–35, 241; in the Second Empire, 158–59, 163; during the U.S.-Mexican War, 120–21, 123. *See also* censorship; licensing; press jury; printing press: seizures of; privileges for printing; responsibility for texts
pressmen, 25, 90, 148, 177
Prieto, Guillermo, 121–22, 123, 169–70; *Elementary Lessons in Political Economy*, 169
print: annotation of, 50–51, 74–75; capitalism, 11; "clandestine," 233; and Enlightenment, 58, 61–62; and the muralist movement, 242; notarization of, 107, 164, 216; official anxieties about, 8, 12–13, 158, 236; and orality, 3, 12, 29, 95, 96, 98, 234; and political authority/ legitimacy, 12, 51–54, 55, 58, 76, 160, 163, 164, 168, 239; and revolution, 52, 76, 230–31; runs, 71, 74, 77, 85, 92, 143, 162, 166, 215–16; social aspirations associated with, 12, 122, 136, 172–73, 187, 192, 194, 201; and social hierarchies, 5, 96, 134, 235–36, 239, 240–41; state archiving of, 2, 4, 143–44, 166; and the urban landscape, 3. *See also* books; broadsides; decrees (*bandos*); forms; newspapers; pamphlets; *papeles públicos*

"print clientelism," 146, 154–57, 167, 215, 236; definition of, 11–12
printers: accusations against, 64–65, 66, 67–68, 86, 90, 123–24, 222, 225; as archivists, 22, 35; autonomy of, 11, 171, 235, 238; as censors, 65, 66, 73, 91, 101, 103, 104–5, 237; census figure for, 168, 180, 212, 296n29; expressive culture and imaginary of, 14, 15, 25–29, 72, 170, 172–73, 182–86, 190–201; impartiality of 15, 86, 100, 103, 110, 137; informal education of, 16, 173, 182, 184, 212–13, 241; as intellectuals, 15, 49, 103–4, 172, 192, 198, 238; legal arguments of, 11, 131–32, 140–41; literary and visual representations of, 47–49, 48*fig.*, 181–82, 183*fig.*, 244*fig.*; as mechanics/ machines, 100, 105–6, 126, 237; and mythmaking, 17, 185–86, 199, 218, 242, 245; negative views of, 7, 83, 86, 122, 179, 243; and partisan politics, 11, 110–11, 120, 124, 238, 239–40; persecution of, 83, 91–92, 109–10, 120, 219–20, 221, 273n37; public personae of, 6, 18, 22, 35, 83, 84, 104, 110, 120, 122, 140, 209, 218, 238, 243; as publishers, 6, 15, 64, 66, 90, 127, 137; women, 14, 24, 26, 205, 286n42, 297n54. *See also* compositors; printing shop: administrators of; printing shop: owners of; responsibility for texts: printers' efforts to evade; *and under names of specific printers*
Printers' Mutual Aid Society, 180, 184
printing, 255n33; and the Bourbon Reforms, 30–32; business aspects of 5, 11–12, 23–25, 85–86, 102, 207–8, 255n30, 271n11; and enslaved laborers, 25, 259n25; historiography of, 6, 243; "job," 208, 213–15, 230, 240; in Nahuatl, 162–63; and narratives of progress, 206, 208, 209–10, 214–15, 229–30, 245; as performance, 67, 187, 189, 199, 239; religious, 11, 30, 149; technical aspects of, 16, 99, 100–101, 148, 149, 174–79, 188, 208; as technology of social trans-

formation, 4–5, 172, 184, 240–41, 245; wartime, 36–37, 54–59, 123, 156–57, 160–63, 230–31. *See also* government printing; halftone (photomechanical reproduction); lithography; printing shops; privileges; proofreading; reprinting; type: composition

printmaking, 242. *See also* lithography

printing press, 123, 216; as evidence in criminal cases (*cuerpo del delito*), 209, 221 222, 224–25, 226, 229; feminization of the, 14, 29; first, in the Americas, 4; mechanical, 120–21, 124, 153, 176, 208, 215; as private property, 226, 232, 241; sales of, 85, 210, 216; seizures of, 19, 92, 164, 205, 219–24, 225, 226–28, 238–39; as symbol of civilization, 5, 229. *See also* advertising: of printing equipment

printing shops: 67, 124, 296n29; administrators of, 25, 71, 72, 90, 174, 177, 188, 201; blurring of social boundaries in, 6, 13–14, 177–78, 181, 203, 240; equipment and organization of, 85, 148, 153, 174–78, 208, 212, 295n13; literary and visual representations of, 202–3, 213–15, 214*fig.*, 216–18, 218*fig.*, 243–45, 244*fig.*; owners of, 25, 90; and political subterfuge, 6, 87, 88–90, 207; sackings of, 221, 238–39, 298n57; sensory environment of, 13, 90, 176; as sites of social transformation, 202–3, 245; social hierarchies within, 14, 25, 29, 174, 177, 201–2, 203; women in, 176, 213, 290n23. *See also* government printing shop

privileges for printing, 21, 22, 24–25, 32, 70, 79, 85, 258n17; conflicts over, 39–40, 41–46

Producer and Importer of Paper (PIPSA), 241–42

pronunciamientos, 84, 231, 239

proofreading, 16, 90, 99, 174, 176

propaganda, 57–59

property: liberal definitions of, 169; the printing press as 226, 232, 241; printed materials as, 18, 117, 131–32, 140–41

Proudhon, Pierre-Joseph, 196

public happiness, 21, 41

public opinion, 1, 5, 22, 42, 60, 75, 151, 159

Public Reading Society, 67, 71

public sphere, 9, 11, 21, 78, 220; and efforts to marginalize printers, 17, 236

public writers. *See* journalists

publishers, 128; Catholic, 210–11; printer-, 6, 125, 126–27

publishing industry, 5, 11, 73–74; efforts to rationalize, 66–67

Puebla, 25, 68, 70, 72, 74, 77, 93

Pugibet, Ernesto, 212

pulquerías, 12–13, 179–80

Rabasa, Emilio, 15, 293n73; *Cuarto poder, El*, 15

radicals (*puros*), 114, 120, 124

Rafael, Rafael de, 123, 127, 155–56, 158; type specimen of, 190–91, 239

railroads, 197

Rama, Ángel, 6; *The Lettered City*, 6

Rancière, Jacques, 16

Read, Ellis, 210

readers, 58, 78, 128, 134, 127; "the citizen reader," 140–41; printing shop workers as, 170, 188–90, 203, 216

reading, 27–28, 30, 96. *See also* Public Reading Society

redacción/redactor, 121, 151

Reforma, La, 142, 146, 154, 169, 199

Regeneración, 225

Renacimiento, El (Monterrey), 228

reprinting, 17, 39, 73, 86; as copying, 43; of literature, 127, 129; of news coverage, 36, 227–28, 230; official fears about, 70–71, 78

republicanism, 81, 120, 196, 203; conservative efforts to end, 84, 110–11; egalitarian language of, 7

responsibility for texts: defined in press laws, 10, 88, 171, 222, 232–34; debates over, 83–84, 90–91, 96, 105–6, 110, 227, 235–36, 237, 241; printers' efforts to evade, 92, 97–99, 109, 222–23, 235

responsivo, 88, 89*fig.*, 233

Restored Republic, 19, 166, 168, 170, 203, 238, 240

Revista de Revistas, 242

Revista de Tabasco, La, 227

Revolution of Ayutla, 146, 155

type, 16, 75, 90, 153, 189; automated typesetting machines, 197, 212, 230; composition, 99, 101, 174, 177–78, 188, 290n25;
founding, 31–32, 51; imports of: 6, 32, 85,
90, 93, 125; pied, 148, 149, 189, 219, 226
typesetters. *See* compositors
type specimens, 10, 26–29, 173, 175–76,
190–92, 192–201. See also *muestra* of
1877
Typographical Brotherhood Artistic Association, 180
typography, 22, 69, 79, 92–93, 147, 160, 188;
baroque, 27, 28*fig.*, 32–33; and literary
and political genres, 16; and neoclassical
taste, 22, 32–34, 33*fig.;* and novelty, 16, 93

ultraje (attacks) against public officials,
221, 224
Union Linotipográfica, 242
United States of America, 84, 110, 127, 160,
194, 197. *See also* U.S.-Mexican War
Universal, El, 124, 127–28, 129, 137
Universal, El (1888), 208
urban landscape: printed texts as actors
in, 3
U.S.-Mexican War, 12, 111, 114, 119, 122–23;
and the Imprenta del Aguila, 152

Valdés, Alejandro, 18, 47, 63, 149; and
conflicts with writers, 64–66, 68; as
imperial printer, 79; *La prensa libre,*
65–66; and reprinting of *El liberal a los
bajos escritores,* 71; on the rights of
printers, 65–66, 232; viceregal regime
and, 53, 72–73, 76
Valdés, Manuel Antonio, 18; business
partnerships of, 37–38, 39, 46; and
conflicts with officials, 40–42; defense
of privileges by, 42–45; and the *Gazeta
de México,* 20–22, 34–36; as a *letrado,*
47–49, 48*fig.;* type specimen of, 190

Vanegas Arroyo, Antonio, 208, 242, 243–45
Vatican, 1
Vazquez, Andrés Clemente, 180
Venegas, Francisco Javier, 45, 60
Veracruz, 45, 107, 156
Verdad amarga, pero es preciso decirla, La
(Dávila), 75, 78
Verdi, Giuseppe, 196
Villaurrutia, Jacobo, 37
Voltaire, 117, 137
Voz de México, La, 210

wages, 85, 153, 177–79, 178*tab.*, 201; discussion of piece work, 170
War of Independence, 50–60, 77
Washington, George, 194
women, 14, 176, 197, 213. *See also* printers:
women
work: complementarity of manual and
intellectual, 31, 45, 170–71; 185–86, 201,
240; creative aspects of, 15–16, 240; as
drudgery, 15; Enlightenment discourses
about: 7, 31, 49; liberal definitions of,
169–70, 185; printers' ambivalence
towards, 49, 172
workers: discussion of the "social question"
by, 184–85; journalistic depictions of,
181, 184; printers as a particular class of,
15, 185–86, 240; and technology, 212–14,
214*fig.*, 218*fig.*, 230. *See also* compositors;
newspapers: for workers; pressmen;
printers

Yorkinos, 87
Yucatán, 84, 88

Zapata, Emiliano, 231, 239
Zarco, Francisco, 171
Zúñiga y Ontiveros, Cristobal, 24
Zúñiga y Ontiveros, Felipe, 24–25
Zúñiga y Ontiveros, Mariano, 63, 79

Founded in 1893,
UNIVERSITY OF CALIFORNIA PRESS
publishes bold, progressive books and journals
on topics in the arts, humanities, social sciences,
and natural sciences—with a focus on social
justice issues—that inspire thought and action
among readers worldwide.

The UC PRESS FOUNDATION
raises funds to uphold the press's vital role
as an independent, nonprofit publisher, and
receives philanthropic support from a wide
range of individuals and institutions—and from
committed readers like you. To learn more, visit
ucpress.edu/supportus.